Jim Murray's

COMPLETE BOOK OF

WHISKY

THE DEFINITIVE GUIDE TO THE WHISKIES OF THE WORLD

With love to my son, James,
a charming and cheerful companion
on my exploration of
the world's whisky outposts.

THIS IS A CARLTON BOOK

This edition published in 1997

10 9 8 7 6 5 4 3 2 1

A CIP catalogue record for this book is available from the British Library

ISBN hardback 1-85868-184-7
ISBN paperback 1-85868-386-6

PROJECT EDITOR: Martin Corteel
PROJECT ART DIRECTION: Zoë Maggs
PICTURE RESEARCHER: Charlotte Bush
PRODUCTION: Sarah Schuman
DESIGNER: Fiona Roberts

Author's note

I have used the spelling "whiskey" or "whisky" depending on how the individual distillers prefer. All Scotch is "whisky". So is Canadian. All Irish, these days, is "whiskey", though that was not always the case. In Kentucky, bourbon and rye are spelt "whiskey", with the exception of the produce of the Early Times/Old Forester Distillery and Maker's Mark which they bottle as "whisky". In Tennessee, it is a 50–50 split: Dickel is "whisky", while Daniel's is "whiskey".

CARLTON

Author's acknowledgements

At the last count there were 411 people I wished to thank individually for their help, one way or another, with this book. Sadly, lack of space prevents me from doing so. Some span back over a decade, others have, month in, month out, been keeping me abreast of what's going on in their sector of the whisky world. With their aid I have tried to keep this book as up to date as possible at the time of going to press. This information was gathered, though, during my day-to-day work as a whisky writer.

But there have been a hard core of people who have gone out of their way to make this book possible with help and friendship that has transcended the professional call of duty. And it would be most remiss of me if they, at least, did not receive my whole-hearted, personal thanks. In the USA there was Ed O'Daniel of the Kentucky Distillers' Association and Chris Morris, Lincoln Henderson and Jimmy Russell. In Canada special thanks to Ron Veilleux and Sandi Bochij of the Association of Canadian Distillers; the Ireland section would be all the poorer but for Barry Walsh, Stephen Franck, David Hinds and Noel Sweeney; as well as the excellent support I received in Scotland and elsewhere from Richard Paterson, Prathmesh Mishrak, Janet Leigh, Jill Preston, Lauchie MacLean, Mark Hunt, Jimmy Lang, Jim Swan, Naofumi Kamiguchi, Max Griggs, Gill Jefferson and Colin Ross of Ben Nevis, in particular.

And there is no way I can thank enough or even attempt to repay the extraordinary kindness of those Aces of India: Alan, Carol and little Emily Don who helped make my trips to the sub-continent as safe and smooth as could ever be hoped. Thanks, also, for your great company and many laughs along the way.

On the production side, I cannot have been luckier to have been landed with a more tolerant and good-natured fellow than Martin Corteel as Editor. Thanks for your amazing support, Martin. Behind him was the hard-working team of Sarah Schuman, Zoë Maggs, Fiona Roberts and Charlotte Bush.

Behind me was my secretary and personal assistant Di Crook who, apart from the 101 jobs she had to do, kept tabs on the thousands of whiskies pouring in from around the world and never touched a drop; while housekeeper Julie Musgrove always made sure of clean clothes at short notice for my next expedition. I would also like to thank my children, Tabitha, David and James, for being so patient when I was locked in my office or some hotel for days – sometimes weeks – on end, and my mum for worrying about me when I'm away and advising me when to get my hair cut. Oh, and for buying me a big dictionary 28 years ago which I still use today.

If anyone feels aggrieved that they have not been included in this list of acknowledgements, then let's meet over a dram and see what we can do for the second edition … .

Jim Murray's

COMPLETE BOOK OF WHISKY

THE DEFINITIVE GUIDE TO THE WHISKIES OF THE WORLD

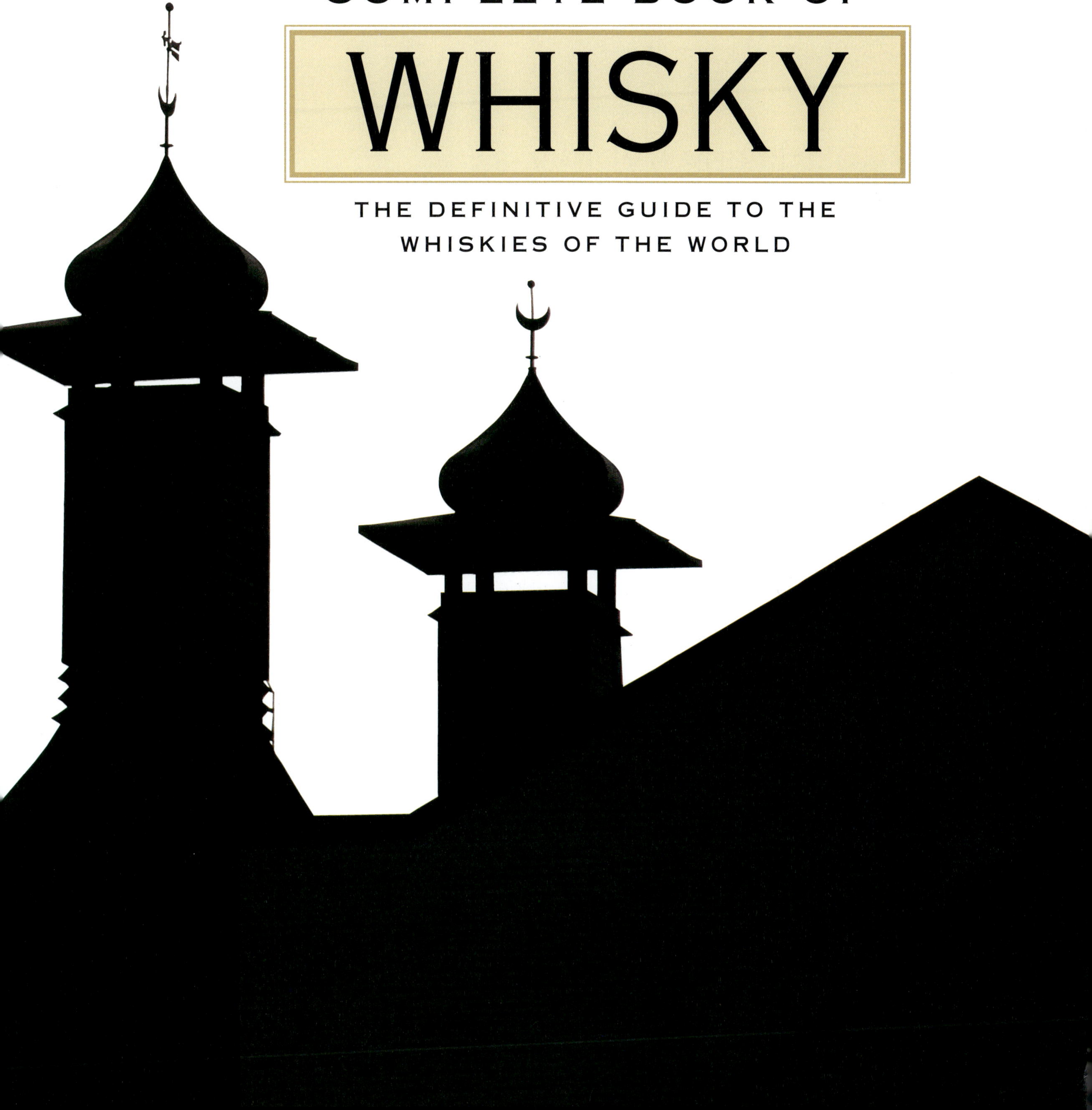

CONTENTS

INTRODUCTION

Twenty-two years ago, when I was a tourist hitch-hiking around the back roads of the Scottish Highlands and Islands, a motorist in a tiny car with an engine which droned like a Second World War bomber changed my life forever.

"Been to the distillery yet?" he asked.

"No. But plan to."

"You're going now, then."

With that, he took a left fork off the road he appeared to have been previously intending to drive along and within a few minutes we arrived at the Talisker Distillery. Little did I know as I walked through that entrance for the first time that I was stepping into the most romantic, most captivating, most delicious, most extraordinary of worlds.

The tour of the distillery lasted 30 entrancing minutes. The taste of the whisky which I had sampled at cask (Semtex) strength lasted even longer. My heart was lost.

Around eight years later I was back vacationing in Scotland again. This time I was on the glorious Hebridean Isle of Islay. I was there for two reasons: the distilleries and the bird-watching. It was the distilleries I found most enjoyable. Even now I can remember the sensation as I visited those great shrines to malt on the island's eastern coast for the first time: Lagavulin, Laphroaig and, of course, the incomparable Ardbeg – still today the maker of my favourite dram anywhere in the world. There, while tasting its beguiling and complex 10-year-old, I realized that what was already an interest was becoming a passion.

Nearby was a piece of jagged land where smuggling had taken place for centuries, the peninsula of Oa. While in this vicinity I decided that, one way or another, I would get round as many distilleries in the world as I could, trying to learn their secrets on the way. Little did I realize that 15 years on I would be putting the finishing touches to my own book of the world's whiskies having just visited a distillery in tropical Goa. From Oa to Goa in – that's neat. Which is just how I like my whisky.

Raise a glass: *The noblest of spirits.*

At some stage following that trip to Islay I decided to give up my full-time job writing for a British national newspaper and enter the unknown by becoming the world's first-ever full-time whisky writer. Since then I have visited the vast majority of the distilleries described – and there are 150 of them throughout 12 countries or principalities – on numerous occasions and have come to know their whiskies very well indeed. Others I have had to make special expeditions to find. This book was totally up to date when completed (stop press: only yesterday I discovered the future of my beloved Ardbeg had been secured by Glenmorangie!) and, as the final words were faxed to my publishers, it became in itself a complete distillation of all the world's drams.

You see, that is the beauty of whisky. There are so many different types, so many different styles, that I defy anyone not to find one that appeals to them one way or another. And that is the major reason for this book: to take the reader on a journey to just about all the world's whisky distilleries, tell something about them and show why each and every whisky is different.

It is a journey that takes you from the shores of Islay, where waves can lap quietly or crash noisily against ancient distillery walls, to nearly 6,000 feet up the serene Himalayas to a forgotten – yet still working – malt distillery dating from the time of the Raj; from the mountain-framed distilleries of Japan to those lost in oceans of corn on the pancake-flat Canadian prairies; from distilleries sweltering in the summer heat and humidity of Kentucky and Tennessee to one in New Zealand so cold that penguins take a daily plunge just a mile or so away; from the rich, honey-sweet malt whiskies of Perthshire to the tangy, mouth-watering malted rye of California; from the light, ethereal Canadians to the pungent, peaty Islays; from the grassy, barley-rich Speysiders of Scotland, to the grassy, barley-rich malt of Pakistan.

Each and every conceivable style of whisky is here, the good, the bad and the indifferent. And if I do feel the whisky is bad, then I say so. But what makes my Complete Book of Whisky a little special, I hope, is that for the first time distilleries never before visited have been described in the detail they deserve. For any writer, it is always thrilling to be the first to break the news about something special. So I do take some pride in being the first writer to visit all of Canada's working distilleries; the first to visit all those in

Silence is golden: *The barrels rest in the warehouse at Jack Daniel's Distillery nurturing their precious contents.*

the USA; the first to taste Czech malt whisky in its own warehouse; the first to discover the one and only distillery working in an Islamic state; the first to venture into the Himalayas to discover a time-warp distillery with 140-year-old, working machinery. When writing about these far-flung distilleries I hope I have tempered my natural romanticism with something a little more analytical. I have tried to place the distillery in the overall context in which it is found which I hope makes for an easy read along the way.

If there is one thing I enjoy as much as tasting and writing about whiskies, it is talking about them. Each year I give dozens of tastings around the world, from New York to New Zealand, to audiences eager to find out more about this enigmatic spirit. They are surprised to discover why I regard bourbon whisky as at least an equal to Scotch and why certain Scotches – including blends – when tasted the right way offer tantalizing subtleties to the palate that, maybe at first encounter, do not seem to be there. At these tastings I get the chance to learn what people want to know about whisky – and it is a lot.

This book is written with the novice, the connoisseur and the plain curious in mind. I have tried to moderate my language when describing the flavours of whisky, but if I ever do go over the top, forgive me. As I say, I do have a passion.

My aim in this book is to take you on a voyage of discovery, and if it makes you want to try at least one whisky from somewhere around the world that you had never considered tasting before, then *Jim Murray's Complete Book of Whisky* has been successful.

Jim Murray
Goa, India
February 1997

I  MAKING WHISKY

Despite what others have written elsewhere over a great many years, the making of whisky, or whiskey, is not a difficult task. The making of good whisky, however, is another matter entirely. From the craggy granite Highlands of Scotland to the gentle limestone hills of Kentucky, you will hear an old adage: "there is no such thing as bad whisky". Well, there is. Fortunately for us, though, nearly all the fruits of the world's more productive distilleries are ripe and mouth-watering, even though they may taste quite distinct and have grown from quite different seeds.

It matters not whether the whisky is made entirely from malted barley, as is traditionally the case in Scotland, or from a mixture of unmalted and malted barley as perfected by the Irish, or from predominantly Indian corn, or sometimes unmalted rye, as in the making of bourbon in North America. The same natural processes have to be gone through to turn basic, outwardly ordinary materials into something which can delight, charm, sometimes absolutely astound you. And although the taste characteristics may be enormously different, depending on which part of the globe they come from, what is beyond doubt to anyone who tastes them side by side is the fact that these spirits are related. And only by tasting these whiskies side by side can you ever genuinely discover the enormous divergence of flavour that makes whisk(e)y the most fascinating, the most enormously complex spirit of all.

Cask strength: *Distillers are still learning the importance of the quality of the oak and the effect it has on their maturing whisky.*

Perhaps the most startling aspect of any distillery you may visit anywhere in the world is that the principal techniques required to make whisky are the same now as when the spirit was first discovered by person or persons unknown in the distant, unrecorded past. The materials are the same, as is the alchemy and the grand order of things. The only difference today is the efficiency and scale.

The first, and perhaps most important, thing required by any distiller, whether he be a fly-by-night moonshiner or part of a blue-chip international drinks corporation, is water. That water has to be clean, preferably, and copious, certainly, as it will serve two, perhaps three, roles each – every one vital to the act of distillation. Next he will require grain. Vessels will be needed to mix that grain with boiling water, the juices from which will be fermented and finally distilled. Even in the murky past it became clear that, of all the metals from which the distilling apparatus could be made, copper inexplicably and consistently yielded the best results. Today some very fine whisky is created from stainless steel stills, yet copper is not only regarded as the golden key to unlocking the most glorious distillate, but even those steel kettles have to include copper in their make-up somewhere if the end product is to be regarded as remotely potable.

No one is able yet to put an exact date on when whisky was first made. What can be sure is that it is only in the last couple of centuries that it came to be regarded as a dark spirit as opposed to a clear, colourless one like gin. The monks and illicit distillers who began perfecting the art would have drunk or applied their water of life within days, weeks or perhaps months of it being made. No warehouses for them. Chances are, the discovery of whisky's ability to mature and improve in the wooden cask was little more than an accident, but one for which we should all give hearty thanks.

Whisky making represents the timeless confluence of art and science. Maybe it is that, along with tales of bothies, smugglers and settlers and the image of secluded mountains, rivers and glens which gave cover and sustenance to those early distillers, which accounts for whisky being the most romantic of spirits, irrespective of the country in which it is made.

THE PRIMARY INGREDIENTS

WATER

There is an old Scottish saying about how to predict that country's fickle weather: if it's not raining, then it's about to. In Ireland, cows are renowned for the quality of their milk thanks to the lush, rain-soaked grass. Canada spends much of its winter and early spring under a blanket of snow which begrudgingly melts only as summer approaches. Kentucky and Tennessee are famous for their stiflingly humid, airless summers, but their ferocious springtime and autumnal thunderstorms are examples of nature at its most spectacular.

Perhaps with the exception of India and Turkey, wherever you go to watch the whisky-maker at work, a raincoat and umbrella need to be at hand. Even when you are caught in a storm between warehouses, rather than curse your luck, you should gaze heavenwards and smile in recognition that you are at the centre of a wondrous creation: this, after all, is how all whisky begins.

For without water there would be no whisky: it is the one non-negotiable element. If you don't have barley, you can use maize; if you don't have maize, you can use rye; if you don't have rye, you can use wheat. If you don't have brewer's yeast for fermentation, you can allow natural spores upon the wind to do the job. But if you don't have water, you can never make whisky – period.

The world's oldest working distilleries are to be found in Scotland and Northern Ireland. Usually they are remote, but what you can happily bet your house on is the close proximity of good, clear water suitable not only for distilling but in enough abundance to act as the cooling agent for the condensers, allowing the alcohol vapours to return to liquid form. Chances are, distilleries began their life as bothies, secret chambers on lonely sites where a nefarious distiller would distil from an illicit alembic so small that he could carry it around with him. When the distiller sought respectability and bought a licence, he would be tempted to build his distillery at the very spot where he had spent many nervous weeks, months and probably years trying to outwit the Excise man, the gauger as he was known, the most notable case in point being George Smith of Glenlivet fame.

Even today, when a new distillery is built, the first thing to be located is the water source. When the Gimli Distillery in Canada was created in the heart of the Winnipeg wilderness, the bore hole came first, the builders later. In Japan, water sources were tested around the islands for two years before Suntory finally settled for the soft waters at Hakushu. The Lochranza Distillery on the Scottish island of Arran was opened in the summer of 1995, but before that there had been several years of planning, with nine different water sites tested not only for the quality of water but for the profusion of it.

Sometimes, though, there are problems. Contamination or an unexpected drying-up of the supply may lead a distillery to switch briefly to town water for mashing, even after it has been chlorinated. Even some of the most traditional of Scottish distilleries have to pass water through a de-chlorination process as the lochs which supply them also supply the community. Some Scottish distilleries use chlorinated town water all the time, quite confident that first the mashing process and then the high temperature of the bubbling pots will get rid of anything that may have an adverse effect on the spirit. Their whiskies can be sensational and it is evident no harm has been done to the quality or character of the whisky on the whole; though in the case of one or two you cannot help but wonder. Generally and globally speaking, it is clear distillers take enormous care to ensure the quality of their water: it is not unusual for them to buy all the land around their source so fertilizers do not accidentally find their way into the supply. Obviously, the water for cooling the condensers does not have to be of quite such a pure standard.

Of all the world's water, the one which has perhaps the biggest say in the local whisky is that found on Islay. The waters which feed the Ardbeg, Laphroaig and Lagavulin distilleries have run over long stretches of boggy peats and picked up enormous turf character. This has a direct effect on the eventual heaviness of the whisky, though it is the kilning process of the malt using peat turf that has the biggest say. Curiously, 150 years ago some

Water of life: *The indispensable ingredient for the making of whisky.*

In the beginning: *Lochs, like this one feeding Glenturret, can be the source of a distillery's water.*

eminent scientists thought it was the other way round: that the kilning had little or no effect and that it was the steeping of the barley in dark, peaty waters which gave the whisky its smoky tang.

But what makes good whisky-distilling water? In the United States, geographically it would make more sense to find distilleries operating out of the north-western states of Washington, Montana, Idaho, Oregon, or even Alaska, where not only are they blessed with chilled snow-melt waters rushing down from the Rocky Mountains, but they are close to vital Canadian grain supplies as well. Where Kentucky and Tennessee score is the limestone shelf on which the states sit. Not only does this soft material act as a natural basin for storing underground all the water the industry will ever require, the inherent chemical deposits which dissolve over the course of many hundreds, even thousands, of years are instrumental in allowing the water to react perfectly with yeast added for fermentation. Yeast, being a living thing, needs its nutrients; limestone-rich water is steeped in minerals many of which are necessary for it to thrive. Fortunately, iron is not among them: if it were, the spirit would not turn gold as it matured, but black.

In Scotland and Ireland, distillers also prefer to draw from their reservoir through springs which allow water stored underground for years rather than weeks to finally escape. At Highland Park on Orkney, geologists estimate that the water which runs from Cattie Maggie's spring to the famous old distillery originally fell on the Scottish mainland sometime in the last century before completing its 200-mile subterranean trek to the wind-swept island.

However, these are worrying times in Scotland. Every time you visit there you may be guaranteed a soaking or two for your troubles, but the indisputable fact is that it does not rain so often as it did even a decade ago – further evidence, many claim, of global warming. For that reason, distillers are looking for divine intervention: that is the use of a diviner to find fresh water sources as older-established ones dry up. This is done by holding a "Y"- or "V"-shaped twig, rod or similar appliance above the ground until it twitches and points to a water source. Since 1995, the giant United Distillers company has been employing someone almost full-time to find fresh sites using this ancient method. He has been his busiest on the Isle of Skye, which has been particularly badly hit by drought. His job has not been made any easier by the fact that the Talisker Distillery there actually sits on land rich in iron deposits. Often water which is sparkling clear when first tapped changes to orange as iron contamination enters the system. Sometimes the spring can be seen to be contaminated at first glance: the moss is bright orange instead of green.

As a rule, though, Scottish distilleries work with soft water (better suited than hard water to steeping barley) which is relatively mineral-free and occasionally as close to pure as you are likely to find. This is because much of the underground water has contact with unyielding, impervious granite. This poses an intriguing question: if Kentucky and Tennessee whiskey benefits from hard water, which, as it happens, the famous English brewing town of Burton is also renowned for, is it really inferior to Scotland's soft water, as the sages have so long claimed?

I can think of only four Scottish distilleries which use hard water, Scapa, its Orcadian neighbour Highland Park, and on the mainland Glenkinchie and Glenmorangie, whose Tarlogie Springs seep at a number of points from an underground bed of limestone, though its mineral content is low compared to that of Kentucky. Highland Park and Glenmorangie, it has to be said, have long been purveyors of two of the most consistently good drams you'll ever find in the Highlands and Scapa's is pretty delightful, too. Glenkinchie is geographically many miles away in the Lowlands: its water actually filters through chalky hills and picks up calcium. Sceptical research scientists may tell you there is little difference between hard and soft water anyway by the time certain minerals have been leached from the grain during mashing. So why do the Scots so vociferously claim their water is best? As one doubting distillery manager once told me: "Probably because it's all we've got and we have to make the most of it!"

GRAIN

Depending on where in the world you live, or are visiting, you will hear strongly differing views on which grain can be relied upon to yield the finest whisky on earth. It is odd that the Scots will, nine times out of 10, tell you it is malted barley from the copper pot still. Odd, because they drink a lot more blended

Scotch than they do single malt, and between 60 and 70 per cent of that blend will contain whisky made from wheat or maize which will have been nowhere near a copper pot.

The Irish, over a stout and Power's chaser, will likewise tell you malt despite the fact that nearly all the home-grown whiskey drunk in the Republic is also a blend. The older generation and a few younger ones in the know will confide that the secret is mixing raw barley in with the malt. Few, though, will be aware that until as recently as the 1950s and 1960s oats also found their way into the leading recipes such as Jameson, as did rye.

Rye was once the pride of Pennsylvania, Virginia, Maryland and to a lesser extent Kentucky, and was the favourite tipple of Humphrey Bogart's Philip Marlow. These days Kentucky and Tennessee distillers will rightly extol the virtues of Indian corn, or maize as it is also known. Even so, they will happily acknowledge not only the truly essential part malted barley plays in fermentation, but also the extra zip it adds to the taste of their whiskey. The Canadians, also, owe their all to maize and rye.

It is this healthy cross-section of grains which sets whisky apart from any other spirit you can find, and guarantees a complexity of taste which offers the broadest spectrum of delicate and delightful sensations a palate is able to detect. The simple test of nosing and then tasting a sample of each country's major style – Kentucky bourbon, Kentucky rye, Scottish single malt, blended Scotch, blended Irish, pot-still Irish, light Canadian and heavier Canadian rye, plus any from the smaller distilling countries like Japan, the Czech Republic and New Zealand – will give a much clearer indication of this than a book, however informative. And, of course, that is telling only part of the story: each country offers a myriad of styles to choose from, even if they do have a certain grain in common. By comparison, sampling brandy, whether it be made from apple, peach or the noble grape, can be a rewarding experience, though by no means as complete as when discovering the beguiling nuances of the world's many whiskies.

Barley

This most durable of cereals was, it is believed, first cultivated by Neolithic man between 5,000 and 10,000 years ago. Certainly, it was a staple of the early Egyptians who made beer from it and it held such an important place in the society of the Metapontumians of southern Italy around 500 BC that they struck coins clearly depicting its proud beard and plump six rows of grain. In Roman Colchester, England, coins were issued with a rather less impressive two-rowed barley on the reverse. Although a four-rowed barley exists, it is the strains depicted in Italy and Britain which have some significance in the current making of whisky. In Scotland and Ireland a two-eared barley is turned to malt; for the making of bourbon and rye the six-eared is preferred. The four-eared is an unusual species these days, growing wild and rarely cultivated. Yet it was from one of these, called bere, that whisky was first made in Scotland, being the hardiest barley of them all but by today's standards of poor flavour and starch yield.

It is barley's ability to thrive on infertile, nitrogen-starved lands that makes it so suitable for brewing. And its suitability for brewing is such that, 100 per cent rye whiskies and most Canadian distilleries (where enzymes are allowed and preferred) apart, barley is found in some percentage or other in just about every type of whisky made. When whisky is made from unmalted corn or wheat, just 10 per cent unmalted barley is sufficient to set off an effective fermentation, so it is useful for more than taste alone.

When distillers buy in barley, not only do they check for mould but also the nitrogen content is assessed. The more nitrogen found within the grain, the less carbohydrate there will be for turning to sugars during malting (see distilling processes). As these sugars are vital for yeast to feed on to produce alcohol, it is not surprising that malted barley finds its way into almost every whisky type. That used in Scotland is mainly grown in Scotland and some smaller distillers over the years have made a point of using local farmers, these days making publicity capital out of that quaint fact.

Since the Second World War there have been huge global advances in the quality of barley as far as sugar yield is concerned, but recent research has suggested that the more carbohydrate in the barley, the less capacity there is within the grain to hold flavour components. This was borne out by tests which revealed that of all the barley grown to make malt whisky, it was a strain from India – which had undergone little or no genetic engineering but gave relatively low carbohydrate counts – which was able to produce by far the most intensely attractive spirit to taste.

Some distillers, like The Macallan in Speyside, have tried to fight this trend towards sugar yield by sticking to trusted strains, in their case Golden Promise, in an effort to keep flavours constant. Theirs is an unusual, noble, though ultimately lost battle. It will only be a matter of time before Golden Promise, like dozens of others before and after, will become obsolete as farmers cave in to the lure of fatter returns for higher yields. It has become a case of John Barleycorn is dead – long live John Barleycorn.

Rye

Used in malted and unmalted form in North America where early Irish settlers, some of whom were vaguely familiar with it from the making of whiskey in their homeland, were aware of its intense flavour. German distillers knew it better still. Brought to America from Europe, it is grown in the northern states, especially Dakota, and Canada. Most Kentucky and Tennessee mashbills (the grain recipe for their whiskey) will include some rye among the more expensive "small grains" to help bulk up the flavour content over the gentler-flavoured Indian corn, as well as add to the efficiency of fermentation. It is used in Kentucky to make straight rye whiskey, where at least 51 per cent of the mashbill has to contain rye. Canadian distilleries traditionally add small percentages of rye to flavour their whiskey, the pick of the crop by far coming from Alberta Distillers who make an extremely oily and fulsome whiskey from 100 per cent rye. Watching this ferment is some experience: the aroma from the fermenters is sharper, fruitier

 Blowing in the wind: *Countless miles of prairie are under a sea of rippling barley in America's Grain Belt.*

and more vivid than any other mash and the colour is significantly darker.

With the exception of heavily peated Islay whisky made from malted barley, there is no other whisky in the world that matches the enormity of character yielded by spirit distilled from 100 per cent malted rye. In the distant past, the very first vodkas were made in pot stills from rye in the Russias, but were never regarded as whiskey as they were never allowed to mature.

Seagram occasionally make a malted rye to use in a blended American whiskey. But, wondrously, in 1996 the new Anchor Distillery in San Francisco brought out the first commercial 100 per cent malted rye whiskey in living memory. Of all the world's whiskies, rye and traditional Irish pot-still whiskey, containing a high proportion of unmalted barley, are the closest in style, both having a hardness to the taste which is uncompromising and more mouth-wateringly flavoursome than any other.

While malted rye whiskey has been returned to us, there is a style that remains lost: blended rye. I am one of the world's lucky few to have several bottles of this, all possibly dating from the 1930s, and the latest I opened shortly before the completion of this book was as spicy-fresh, sweet, rye-rich and clean as the day it was bottled. To my mind, rye whiskey – whether straight, blended or malted – remains the world's most underrated spirit and, as a style, perhaps the greatest whiskey of all. One, certainly, just waiting to be re-discovered. (See rye whiskey section.)

Maize *(Indian corn)*

Until very recently, this was easily the most commonly used grain to be found in the world's whiskies. Not only did it provide the meat for bourbon, which by law contains 51 per cent corn, but it was also used in Scotland and Ireland to produce the soft, continuously distilled (see distilling process) grain whisky used to bulk up blends. That has changed now, with all but one Scottish grain distillery switching to (theoretically) cheaper wheat and the Midleton Distillery in Ireland alternating between the two, depending on market prices. With Canadian whiskey continuing to use corn, it may still be ahead of barley and wheat, but only just.

At the turn of the twentieth century, it was by the far the most widely used grain as cheap straight grain whisky was usually served as a matter of course in British bars with not a molecule of tastier pot-still in sight, leading to so much anger and outrage within the malt-distilling industry both in Scotland and Ireland that a Royal Commission was set up solely to answer the simmering question "What is Whisky?"

After lengthy and learned debate it was decided, not without some controversy, that Scotch and Irish whisky could contain this most un-British of products. It is thought to have first been used in the making of Scotch whisky in about 1850, but took a further 10 to 15 years to become established. Being cheap, it was found to be perfect fodder for the new-fangled, continuous patent, stills of the time, stills that produced spirit at a fraction of the cost of much smaller pot stills which had to be re-cleaned. So by the time the Whisky Commission was set up in 1908, most of the whisky consumed in Britain's bars was maize, as was pointed out in the hearing. Samples were taken from public houses throughout the British Isles which when analysed showed that all 39 samples taken in England were patent-still whisky, as were the 23 in Scotland, while Ireland was split 21 patent- and nine pot-still.

In North America, there was never any such problem regarding the use of maize. From the late eighteenth and early nineteenth century on, Indian corn, rich as it was in starch, was accepted as a fine ingredient for the making of whiskey and today corn whiskey is still being made, which by definition is made from a minimum 80 per cent corn.

To avoid mould, corn used in the distilling of North American whiskey has to be dried to a maximum of 14 per cent moisture content. As it is an indigenous plant of America, the US states of Indiana and Illinois once supplied the needs of Kentucky, Tennessee and Canadian distillers. But today, Canada produces its own on the plains of Ontario, Manitoba and Quebec. That grown around the Gimli Distillery in Manitoba is particularly interesting: it was specially engineered to thrive in those chilly climes from a plant that had partially originated in the Andes Mountains of Peru. Meanwhile, maize used in the making of Scotch and Irish is likely to come from the warmer climes of France, with some grown, ironically, in the Cognac region. The maize used in Kentucky's distilleries is larger than that found in Scotland and Ireland and looks a little like a discoloured tooth. This is known as dent corn, due to a dent in the crown of the kernel.

In North America the use of maize for the making of whiskey became more widespread as settlers moved west and south west. The further away from the Atlantic coast they moved, the harder it became to cultivate barley, wheat and rye. For that reason, maize became a staple of their diet, with bread being made from it and any spare coming in useful for distilling. Although barley and rye was considerably more expensive to procure, distillers still had to do so, because a fault of maize is that it doesn't naturally ferment without persuasion and cannot easily be malted. Therefore the smaller grains were used not only to add flavour but, more importantly, to get the fermentation process started.

Wheat

This is always a secondary grain that is constantly doing battle with rye or maize as a preferred item. In Scotland there is no doubt blenders prefer to work with grain whisky made from maize as it has extra body and a subtly richer flavour. Only subsidies from the European Commission brought wheat into the reckoning, making it cheaper to buy in than maize. Over the last few years that has changed and there is now very little difference to be found price-wise. Many a Scottish grain distiller is now looking to see if it is viable to switch back to maize. And not only do distillers prefer the taste of maize but wheat, having no husk, is considered a messy grain as well.

Across the Atlantic there are two distilleries which work with wheated bourbons, Maker's Mark and Bernheim, which has taken

Recipe for success: *Various grains (from left to right) barley, maize and rye.*

over the production of the Stitzel Weller brands. The idea of substituting wheat for rye was, so legend has it, to produce softer whiskeys lacking the traditional rye ebullience and hardness on the palate.

What the Maker's Mark, Rebel Yell, Old Fitzgerald and Weller brands all seem to share is a spiciness which lightly peppers the tastebuds. Outside of Kentucky and the grain distilleries of Scotland and Ireland wheat is hardly known at all in the making of whisky.

Oats

American distillers of the early nineteenth century swore by the stuff; indeed, one of the most flavoursome whiskeys made at the time, it was reckoned, was made from two parts maize and one part oats. But not any more. Its sticky nature meant distillers were on full alert as there was a danger of stills exploding from becoming too clogged. Oats are no longer used in the making of whiskey. The art finally died out in Ireland, where it had been commonly used, in 1975 when the old Midleton Distillery was closed and production was switched to the new oat-free plant next door.

YEAST

Of all the ingredients that go to make up whisky, the one which is least discussed has to be yeast. Yet this is the vital catalyst which turns an otherwise docile soup into a cauldron of seething alcohol. Sounds dramatic? Just go and see a Scottish washback in full action and you will know what I mean. But not only is yeast a catalyst, it actually adds a defining character to the whisky, as well. That characteristic can be a milkiness, fruitiness, occasionally bitterness or sweetness.

The distillers of North America are a bit more precious about their yeasts than distillers elsewhere and they go to great lengths to keep the same strain for decades, though when accountants get to work the hereditary importance can get lost in the red ink of the bottom line. In Scotland, the character it imparts to the whisky is lower down the order of priorities.

Yeast is a living thing, neither plant nor animal, but a fungus. Just as scientists had long considered the world to be flat, so too did they consider yeast as an inanimate but highly useful tool, and it took Louis Pasteur to recognize that this was a single-celled organism that fed upon sugars and gave off alcohol and carbon dioxide as a by-product.

A century ago, the operation of skimming the yeast from the top of the frothing washbacks was as common and vital as firing the still. Today, however, no distilleries in Scotland or Ireland produce their own yeasts and instead buy in a dried form which they blend to their own requirements. There is the more expensive distiller's yeast and the cheaper brewer's yeast, which has been skimmed off a fermenting beer and is capable of adding some richer flavours as well as "kick-starting" the fermentation process. These will be mixed in anything from a 58:42 to a 70:30 ratio. However, there is a little nervousness that these brewer's yeasts may be more open to contamination and extensive work is going on to make 100 per cent distiller's yeast a more attractive proposition. For years many distillery managers in Scotland made great whisky without knowing the first thing about yeast. Today, the new breed of distillery manager takes a far greater interest; one, at Glenmorangie, even obtained his PhD in the subject.

Over in Kentucky a number of distilleries still happily produce their own yeast, though a number are now buying in. Strangely, some of these yeasts contain hops, more commonly associated with beer. This stems from experimentation among American distillers in the early nineteenth century which showed, against the received wisdom of the time, that yeast with hops added actually fermented a whole 24 hours faster than that without. It was also used in summer to help preserve the fungus during the hot summer months. You will be relieved to learn, though, that there is no detectable hop bitterness in any of the whiskeys produced by these most old-fashioned of distillers.

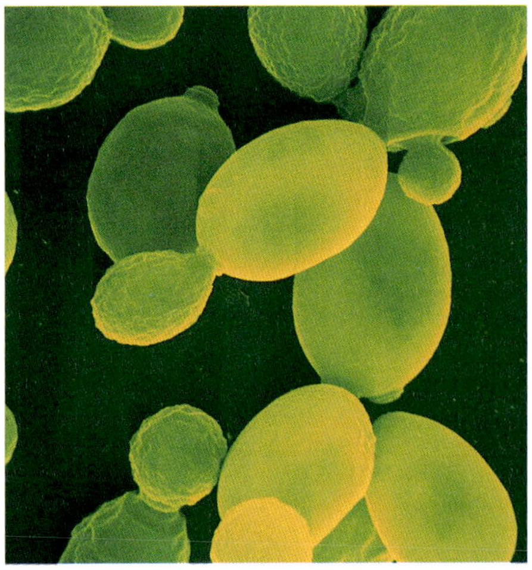

Culture: *Yeast converts sugars to alcohol.*

THE BASIC PROCESS

No matter which whisky you prefer, be it Irish, bourbon, Scotch, Canadian, Welsh or whatever, the methods used to arrive at that spirit in the glass will be very similar. It is simply a case of taking grain, some of which must be malted, crushing it, adding it to boiling water, draining off the sugar-enriched water before adding yeast to it, then distilling the beer made from that, preferably a minimum of twice, and sometimes three times. The spirit produced is then placed into an oak barrel where it should be left for a number of years to react with the wood, taking on colour and a defining character. That, in a nutshell, is how ALL the world's whiskies are made. But from country to country there are slight variances in each step, as we shall see.

Malting

Nature is the most accommodating of mothers and mankind the most inquisitive of her children. So when each year barley germinated, someone, somewhere, discovered that the grain had changed in a way in which extra, magical use could be made of it. The first beers were probably brewed soon after.

Obviously, people making malt liquors could not wait until each grain germinated naturally, which would have been a messy and labour-intensive affair. So they devised a way to trick that grain into thinking summer had arrived when it was away from its earthy habitat. As Irishman John Long observed in his *Treatise on Malting* as far back as 1800: "Malting is a chemical process, and in that light not so generally understood as it could be wished: it is in some measure a kind of forced vegetation, and the nearer we follow the laws marked out by nature, the more certain we are of arriving at the highest state towards perfection, that humanity is capable of obtaining."

Just what is malted barley – and why is malting so important? The answer lies in both its flavour and, more importantly, its chemical properties. Freshly picked grains of barley, like all cereals, are rich in starch and as the grains germinate those starches change molecular structure to become more sugar-like in composition. It is these sugars which are the key to producing alcohol as they are the vital foodstuff of yeast.

One method of malting barley has changed little over the two centuries since Long's time: the grain is steeped in cold, regularly-changed clear water for 48 to 60 hours, allowing the grain to fatten and increase in weight by half again. Then it is spread thinly and evenly over a floor. This is called a piece. In this saturated state the barley at the bottom begins to warm and so the maltman turns the barley over to even out the temperature. Traditionally a malt shovel called a shiel, made from wood to inflict minimum damage during this process, would be used. Today there are automatic ploughs which do the job for a fraction of the effort and time, though I know maltsters who occasionally take up the shiel just for old time's sake.

Piece-ful place: *A floor malting.*

Only a handful of distilleries in Scotland still carry out this most traditional of preparations, and even they are a dying breed. Only Springbank malts all its barley by traditional floor malting. The others supplement their own produce with malt bought in from large, professional maltsters. These establishments, which supply all the barley required by other distillers, are large concerns which use cylindrical bins to turn the malt mechanically.

Whichever method is used, when shoots have started to grow and have reached a certain length, the maltman knows that the sugar levels within the grain are at their optimum point. Now it is time to dry the malt vigorously to arrest further development which would see sugar levels in the grain drop. In this state the grain is called green malt. At certain grain distilleries in Scotland, where whisky is made as cheaply and efficiently as possible for blending purposes, green malt is used in the distillation process.

What both old and new maltings have in common is the kilning, where the grain is dried by passing very hot air from the fires below to the chimney above. This way the grain not only dries but becomes very lightly toasted and brittle.

In North America, not only barley but also rye is malted in this fashion. In the making of bourbon, around 10 per cent of the mashbill is malted barley to assist fermentation. But whether barley malt or rye malt, it is then ready for the next stage in the whisky-making process: milling.

Peating

In Scotland, Australia, Japan and occasionally Ireland, peat – a solid fuel made from decomposing vegetable matter – is sometimes added to the kiln fire to give that malt a distinctive smoky flavour. Some Islay distilleries use malt which has been subjected to heavy peating, with phenol levels – by which steamed distillable compounds of smoke are measured – as high as 50 parts per million and sometimes even beyond. By stark contrast, the average found in, say, Speyside is around 2–3 parts per million. Some Scottish distilleries insist on using malt that has not seen any peat at all, while peat is never used in North America and very rarely in Ireland.

Once upon a time, each distillery cut its peat from its own special area and the friable qualities of that peat helped give the whisky

Fiery spirit: *Hot air dries the malt above.*

its own slightly different character. On Islay in particular, it was well known that a distillery's whisky could dramatically alter should the source of the peat change. These days the maltings plant at Port Ellen on Islay gathers its peat from one area of the island so the flavour and aroma will be pretty uniform.

What the maltster is looking for when firing the kiln is smoke. The usual smoking time is 18 hours. At Port Ellen 5-6 tonnes of peat will slowly cure 48 tonnes of barley. At other maltings where a very low phenol level is required, the smoking time will be the same but 2-3 tonnes of peat will be used for 300 tonnes of malt. This is usually carried out using the GKV method, where Germination Kilning Vessels not only allow the barley to germinate by mechanical means but the malt is dried in the same chamber without having to employ a kiln.

Milling

To help extract the highest possible amount of fermentable substances from the malted and unmalted grains, they are next crushed, using either hammer mills or softer-action roller mills. Some very small distilleries buy their grain in ready-milled, but the vast majority have their own mill rooms. The very latest to have been built in Scotland are time-locked because of the danger of explosion caused by particles released in the milling process. Theoretically, the finer the grist is milled the more alcohol can be yielded.

Cooking

In distilleries where unmalted corn is used a cooking process has to be undertaken. Malted grains are never cooked as this would destroy their enzymes. The purpose of cooking grains is to help break down the tough walls that hold in the starch which will eventually be released for fermentation. There are two principal cooking styles. One is old-fashioned batch cooking, often carried out in cylindrical tanks. The other is pressure cooking, where the grain is pressurized at high temperature and forced through narrow pipes.

Mashing

This is another, much less vigorous, form of cooking carried out at all whisky distilleries the world over. Just as in the making of tea, hot water is infused with the grain so all the fermentable materials are eventually absorbed into the water to form a sugar-rich liquid called wort.

Particular care is taken in Kentucky where three types of grain are mashed together – corn, malted barley and rye/wheat. To accommodate the different make-ups of these grains they are introduced to the water at differing temperatures: corn initially at 120°F rising to 212°F maximum; rye when the water has cooled down to 180°F and finally the malt at around the 152°F mark. Wheat, if required, may be added at between 145°F and 155°F. If the water was any hotter, enzymes within those grains would be destroyed, rendering them unfermentable.

In Scotland there are usually three mashes, with the final, weaker, one being used to begin the next round of mashing. The process takes place in a large, circular stainless steel or sometimes cast-iron vessel called a mash tun. In malt distilleries these have false bottoms to separate the spent grains from the wort. In North America and some grain distilleries the wort contains whole solids and this is pumped through to the fermenters.

Fermentation

This is a process by which yeast is added to the sugar-rich wort to form a heady cocktail of alcohol and lethal carbon dioxide. Although fermenters can today be quite massive (in America it is normal to find them holding in excess of 20,000 gallons each), the first commercial distilleries employed hundreds of barrels to do the same job. Known in Scotland as washbacks, these fermenters can be made from Oregon pine, larch or stainless steel. Although stainless steel washbacks and fermenters are much easier to clean and less susceptible to infection, there is a school of thought among

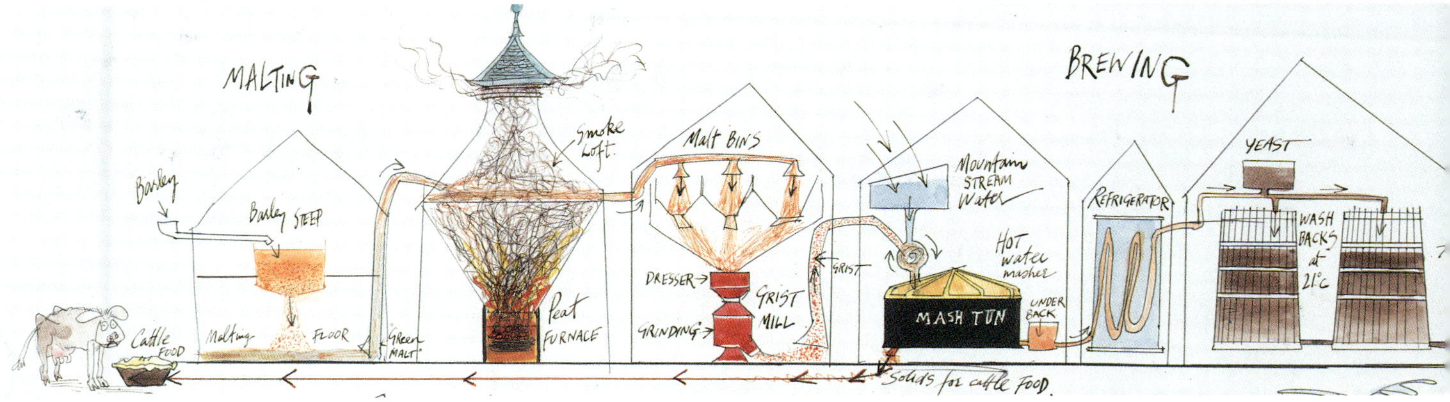

 Production line: *Cartoonist Ralph Steadman's idiosyncratic view of how whisky is made.*

some, though by no means all, older hands that fermentation carried out in wood produces a better product than that using metal.

Fermentation can take anything from 40 to 72 hours, sometimes longer if the distillery is closed over the weekend. Then the mix is cooled to slow the fermentation rate.

In Scotland fermentation is a violent affair because of the exclusive use of malted barley, and switchers – slow-turning propellers – are used to cut through the foam to prevent it from spilling over the top. In North America fermentation is much quieter and usually, though not always, carried out in open-topped vessels.

During this time, the seething contents of the fermenter changes from wort to "wash". Just how far along this route it has gone can be discovered by tasting the liquid directly from the fermenter. If it is sweet, fermentation has just begun because the sugars are still present. When it becomes sour and bitter, fermentation is coming to a close because the sugars have been used up by the yeast. The murky yellow/brown (depending on the grains used) liquid is sometimes described as a weak beer. A beer it is; weak it isn't – unless you consider a beer holding 8-9 per cent alcohol weak.

Distillation

The wash, solid in North America but clear in Scotland and Ireland, is now ready to be pumped into a still for distillation. The process of pot-still distillation is fully explained on the next pages. Here we shall look at continuous stills responsible for the bulk of whisk(e)y made around the world. But whichever type of still is used, the principle is the same: distillation is the strengthening of a weaker alcoholic liquid into a stronger one by the stripping away of water by some form of heating. In column stills the heat source is steam, though not in the same way that steam is often employed, inside copper coils, within pot stills. In column stills naked steam interacts with the alcohol, a practice which the early-20th-century guru of whisky, J.A. Nettleton, felt disqualified the resultant spirit from being called whisky at all.

Copper pot stills can move even the most ardent teetotaller, thanks to their charm, gleaming beauty and sensuous curves; column stills, lank, stark and shapeless, only ever thrill the whisky lover. These stills are tall, anything between 60 ft and 80 ft is not uncommon, and cylindrical. There are no mysterious curves visible, though what actually goes on inside is fascinating enough. Whether in Scotland or North America, where they are known as beer stills, the principle, in its simplest form, is the same: the wash is fed into the top of the still and runs through a number of copper plates. On its journey it is met by an upward draught of steam which strips alcohol from the wash as it travels up before entering a condenser.

In Scotland, Ireland and Canada these vapours are re-distilled to a higher strength using a second and sometimes third column still. In Kentucky and Tennessee, where a heavier spirit is required, the spirit enters a form of pot still called a doubler where the alcoholic strength is fractionally increased without stripping away much of the heavier components of the spirit.

A name you will see attached to most whiskey stills in Kentucky and Tennessee is that of Vendome, a family coppersmith that has been situated in the same block or two in the east of Louisville since 1904. The sons of company president Tom Sherman represent the fourth generation to be in the still-making business. In the early 1960s some 85-90 per cent of their business was whiskey-related. Today it is 20 per cent maximum (including the odd copper toilet seat for an overweight whiskey executive!), though the disastrous fire at the Heaven Hill Distillery in the winter of 1996 means that some unexpected work has come their way as the long process of rebuilding begins. Kitting out a bourbon distillery is not cheap: a complete unit consisting of a pre-heater, column still, doubler and two sets of

End of the line: *Bottling whisky.*

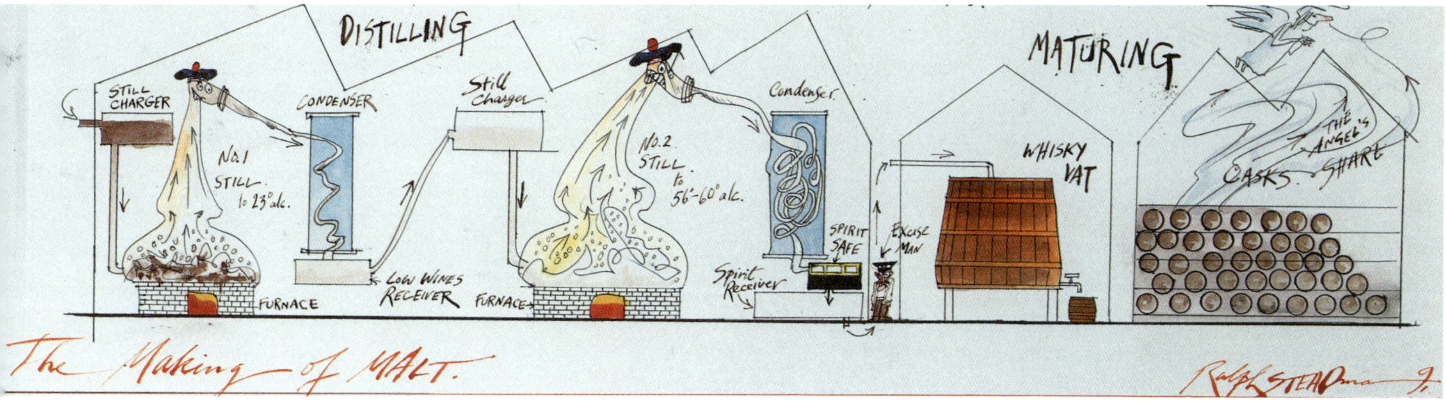

condensers would set a potential customer back $200,000. It would take four craftsmen six weeks to assemble the stills, though when there is a dire emergency, work can be completed in days rather than weeks.

These stills are usually made from that most pliable friend of the spirits, copper, though over the years the invasion of company accountants into the whiskey-making process has seen an increase in demand by some for stainless steel to be used where possible as this has a much longer life. But, as Tom Sherman says with a hint of embattled weariness: "It's curious how those who buy stainless steel stills then spend the rest of their life trying to run them like copper ones."

POT STILLS

Perhaps, when it comes to malt whisky, distillers should dispense with the term "Stillhouse" and re-name the room as "The Gallery". After all, that is where you go to inspect works of art, and is there in the industrial world so beautiful an appliance as a gleaming copper pot still, a sculptured form that soothes the eye and with its gentle hiss, the soul, too.

Where column stills are dramatic yet austere, pot stills seem to have their own personality and character, a shape and independence of their own. When working, they are hot thanks to their alcohol-rich blood pumping around inside them. That is why, no matter where in the world you are, the sight of a pot still leaves a visitor momentarily transfixed, be you a casual tourist or a whisky writer.

In Scotland pot stills may be dwarf-like, as in the case of Edradour and to a lesser extent at Glenfiddich, The Macallan, Speyside and Isle of Arran, or they may be giants, tall and gangly like those at Glenmorangie, or plump, chunky and expansive like at Auchroisk and Glenrothes. Usually, however, they are something in between. Around the world, pot stills also differ. In Ireland they were once rotund and bulbous, though today they are more similar to average Highlanders. In Canada and the USA they are small and Celtic in style; in Spain the one whiskey distillery has seven pot stills all haphazardly different. Japan's pot stills are generally large, while India shies away from smaller stills. One Australian pot still is tiny, while a redundant New Zealander is bizarrely fashioned from stainless steel into the shape of a lunar capsule.

Still life: *These gleaming copper pots give a tiny part of themselves to each distillation.*

It is this rich tapestry of pot still styles that helps malt whisky enjoy such a divergence of character. However, as beautiful as these stills are, they are an inefficient means of distillation, having more to do with the preferences of Scotland's and Ireland's illicit distillers, who would buy a still from the coppersmith as large as he could carry and afford, but no more. In the United States it became evident that if you were in the business of making whiskey simply to make money, then patent, continuous stills were what was required. Stein and Coffey are names synonymous with this type of still, but by 1818 Harrison Hall was already discussing the considerable merits of patent against pot and was impressed by the invention of a Colonel Anderson, who had devised a method of carrying out nine distillations a day against the usual three. However, where quantity was paramount, quality frequently wasn't, and it was the desire of Irish and Scottish distillers to guarantee the quality of their whisky that ensured that pot stills are still around today.

Pot stills have changed, though. Today they are bigger and usually steam-heated by copper coils at the base of the still. Some distilleries, like at Glenfiddich, still use direct coal fire heating, with clanking, churning rummagers being used to prevent the burning of the heavier solubles that congregate at the bottom of the still. This invention was a great benefit to distillers who before then had to employ a man with a broom or an oar to keep scraping the base of the still until the solution came to the boil.

No matter how they are heated, the principle of the still remains the same: the alcohol in the solution held within the still is heated until vapours are given off. These condense at the head of the still and run down an arm into a condenser. This liquid can be distilled again, and each time the strength of the distillate increases. The angle of the arm is important. The higher it tapers off towards the worm or condenser, the more the distillate is likely to run back into the still for re-distillation (the reflux), which will lead to a lighter, less complex spirit. That is the theory, anyway.

Copper being a relatively soft metal, stills do wear thin, especially around the head (the reflux area), the condenser and on the shoulders of the still where the boiling wash or spirit inside has most contact. It is this contact and the dissolving of the metal that enriches the spirit: there is no doubt that the more contact a spirit enjoys with copper the more flavoursome and heavier in character it eventually tends to be.

Gradual erosion of the pot stills keeps the coppersmiths busy, even if no distilleries are being built. In the Speyside town of Rothes there are a number of distilleries, each using copper pot stills. But around the back of one of them, away from the main road bisecting the town, is a large factory hidden out of view. This place is not on the Whisky Trail, but it should be by statute. No matter where you seem to go in the world to inspect distilleries – be it Canada, New Zealand, Japan, Northern Ireland, South Korea, India – there is a name you will spot on the stills: Forsyth's. This, then, is their headquarters.

Unless you are profoundly deaf, a few yards into the entrance and you will be able to discover the plant's purpose in life. No one else makes as many stills in the world as Forsyth's and in its managing director Richard Forsyth is a man used by the malt whisky industry worldwide to put plans into practicality: not just for pot stills, though, but also column ones. First, they might call upon top whisky scientists like Jim Swan and Harry Rifkind to listen to the impeccably researched theory. But for sheer day-to-day experience Richard is also often brought in to make suggestions regarding financial and logistical constraints.

There is little that can beat experience and the Rothes copperworks has been going a long time, being in the Forsyth family for over 60 years. It was Richard's father Ernest who changed the face of the pot still by devising a way of welding plates together rather than riveting them. Until this breakthrough just after the Second World War, all pot stills, though still beautiful, had a look of Herman Munster about them.

Richard Forsyth has been in the trade himself since he was 15 and completed an apprenticeship in coppersmithing. That's why his hands-on style is so appreciated by distillers and why a walk around the plant with him can be such an invigorating experience, even for experienced distillery managers. The last time I was there I watched as the stills for the brand new Isle of Arran distillery were being fashioned into shape amid a head-spinning cacophony of creativity, and whenever I visit that particular distillery I always get an extra kick having seen the stills in their embryonic state.

Pot stills, being living things, die as well. The compound directly outside Forsyth's and backing on to the Caperdonich distillery resembles a graveyard. Stills of all shapes and sizes, some worn within a millimetre of exploding, stand in the Highland drizzle, sad and a little ugly away from the warmth of the stillhouse, but life begets life and these stills will become scrap and get re-cycled, perhaps to be hammered back into being as a still in another part of Speyside or some distant land. Still life: a work of art, indeed.

MATURATION

The final – and some may argue – most important part of the whiskey-making process happens away from the distillery building itself. Certainly, it is vital that the stillman selects the very finest part of the spirit as it trips off the stills. The first spirit to show contains some unpleasant oils which will taint the whisky as it matures; similarly, the weaker spirit at the finish is also unpotable. Both will be re-distilled. It is the middle cut, the heart of the run, which is filled into barrels and then stored in warehouses.

It is only in the last decade or so that the importance of maturation has been properly addressed. These days distillers may employ someone solely to buy casks, his duty being to ensure that they are of good enough quality for maturing spirit to develop and prosper.

In Kentucky, law demands that for bourbon to be bourbon the spirit must mature in virgin oak casks. This is handy for the world's other distillers, especially the Scots. They then buy these casks to fill their malt and grain. The outcome of these whiskies may depend slightly on how long bourbon has been kept in the cask. You may taste a dozen Speyside malt whisky samples side-by-side after they have matured together for a dozen years, but they will each taste a little different. A sample which has matured in a cask which held bourbon for four years is likely to have an oakier outline and be darker in colour than one that kept bourbon for 10 years: there were more chemicals remaining in the wood for the spirit to leach out. However, the taste of the bourbon will not be reflected in the whisky. That is unlike the case of sherry and other fortified wines, which can be detected in the whisky if a distillery has chosen to mature spirit in casks that have come direct from Jerez, Madeira and Oporto.

Whisky will also mature at a faster rate if the climate is hotter. For that reason Tennessee, Kentucky, Indian, Turkish, Spanish whisky, etc., matures much more rapidly than that distilled in Scotland, Canada and New Zealand. The geographical location of the warehouse may also have a say in the whisky's outcome: dank, draughty warehouses by the sea do help impart a salty character to the spirit as it develops; a Canadian warehouse that has been all but hermetically-sealed and temperature-controlled will produce a whisky devoid of natural interference and local character. Likewise, some bourbon and Tennessee distillers like certain casks to cook in the sun and deliberately place them at the top of the warehouse under the rafters. One way or another, the whisky will be shaped by whichever route its maturation process takes.

2 SCOTTISH MALT WHISKY

Offer a visitor a wee dram of your favourite blend, and if he's a whisky drinker he'll be grateful. Offer him a malt, and he'll be honoured. Such is the average person's perception of Scotch single malt whisky. Yet it was not always so. For the best part of a century the world's most noble spirit was kept back from the masses by distillers who felt that malt was too full-bodied and complex to handle. Instead, blends – a mixture of predominantly grain whisky, continuously distilled and of relatively light character, with the maltier, fruitier, earthier more complex malts – were all the rage.

That is not to say that blended Scotch is a poor substitute for a single malt. Admittedly the cheap blends, holding 75 per cent or more of just three-year-old grain, do not bear comparison. But when I was asked to write a "Desert Island" list of Scotch whiskies I would wish to be cast away with, exactly half of my choices were blends, two of them standards. For those blends to have been so complex, so deep and labyrinthine, very good malts had to be in there somewhere. Here malt whisky scores against any other whisky in the world. No other nation on earth can produce a spirit of any type that boasts such enormous diversity of style as Scotch malt whisky.

There are whiskies produced in Kentucky, Tennessee, Canada and Ireland which for sheer class and elegance contemptuously wipe the floor with all but a handful of the best single malts. For while some of the single malts produced in those gleaming, bulbous copper pots mature after eight to 21 years into something that exceeds the sublime, there are many which are at best ordinary, at worst plain awful. For this reason it is dangerous and perhaps ill-informed to make the blanket assertion that Scotch is the greatest of all the world's whiskies. But the best of Scotch malt whisky offers something to the drinker that takes time and patient study to fully understand. And the learning process is as enjoyable as any you are likely to undertake.

Those which take longest to master are usually the Islays, most of them heavily peated and medicinal in character. Once the drinker can get past the shock of taking them on board, silent appraisal will bring its own rewards. The Perthshire region is brimming with distilleries whose spirits have a rich, honey theme to them and appeal to the sweeter tooth and often the fairer sex. The lightest in character are the few remaining Lowlanders; but there are light Speysiders, too – these can often give the tastebuds a sharp, fresh grass jolt. North of Inverness are a clutch of distilleries whose products are at once earthy and slightly citrus-fruity; over at Campbeltown is a single distillery which produces a salty, intense whisky set apart in sheer complexity from any other spirit, let alone whisky, in the world.

Precious goods: *From tiny oak barrels great whiskies grow.*

The wonder of Scotch single malt whisky is that just about every palate will find one somewhere to suit it. And if not, there are numerous underrated blends which most certainly will.

It has only been since the very late 1970s, after a path had been cleared by first Glenfiddich, then Glenmorangie, that single malt Scotch has been looked upon by distillers as a way of keeping drinkers loyal to their products. Today, malt whisky is universally available. Distillers are marketing their malts now with different ages, different strengths and different maturation techniques. Never have whisky drinkers had such an enormous variety of whiskies from which to choose.

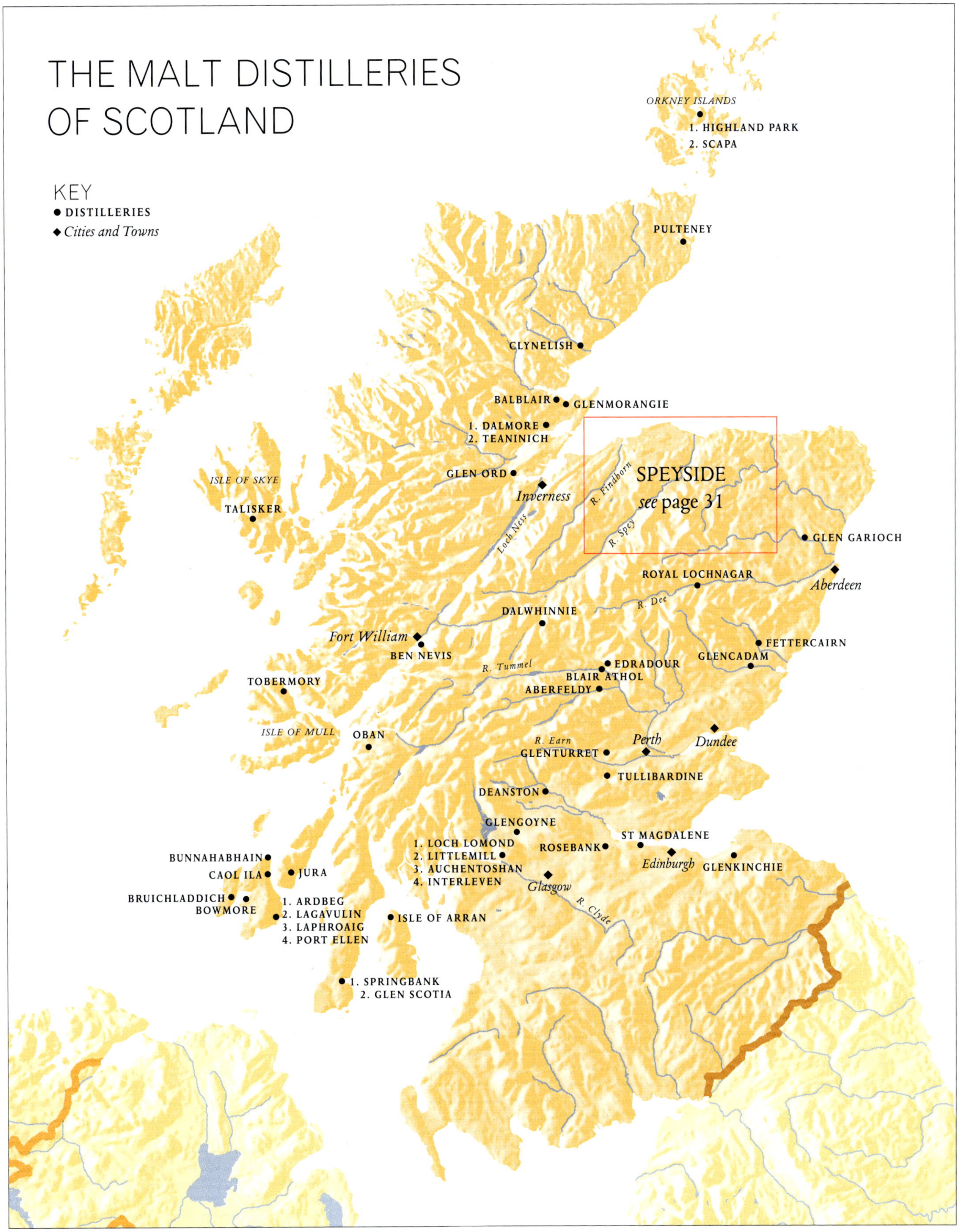
THE MALT DISTILLERIES OF SCOTLAND
KEY
● DISTILLERIES
◆ Cities and Towns
ORKNEY ISLANDS
1. HIGHLAND PARK
2. SCAPA
PULTENEY
CLYNELISH
BALBLAIR
GLENMORANGIE
1. DALMORE
2. TEANINICH
GLEN ORD
Inverness
Loch Ness
R. Findhorn
R. Spey
SPEYSIDE
see page 31
ISLE OF SKYE
TALISKER
GLEN GARIOCH
ROYAL LOCHNAGAR
Aberdeen
R. Dee
DALWHINNIE
Fort William
BEN NEVIS
FETTERCAIRN
GLENCADAM
R. Tummel
EDRADOUR
BLAIR ATHOL
ABERFELDY
TOBERMORY
ISLE OF MULL
OBAN
R. Earn
GLENTURRET
Perth
Dundee
TULLIBARDINE
DEANSTON
GLENGOYNE
ST MAGDALENE
1. LOCH LOMOND
2. LITTLEMILL
3. AUCHENTOSHAN
4. INTERLEVEN
ROSEBANK
Edinburgh
GLENKINCHIE
Glasgow
R. Clyde
BUNNAHABHAIN
CAOL ILA
JURA
BRUICHLADDICH
BOWMORE
1. ARDBEG
2. LAGAVULIN
3. LAPHROAIG
4. PORT ELLEN
ISLE OF ARRAN
1. SPRINGBANK
2. GLEN SCOTIA

THE HISTORY OF SCOTCH

It may come as a surprise to many that Scotland was not the cradle of whisky; it has been the Scots' Celtic cousins across the Irish Sea who have claimed that distinction. But in my youth one of the first distillery managers I ever met told me, "Aye, the Irish may've have invented the stuff. But, by jings, man, we were the ones who perfected it" – a saying that has been repeated to me countless times since. Actually, once you cut through the hearsay and legend, I have yet to find any proof of the Irish beating the Scots to whisky and there is a move afoot to claim that it may have been the Welsh who first distilled from malt. But that's another story...

James IV: *Drinker or doctor?*

What is certain is that by the year 1494, the art of turning barley into malt and then malt into a water-clear, fiery liquid had arrived in the mountainous, wild, warlike land north of Hadrian's Wall. A couple of years ago, the Scotch whisky industry was celebrating its 500th birthday, and at the epicentre of their toasts and gratitude was a monk far more famous in this age than he was in his own, one Friar John Cor. "Eight bolls of malt to Friar John Cor, by order of the King, wherewith to make aqua vitae," reads an extract in the Exchequer Rolls for 1494. It was not unknown for monks to make *aqua vitae* as a medicine; that had been happening throughout the length and breadth of the British Isles for centuries before. What made this so important was that it was the first-ever reference to barley being the principal ingredient to make it with; until then, *aqua vitae*, Latin for "the water of life", had been made from wine.

The Gaelic term for aqua vitae was *uisge-beatha*. This, when spoken over the years, was shortened and pronounced "usky". Thus was derived the name whisky. The fact that Friar John was given the equivalent of well over 1,000 lbs of malt to distil from meant this was no part-time hobby. It has often been stated that the king in question, James IV of Scotland, was known to enjoy his drink and that much of Friar Cor's spirit may have found its way into his stomach. That may be the case, but what is rarely mentioned is that at this stage the king was in his early twenties and considered himself something of a doctor. It is equally likely, then, that much was for His Majesty's medical requirements. A further point, and one that will further jar with the traditionalists, is that Scotland's first known malt whisky was Lowland, not Highland, in make.

After that first reference, other mentions of whisky became more common. Today we travel the Highlands by car or bicycle, taking in the beauty and the glory of mountain, glen and coast and leave with fond memories and a sense of well-being. But for the crofter living between the sixteenth and nineteenth centuries, who somehow had to eke out a living for himself and his family on weather-ravaged, often unyielding land, life was hard. So when he had the opportunity to make a spirit from barley that may well have rotted if not put to other use, he did so. This spirit was priceless in the long, hard winters. And when his harvest failed, he could sell his whisky to raise the money needed to make ends meet. It was this understanding of the situation which led to the crofters' landlords openly encouraging them to distil.

With so much alcohol being made in the Highlands, it was only a matter of time before governments on both sides of the border decided they could make some serious money out of it in the form of Excise taxes, and made a particular point of enforcing them when there were wars to be paid for. The early history of Scotch whisky is one long series of taxes – even malt was taxed for a while. Smuggling became a major industry in the Highlands; a bloody one, too, as the illicit

Roman remains: *Would the Wall have been built if Hadrian had known of "uisge-beatha"?*

distillers tried to outwit the "gaugers", as Excise men were called.

The Revenue men were paid only a pittance by their masters and as such they became bounty hunters, receiving from the government half the value of the spirit seized. The wages and lodging of the assistant who patrolled with the Excise man were paid from his own pocket, not the government's. So the battle between the gauger and the smuggler became a personal one between two parties whose living depended on the outcome. It was not surprising, then, that sometimes lives were lost on both sides, or horrific injuries were sustained.

Furthermore, the Excise man was hampered by the simple fact that it was the same powerful landowners, who encouraged and often benefited from the locals making their illegal whisky, who were asked to preside over the courts that determined the fate of smugglers and illicit distillers once they were caught. One of the reasons these distillers had been so prolific was because their landlords had often turned a blind eye to their nefarious practices in the first place.

All this changed radically in 1823, when a piece of government legislation was introduced which was to alter the course of whisky distilling in Scotland permanently. This Act made it easier and cheaper for the legal distiller to operate than at any time before. The main drawback was that they had to operate one still that was of at least 40 gallons capacity – far too large to be hidden away in a barn or gully and carried about from bothy to bothy. A consequence of this legislation which was often overlooked was the pressure it now placed on the landowners: they were liable to be prosecuted for illegal stills found working on their lands, whether they knew of them or not. Hence many illicit distillers turned respectable and were helped along the way by their landlords. Even so, some smugglers and distillers refusing to pay tax responded by burning down the new legal distilleries and threatening the proprietors. It was in this atmosphere of hostility that John Smith famously kept a packed pistol as he set up what is now the Glenlivet Distillery.

Naughty but nice: *Making illicit whisky was a major industry in the 18th and 19th centuries.*

With distilling becoming more widespread, inventors were looking at ways to distil more efficiently, and thus more economically, than the very slow pot-still method. Robert Stein had a number of distilleries in the Lowlands of Scotland and devised a method of continuous distillation which was crude, though ingenious. An Irishman, Aeneas Coffey, had been thinking along the same lines and made a more efficient model. Soon distilleries in the Lowlands were employing these stills to supply cheap whisky to the markets of Glasgow and Edinburgh in particular.

It was when this light whisky was blended with the more pungent malts that whisky as a spirit began to take off on an international scale. Until then, malt whisky had been considered far too much of an acquired taste for nations like the English, who were more used to softer, sweeter brandies from France. However, the arrival of the *phylloxera vastatrix* louse, which devastated the grape crops of France, led to a shortage of wine and brandy. First Irish whiskey and then Scotch blends took their place.

Not all publicans, or blenders come to that, were scrupulous. There was a demand for single malt as well as blended whisky, but occasionally what people received was young, pure grain whisky while brandies, like malt pot-still whiskies, were also adulterated with grain spirit without any warning given. By the turn of the twentieth century, the practice had become endemic, and it was one small London borough which bravely decided to act as watchdog for the nation.

In 1905, Islington Council in North London began issuing summonses to traders who they felt were duping the public with what they considered a vastly inferior, neutral spirit which was anything but what the customer had asked for. These successful prosecutions were the first skirmishes in the war which was eventually to culminate in the "What is Whisky?" case. After Islington's stand there was such heated debate about the subject that two years later the government agreed to set up a Royal Commission which sat through much of 1908 listening to experts in the field of health, engineering, chemistry and whisky distilling itself, from both camps of malt and grain distillers.

By the time the malt distillers were heard they themselves had adopted a softer line on the grain producers. While Islington Council fought for spirit made only from malted barley and in pot stills to be deemed Scotch whisky, the pot-still distillers torpedoed the case somewhat by accepting that grain whisky

A wee dram: *The revelry of Scotsmen partaking of their national drink became an oft-depicted caricature.*

spirit could be called whisky, providing it did not make up more than (as Alexander Walker of Johnnie Walker was one of many to suggest) half of the blend. It was John MacDonald of Ben Nevis Distillery who perhaps summed it up best when he told the Commission, "If it were not for the Highland malt, Scotch whisky would be practically non-existent and but for the toning-down by Lowland grain whisky, it would not have obtained its world-wide popularity. I have always found that our self-whisky did not sell so well in the south as in the north."

Why had the malt distillers become quite so accommodating? Perhaps it was the gradual realization that they would need blended whisky to survive. The entire whisky industry was still feeling some of the shockwaves of the Pattison crash of 1898 which had ended the days of Scotch being a gold nugget industry. For a decade up till then investors had poured many thousands of pounds into building new distilleries and producing as much spirit as they could. One of their main customers was a firm called Pattison, Elder and Co., run by a pair of rogues, brothers Robert and Walter Pattison. In a style of which Robert Maxwell would have been proud, they did everything on an enormous scale and their business became so enmeshed in credit that they gave the appearance of stature, yet had no substance at all. They built up enormous stocks of malt, but were not using anything like the amount they needed, as their blends got away with the minimum required to give flavour.

Some in the industry had warned of the Pattisons' financial situation. Yet they were sucked in nonetheless, fearing that they might lose out. In the end, the Pattisons went down for the then massive amount of £250,000 with distillers owed the vast portion of it. It was that which had heightened hostilities between the grain and malt makers. But some blenders remained in a powerful position. The late nineteenth and early twentieth centuries was the era of the whisky barons, men who made vast fortunes by selling their blended whisky worldwide. They were led by the flamboyant Tommy Dewar, followed by James Buchanan of Black and White fame, Peter Mackie with his White Horse, John Haig and Alexander Walker of Johnnie Walker – names which are still famous today.

Fearing that their malts might be cut out of these blends, distillers reluctantly faced up to the truth: the world preferred a lighter spirit. And in 1909 the Royal Commission agreed, allowing spirit made from cereals other than pure malt to be produced in continuous stills and call itself whisky. It was later that a three-year-old stipulation was added.

Scotch whisky is doubtless better than it was a century ago. Customers demand and expect better quality. And there is no doubt that without blended whisky there would be very few malt distilleries surviving today.

Whisky baron: *Lord Dewar gained wealth and respectability on the back of his blending empire (above).*

ORKNEYS AND NORTHERN

There is probably no better place to start a grand tour of those palaces of industry known as Scottish malt whisky distilleries than in the Orkneys. Not necessarily because the very best whisky is made there, because it isn't – though daily they have a damned good try. No, it is because the fate and the practices of its two distilleries can be seen as a microcosm of the industry as a whole.

On the one hand there is Highland Park, a traditional, big-stoned, twin-pagoda Victorian-style distillery, right down to its unique and mysteriously "Y"-shaped active floor maltings, which enjoys a worldwide reputation for its velvety, heathery make. On the other, there is Scapa. Except for blenders and a few connoisseurs in the know, it is virtually unheard of, despite the fact that the maturing spirit in its warehouses is rarely anything less than excellent. But from the outside it is a somewhat characterless, functional-looking building, its ugliness cruelly exposed against the deceptively tranquil setting on the shores of Scapa Bay, close to where the German fleet was scuppered in Scapa Flow in 1919.

While Highland Park thrives, its owners using it as their flagship malt to be carried like a torch across the markets of the world, Scapa has been closed since the early 1990s and, inevitably, there are questions about whether it will ever distil again. So there you have it in the space of a mile or two: two distilleries separated not just by peat and burn but by the aspirations of their parent companies. Highland Park, famed for its superstar 12- and 25-year-old single malts, is a big wheel in a relatively medium-sized concern. Scapa is a tiny, though (we hope) not totally expendable, cog in the massive machinery that is Allied Domecq – a pit pony distillery valued only for its contribution to an interminable number of blends.

HIGHLAND PARK

The Orkneys are a group of islands in the northeastern corner of Scotland, famed for their standing stones and carefully preserved Viking settlements. Highland Park is found on the outskirts of the islands' capital, Kirkwall. It is old, dating back to 1798, and has the proud claim of being the northernmost distillery in Scotland, just a fraction further north than Scapa. It was once also slightly further north than a third distillery, Stromness, to the west, which Barnard regarded, when visiting the islands in the mid-1880s, as "the most remote Distillery in the kingdom". Its output was about equal to that of Edradour, today the smallest distillery in Scotland by far. That was not altogether surprising: one of the stills used, a strange pumpkin-shaped affair, was originally the apparatus of an illicit distiller. This is in keeping with Orkney. Of all the hundreds of old smuggling tales of the Scottish isles I have been told or have read about, those involving the Orkneys outnumber all the others. Stromness Distillery, later renamed Man of Hoy, limped to its centenary but closed for the last time in 1928.

The geographical honour held by Highland Park has been served with great distinction. It insists on embracing many of the customs held dear, such as cutting local peat from Hobbister Moor for use in the malting process, which means that the pagodas are not mere ornamental appendages to the old building like so many others around the land, but actually serve their intended purpose. This peat helps to give the malt a delicious heatheriness and a full, sweet, yet oddly understated smokiness. The malt, smoked to a heavy phenol level of 20 ppm, is then blended with unpeated malt which is shipped to the island. The result is an Orcadian delight – a character which sets it apart and has won many admirers over the years.

In the manager's old-fashioned office framed letters of testimony and allegiance hang dustily above the fireplace which holds a busy, crackling hearth. Among them is one from Winston Churchill, a black sheep from brandy-drinking stock. If he had still been around, he might have noticed a slight wavering in the distillery's consistently high-quality output. For a year or two I detected an

> *Connoisseur's Selection*
>
> **HIGHLAND PARK** – AT BEST AS 12-YEAR-OLD DISTILLERY BOTTLING. OUTSTANDING BUT NOT AS PEATY AS IT USED TO BE.

Golden memories: *(Above) Yet the distillery was by this time 150 years old.*

uncharacteristic harshness. It has gone now, doubtless a temporary blip caused by the use of some sub-standard casks during a wood shortage of the early 1980s. I will be surprised to see it reappear.

SCAPA

If only dodgy casks was all that poor Scapa, with its manager banished to Speyside, had to worry about. It is unlikely the general public will get the chance to discuss its form. Apart from some independently bottled efforts, the most notable by Gordon & MacPhail, it is a malt rarely seen, although it is finding its way into supermarkets here and there as an own-label. Allied have recently launched it into duty-free as a 10-year-old, which perfectly captures the lightness and sophistication that is the distillery's hallmark and shares with Highland Park a honeyed theme.

Because Allied wanted to present Scapa as an attractive proposition to blenders, they insisted on making the whisky there with completely unpeated malt. Even so, Scapa defiantly hints at something smoky, possibly thanks to the water which once bubbled in a redundant wash still of the squat, slightly deformed-looking Lomond variety.

Orkney, treeless and windswept, has a melancholy air, despite its beauty and rich historical pickings. Sadly, the same could be said for the silent stillhouse at Scapa.

PULTENEY *(Pult-nay)*

While Highland Park revels in its fame as Scotland's most northerly distillery, Pulteney goes about its business as the mainland's with quiet dignity. Like Scapa, it has never gained much notoriety as a single malt beyond its own community, but has produced, year after year, a very decent dram for blending and one not short on character.

It is a major trek to visit Pulteney: there is no strong reason to go there other than as on a holiday or in order to visit the distillery. Perhaps you are nearing completion of a walk, jog or cycle from Land's End to John o' Groats and passing Wick on the very last leg of your journey up the A9. At one time you would have found any number of distilleries operating north of Wick in the bleak openness of Caithness. There were stills at Brabster, Murkle, Greenland and Gerston near Thurso, the last one dying out as the twentieth century dawned. But these were just shooting stars compared with the perpetual northern light of Pulteney.

You have to lurk around the back streets of Wick for a while before finally locating Pulteney. No pagodas or any of the frilly stuff here. Despite being the home of only two stills, it is a substantial old distillery, complete with a courtyard, but has been subjected to the same pragmatic approach as Scapa. Indeed, it was owned by the same company. Today, though, it is under the control of Inver House Distillers, who are making a habit of acquiring fine, undervalued distilleries. They have wasted no time in unleashing an impeccable 12-year-old, exceptionally busy on the palate with a brininess that mingles gratiously with the tingly malt and faint peat and coffee. It may also be one to keep in the medicine cabinet. The barmaid of the hotel at which I stayed some years back told me that her mother owed her life to the drink. When she was born, she was very weak and there were fears that she would not survive. So her mother applied a mixture of tepid water and straight Pulteney to her ailing daughter, who pulled through against all the odds: "My gran always said it was down to the Pulteney." Ah, *uisge beatha*: water of life, indeed.

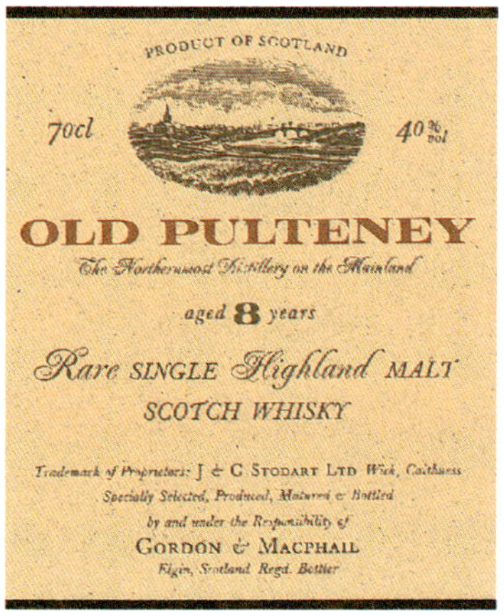

CLYNELISH *(Kline-leesh)*

Despite recent road widening, the journey down the A9 to Sutherland, with the sheer drop to the ocean on the left, can be a heart-in-the-mouth affair, especially when the sea mist rolls in, as it so often does. Clynelish Distillery can be found on the right on the approach to the charming town of Brora. As you follow the sign to the distillery you are met with perhaps the most classical example of a large Victorian pagoda distillery still standing in Scotland. Despite its size it is a masterpiece of elegance in stone, even down to the massive warehouses.

Sadly, however, it is no longer the Clynelish Distillery. It held this distinction until 1968 but was superseded by a box-shaped monstrosity which the old Scottish Malt Distillers company considered a worthy replacement. The whisky produced there is, admittedly, pretty fine and highly prized by a number of blenders. But it is not a patch on the original distillery's make, which was fruitier and slightly peatier, perhaps because its water came from a different source.

Even in that bygone age of the 1920s, when it was not seemly to try to explain what one felt about one's whisky, George Saintsbury, one of Britain's most respected palates, swore by Clynelish. It is quite a while since I found some of its traditional make, but what a full-bodied, rich dram that was and, to a lesser degree, still is. The whisky made at the old distillery is still to be had, though not in that form. It comes under the name of Brora and is probably among the most superb single malts to be found today. It is about the peatiest mainland malt you will find, registering a massive 40 ppm as part of an Islay-style experiment. During that time it was distilled as Clynelish B, as the new, shoe-box style distillery produced Clynelish A. Customs and Excise, following the rule set at the turn of the century at Glen Grant, insisted that the two whiskies should be called something completely different. So the proud old Clynelish had the ignominy of being renamed Brora before it was closed down altogether on March 17, 1983.

Clynelish: *Rolling hills by a rolling sea and good whisky to boot. Shame about the building.*

Local people certainly know the value of the malt. A few years back it was thought that the angels who took their share of the evaporating whisky in one of the warehouses were an unusually greedy lot, since the casks seemed to be reducing in content at an alarming rate. The mystery was solved when some men were discovered in the warehouse helping themselves to a free dram or two. They had entered via a tunnel they had secretly dug. Meanwhile, the old distillery, despite being a listed building, is falling into a state of disrepair. The distillery manager, Bob Robertson, who was here before the present distillery came on stream, has long tried to find funds from his maintenance budget to keep it from caving in, but is fighting a losing battle. This is a shame because, despite everything, it could still operate. The stills are there; the wash could be piped from the new distillery. All that is missing is a spirit safe, a holding tank, feints charger – and a miracle.

Connoisseur's Selection

SCAPA – HOLDS UP BRILLIANTLY AS A 15-YEAR-OLD WITH STRONG CHOCOLATE CHARACTER.

PULTENEY – YOU DON'T HAVE TO WAIT TOO LONG FOR THIS ONE TO MATURE. EXCELLENT AT EIGHT YEARS.

CLYNELISH – THE MAGNIFICENTLY PEATED BRORA IS WORTH THE INVESTMENT: IT WILL NOT LAST FOREVER.

NORTHERN HIGHLANDS

To the south of Clynelish, but before the sprawling bridge which carries you into Inverness, is a quarter of Scotland blessed with some of the most glorious of the country's distilleries and as yet still relatively undiscovered. These are the five distilleries found in the area around the Dornoch and Cromarty Firths, north and west of the appropriately named Black Isle. Two of these distilleries, Balblair and Dalmore, are about as classic and aesthetically perfect as you could possibly wish for. The two which were once in the hands of Scottish Malt Distillers, Glen Ord and Teaninich, have something of the ugly duckling about them while the best-known of them all, Glenmorangie, remains a little gem by the sea despite all its fame. Together they form a style of whisky quite unique in its earthiness and certainly worthy of its own region.

BALBLAIR *(Bale-blair)*

Balblair, to the north of the village of Edderton, stands proudest of all. It has barely changed a granite slab since being rebuilt at the end of the last century in that elegant style which has since become the architectural benchmark for all of Scotland's, and in some ways of the world's, malt distilleries. Originally dating back to 1790, it is the second or third oldest distillery in Scotland, depending on whose evidence you listen to, and has a rather confusing past as there was once, apparently, a Balblair distillery a few miles south on the Black Isle as well. The pedigree of the current distillery, though, is now beyond doubt. In 1990 a local farmer contacted long-standing and recently retired manager Jim Yeats and asked if he was interested in some old books he had found: they turned out to be the earliest ledgers of the distillery, a remarkable find and one that keeps that farmer well stocked in whisky each Christmas.

While it is doubtless impossible to find two identical whiskies from the hundred or so made throughout Scotland, there can be similarities in the buildings themselves. The hamlet and lands next to Balblair Distillery are called Ardmore, which is a coincidence because the Ardmore Distillery in Aberdeenshire could almost be its twin. Not only are their designs very similar, but both distilleries have railway lines running directly past them at exactly the same angle to the still-house and old maltings. Ardmore has had its stillhouse increased three-fold, but Balblair continues to make do with just the two coppers, although there is a second spirit still which, though redundant for the last 20 years or so, would be the last working riveted still in Scotland if called back into action. And where Ardmore's whisky is peaty, Balblair's once used to be: the area the distillery was built in was once known as the "Parish of the Peats".

I have always admired Balblair's whisky, which for many years found its way into Allied's blends. But early in 1996 it was mothballed and in danger of the same fate as befell it in the years from 1915 to 1947 when it was closed down altogether. As then, a white knight charged to its rescue. This time it was Inver House which, having just secured Pulteney, stepped in with a surprise bid for this wonderful old distillery which became theirs during the summer of 1996. Enchanted with their newest purchase, Inver House intend to bottle Balblair as a single malt: a wise choice. Allied had left it to Gordon & MacPhail to keep the flag flying, which they did with panache. It is a malt with no qualms about being tasted young: at six or seven it has already attained a firm spiciness. Gordon & MacPhail excelled with a crisp 10-year-old, citrussy sweet in parts and not a little phenolic in the finale; while samples I have tasted over the years at 13 and 16, in particular, have been quite superb, the former absolutely brimming with a delicious cocoa bitterness and subtle hints of top-quality bourbon. I could never quite understand why Allied never made this one of their principal single malts. After over 200 years, Balblair's time could just be arriving.

GLENMORANGIE *(Glen-Moranjee)*

A little matter of five miles away, to the south-east, the most popular malt whisky in Scotland is made. Glenmorangie is also perhaps the most mispronounced distillery in the land: the accent falls on the "m", not the "a". Despite Glenmorangie being Scotland's best seller and a common feature in Britain's pubs and clubs, the parent company has not been having the happiest time of it and, after a period of refusing to allow the spirit from Scotland's tallest stills – at a fraction over 17 feet 10 inches – to become part of the blends of others, at last they are taking orders. This is being filled into casks under the uninspiring name of Westport. The tiniest fraction of Glen Moray is tipped into the filling tank – not enough to have any effect on the flavour of the maturing whisky but sufficient to prevent independent bottlers grabbing hold of a cask and selling it under the famous Glenmorangie name as a single malt.

The distillery sits comfortably by the sea, but is fed from a group of springs at Tarlogie which give an unusually hard water. It seems to like those amazingly slender stills and its coastal position, because after 10 years a malt arrives which, to nose, has all the charm of an evening garden in early summer. And to taste, the malt itself is magnificently rich, complemented by a spice and citrussy tang found among most of the distilleries north of Inverness, yet this is still naturally the lightest in the region.

Despite the great play made of the stills, it is the contents of the Glenmorangie warehouses which impress me most. There has been some remarkable experimentation in rounding their whiskies off in different casks. It all started with the 18-year-old; all Glenmorangie new make is filled into ex-bourbon cask. To take out some over-woodiness for the 18, it was decided to allow it to soften and sweeten a little in ex-sherry butts. The results were sensational. Now they have them out in Port Wood, Madeira Wood and Tain L'Hermitage.

The latter is the one I think works least well. It possesses an austerity which actually reduces the complexity of the whisky and makes for the most disappointing, quite ordinary Glenmorangie I've ever tasted. Much better is the Madeira finish where we are back to sweet, floral notes and a lingering, almost herbal finish: fascinating. By far the pick of the bunch, though, is the Port Wood. It can differ slightly in character and colour from bottle to bottle. But never, ever, drink when cold; always warm up to body temperature. This is the Rolls Royce of all Glenmorangie's output, breathtakingly complex and multi-layered in its gentle assault on the tastebuds. At cask strength it is even more astonishing, with deep spices and buttery notes, but unfortunately it is not yet available for general consumption in that form.

No one knows exactly why Glenmorangie, even in its normal 10-year-old incarnation, is so distinctive. Maybe it's the micro-climate: recently I was trapped in a warehouse there due to a hailstorm sending down ice the size of musket shot; some years back while walking back from Tarlogie I was caught in a ferocious rainstorm but when I looked up the distillery was at the very end of the most vivid rainbow I had ever seen. You see, there really are pots of gold...

Glenmorangie: *Its old buildings are as stylish as its whisky.*

Connoisseur's Selection

BALBLAIR – EXCELLENT RESONANCE AT AROUND 15-YEARS-OLD.

GLENMORANGIE – SPOILED FOR CHOICE. YOU CAN'T GO WRONG AT ANY AGE BUT DO TRY THE ASTONISHING PORT AND MADEIRA CASK FINISHES IN PARTICULAR.

DALMORE – IF YOU SEE THE ULTRA-RICH 12-YEAR-OLD GET TWO BOTTLES – THE FIRST WON'T LAST LONG!

DALMORE *(Dale-more)*

As the main A9 trunk road swings round to follow the peninsula sandwiched between the Dornoch and Cromarty Firths it eventually arrives at Alness. The younger of the two distilleries here (though to look at them you would never credit it) is Dalmore, another cluster of old stones set with magnificent taste a century or so back next to the sea, its aspect beyond the shell ducks and oystercatchers spoilt somewhat by oil rigs further down the Firth. Classic is a grossly over-used phrase in the drinks world, but make no mistake: Dalmore is a classic whisky.

I have never really understood why this malt has failed to take the market by storm. Despite their acquisition of the Invergordon distilleries, Dalmore remains the crown jewel in Whyte & Mackay's portfolio. None of their other distilleries offers a malt which is outwardly so macho, but on further study, preferably late at night with a friend or alone after a tiring day, offers a subtlety and grace available only in the world's finer whiskies. Ten years back the 12-year-old malt was lighter in style with a bigger, citrus-type fruit. Today it is weightier, in a sherrier kind of way, more lush

Dalmore: *An ancient distillery looking out onto the Cromarty Firth and still awaiting discovery.*

and muscular (and none the worse for that). It is also a very consistent dram and I cannot remember the last time I found one that was out of true.

The distillery itself offers the quirkiest of stillrooms. Barnard must have seen it when he visited in the mid-1880s, but he doesn't mention that the spirit stills are shaped like the trumpet of a daffodil or the funnels of a steam train. These are copper-clad cooling jackets. The original has the date 1874 on it and is still doing its job today, allowing water to fill inside and assist early condensation. With that and its eight wooden washbacks, this is a great distillery both to visit and to sample the fruits of. The malt does change quite dramatically between 20 months and 20 years and stands up well to age. But a dozen years in the cask is just about spot-on, as the finish at this age just goes on and on...

TEANINICH *(Te-an-in-ick)*

Just up the River Alness is a distillery that finds itself slap in the middle of an industrial estate; when it was built in 1817 it was on the outskirts of town in the middle of a laird's estate. This is Teaninich, another distillery reprieved from possible closure after being mothballed for six years until 1991. This time, rather than sell or close, someone at United Distillers recognized this as a distillery that was simply too good to die. The style when bottled as a 10-year-old is remarkably close to how Dalmore's was 10–15 years ago: lots of citrus and spice but with that rumbling hint of peat which always seems to crop up in these most northern of malts, despite the malt used being almost unpeated.

Like those other old DCL houses, Clynelish, Glendullan and Linkwood, the distillery found itself with two separate stillhouses, making slightly different spirit, following rebuilding. Only the new stills are currently in operation, though the older stillhouse, which makes a slightly fatter whisky, could still be operated. One of the people in charge of them is a new breed of production manager, the female. Soon, one suspects, Cathy Earnshaw will be leaving to take over her own distillery having proved, just like Bessie Williamson did at Laphroaig a generation or two before, that making whisky is not necessarily a man's game. She will be lucky, though, to find one making whisky quite as well as Teaninich.

GLEN ORD

The most southerly of this cluster of distilleries is found at the Muir of Ord near Beauly. You can forgive those at Glen Ord for experiencing a personality crisis. Not that long ago the distillery was called Muir of Ord, then Ord and now Glen Ord. For a spell the whisky was sold as Ordie and to confuse matters further, the style of the bottled whisky has changed as well. At its best it is brooding and combative on the palate, full of the earthy, rooty spices which set this region apart. That character is still in there, but has to be searched out more than of old as there appears to be a kind of sherry-esque interference which flattens out the naturally occurring peaks and troughs. Tasted blind it's OK, but, knowing what it is, I don't much care for the sherry intrusion as I can remember how good Ord was without it. Today if I drink Ord, it is usually from very old, dwindling stock of samples from ex-bourbon cask, often quite excellent, obtained elsewhere. For once I feel United Distillers have got it badly wrong. It is as if someone wishes to obliterate a generic style.

Still, the distillery remains a good place to visit. Although it is not exactly the prettiest you will find, overshadowed rather by the massive industrial maltings next door, for anyone needing to learn very quickly how a malt distillery operates, this is it. Everything is done on a single level, you can see the next process from the last one, and the guides are usually superb.

Try and find some independent Ord. For many years until his retirement in 1995, the distillery was run by Willie Meikle, one of the most technically gifted of all Scottish distillery managers. During his time he made some cracking stuff there. If United Distillers would drop the off-key sherry approach, we would all be able to experience just how good it was.

Connoisseur's Selection

TEANINICH – SO RARE. GET AT ANY AGE.

GLEN ORD – LOOK FOR AN INDEPENDENT BOTTLING.

SPEYSIDE

The coastal route west of Inverness toward Fraserburgh is a satisfying one. There are a number of extremely agreeable fishing villages, beaches and heads to make the trip here really enjoyable. There are two particularly charming villages: Portsoy, which specializes in the fashioning of crystallized rock, and cliff-framed Pennan, a village which gained international immortality thanks to the film *Local Hero*.

There are also distilleries on this coast, which is to be expected given that such rivers as the Spey, Deveron, and Lossie all empty into the Moray Firth, an expanse of sea whose

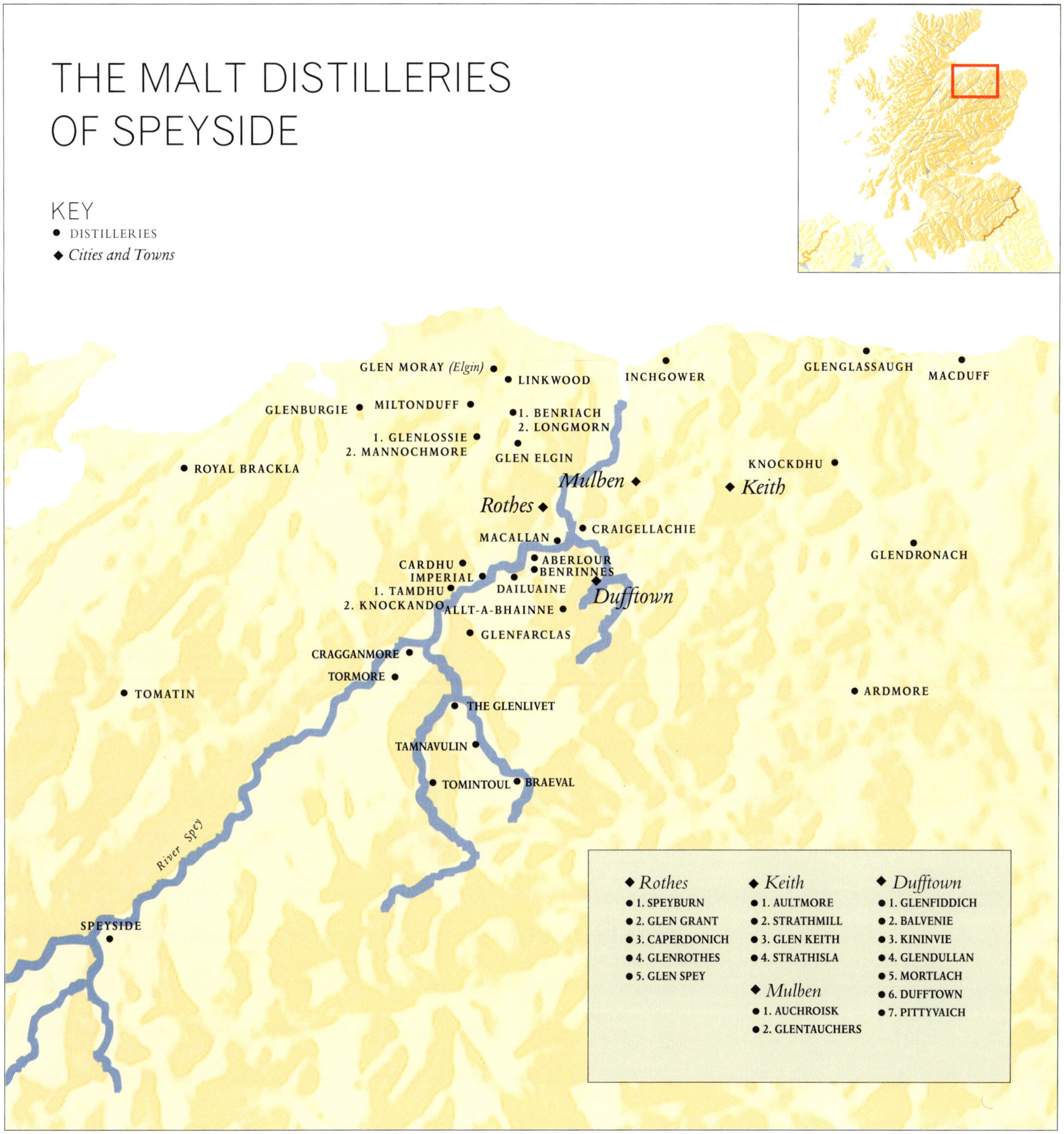

tranquillity is regularly interrupted by the dull thud of training runs by RAF bombers. And just like the distilleries north of Inverness, this group have something in common: this time it is near-anonymity. If you can name all the distilleries, working and mothballed, which run along this coastline, give yourself a pat on the back.

ROYAL BRACKLA

From Inverness, the first you will reach is Royal Brackla. To describe this as a coastal whisky is stretching the point a bit because it is a few miles south of Nairn. Like Teaninich, it has been producing busily since 1991 after six years of silence.

It is one of three Scottish single malts available today with either a prefix or a suffix which links it to royal patronage (the others being Royal Lochnagar and Glenury Royal), this one dating all the way back to 1835 and King William IV. Some books I have read mysteriously suggest the distillery is close to the River Findhorn. In fact, the Findhorn is many miles away to the east and Royal Brackla sits close to the lonely and beautiful spot where the Allt Dearg swells the River Nairn, though its sweet waters emanate from the Cawdor Burn. The buildings, housing four neat stills, are a mix of the old and new and for the last few years the malt has been available first as a 10-year-old for their Flora and Fauna range, then seemingly used by United Distillers to fill a gap in the economy-priced malt market.

Don't be fooled: the price does not reflect the quality. There is no age statement, but it is a beauty. As a character guide, this is a delicious whisky when at 10 years, light when compared to the northern drams of before, but well in tune with Speyside. The malt is intense and sweet and there is a wonderful chocolate-oak finale with traces of peaty earthiness at the very end. Even at eight years it contains a flighty youth, certainly, but there is maximum complexity for its age.

GLENBURGIE *and* BENROMACH

Offering not quite such a good malt is Glenburgie. Before you reach there you pass through Forres where there are the silent distilleries of Dallas Dhu and Benromach. It is understandable in harsh commercial terms that distilleries should close due to overcapacity. But why Dallas Dhu, now a public-owned museum, was sacrificed is open to hostile debate. Its labyrinthine, roasted-coffee-ish malt was easily the finest made in this part of Scotland and possibly one of the top 10 in the country. It is still available, as is Benromach, which was also pretty decent, a fuller-bodied affair with a lovely salty, oaky tang. The independent bottlers Gordon & MacPhail have bought the gutted buildings and, having removed several tons of bird droppings, are embarking on a plan to install a very small plant which should be operational by 1998, but producing a different make entirely.

 Royal Brackla: *Back in production having been silent for six years.*

And so to Glenburgie. This being an Allied distillery, two things can be guaranteed. First, it is as neat and tidy as any you will find. Second, they have left it to Gordon & MacPhail to push as a single malt. A third, additional point, is that an alternative whisky, called Glencraig, was made here from Lomond stills. With the stills being removed in the early 1980s, that is now a very rare whisky indeed.

I can never resist popping into the distillery grounds when I'm passing just for a second or two's glimpse. Close by the office buildings is a tiny, stone, hut-like construction with stairs taking you below ground level. This, remarkably, is the site of the first stillhouse when it was built in 1829 as the Kilnflat Distillery. With such an evidently tiny output, it is hardly surprising that it went out of business before the current distillery was constructed around it in the 1870s.

The Glenburgie whiskies marketed by Gordon & MacPhail are varied. Allied themselves once marketed a very fizzy and under-ripe five-year-old and Gordon & MacPhail bottle at eight. This can sometimes be quite lush and sweet, but I have sampled rather disappointing, feinty, vattings. They have also brought out a welcome 10-year-old from three casks at a fraction under 60 per cent proof and here we are getting to the distillery's optimum age. So well do Gordon & MacPhail regard Glenburgie that, as part of their Centenary Celebrations in 1995, they offered a 1948 version, full of honeysuckle and oak on the nose and delicate grapey, malty notes on the palate, with a refined, sweet finish: a remarkably well-kept malt for its age. Much more thick-set and bouncy is the Glencraig, as one might expect from a Lomond still. I must admit I prefer this rich, sweet, oily monster with all its surging fruit and malt notes. Although part of the Glenburgie site, it really must go down as another lost – and lamented – distillery.

Connoisseur's Selection

ROYAL BRACKLA – THE UNAGED VERSION IS CHEAP AND VERY CHEERFUL.

GLENBURGIE – HUNT THE GLENCRAIG OR SETTLE FOR SOMETHING AROUND 12-YEAR-OLD.

BENROMACH – MOST OF GORDON AND MACPHAIL'S BOTTLINGS SHOW ITS WEIGHTY CHARM.

INCHGOWER – THE 14-YEAR-OLD MAY BE FLAWED, BUT STILL FASCINATING.

GLENGLASSAUGH – AT 12 PLUS, YOU WILL BE GIVING YOURSELF A MAJOR TREAT.

INCHGOWER

On the other side of Elgin, where the A98 skirts around Buckie, is arguably Scotland's most attractively constructed distillery, Inchgower. It is now part of the United Distillers empire, but escaped harm as it was acquired by them when the Bell's organization joined the fold and so had never been subjected to Scottish Malt Distillers' rebuilding programme. What makes the distillery almost unique in style anywhere in the world are the low-slung buildings which mean the distillery takes up a large area of ground. When Bell's produced a delightful little booklet about their company in November 1935, there was a lot about the Dufftown and Blair Athol distilleries, but not a jot about Inchgower. That is because it came under their auspices the following year, picked up for the princely sum of £3,000 from the owners, the local council. AK Bell, hearing that the mansion house next door was also on offer, added a further £1,000 for that as well. Reportedly, the provost who accepted the deal was later heard to remark, "That was the first time I had been done twice in one day."

Bell's were by then already a successful company, but were nowhere near as powerful as in the 1960s and 1970s when their blend took the British market by storm. Such was the demand for their whisky that shortcuts were taken in both its manufacture and maturation and the apparatus's upkeep. Even now I shudder at the thought of the 12-year-old Inchgower marketed by Bell's. Fiery and "dirty" to taste then, its fresh spirit has picked up now under the new owners and, though the 14-year-old – made during Bell's reign – can on the nose remind you of some of its failings, its salty character and dry maltiness with buttery oak and faint hint of peat are quite a delight.

GLENGLASSAUGH

(Glen-glas-soph)

To continue along the coast road will take you past Cullen and, before you come to Portsoy, a small turn to the left will take you to the cliff edge and the Glenglassaugh Distillery looking forlornly out to sea. It has been mothballed by owners Highland Distilleries since 1986, and I wouldn't put money on it ever opening again, unless it is bought by someone else. Which is a pity. The distillery gives little hint that it dates back to 1875 as it is a rather tatty place, the victim of the whims of unsympathetic architects. And blenders were not too happy about the new make either, hence the decision to silence it.

Yet give the whisky time to mature in the briny air beside the storm-lashed cliffs and Glenglassaugh becomes one of Speyside's most distinctive, and classy, whiskies. At between 12 and 16 years it takes on a lovely nose, a mixture of malty biscuit and fine Canadian-style toffee-oak. On the palate it

 Whisky country: *The rugged beauty of Findhorn Valley in Speyside.*

takes on an extreme saltiness, as one might expect from its location, a counter-balancing sweet malt and a weighty smokiness. This is magnificent stuff. The trouble is, a distillery cannot wait 12 years for its malt to pick up the finer points of life. Still, an un-aged version is occasionally seen outside the British Isles – only a few thousand bottles are vatted each year. Buy it, it's a stunner.

MACDUFF

Travelling further east, you will come across the twin towns of Banff and Macduff, interlocked as the twin cities of St Paul and Minneapolis are in the United States, only on a far smaller scale. The old Banff Distillery has been torn down now, paying the ultimate price for the constant production of some pretty naff whisky. Much better is the honey-rich malt from the Macduff Distillery, bottled under the Glen Deveron name. Macduff, built in the early 1960s, is a relatively new distillery and designed, from the outside, at least, with little heed to the traditions of Scotland's glorious homes of malt. But you cannot fault its make, which goes on to become the core ingredient of its owner Lawson's blends. Indeed, William Lawson's 12-year-old is remarkable for being virtually peat-free yet, for all its lightness, rich enough to be one of the top half-dozen blends I have ever tasted. The honey-silk nose on Glen Deveron is evident in the great blend and it is a malt you keep on the palate for longer than usual to allow its delicate sweetness to infuse with the dry maltiness which runs as an undercurrent all the way to the embers of the finish. It may be the end of the trail as far as the malts of the coast road are concerned, but what a majestic finale to such a varied journey.

Connoisseur's Selection

MACDUFF – THE 12-YEAR-OLD IS SILK-SOFT AND SWEET.

GLEN MORAY – AT 12 YEARS OLD, THIS IS AN ESSAY IN MALTY ELEGANCE.

MILTONDUFF – TOO TEMPERAMENTAL TO RECOMMEND; THE OCCASIONAL 12-YEAR-OLD CAN BE STUNNING – BUT ALL TOO RARELY.

GLEN MORAY *(Glen Murray)*

There is an aura of gentility about both the buildings and people of the cathedral city of Elgin that makes you somehow feel that the history in which it is steeped has more than a chapter or two including the making of whisky. In fact, the city centre itself boasts just the single distillery, Glen Moray, but a mile or two to the east, west and south Elgin is served by a number of satellite distilleries.

Despite Elgin's importance as a distilling centre, whisky-loving tourists who pass through the elegant seventeenth-, eighteenth- and nineteenth-century streets usually make for a shop rather than a distillery. This is Gordon & MacPhail, a grocers on South Street which in 1995 basked in well-deserved centenary celebrations. On entering the old shop, you are met by a wall of hams to the right and shelves of clootie dumplings and other savouries. Turn to the left past the chocolates and you will find what all the fuss is about: a display of rare malts sufficient to make the most ardent connoisseur first gasp and then salivate at the prospect of the malty or peaty delights ahead.

After the Second World War, Gordon & MacPhail's Connoisseur's Choice range was often, internationally, the malt lover's only safety net between them and a diet of blended Scotch. We all owe Gordon & MacPhail a debt of gratitude. Beyond even Glenfiddich and Glenmorangie, the present-day appreciation of Scotland's great malts owes more to them than to anyone else.

The lovely old grocers is still operating from the same site. But the whisky section has moved elsewhere in the town, with warehouses overlooking Elgin City's football ground. Inside these warehouses are casks from long-lost distilleries and some from better-known ones dating back before the war. The company's head, George Urquhart, or Mr George as he is affectionately known, still remembers deals struck between himself, his father and hard-up distillers during the 1930s which on more than one occasion saved a local whisky producer from going out of business. Mr George's father, John, had been one of the shop's very first apprentices, rising to the position of partner, then owner, and today the company remains very much a family concern, with John's grandsons and granddaughter each holding executive posts.

A distillery from which they often bought malt in its earliest day was Glen Moray. This is a typical distillery which began life as a brewery before being converted during the great whisky boom of the late 1890s. It is today owned by the same company which owns Glenmorangie and, since little of the Tain distillery's malt is released for blending to outside companies, Glen Moray, which celebrated its centenary in 1997, is used as a workhorse distillery within the group. Its make is absolutely perfect for blending, being of a clean, sweet and unenergetic malt style. The intensity of malt, not unlike a Cardhu, also makes it a fine single malt at 12 years. The big surprise is that it has body enough to reach 21, but it does so with a touch of finesse if, admittedly, very little complexity. There are much better malts around but this remains a personal favourite of mine for its simplicity.

MILTONDUFF

An older and bigger distillery close by is Miltonduff. Where Glen Moray's buildings retain a formal compactness, Miltonduff's have an expansive feel, though it enjoys a more rural setting southwest of the town in the village of that name. Again, Miltonduff is a blending malt used for any number of Allied brands and others besides. It has been pushed as a single malt, but I never thought it quite had the personality on the taste, even though the grapey nose is rather beautiful. Bottlings of its 12-year-old can vary between sweetly enjoyable and harsh and acetic but nearly always with a pretty awful finish. You can see its merits for blending: light enough not to rock the boat with, perhaps, just sufficient character to breathe life into some dull malts. And, of course, it offers a lot on the nose. But as a single malt there are limitations.

Connoisseur's Selection

LINKWOOD – IF YOU FIND ANY STORE WITH A 15-YEAR-OLD, GET IT – WHATEVER THE PRICE.

BENRIACH – THE 10-YEAR-OLD CAN BE IN YOUR FACE – BUT GROWS ON YOU.

LONGMORN – TALK ABOUT THE 15-YEAR-OLD, AND YOU ARE TALKING ABOUT MULTI-COMPLEX CLASSICS. MAGNIFICENT.

GLENLOSSIE – QUITE IMPRESSIVE AT AROUND 11 YEARS OLD AT CASK STRENGTH FROM THE INDEPENDENTS.

MANNOCHMORE – THE 12-YEAR-OLD DISPLAYS FLORAL LIGHTNESS AMID AN OILIER BACKGROUND.

Personally, I preferred the make from the now discontinued Lomond stills. That was called Mosstowie and was regarded as an altogether different distillery. By comparison, at 12 years it was a much richer, fatter dram, with an oily sweetness and a malty, burnt-toast dryness after a fanfare of apples and peat. If you ever find any, you will notice that the oiliness almost shimmers in the glass.

LINKWOOD

To the south-east of Elgin, and for a few miles down, lie the distilleries on which greatness should have been thrust, but never really has been. One such is Linkwood, these days on the outskirts of town, hanging on by a thread to a rural setting. As a malt found in United Distillers' Flora and Fauna series, it has adopted the swan as its crest. Really, it should have been a spider: after the war the then manager, Roderick Mackenzie, believing the final say on the quality of the whisky was with the environment in which it matured, banned his employees from tampering with anything inside the warehouses. Even dusting off cobwebs was outlawed!

Linkwood is another which dates back to 1824 and came on-stream a year later. Some of the older Victorian buildings are still in evidence, one of them housing the original stillhouse. Oddly enough, there are, in a way, two distilleries on this surprisingly rustic site: a new stillhouse was built in 1971 and the old one is called into action from time to time, the makes being called Linkwood A and Linkwood B. The idea is that they make close-to-identical whiskies and when both are operating their spirits are mixed together. For me, the new stills make a whisky of pronounced lightness in comparison to their older brothers. It would be great if the two were casked separately and I think there may be a move afoot to do just that.

For years, Gordon & MacPhail pushed Linkwood as one of their major malts. Their 15-year-old wallowed in oak, but not in a way that made the whisky feel tired. With sherry in evidence, too, it offered quite a spicy, mouth-filling dram of considerable weight and distinction. The current Gordon & MacPhail boasts neither the sherry base nor spice, with the straightforward malt having greater impact. United Distillers bottle their own 12-year-old, which is nothing like as sweet on the nose, though the impact on the palate is one of intense malt which is just a fraction off-key. Other samples I have of Linkwood are much cleaner-nosed with greater spice. None, though, is a patch on the old Gordon & MacPhail 15-year-old sold in the early 1980s. Perhaps that is because the malt came from the original stills.

BENRIACH

Heading southeast down the A941 to Rothes, following the low-lying contours of the Lossie Glen, there is to the left a massive sign announcing Queen Anne whisky. This is the entrance to Benriach Distillery, itself a kind of working gatehouse for the comparatively palatial Longmorn Distillery. Both are owned by Seagram and Benriach remains a bit of an oddity. Seagram have, over the last decade, undertaken a massive programme for improving efficiency, pioneering the one-man operation of distilleries. Nevertheless, here at Benriach can be found the smallest floor maltings in all Scotland, employing just 10 tons of barley a week to produce 8.5 tons of malt – only about 8 per cent of all the malt used there. The distillery itself is delightful in its Victorian compactness. Yet the fact that it is operating at all defies logic. After opening in 1898, it closed down almost immediately following the Pattison crash and the subsequent shockwaves which hit the market. The distillery stood silent until 1965 when it was re-equipped and re-opened. The malt has never been quite of classic proportions, a light, breezy, slightly thin cerealness being its main signature. Experiments were conducted there with some very heavily peated whisky on one

occasion, but that is unlikely ever to be seen by the public. A little surprisingly, perhaps, Seagram have belatedly begun bottling Benriach as a 10-year-old single malt. The first bottlings were not really in tune, but lately Benriach has become quite a character. Although now a competent dram, it can still be best enjoyed by opening and pouring half into another empty bottle and leaving for about six months to a year. The slight oxidization which takes place removes some of the harsher notes and leaves behind a surprisingly attractive, better-proportioned dram in which soft malts dominate before the harder finish. When cold in the glass it is, if anything, the most Canadian-style whisky produced in Scotland and I do admire it for its singular disposition.

LONGMORN

However, all this pales by comparison with Longmorn, easily the proudest and most domineering of whiskies to be found in this sector of Speyside. It has never quite received the plaudits it deserves and I remember the surprise in the Perth whisky shop which gave me the pick of their range when, back in the early 1980s, I won my first-ever whisky prize by being the only person able to name the six whiskies which they were blind-tasting that day. As my reward, I chose the Gordon & MacPhail 12-year-old version of Longmorn. Since then Seagram have done a better job promoting a 15-year-old with a sensible 43 per cent abv which allows greater say to the oaky complexity.

Until 1993 the distillery, which has operated on the site since 1894, used coal fires and rummagers to prevent burning inside the pot stills. More efficient steam coils are now the order of the day. This is a bit of a gamble on the part of the owners. Most managers I know reckon that their whisky lost something when direct firing was removed and I cannot help thinking that Longmorn is just too complex, too magnificent a whisky to take chances with. We shall not know the overall outcome for another dozen years or so. So until then there is still plenty of time to celebrate the majestic make from this old distillery, complete with its delightfully maintained, cream-painted, redundant, railway station. The land in which the distillery is sited is rather flat and featureless by Highland standards, but it is the heart of one of the best barley-growing regions in Great Britain. The distillery stands proud against it in its orangey sandstone, many shades lighter than Benriach's. The larch washbacks are an interesting feature but it was, until recently, those stills sitting above the well-stoked fires which had the spell-binding effect. Time to cross your fingers.

GLENLOSSIE *and* MANNOCHMORE

Heading west out of Longmorn, a pair of distilleries are to be found half-way to Miltonduff and due south of Elgin. Glenlossie and Mannochmore sit side by side, both making floral, high-grade Speyside whisky and I have never really been able to decide which is superior. Maybe it's because they are fed by the same waters from the Gedloch Burn in the Mannoch Hills and supplied with the same malt, but to nose at least, there is a great similarity between the two, with the Mannochmore the heavier by a primrose. The two distilleries also share the distinction of being virtually unknown by other than the most interested of whisky lovers. Both, however, are worth seeking out.

The elder distillery is Glenlossie by the best part of a century. Dating from 1876, the distillery originally operated, as so many did at the time, from water power (it was another 84 years before electricity finally arrived). In 1929 Glenlossie was severely crippled by fire, though it remains a pretty distillery to visit. Its most impressive features are the stills, highly unusual for being fitted with a mechanism called a purifier to lighten the distillate.

Perhaps that is why, then, I have come off the fence to side with Mannochmore. Where

Peering into the past: *Longmorn's stills are no longer coal-fired but the whisky that was is found in every bottle.*

Glenlossie is as delicate as a young Victorian maid, Mannochmore has that extra fatness which allows it to sit longer and sweeter on the palate. Considering it was built in only 1971, it has long enjoyed high status among blenders. With Glenlossie, it had strong links with the Haig brands.

Like twin stars circling around each other, Glenlossie and Mannochmore share one of the strangest relationships between two distilleries. Mannochmore was mothballed in 1984 amid very strong rumours it would never start again. However it did, thankfully, in 1989. Immediately, Glenlossie closed for refurbishment and re-opened in 1991. Now the distilleries each take turns at operating for a 12-month period from September to September, with the staff moving between the two.

Mannochmore has also, inadvertently, gained reflected fame for being the supplier of the malt from which the first black whisky, Loch Dhu, derived. United Distillers won't say how they achieve its darkness, denying caramel is the reason. From the nose and taste, sherry influence can be ruled out, too, as the Mannochmore character comes through powerfully, though not as intensely as with the luscious 12-year-old.

GLEN ELGIN *and* COLEBURN

Had you headed south out of Longmorn, rather than west, the Rothes road would soon have taken you to the curiously named village of Fogwatt, where there is a left-hand turn to the Glen Elgin Distillery. Once more we are talking superstar whisky. If you are looking for a definitive Speyside malt – not too dry, grassy but not too tart, very faintly peaty but not particularly earthy, clean but not characterless, rich but not overly fat, full of complexity but still light enough not to upset a blend – this has just about got to be it.

The manager these days is the same Harry Fox who manages Linkwood and learnt his trade with Glenmorangie manager Dr Bill Lumsden. Both think Glen Elgin is something else, and I can only agree. It's a pity it hasn't quite kept the same originality as the closed Coleburn Distillery just down the road. When the final slate was hammered into place on the building begun in 1898, the topping-out ceremony was for the entire wave of distillery building in Speyside. It would be another 60 years before the region was blessed with another. There is nothing about the Glen Elgin Distillery to notify you of the cracking whisky it makes, except that you might recognize some of the staff from Linkwood who alternate every few weeks between the plants.

The Japanese have just lost out. For a few years United Distillers sent over to Japan a 12-year-old of distinction, but not any more. Now if you want to find Glen Elgin, it is only available from the distillery and very specialist outlets. The nose is little short of sensational with just the right amounts of everything, bulked up by generous dollops of heather and acacia honey. Everything is soft on the palate, a kind of unoiled version of Mannochmore, but with more subtle malts. Other independent bottlers have brought out some fine samples over the years, though a 1968 by Gordon & MacPhail still doing the rounds glories in the intense honey and melt-in-the-mouth oak. Other samples I have in my library have over the years suggested ripe melons and sometimes quite powerful peat. Had Coleburn with its sweet but mustily flawed make been only half as good, that distillery might not have perished in 1985.

SPEYBURN

Passing on the right the magnificent Rothes Glen Hotel, designed by the same architect as Balmoral, and where I have enjoyed many a whisky-induced evening of fun, Speyburn Distillery is spotted in an impressive tree-shrouded gully to the left, a mile or so on along the Glen of Rothes. To enter it, you must negotiate the new roundabout in the town. A monstrosity of construction finished in the early summer of 1996 and totally out of keeping with the town, it does, at least, make it easier to locate Glen Grant, though trying to find it was always half the fun. Speyburn, however, can be found by taking the first exit off. This was Inver House's second purchase in January 1992 and, while it looks neat and compact when you are there, it is worth viewing from the Elgin road first. From there Speyburn, with the waters of the Broad Burn

Glen Elgin: *The home of one of Scotland's most ridiculously rare malts.*

Speyside: *An area criss-crossed by snow-melt rivers and charming bridges, like the one which fords the Lossie near Elgin.*

and the Small Burn flowing through it shortly before their rendezvous with the Spey, presents the quintessential image of a Speyside distillery. In a wooded glen, hemmed in by escarpment of forest, it looks exactly the same now as when it was built in 1897.

Inside, everything is on the grand, confident scale of the time: it even has its own drum maltings, the first to be constructed in any of Scotland's distilleries, with large metal vessels doing the same work as a floor. They have not been used for 30 years or so and the malt brought in is virtually unpeated. The 10-year-old launched by Inver House has already won an award but, pleasant as it most certainly is, Speyburn strikes me as classic blending malt: light, with a big cereal note and, when around the 13–14-year-old mark, not without a touch of pepper to warm things up a little. In essence, a charming, easy-going malt from a charming, easy-going distillery.

Rothes is one of the most important distilling towns in the world. I tell you that because if you have driven, even walked, through it, you may not actually have realized this. Where the distilleries in nearby Dufftown are there on show for all to see and admire, the making of malt in Rothes is a covert affair. There are four distilleries in the town centre, though you would never know. There is even Forsyth's, the world's foremost manufacturers of copper pot stills, though, again, it will take a scout around the back streets before you find their headquarters – a hubbub of clattering craftsmanship.

With Speyburn down on the left as you enter the town from Elgin, many tourists are mistaken in thinking that there is a distillery at the crossroads. That steaming, smelly affair is actually a dark grains plant where spent barley solids from the mashing process are turned into animal food. It constitutes such an overwhelming presence, both to the eye and the nose, that until the roundabout it is all too easy to overlook the small ramp to the right which takes you to Glen Grant. This is the town's one and only true first division distillery and to miss that turn would be a costly mistake for the whisky lover in search of something a little special.

Connoisseur's Selection

GLEN ELGIN – BEAUTY AND SUBTLETY ARE THE HALLMARKS OF THE QUITE BRILLIANT 12-YEAR-OLD.

COLEBURN – POOR STUFF. DON'T BUY EXCEPT AS A COLLECTOR'S ITEM.

SPEYBURN – THE 10-YEAR-OLD IS A GOOD CHOICE FOR THOSE LOOKING FOR THE LIGHT AND WELL-BALANCED.

GLEN GRANT

Dating from 1840, this distillery is as old as the British postal service. And the distillery itself has a uniquely municipal feel about it, with its clock in the centre of the turreted, granite office building which faces out into the courtyarded entrance like a Victorian town hall overlooking the local market square. This elegance is transferred on to every bottle bearing the Glen Grant name. This is my favourite of all labels to be found in Scotland: a line drawing of two kilted, bearded Highlanders at the ready with sword and gun – and a glass and bottle of whisky on a barrel. The name on the cask is "J&J Grant", two one-time illicitly distilling brothers who founded Glen Grant nearly 160 years ago after their tenancy of the original Aberlour distillery expired. The brothers, John and James, rose to prominence and were wealthy enough to install electric lighting in the distillery in 1861, making it the first industrial premises in the whole of the Scottish Highlands to take advantage of post-gas technology.

The Grant family became something of a dynasty and the distillery has possibly more weird and wonderful stories told about it than any other. Whichever member of the family was in day-to-day charge of the distillery was known by those about them simply as "Glengrant". First it was John, then, when brother James died in 1872, it was the turn of his son, also named James. Today visitors to the distillery can see two features that James the Younger, or the Major as he was later known, bestowed upon the distillery. This Major Grant, like so many of his contemporaries, enjoyed hunting and on one expedition to Africa found a young Matabele orphan sitting abandoned by the roadside. Giving him the name Biawa, he brought him back to Rothes where he put him through the local school and then employed him as his butler. Biawa, who spoke with a broad Rothes accent, supported the local soccer team until his death aged 84 or 85 in 1972 and once confounded a local laird who addressed him in fluent Swahili, only to be told by Biawa, in his thickest Highland-speak, that he did not understand a word of what he was saying.

The current owners, Seagram, have just completed a massive programme designed to restore the distillery's grounds to their former beauty. And in those grounds, above the teaming waters of the Black Burn as they hurtle towards the Spey, a safe was long ago built into the rocks. In it there is always a bottle of Glen Grant and a couple of glasses, cleaned by the running burn. Seagram have been owners of the distillery since only January 1978, by which time J&J Grant had teamed up with Glenlivet, and later Longmorn, to form a small company with, pro rata, the best-quality distilleries in the world. Glen Grant whisky had long been used for blending into Chivas Regal and when James Grant's grandson, Douglas Mackessack, signed the contract to sell, his own 47-year tenure of the distillery came to an emotional end. He bowed out by handing each of the distillery workers an envelope containing £100.

It had been left to the Elgin independent bottlers, Gordon & MacPhail, to advertise the Glen Grant name far and wide as a single malt. Even today, bottles of pre-war and wartime Glen Grant can be found, rich and sweet in character, and the same could be said for many vintages since. A 1952 brought out by Gordon & MacPhail is the peatiest Glen Grant I have tasted, a sublime mixture of the gentlest sherries and oaky malts, with the smoke sitting confidently among the chocolate and cocoa.

Seagram have placed their eggs in two baskets: a 10-year-old and one half that age which enjoys phenomenal success in Italy where young whiskies are cherished. The five-year-old keeps the stillhouse on the nose and is delightfully playful on the palate, with its rigid, crunchy maltiness softening towards a little toffee on the finish. The 10-year-old, meanwhile, is one of the few malts I would recommend to drink at room or cellar temperature and not warm in the hand. When cooler, it retains an astonishing brittleness. For me, it is the closest thing to Irish pot-still whiskey: that mixture of malted and unmalted barley

Glen Grant: *Quintessential Scotland and a quite essential malt.*

Glen Grant: *The old-fashioned – and time-consuming – method of racking barrels. This great malt dates back to 1840.*

which simply makes the mouth water.

This is a truly superb malt, so it was little surprise that the Major wished to make more of it. In 1898 he built a second distillery, called Glen Grant No 2. The stills were of the same style, the water source, the Caperdonich Well, was the same, the barley came from the same supplier, yet...

CAPERDONICH *(Capper-donick)*

At first Customs and Excise insisted that the make be pumped across the road to the original distillery, Glen Grant No. 1. This was achieved by a metal pipe which bridged the road, and the famous whisky pipe was for a long time a feature of Rothes. But from day one it was known that the whisky was not living up to expectation and, with the advent of the whisky crash, a perfect excuse was found to close it just four years later. It sat silent for 63 years, hidden by a row of buildings, before being revived by Glen Grant's parent company. This time it was called Caperdonich: different name, same old inferior whisky. The outside of the distillery is unattractive, yet I have enjoyed spending a cold winter's evening sitting in the stillhouse there. Stills, mashtuns, washbacks – everything is in close proximity and it feels good. The malt, though, even samples I have tasted from sherry cask, are as featureless as the distillery's exterior. It is a dram that Seagram have never once felt inclined to bottle, and that is a wise choice. It is not so much a bad whisky as a boring one. Its vague pine aroma and sweet maltiness are fine for the anonymity of a blend but, because of a near non-existent finish, it remains an under-achieving disappointment beside its brilliant older brother.

At one time the stillhouse at Glen Grant was famous for having two sets of stills: one, "Big Geordie" was enormous, the other, "Wee Geordie", much smaller. When a total of eight stills had been installed, it was about the noisiest stillhouse I had ever visited, thanks to the clanking of the steam-driven rummagers working in tandem with the coal fires under the four most traditional of stills. But now the rummagers have gone and with them, sad to say, a sooty, screechy but genuinely fascinating part of Scotland's distilling heritage.

GLENROTHES *(Glen-roth-ez)*

Just a few hundred yards along the main road you take a right turn beyond the police station and there, across the river-sized Linn burn, is another truly magnificent stillhouse, cathedral-like in its dimensions. This belongs to Glenrothes Distillery, part of Highland

Connoisseur's Selection

GLEN GRANT – I JUST ADORE THE UN-ALED VERSION FOR ITS CRISP SIMPLICITY.

CAPERDONICH – IMPOSSIBLE TO FIND AND ONE WORTH MISSING.

GLENROTHES – THE OCCASIONAL CASK-STRENGTH BARREL AT AROUND 12 YEARS OLD IS SUPERB.

Connoisseur's Selection

GLEN SPEY – FOR CHARACTER HUNT IT AT A DOZEN YEARS.

AUCHROISK – THE SINGLETON IS ALWAYS A JOY FOR ITS CLEAN SIMPLICITY.

GLENTAUCHERS – BLENDS SMOKE AND PERTHSHIRE-STYLE HONEYNESS WITH THE OILY, HEATHERY WEIGHT. ONE OF THE LAST GREAT MALTS TO BE FOUND.

AULTMORE – GRASSY AND MOUTH-WATERING AT 12 YEARS OLD.

Distilleries which, with its complex structure of who-does-what-with-what, allows the marketing of the malt to fall under Berry Bros and Rudd of Cutty Sark fame. The still-house really does take you aback with its enormity, where five pairs of very large coppers hum and hiss gently away.

With such large stills and its massive capacity, you might be forgiven for thinking that this old distillery, dating back to 1878, would make a malt of little consequence. You would be wrong. If it were a Bordeaux, it would be a second growth. Blenders adore it and I personally believe that at five years it has already taken on a maturity and malt-smoke complexity, with the faintest touch of cinnamon thrown in, that makes it as good at that age as anything in Speyside. Unfortunately, you're unlikely ever to find it in that form. The official bottling at 10 or 11 years is pretty impressive stuff, with clever use of sherry cask helping to weigh down the smoky spices. Some individual bottlings, especially by the Malt Whisky Society, have been stupendous.

GLEN SPEY

All this rather leaves poor old Glen Spey in the shade. Tucked around the back of Glenrothes, it is out of bounds to the public – a shame really. It is a lovely old place, clinging on to that quaint air of Victorian expectation. After years as a backwater distillery, it received a little publicity recently when the owners, IDV, who use the whisky as fodder for their J&B blends, launched their special blend of 100 different whiskies from one of the warehouses. As a single malt Glen Spey can be found as a somewhat bland eight-year-old at the budget end of the market. I think it peaks at 12 or 13 when a fine, clean harmony between malt and smoke has been reached. But like everything else in Rothes, it seems determined to hide itself away and hope not to be noticed.

On leaving Rothes you have a choice. You can chance it back past the dark grains plant, making sure your windows are closed, or you can head toward Dufftown. The road past the dark grains plant also leads you to the entrance to Speyburn and, as the road enters open countryside, you take a right turn opposite the crumbling remains of a crofter's cottage and head toward the bridge which spans the River Spey. Within touching distance a railway bridge keeps it company, the last in the area that is still operational. The road to Keith is undulating rather than hilly, but is truly charming, nonetheless. It is a road I have driven along so many times now that I cannot remember the last occasion I used a map. Yet, irrespective of the time of year, it is a land I have grown to love with a passion. This is the back road to Keith and soon, on your left, a distillery comes into view, startlingly different from anything else in Speyside. It was build by IDV in 1974 to produce a malt to keep their stocks for J&B replenished. J&B being J&B, a light malt was required. And that is exactly what they got.

AUCHROISK *(Arth-rusk)*

The aspect of the distillery is a curious hybrid of futurism and functionalism, with traditionalism in the shape of a small, useless turret thrown in for good measure. Set amid manicured lawns, it presents a slightly sanitized figure. Inside, however, the distillery shows little willingness to comply with the Victorian determination to save space and the feel is sumptuous. However, with the stainless-steel washbacks and eight bulbous, highly polished stills, you cannot help thinking that, if you are looking for a rich-textured, oily, heavy kind of malt, you have come to the wrong place. Indeed, the malt is absolutely perfect blending whisky, its lightness ensuring that you can bulk up with it without any fear of disturbing the main characteristics provided by the distillates from elsewhere. This posed a problem for IDV when they wanted to bottle it as a single malt. Frankly, it was too light. So their then blender, Jim Milne, hit upon the ingenious idea of allowing it to "round off" for 12 months in sherry cask. The result was a heaviness and fruitiness that the original malt, maturing in ex-bourbon cask, came nowhere near matching. This was first launched, as a 12-year-old, in 1986 under the name "The Singleton of Auchroisk".

The idea of calling it the Singleton was to avoid putting people off with the name Auchroisk (pronounced "Arthrusk"). At the time, one or two experts made a great song and dance about it, claiming in their drinks columns that it was one of the greatest malts ever. I did not see what all the fuss was about, and I still do not, even though it has won various awards. It is a soft, gentle dram, inclined these days toward an attractive spiciness in the finish and one now brought out as a 10-year-old rather than in vintage bottlings. Even in this younger mode it is a fine, enjoyable malt, but not a classic. Its appeal is to those who enjoy a sherry-like dram, but I think I prefer it natural, direct from bourbon cask where the undeniably sweet, crystal-clear waters of Dorrie's Well seem to hang on the lips. It was the discovery of this exceptional water source, followed by successful test runs at Glen Spey, which led to Justerini and Brooks buying the lands including the waters and the site on which the building of the distillery took place. And just as well they did.

Auchroisk: *The distillery is stark and well-manicured, typical of 1970s design.*

one of the last great malts yet to be properly discovered. It is from the oily and heavy and slightly heathery school, blending in smoke and a Perthshire-style honeyness to add to the weight. On the palate it begins beautifully sweet, then darkens and becomes heavier, the oiliness ensuring a long, satisfying, malty finale. This is an old-fashioned, earthy dram to be cherished.

GLENTAUCHERS *(Glen-tuckers)*

However, the one truly magnificent whisky produced in the outer reaches of Keith can be found a couple of miles down the road at Glentauchers, the other side of the village of Mulben. At one time its approach, with the workmen's cottages in a neat line beside the distillery, was as proud as any in the Highlands. But, with the levelling of those old homes and the passing of the last vestiges of the community which had thrived around the distillery, there is now a feeling of desertion and desolation. It is, therefore, a welcome surprise to see steam rising from the distillery showing that it is still alive and well.

But without the intervention of Allied Distillers, that might not have been the case. In the mid-1980s Scottish Malt Distillers had discarded Glentauchers from their plans and the distillery, dating back to 1898 when it was built by James Buchanan to help supply malt for the Black and White blends, looked to be heading for closure. Allied, showing sound judgement, stepped in to buy it. There are many mysteries surrounding the making of whisky. One is why Allied have made a point of buying top-grade distilleries but promoting their inferior malts. Once again it has been Gordon & MacPhail who have made this malt available, although in limited supply, around the world. The inside of the distillery, despite having seen its capacity tripled in 1965, has retained the same old-world feel as the front exterior with its two resplendent, though redundant, pagodas. Do not, however, look around the back. SMD architects have been at work. Even so, once again one of the more attractive distilleries is off-limits to tourists and so they can only taste the whisky,

AULTMORE

Follow the road into Keith and take the immediate left turn over the railway which once served Glentauchers, then follow the B road to Buckie and you will find the distillery in the area Scottish Malt Distillers wanted to keep – Aultmore. Although it, too, dates back to the whisky-boom years of the 1890s, a rebuilding 80 years later demolished much of its sense of history. It is located among the very flattest lands this part of Speyside has to offer and its low-slung, box-like appearance does little to raise the heart but, rather, convinces you that the architect was probably a gin or cognac drinker. Behind it to the south-west is a small, forested hill, the Wood of Mulderie, beyond which sits Glentauchers. Until United Distillers took control of matters, Aultmore was just another malt sold by SMD and probably their feeblest. Again, it was a pleasant enough dram, but the SMD effort did little to reveal some of the hidden talent that Aultmore does actually possess. More recent samples of this make I have tasted suggest that the whisky may not be quite so bland as the distillery. There is even a certain fatness and cereal sweetness in the understated complexity which appears to have been vatted out by SMD. It has taken me a few years to come to terms with Aultmore, the SMD bottling having turned me against it. But sampling it at varying ages has helped me spot some of its finer points, such as the very faintest traces of peat which seem to have been gathered on the short journey from the Auchinderran Burn. This rises a mile or two to the north of the distillery and runs down, away from the sea, past the stillhouse eventually to join the Isla.

STRATHMILL

The Isla is the river which runs through Keith and gives its name to the most sensational of all the area's whiskies, Strathisla. In 1891 it also gave its name to the Glenisla distillery, which four years later was sold and renamed Strathmill. For the best part of a century this has been a distillery whose malt has been extremely rare. Although in Keith, Strathmill enjoys a position on the edge of the town which, coupled with its almost unspoilt period buildings and classic interior, makes this a distillery that just has to be seen. In its unusual green livery, the distillery has been designated by the owners Justerini and Brooks for one of their more glamorous showpieces, Dunhill. The malt goes into their first-rate Old Master and Gentleman's Speyside blends, which enjoy great popularity in the Far East especially in duty-free.

In Strathmill's Number One warehouse, cordoned off from the Plain Janes awaiting to be tipped anonymously into any number of blends, are casks worth a small fortune. In them is a mould-busting blended whisky, the vanguard of the Peasants' Revolt which is bringing to an end a decade's cap-doffing subservience to the aristocratic single malt. To mark the centenary of Alfred Dunhill in 1993, 100 casks were filled with the maturing spirits of malt and grain distilleries which were operating at the time of Dunhill's foundation. To buy a cask will set you back £43,000, making it the most expensive unbottled whisky in the world. You do get a flight included if you wish to come and visit your cask, but there are less than half still available. Typically, the first sample they ever sent me perished in the post. As you might expect, it is a long way removed from the clean, softly oily and malty make which is maturing elsewhere in the warehouse. Strathmill is different from most malts as it possesses that delicious flour character of the crushed malt from the Porteus Mill in the way that Port Ellen does on Islay, though with only the most distant hints of peat. At 12 or 14 years, this is a dram IDV ought to think seriously about bottling for themselves since that wonderful sweetness makes this a drink which would appeal far and wide.

Glen Keith: *Speyside's first distillery of the 20th century began life as a corn mill.*

> *Connoisseur's Selection*
>
> **STRATHMILL** – PEAKS AT AROUND 13 YEARS OLD, BUT ONLY A CITRUSSY, LESSER 11-YEAR-OLD CAN BE FOUND.
>
> **GLEN KEITH** – UNINSPIRING AND WORTH A MISS.
>
> **STRATHISLA** – THE HEAVYWEIGHT 12-YEAR-OLD HAS A BREATH-TAKING COOLNESS. SUPERB.

GLEN KEITH

Its neighbour, Glen Keith, has already climbed the dizzy heights from the unknown to the corporate star. Until 1957 this was the site of a corn mill and was rebuilt by Seagram in local stone. Today it is a massive edifice, and, with its lawn and trees to the front, slightly sinister in appearance. By wonderful juxtaposition, the stills have been crammed into a building which is tiny by comparison and today six of them work in three tandems, whereas for the first 13 years it boasted just the three stills which operated in triple distillation. For some reason most books will tell you that this was the first malt distillery to be built in Scotland this century. In fact, it was the second after Inverleven. But you are unlikely to be told about the experimental whisky which was made here and filled into cask under a different name. This sits in Seagram's warehouses – Glen Keith has none of its own – and is called, confusingly, Glenisla. During the 1970s, many distillers experimented with producing an Islay-style whisky of their own, and this was one of Seagram's. It was finely peated, but with an excellent though unusual oiliness and mouth feel. This sweet dram is one of the rarest whiskies on earth, and is unlikely ever to be bottled by the distillers since very little of it now remains. The usual Glen Keith whisky can be variable, but the best casks are very good, offering a starburst of shimmering complexity. The official bottling, however, is a lighter, less impressive affair which offers an attractive grassiness but little else to genuinely excite the palate

STRATHISLA *(Strath-eye-la)*

On the opposite banks of the Isla is Keith's recently polished gem of a distillery. At last Seagram have begun to promote Strathisla's malt with the verve that such a truly great whisky deserves. For once, Gordon & MacPhail got it wrong by selling Strathisla as an eight-year-old, long before the complexity of this malt had a chance to unfurl like a flower in bloom. To back up Seagram's promotion they have spent hundreds of thousands of pounds turning the distillery into their flagship visitors' centre for their Chivas Regal blend, while essentially retaining the quiet individuality of its elegant buildings.

Strathisla dates back to 1786, making it easily the oldest still operating in Speyside. The open-beamed stillhouse, with its four stills crammed into just about every square inch available, is as atmospheric as any in Scotland and the squat stills and the sharp down-turn of the neck for the spirit still suggest that a very distinctive, heavy malt is likely to be made there. Originally, it was called the Milltown (sometimes Miltown) Distillery and, over its 200 years, successive owners have changed its name to and fro. Between the 1870s and 1890s it was called Strathisla before reverting to Milltown. In 1951, with Seagram now in charge, it was again called Strathisla and, with the investment that has been made to turn it into a major brand and tourist venue, it looks as though it will be keeping that name for the foreseeable future.

Perhaps the most striking thing about the distillery is its quaintness. It is not a large one and the waterwheel beneath the twin pagodas is as romantic as it is aesthetically pleasing. These were Victorian additions to the distillery first founded by a local businessman, George Taylor. He had raised sufficient capital in the flax industry to make use of the Wash Act that had been passed two years earlier to allow the easier distillation of legal spirit. The fact that he was a banker probably also helped to oil the wheels.

Even now it is hard not to believe that George Taylor, should his spirit roam those ancient buildings, would find his way around Strathisla. He would be impressed by the stone from which the distillery continued to be built, retaining a softness to the eye which elsewhere distillery architects altogether failed to achieve, with their appallingly tasteless attempts of the late 1960s and early 1970s. However, Old George would have difficulty in recognizing the matured spirit. In his day peat was copiously used in the kilning of the malt and Speyside whisky was a lot smokier then than now. That does not mean to say he would like it any the less. Strathisla has maintained its traditional wooden washbacks and the water from Fons Buliens Well is soft and sweet. But, most of all, he would appreciate the relative compactness of the stills, their bulbous shape and the weight of the spirit they produce.

It is here that Strathisla comes into its own. Gordon & MacPhail may have made the mistake of bottling too early, but they also produce a 25-year-old of distinction and other specials of varying vintages. A cognac-like 1963 from sherry cask is among the pick of the bunch, notably for its ability to show shape and sophistication despite all the grape

Strathisla: *Perhaps the one thing that outdoes drinking this classic 12-year-old by night is actually the distillery that makes it after dark.*

present. However, the Strathisla 12-year-old, as found in Seagram's curious, amber, "give-it-to-me-in-a-dirty-glass", bourbon-type bottle really is a class act. Independent bottlers may have some decent old Strathislas floating about their warehouses, but nothing compared to the stocks held by Seagram. There undoubtedly appears to have been some judicious vatting when they put together this hefty classic. It is heavyweight whisky, a touch feinty on the nose, perhaps, but on the palate there is a hint of mint and eucalyptus merging with intense malt to give an initial coolness, counterbalanced by an oily, sweet loftiness that also tingles with a touch of spice. If anyone thinks Speyside whisky is one-dimensional, they should get hold of some of this.

KNOCKDHU *(Nock-doo)*

Head east out of Keith and you are taking Speyside to its furthest limits. You are also on course for a little-known distillery which in many ways epitomizes what Scotch malt whisky is all about. It is easy to find. Just head for the bleak, treeless escarpment of Knock Hill, over 1,200 feet high and visible for miles around. A number of springs run from there, making the hill soggy in places, and some of this water collects and moves south toward the tiny hamlet of Knock. Feeding into this water supply is Knockdhu Distillery, a picture of late Victorian splendour. It is another distillery built in the boom years, but with near faultless taste. It has probably never looked better. Its owners, Inver House, gave it a fresh lick of paint to mark its centenary in 1994 and when the sun glints on the freshly golden-tipped pagoda all seems right with the world. Yet this was another distillery whose days seemed to have been over when it fell victim to the SMD purges of the 1980s.

But Inver House are a canny company. After their management buy-out they needed a malt distillery and their marketing director, Graeme Thomson, also doubles as a fine blender and knows more than the average marketing man about a half-decent malt. His choice of Knockdhu was inspired and the further acquisitions of Speyburn, Pulteney and

Connoisseur's Selection

KNOCKDHU – AN CNOC IS A SPLENDID HONEY-RICH MALT OF QUALITY.

GLENDRONACH – AT 19 YEARS OLD, THIS WHISKY TAKES ON A PEATY DIMENSION SET TO STUN.

ARDMORE – ONE OF THE GREATS. GET AT ANY AGE, PREFERABLY NOT MUCH BELOW 10 YEARS OLD.

Balblair put the distillery at the heart of a quartet of tiptop if unspectacular malts. The inside of the distillery still bears the navy blue of a SMD director who was a fanatical supporter of Glasgow Rangers football team, and it is always pleasant to find a distillery with just the two stills. Its new make is something else. This is among the fruitiest you may find, but in a distinctively stewed way with added rice paper and smoke. It is a different animal by the time it reaches a dozen years. Then it is bottled as An Cnoc to help distinguish it from IDV's Knockando. That smoke hangs on the nose and palate but it has become a sweeter, richer dram, with a golden thread of honey running teasingly through it. In every way it is whisky and distilleries like this that give the Highlands such superb character.

GLENDRONACH

To get some idea about what Inver House's latest distillery, Balblair, looks like, just pop along to Ardmore. It is some drive away, but now you are reaching the outer limits of Speyside where distilleries are few and far between. Not only are you entering what has to be the most attractive of all the lands regarded as Speyside, but you are now stepping into Teacher's country.

On the way to Kennethmont, take a slight detour off the A97 and into the rolling hills of Glen Dronach. The famous old distillery of that name awaits you there, though at the moment all is quiet. When I first began looking into the mysteries of Scotch whisky over 20 years ago, I remember a distiller calling Glendronach a "Bank of Scotland" distillery. In other words, it was safe, one that would never close. The reason was that it had been bought by Teacher's in 1960 to produce the malt needed to either put into Teacher's or exchange for the other malts which would accompany it. But in 1976, Teacher's approached Allied, asking Allied to take them over. Allied duly accepted. Since then Glendronach has not been anything like as important and in 1996, to mark its 170th year, it was mothballed – much to the surprise of many in the industry.

Knock Hill: *One of east Speyside's most brooding landmarks.*

Cold stillness: *The delightful Aberdeenshire distillery of Glendronach has been frozen out for a year or two.*

Its location, snuggling into the glen and with red-eyed Highland cattle feeding at its front, makes it one of Scotland's more attractive places to visit – that, plus the fact that you used to be able to see the maltings, marked by its strangely oblong pagoda, in full flow. But no longer, though there is still plenty of its malt around. In the early 1990s it offered a choice between "Original" and "Matured in Sherry Casks". Both were 12 years old and the "Original", including just enough sherry to add the subtlest hint of fruit, won hands down as a quite superb, multi-faceted dram. Those two whiskies have gone, replaced by the "Traditional", also 12 years old but too sherry-dominant, dry and hardly impressive at all. The 1968 Glendronach that has been brought out has a much cleaner sherry character, but the pick of the bunch is the Glendronach 19-year-old. Again the vatters have gone sherry-mad; this time, though, there is a thumping peaty character to show the malt and constituent parts are alive and kicking. This replaced the 18-year-old which was so sherry-dominant and thick that it was impossible to discern anything else and made for one of the worst drams I have ever encountered. Even so, one can only hope that the silencing of the Glendronach stills is a temporary phenomenon. There will be no finer sight than seeing again the raw malt spirit dancing into the two spirit safes, standing side by side and built with great pride and a generation apart by father and son.

ARDMORE

Making something completely different is Ardmore. Another Aberdeenshire distillery, this was Teacher's first foray into whisky-making. Built in 1898, it placed a financial burden on the company as the man who planned it, Adam Teacher, son of founder William, died before its completion. Unusually for a distillery in this part of Scotland, it took its name not from a point in the surrounding area but from one near the Teachers' ancestral home on Scotland's west coast.

There is a solidity about this distillery which bodes well for the whisky made there. The countryside all around is prime barley-growing land, except for the Knockandy hill from which the waters from 14 springs tumble toward the distillery before being piped the rest of the way. Inside the distillery the mash-tun, with its copper dome, is magnificent. Set on the wall around it are fragments of the original tun's false bottom plate, and a cast-iron side plate dated 1898. The stillhouse is larger than it once was, having been completely rebuilt, but everything looks in place and traditional, mainly thanks to the use of coal-fired stills which have prematurely aged the new buildings with a layer of dust and soot.

But it is the spirit produced at the end which guarantees this distillery a special place in my heart. Manager Jim Sim is still using well-peated malt with a phenol level of about 10 parts per million. And it shows. It has oomph in a way other Speyside whiskies would once have found quite natural.

Because this is perhaps the last of a dying breed, and because I love it so much anyway, Ardmore is one of my regular drinking whiskies. As with nearly every other whisky worldwide, I have dozens of samples spanning many years. What is so different about Ardmore is that I don't have a dud amongst them. Gordon & MacPhail bottle a steady 14-year-old but the best I have ever tasted was from Cadenhead. Distilled in 1977 and bottled at 60 per cent ABV, this has a spectacular sweetness which complements the peat like a fine Port Ellen. The phenol levels also seem to be somewhere in the mid-teens.

For years I have been able to spot Ardmore in Teacher's. At the end of that blend you might detect a certain kippery flavour. That's the Ardmore, a malt which – frustratingly and ridiculously – is still not bottled by Allied, much to everyone's loss.

Macallan: *The offices of Easter Elchies House give a clue to the distillery's antiquity.*

MACALLAN

When people think of Speyside whisky, there are two distinct styles which may spring instantly to mind. The first is the grassy, clean, light, bristling style of a Glenlivet or Glenfiddich. The other is polarized: heavy, clingy and smooth with a towering, sherry-induced fruitiness – in other words, The Macallan. To find the distillery you must head south out of Rothes rather than take the road to Keith. Before you reach Dufftown, a signpost points the way to Archiestown and, after heading steeply uphill with the Spey and the village of Craigellachie located vertically beyond the crash barriers, you can eventually take a left and head down the kind of long, straight narrow driveway more usually reserved for Kentucky and Tennessee farmsteads – and distilleries. The drive is a glorious one, especially in deep winter when snow has piled high. You are heading directly toward the highest point of Speyside, Ben Rinnes, and in its foothills the distant buildings of the distillery of the same name can be picked out several miles away. The Macallan immediately confronts you when you sweep over the brow of a small hill.

It is highly unlikely that any other Scottish distillery has so successfully carved out such a niche as The Macallan, the very reason it was bought in 1996 by Highland Distilleries. For years it was just another Speyside distillery, always renowned for producing a better than average dram, and experiencing its nasty moments like all the others when the recession came. It began life in around 1824 as Elchies Distillery, being re-named after the church that had stood on the site when it was rebuilt in 1892. Like other mortal distilleries it changed hands a number of times, was on the brink of closure during the course of this century, but somehow found just enough orders to keep it going when times were at their worst. Its remarkable transition took place after it had become a private company in 1966, having long been part of a trust. Eventually it was decided to market the single malt, but to make it different from anything else the malt selected for bottling was to come from only sherry cask, mainly *oloroso*. Since then Macallan has become a byword for sleekness: it is a malt seemingly made from silk couched in velvet. Ask any distillery manager his second favourite dram and, as often as not, The Macallan is it. It does have its detractors who claim, with some justification, that if you want a drink to taste this way then you pour yourself a sherry. But the point they are missing is that this is not sherry, it is whisky and the spirit is of such excellent quality before being filled into the dripping butt that its slightly peaty, spicy character shines brightly through.

The distillery itself has undergone so many alterations over the years that it is no longer pleasing to the eye – certainly at least, from the outside. This explains why the carton the whisky comes in promotes the old office building, Easter Elchies House. But go to the No. 1 stillhouse and you will see something truly unique. Macallan's stills are among the smallest in Scotland. Only Edradour's are smaller, but the two stillhouses are bursting at the seams with them. The stills are divided up, nine one way and five more at right angles. They are mostly of similar shape, but look closely and you will see that they are different and, with their gnome-like stature, are treated as individuals, each with its own unique personality. Chat to the stillman, or to former blender, Frank

Newlands especially, and they will tell you which stills (such as wash and spirit No. 3) hold pride of place and which ones, especially spirit No. 1, are distrusted, disliked even, for the quality of their spirit.

The warehouses are also in a league of their own. The rows of *oloroso* butts ensure a richness, a tangible thickness in the atmosphere that you almost have to cut through. On some butts the brightly coloured stickers of their original *bodega* can still be read, even after a dozen years or more in the dank Highlands. But what of the whisky? Frank Newlands and I crossed swords over the years on this subject. He reckoned that vertical tasting guarantees that every bottle of Macallan is as close to the last as makes no difference. I have always disagreed. Indeed, I feel that unless they came from the same vatting no two Macallans are really a match. Vatting sherry with sherry must be about the most difficult thing to achieve in the world of whisky. Yet it is this slight variance in The Macallan which I find most intriguing and which impresses me above all else.

Other distilleries have tried to create their own Macallan-esque whisky – and failed. The Macallan, however, hits the bull's-eye time after time. What is noticeable, though, are the changes to the malt when it reaches certain levels of maturation. To fully understand The Macallan it helps to have known it as it matured in ex-bourbon cask. Only then can you wholly appreciate the subtle, spicy nuances which make this malt so special and why this particular malt has sufficient character to bond with the sherry rather than submit to it.

Depending on which part of the world you live in, a slightly different Macallan may be offered to you. The seven-year-old for Italy is as clumsy as a newborn giraffe, falling about the palate without having reached a rhythm. In Great Britain the 10-year-old is the standard model and the transformation over three years is extraordinary. The finished article? Yes, but the 12-year-old sold commonly outside Britain is much deeper, a touch sweeter and a little more spicy and satisfying. It is when you reach the 18- and 25-year-olds that The Macallan shows superstar quality. A few years back I thought it was the 25-year-old which possessed it. In fact, one bottle I tasted ranks among the top five whiskies I have ever come across. The sherry had died down a little and the malt sang a perfect harmony with the grape and peat. At the moment, though, the 18-year-old is in top form, providing the *oloroso* does not become too dominant.

CRAIGELLACHIE *(Kray-gell-akey)*

An investigation into the complexities and secrets of The Macallan could occupy many pages of this book, as could the merits, or otherwise, of buying a 60-year-old for £10,000 as one Japanese businessman did at Heathrow Duty Free in 1996. The debate over the role of the sherry cask would fill many more. Yet, if you head back down the clifftop road and take a right at the main road and then a left into Craigellachie you will find another distillery, virtually unheard of. But if you were to offer me a dram against The Macallan, I would probably choose it every time. Craigellachie Distillery loudly displays its White Horse allegiance for all to see, and when the capacity of the stillhouse was doubled from two to four stills in the mid-1960s, the building was redesigned, so at night as you drive past, the chunky stills gleam golden for all to see. Its make is blended away by blenders who quietly admire this whisky. However, marketing men have found little time for it and its centenary went past in 1991 with hardly a murmur. So it is when you find a bottle, either the one sold at the distillery and proffered at the stately Craigellachie Hotel, or from an individual bottling at cask strength by Jack Milroy in London's Soho, you grab what you can when you can and run. It is a dram that I have often bought for others as a present. Its beauty lies in its creamy softness, an oiliness which clings to the mouth, so that when the long, sweet malt has died, a wonderful smokiness lingers on. It boasts immense character from about eight years on, but at 12 the balance is pretty close to perfection.

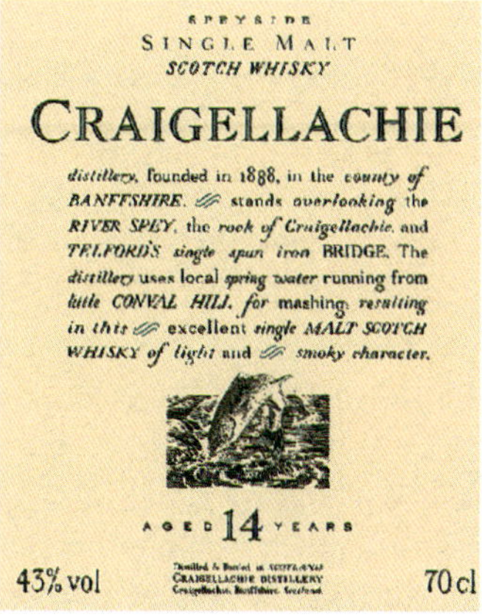

Connoisseur's Selection

THE MACALLAN – THE 12-YEAR-OLD, ENJOYED IN THE USA, IS A GREAT HOUSE WHISKY.

CRAIGELLACHIE – THE SMOKY 12-YEAR-OLD IS FABULOUS.

ABERLOUR – THE 100 PROOF 9-YEAR-OLD HAS MOST OF WHAT CAN BE ASKED OF A SPEYSIDER.

ABERLOUR

Another wonderful malt is found a few miles along the Speyside road which takes you into the wide main carriageway of Charlestown of Aberlour. At the red and black gates toward the end of the village is Aberlour Distillery. It does not grab your attention like a Speyburn steaming dreamily away in an exposed, romantic glen, or cut the same dramatic silhouette against the sea as an Ardbeg or Laphroaig. Nor does it gloweringly stand its ground like Dalwhinnie or Glentauchers. Instead it suffers from the same utilitarian appearance as many others that underwent thoughtless change and expansion, though the waters gushing over the waterwheel inside the distillery make a charming sight. It is worth seeking out St Drostan's Well, which was dry for generations until the distillery won its first international award and then mysteriously spouted water again. Back in the 1970s and early 1980s I did not much care for Aberlour as a malt and was put off by its bitter, almost astringent finish. However, it was decided to take the Macallan route by adding more and more sherry cask into the vatting, and this has worked a treat. Aberlour, not least the humble, day-to-day 10-year-old, has quite a lot to offer. It has changed dramatically, even over the last half-dozen years, and today is the creamiest and most toffee-like of all the cream-toffee style malts. You might even think of mint toffee because, although there does not seem to be quite the same size sprig as formerly, it remains to add a touch of quirkiness to the spirit. Surprisingly, the back label describes Aberlour as dry. When cold or chilled, it is; when warm in the hand, it is as sweet as your first love.

All casks from which Aberlour single malt is chosen were laid down by the late Ian "Puss" Mitchell, the last distillery manager in Scotland I can think of who was born at the distillery where he was to spend his working life. His second in command was brewer Kenny Fraser, who shattered the silence of the warehouses by practising his bagpipes in them for perfect acoustic effect, with a bit of PR thrown in. Kenny has now retired and the distillery has a slightly different air, though the whisky just goes on getting better. Two relatively new bottlings have been launched for duty-free. One is Aberlour Antique, in which whiskies aged up to 24 years have been added to provide oaky weight and bring glorious subtlety to a zesty spiciness. The real showpiece, though, is their 100 proof. Although this is aged around nine years, the fact that it is 57 per cent abv gives the massive spiciness every chance to flourish and you are left with the closest thing to a mainland Talisker in its explosiveness, from its tingly nose to its full-frontal assault on the tastebuds. Of all the enormous variety Speyside has to offer, I rank this as a beauty, especially on days when I am frozen solid or tired and in need of a slap across the face. Old "Puss" had some vivid ideas about maturation and was perhaps too much in love with the idea of developing the sherry theme. But, whichever stillhouse in heaven he happens to be running in his immaculate suit and perfectly coiffured hair, he can look down from above and receive his angel's share with pride. For, thanks to him, of all Scotland's distilleries this is probably the one which has risen from an also-ran to undisputed classic in the shortest time.

Head back to Craigellachie, so that one of Scotland's most historic, fairytale structures, the Telford Bridge, comes into view, and then take the high road back past Craigellachie Hotel and the distillery, passing the Speyside Cooperage to the left. On the official whisky trail, it is worth a visit, especially if you are already deaf. The more interesting route is to take the right before reaching Craigellachie, bypassing the village on the little road up to Blue Hill. This time the cooperage is passed on the left and you will be able to see the thousands of casks stored. If there are not many casks to be seen, things in the industry are going well: distilleries are working flat out and casks are being filled quickly. If they form a group of oaken mountains, then demand is low and Scotch whisky is feeling the pinch.

GLENFIDDICH *(Glen-fid-dick)*

As you continue down the hill into the outskirts of Dufftown, the exhausted shell of Convalmore is to your left. Once part of the United Distillers empire, it has now been claimed by the advancing William Grant. As Grants have three distilleries already, Convalmore will never work again but the warehousing and land are priceless, and can be used to store perhaps the most famous malt of all, Glenfiddich. Beyond Convalmore is a complex which houses three distilleries, Glenfiddich, Balvenie and Kininvie. The last one was only built in 1990 and very few people are aware of its existence. The same can hardly be said of Glenfiddich. It was this distillery which pioneered the mass marketing of single malt whisky and every year well in excess of 100,000 people arrive from all over the world to see where and how the whisky is made and, in some cases, to pay homage.

> *Connoisseur's Selection*
>
> **GLENFIDDICH** – WONDERFUL OAK-MALT BALANCE AT 21 YEARS OLD.
>
> **BALVENIE** – THE 21-YEAR-OLD PORT-WOOD FINISH FRESH OUT, EXOTIC, GLORIOUSLY AND DELICIOUSLY BALANCED – A TRUE MASTERPIECE.

Sadly, it has become something of a sport among the *cognoscenti* to dismiss Glenfiddich as a joke whisky. A number I have met over the years work on the principle that if you think Glenfiddich makes good whisky, then no way can you be considered a connoisseur of malt. Well, I am obviously no connoisseur because Glenfiddich makes very good whisky. To be sure, the day-to-day stuff we find on the shelves does not bear comparison with Speyside's finest. It is too young and vibrant. Yet I find it a refreshing dram with its lemon-drop fruitiness, although the occasional batch can be flat and a touch lifeless. However, select whisky from this distillery from 12 years onwards and we are talking first competence, second excellence.

As for the distillery, most of its visitors wander from the car or coach park past the ducks and into the entrance during the summer months. However, for me, Glenfiddich early on a late November or December morning is the very essence of Speyside. With the sun reluctantly rising to offer a watery glare and the steam from the distillery ascending into the shimmering blue, the grey-tiled pagodas jut with crystal clarity and there's a twinkling of frost above the vague darkness of the gentle hills beyond. On a morning like this, when thermometers are barely troubled as the mercury huddles below zero and the silence of the leafless trees shows there is not even the murmur of a breeze, the biscuity aroma of the mashing malt hangs in the crisp air and gladdens your heart. This is not just Speyside, this is the making of whisky: a vision, a taste, an aroma of timelessness.

No single detractor can take away from Glenfiddich the enduring excitement of the stillhouse. Ever since William Grant drew his first drop in this building on Christmas Day 1887, copper pot stills have been heated by open coal fires and the rummagers have ground on. Of course, there were not 28 stills when William Grant allowed his first make into the receiver. But the stills at Glenfiddich are tiny and that always augurs well for the maturing spirit.

Glenfiddich has never done itself any favours by announcing on its label that the standard whisky is "Special Old Reserve". It is unlikely that much of what goes into that brand is anything above seven or eight years old. And they are equally coy about the age of their "Classic", though the malt will be 10 and 20 years old. However, if you spot the 18-year-old "Excellence" you are getting an insight into why this whisky is so different. Glenfiddich takes an enormous time to mature. The 21-year-old is as complex with its chocolate malt, smoke and raisins as you could wish for and some samples of 30-plus whisky I have tasted from individual casks have displayed breathtaking composure – and peat! – for a malt that ages with little oak in sight. The most expensive malt ever auctioned was, indeed, a Glenfiddich 50-year-old, though it is a dram I would leave in the bottle. What I have tasted of it displays more wood than a bowl of stewed sawdust. As a relatively sprightly 30-year-old, however, the oak is not only as far as you would want to go but fuels a nose that ranks among the most complex as can be found in Speyside, thanks also to the near perfect use of sherry cask. Despite the lengthy oak on the palate, to taste this has a touch of everything, and I adore the peat-chocolate-apple-grape-malt richness that covers the entire spectrum of the tastebuds.

So with all these Glenfiddichs to choose from, which one captures its character to the fullest? Apart from the 30-year-old which operates in a league of its own, it just has to be the 15-year-old, bottled at "cask strength", which in this case is an inoffensively tame 51 per cent abv. The 18-year-old certainly has a gorgeous zip of spice, but for the 15-year-old, with or without a splash of water, there is a peatiness present which the founder might have expected to find a century ago. Perhaps the most extraordinary thing about it is that it still has the feeling of youth as against the standard bottling which is positively pre-pubescent. And, of course, the beauty of youth is its appetite for life and energy coupled with an un-hardened maturity. But, in the end, there is the peat, though heaven knows from where it stems. The barley is all but peat-free, but the water may have a little say in the matter. The 18-year-old may have the edge in the complexity and balance stakes, and to appreciate it at its fullest you have to hold your nerve. It is not a cheap whisky, but take a pretty large mouthful and keep it on the palate as long as you can. With that and the 15-year-old the message is clear: dismiss Glenfiddich at your peril.

BALVENIE *(Bal-ven-ee/Bal-vee-nee)*

That said, you have only to walk a matter of a few hundred yards under a small bridge and you are at the home of arguably the very finest malt whisky, if not in Speyside, then in perhaps the entire Highlands. This is Balvenie. It does not matter how you pronounce it: "Bal-ven-ee" or "Bal-vee-nee", the whisky is the same – a rhapsody on a theme of distillation. Like me, you may argue that other malts are better, but put a glass to your lips and you will find yourself only too willing to concede.

Like Glenfiddich, the buildings are an object lesson in the beauty of late-Victorian, whisky distillery architecture. In the case of Balvenie, some of the distillery came from the remains of a castle, though not from the one opposite Glenfiddich actually called Balvenie. William Grant built the distillery in 1892 to give spare capacity after a fire at the rival Glenlivet Distillery meant that his entire Glenfiddich output was being sold to compensate for the shortfall. He even bought a secondhand still from Laphroaig for £47, less than half what it would have cost to make brand new.

Balvenie: *Speyside's masterpiece is hidden under the shadow of Glenfiddich.*

The irony, though, was that while Grant pushed Glenfiddich as the single malt, everyone in the industry knew that the undisputed whisky of quality came from Balvenie. It is only in the last decade that it has ever really been pushed as a malt of its own and, although tourists are not discouraged from visiting, those who sneak away from Glenfiddich's official tour are in for a treat. The floor maltings are still in operation and are the most picturesque in Scotland, especially when you enter from the doorway opposite the furnace, which is greedily devouring shovelfuls of coal and peat in its yellow and crimson flame. The old walls are slightly bowed and uneven, the windows tiny, allowing the light in with a miserly reluctance, but just enough to give a golden-green haze to the room as the living barley lies dank and slightly warm around the squat pillars which prop up the floor above. Nearby, the wooden washbacks enhance the traditional work patterns and the stills, coloured a ruddy brown like old boots rather than the burnished copper next door at Glenfiddich, complete the picture. Actually, not quite. Some of the Balvenie warehouses are the best I have ever seen. They are attached to the remains of old Balvenie House and the walls, despite their thickness, couple with the gravel floor to give a freezing dampness absolutely ideal for the maturation of classic whisky.

Give me the right day and the right bottle of Balvenie, and I will be its loudest advocate. Some individual casks I have tasted have been stunning, absolutely faultless. It is never easy to pinpoint why it is so fundamentally different from Glenfiddich. Yes, they do mix their own malt with that brought in and I am sure that this accounts for a touch of extra peatiness. Maybe it is the yeast or the shape of the larger stills, while the water, though from a different source, is probably the same (no one is quite sure!). As a 10-year-old it can still offer a shade of youth on the nose; some can be a trifle sweeter and/or smokier. With a malt as delicate as this, it is little wonder. But on the palate the result is roughly the same: an early spice attack followed by dazzling malts and a rumbling smokiness. The 12-year-old version, called Double Wood, is transferred from ex-bourbon to sherry casks for a spot of rounding, in the style of the Glenmorangie 18-year-old and The Singleton. It works particularly well here because at this age the oaky spiciness is so busy flitting across the palate that it has no problems penetrating the sherry which softens the impact. Pride of place, however, goes to the 15-year-old. The nose is as enticing and truly sexy as you

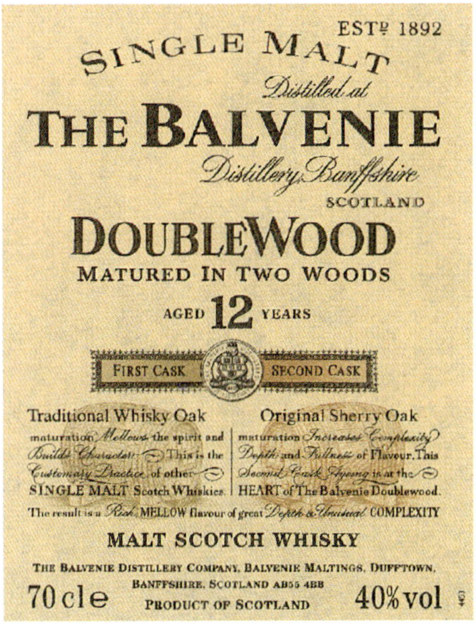

could ever wish for. It comes from a single barrel. I have so far tasted six samples, and a 1980 is the pick of an exceptional bunch. The aroma shows why oak is so vital for balance, and why peat can be as soft as it is earthy. But it is the honeyed tones which ensure that this malt will never be forgotten. It is bottled at a fraction over 50 per cent abv, powerful enough for the qualities on the nose to come through on the tastebuds with a confident intensity that makes you close your eyes and submit willingly as all your senses are drawn toward the brilliance of the performance on your palate. This, ladies and gentlemen, is Scotch.

KININVIE *(Kin-in-vee)*

Considering what happened to the last "Whisky Capital" of Scotland, Campbeltown, it has to be said that its usurper Dufftown has fared a lot better. Apart from the recent demise of Convalmore, the only other distillery to have failed there this century is Parkmore. And remarkably enough, despite having been silent since 1931, the latter is externally one of the most beautifully preserved late-Victorian, whisky-boom distilleries to be found. Because of all the other distilleries, Parkmore has been used for warehousing and so been maintained.

To add to this good news, the town has also seen the building of two new distilleries. It is just as well, so keeping alive the splendid old saying: "Rome was built of seven hills and Dufftown stands on seven stills." The distillery to preserve the adage, Kininvie, is found tucked behind Balvenie. In reality, it is nothing more than a stillhouse: the milling, mashing and fermentation is all carried out at Balvenie though from different apparatus. The mashtun is open traditional, the washbacks, like its sisters, are made from Douglas Fir. The water source is also shared with Balvenie.

Kininvie's first distillation was on July 4, 1990 and three years later Grant's blender David Stewart and I met by those four slightly chunky, thick-necked but modest-sized stills (the spirit still is only 8,400 litres) to taste the spirit as it legally came of age. He had told me years before that the plan was to produce a malt not quite so heavy as Balvenie, but more substantial at younger ages than Glenfiddich. He brought a sample from cask 21 and we were both knocked out by its intense maltiness. It was neither sweet nor dry, but held on the palate superbly. This is going to be a pretty good malt when it reaches 10 years old.

It has already been added to Grant's Clan MacGregor blend for the US markets, so it is in circulation. But they are not releasing any for bottling as a single malt until they are happy that it has reached an optimum age. At the moment they are learning. It certainly won't make a five-year-old. By that age it enjoys a sweeter edge and has already picked up some impressive oak. But the finish is flatter and less complete and some of the balance has been lost. It will return, though, either the next year or the year after.

GLENDULLAN

If Kininvie ends up in the same league as its neighbour to the other side of Balvenie Castle, Glendullan, then I for one will be delighted. Once it was among the quaintest of Speyside distilleries. Where Glen Grant had begun to take advantage of electricity way back in 1861, at Glendullan the River Fiddich was used to supply power until just after the Second World War. There is nothing particularly pretty about Glendullan now, except its whisky. It was yet another victim of Scottish Malt Distillers' desire to wreck the aesthetics of its distilleries when a new stillhouse was completed in 1972. For 13 years the two stillhouses worked together until the old one, inevitably, was closed down. It is said there is no difference between the whiskies from the two stillhouses, but that is not the case. I much prefer the old make

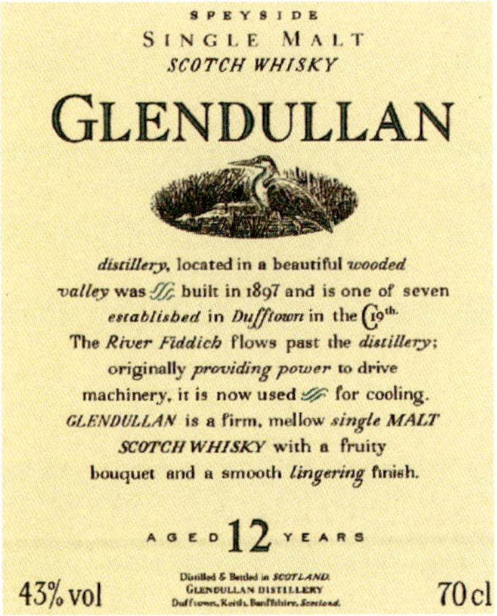

which was fatter, silkier with more confident malt and had the very unusual property of turning from sweet to powder-dry in seconds in a way in which you could almost feel the change. It was the most simple of complex whiskies.

It is a peculiar fact that Glendullan has produced three quite distinct types of malt since 1972: there was the original stuff, then the mixture of the two stillhouses and, from 1985, malt from the new stillhouse only. Some eight-year-old Glendullan shows maturity for its youth with some surprising peat at this early age, sitting heavily on the palate and full of brooding good intention. The standard bottling at 12 may not be as good as the pre-1972 malt but is a beautiful malt nonetheless – pretty dry throughout but still offering decent weight. A 22-year-old has the mouth feel of a Caol Ila without the peat but carries a concentrated vanilla finale. The old stills certainly play their part in its character. But what all three styles have in common is that there is nothing quite like them in the whole of Scotland.

MORTLACH

There is, however, one other malt from Dufftown which is better than Glendullan – much better. It is called Mortlach, a distillery very few people have heard of, but which simply has to be included among the great whiskies of the world. When United Distillers chose their Classic Malt range, Cragganmore pipped it for the Speyside region and there is no arguing that malt's class. But many distillery managers and a few blenders were a touch surprised. Had there been a referendum, Mortlach would probably have won.

It was Dufftown's first distillery; indeed, the town dates back to only 1817 and whisky was first legally distilled on the site just six years later. There is an often repeated claim in whisky books that Mortlach means "bowl-shaped valley", which does describe its location, to a degree. I am more inclined, though, to believe that the "mort" is taken from the Gaelic for massacre with "lach" meaning "wild duck". For it was on this site in 1010 that King Malcolm II of Scotland routed the Danes. The thought of the slaughtered invaders being referred to by the victors as wild ducks massacred there does not seem too far-fetched.

As for the distillery, it has an impressive history of its own and has been the training ground for some outstanding distillers including William Grant of Glenfiddich fame. It is the

Connoisseur's Selection

KININVIE – WILL PROBABLY BECOME AVAILABLE AROUND THE TURN OF THE MILLENNIUM.

GLENDULLAN – ALWAYS LOOK FOR PRE-1985 DISTILLATIONS.

MORTLACH – HUNT FOR SOMETHING AROUND THE 12-YEAR-OLD MARK. THEY ARE RARE, THOUGH.

Mortlach: *For nearly two centuries, the distillery has offered an imposing entrance to Dufftown.*

only one I can think of that has doubled up as a church in the days when it was silent between 1837 and 1851 – but later investment turned the distillery from a failure into the most state-of-the-art of the mid-nineteenth century. Since then Mortlach has never looked back and the quality of its whisky has only ever been praised – by blenders, that is. Its very success as a blending whisky meant there was never really enough around to promote it as a mainstream malt. The type of whisky it produces happily defies logic: being partially triple-distilled it should be lighter. Just like Springbank, though, it is anything but. And, like Springbank, the distillery's inner workings are just great to inspect: the chocolate-painted metal ribs pleasantly set off the dark-stained wooden washbacks. The six stills are bizarre, apparently shaped at random, none looking anything like another and the swan necks lead off to the old-fashioned worm tubs at strange, haphazard angles. For years they operated in two different rooms, though they have now been introduced to each other. Add all this to the peculiar cream colour in which the distillery has been painted, and Mortlach is a one-off in many senses of the word.

At the moment, United Distillers have a 16-year-old available. The nose has gone as far down the oaky road as I'd like to see it go, but is otherwise fine. Gordon & MacPhail regularly bottle a 15-year-old that is similar in style. With both, though, this is a malt that defies you to put the bottle down. Their weakness is that the finish is shorter than other Mortlachs you may very occasionally find from independent bottlers, but the start and middle are of the eyes-closing-head-nodding-lip-smacking school. In the case of the 16-year-old, it's honey with a hint of marzipan and mint yet with a dryness hanging around – and as enjoyable as it is, I'd prefer to see them drop about four years off it and serve it when the malt has a bigger say, is sweeter and the complexity is busier and more intense. Sadly, as Gordon & MacPhail reveal, even the independents (perhaps with the exception of James MacArthur's) are usually seduced by age on this one. But I am nit-picking. This is quality and is enjoying a growing following in the United States. So at least somewhere people outside the industry are beginning to experience one of the last, truly undiscovered classics of the whisky world.

DUFFTOWN

Take the road uphill behind Mortlach and you will arrive at the town's last two distilleries. The first you see is called Dufftown, a pretty distillery which has long been part of Bell's, who successfully avoided the dramatic structural change brought about by other companies equally keen to invest in the expansion of their distilleries. The buildings had begun life as part of a corn mill and, despite its close proximity to Dufftown, with its toy-town granite clock tower and small shops, the distillery manages to give some impression of being in the country. It looks as if it was the natural home of good whisky, though some of what it made left something to be desired.

For years Bell's promoted it as a low-budget, single malt alongside its sister distillery Blair Athol. Their whiskies had four things in common: their price,garish labels, owners and poor quality. A lot of work has gone into improving things at Dufftown and United Distillers are producing a small-batch 15-year-old which must come from some very cleverly selected casks. The nose is at first a little unpromising but there is compensation in the mouth. With it being one of the mealiest malts to be found in Speyside (strangely appropriate when you consider the distillery's former occupation), there is a biscuity feel to this malt mixed in with toffee-nut and dark sugar. Hardly an old smoothie, but it does offer something away from the norm.

PITTYVAICH *(Pitty-vakh)*

Although Bell's showed commendable compassion when they set about expanding Dufftown from two to the current six stills, the textbooks on building to suit the environment were left on the shelf when the construction of Pittyvaich got underway. This is the most functional of functional distilleries, erected on the site of one of their existing distilleries to save in delivery and labour costs and to produce a journeyman malt to exchange with other distillers to keep stocks high for Bell's. Built in 1975, it produced non-stop until United Distillers mothballed it in 1994 along with Dufftown. Such was the quality of Pittyvaich that the blenders were not too bothered whether they saw it again, and today it operates for part of the year for experimental purposes, while Dufftown is back onstream producing its normal make.

My first encounter with it in the 1980s was at the distillery with some nine-year-old that blasted my insides out, thanks to an almost vicious, Semtex-like spirityness. It quietens down by the time it reaches 12 or 13 and as it gets older, but such is its original shortage of breeding that its spirit, matured in American oak, becomes pleasant and attractive but noses and tastes more like bourbon than Scotch. The occasional half-decent bottling can be found, but they are as rare as hen's teeth and nothing like so interesting.

BENRINNES *(Ben-rin-nez)*

The road that takes you past the Aberlour Distillery and toward Grantown has two left turns, each taking you to a distillery. The first,

Connoisseur's Selection

DUFFTOWN – THE 15-YEAR-OLD IS NOT GREAT, BUT IT DOES HAVE A PRESENCE.

PITTYVAICH – DON'T WASTE YOUR MONEY ON THIS ONE.

BENRINNES – LOOK FOR A 10- TO 12-YEAR-OLD.

DAILUAINE – TRY AND FIND A 10-YEAR-OLD FROM THE INDEPENDENTS.

IMPERIAL – BRIMMING WITH BRILLIANT, MOUTH-WATERING QUALITIES – SHADES OF GRASSINESS WITH WEIGHTIER, SMOKY, BUTTERY, FAT NOTES. ANYTHING BETWEEN 12 AND 15 YEARS OLD CAN BE IMPERIOUS.

CARDHU – AT 12 YEARS OLD, THIS IS AS SOFT AND MOREISH AS THEY COME.

as we have seen, brings you to Glenallachie, once famous for the ducks at the front of the otherwise unromantic 1960s distillery, though since Christmas 1996 they have mysteriously vanished. Equally elusive is the malt, sadly nothing like as colourful or tasty as a mallard, due to a metallic harshness which rightly confines its expectations to filling blends. The second starts an uphill climb to a distillery at the foot of the mass of Ben Rinnes. From the Macallan Distillery you might already have spotted it: it is Benrinnes Distillery. As is becoming clear, all distilleries have their own little foibles. Benrinnes' is to distil its spirit more than twice, but not quite three times. It dates back to the 1830s, possibly a decade earlier, but rebuilding in the 1950s has left it with that hallmark Scottish Malt Distillers' messiness. It also has its own mechanical maltings.

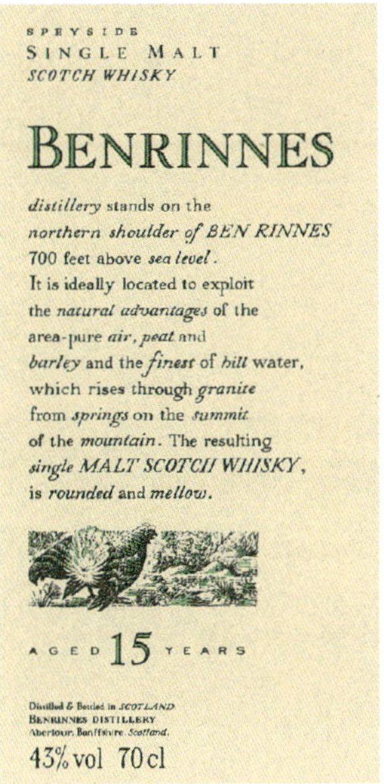

For whatever reason, a distinct peatiness often hangs in the glass when a sample is poured and, despite the fact that reason says the malt should be lighter by being distilled to a higher strength, in fact it is quite a beefy dram, though one better appreciated by blend-ers than it ever will be as a single malt. The distillery does bottle an acceptable, sometimes quite stylish, 15-year-old. But its occasional outings as a British supermarket own-label Speyside have not brought much reward.

DAILUAINE *(Dale-yewaine/Dale-yewan)*

A much more impressive dram comes from the other side of the Grantown road. If you head along the connecting byway between that and the north Speyside road before you reach the great river, the entrance to the impressive pile of Dailuaine Distillery is to your right. The sheer size of the place fair takes the breath away, hidden away as it first appears to be, and things are made more impressive still by the chunky stone with which it is built. It has been around since the 1850s and much of what can be seen dates to the late nineteenth century and post-1917 when the distillery itself was gutted by fire. Oddly enough, for a long time Dailuaine was tied up with the Talisker Distillery, which later suffered the same fate.

Dailuaine is a wonderful blending whisky, and just a small sample of it at any age shows why. It has a solidity which matches the distillery walls, and the Dewar's brands with which it has been associated have benefited from this rod of malty steel as a backbone support for lesser malts and grains. United Distillers' own version is a disappoint-ment. It is 16 years old and the sherry which bursts through on the nose, palate and finish completely overwhelms the finer points of the toffee-malt which shines through from ex-bourbon casks.

Back at the distillery, there is much flat ground surrounding the buildings on account of the large railway sidings that were once there. Dailuaine once had its own small locomotive called a puggy, which shunted empty barrels in and full ones out, plus grain to keep the maltings going. The puggy, named after the distillery, is now being rebuilt outside the Aberfeldy Distillery in Perthshire.

IMPERIAL

Much closer, though, is another distillery built to gigantic proportions, and this time, unusually, from Aberdeen brick. The Imperial Distillery was not only built at the height of the distillery-making craze, but in the same year as Queen Victoria's Diamond Jubilee, 1897, and on a prime site beside the Spey at Carron. The distillery was given its name to honour Her Majesty's Empire, and for good measure a striking metal crown was placed glittering and glinting in the sun atop a maltings chimney. Sadly, following the whisky crash a year later, Imperial found itself closed and the gleaming crown had turned a murky green before the stills hissed again in 1919.

Things didn't run too smoothly after 1919, either. Imperial fell silent between 1925 and 1955; the whisky was not the problem, it was the effluent. And in the mid-1980s it was mothballed by United Distillers before Allied did a very good piece of business by buying it and bringing it back into action. They could do even better for themselves by bottling at around 12 years and dropping Tormore or Miltonduff. Again it is trusty Gordon & MacPhail who are saving the day, currently with a rather over-aged and slightly flat 1979. About the best on the market is a 15-year-old from the small independent, James MacArthur. That is also a 1979 but is brimming with brilliant, mouthwatering qualities, those lovely shades of Speyside grassiness alongside weightier, smokey, buttery, fat notes. The crown on the chimney may have gone and been replaced by a television aerial to give the locals a half-decent picture – but now is the time for Allied to tune in to see what a classic malt they have on their hands.

CARDHU *(Kar-doo)*

From Carron it is an easy matter to reach the village of Knockando. The first distillery you will find is Cardhu, famed for its alliance with the Johnnie Walker brands. It is a lovely distillery, though tarnished a little by alterations made to accommodate tourists. They say a dog looks like its owner, or vice versa, and the same can be said about Cardhu and its whisky. The distillery's bottling is a 12-year-old which is about as clean, neat and tidy as any in Scotland. I can think of no other dram where the unspoiled intensity of the malt has such a big say.

It is great to know that a distillery which started life as an illicit bothy is still going strong. In 1813, John Cumming and his wife Ellen moved to Cardow farm and from time to time played host to the local Excise man. While he was tucking into his dinner, Ellen would claim to be in need of feeding the hens, or make some such excuse, vanish outside and hoist a red flag warning all the other illicit distillers that the gauger was among them. However, in 1824 the Cummings turned legal. The distillery was completely rebuilt on a new site in 1884 and remained in the family until Johnnie Walker bought it nine years later. It was re-named Cardhu only as recently as 1983 and then only to keep in line with the name of the single malt which had been launched. Today Cardhu is United Distillers' principal malt outside their Classic Malt range and a sure winner as a gift for anyone who likes their malt classy, uncomplicated, unpeated and clean as a whistle.

Sunset silhouette: *The twin pagodas of Tamdhu Distillery point towards the Speyside sky.*

TAMDHU *(Tam-doo)*

Down the hill from Cardhu, you must take a hairpin bend into the Spey glen which accommodates Tamdhu and Knockando distilleries. Together these three distilleries produce about as wide a variety of Speyside malt as you are likely to find in such a small area. Tamdhu makes a rich, oily malt, sweet and fruity, which clings purposefully to the roof of the mouth. It has never grabbed the limelight as a single malt, though I admit I find it very attractive and am confident I can spot it plying its trade in the excellent Grouse blends.

The distillery buildings are a pretty crowded affair, thanks perhaps to their proximity to the Spey. The distillery is of that unmistakable late-Victorian style, and is the only one in Speyside to produce all the malt it needs. In fact, it produces more than it needs, employing Saladin mechanical maltings, and sends its excess to other distilleries within the Highland Distilleries group.

Connoisseur's Selection

TAMDHU – RICH, OILY, SWEET, FRUITY, THIS CLINGS PURPOSEFULLY TO THE ROOF OF THE MOUTH. AN ATTRACTIVE MALT AT 10 YEARS OLD.

KNOCKANDO – AT 25 YEARS OLD, THE OAK IS CHEWY BUT NEVER SAPPY.

GLENFARCLAS – SAVE UP FOR THE 30-YEAR-OLD. IT IS A SUPERB TREAT.

CRAGGANMORE – THE CLASSIC MALT AT 12 YEARS OLD IS JUST THAT.

KNOCKANDO *(Nock-an-doe)*

Literally next door is Knockando, run by a now-retired Highland League soccer linesman. For years he has successfully produced a dapper, sometimes bone-crushingly dry malt from another charming little distillery built at the end of the last century, just a year after the completion of Tamdhu. For all but a handful of years this century it has been part of the Gilbey company and today its crisp make is a vital cog in the J&B blends which thrive on Knockando's concentrated maltiness. As a single malt it is marketed as a vintage rather than an age, though by the time it is reaching the mid-20s, it has become very dry – almost salty.

A few years back I had been giving a talk on Scottish malt to a number of whisky executives who had flown into the Highlands from all over the world, including downtown Fifth Avenue, New York. It was the night before mid summer's day and the conversation went on long into the night ... and morning. Finally, I told them the only way to learn about whisky was to experience it in its purest form. So, at four in the morning and with the sun already risen, I marched the group down to the banks of the River Spey, a bottle of 25-year-old Knockando in one hand and a glass in the other. I invited them to fill their tumblers, take a full mouthful and listen to the rush and gurgle of the passing river against the backdrop of the dawn chorus as they slowly swallowed. Their senses were fully awakened by the cool breeze which bounced off the chill water, but many were speechless afterward. It was an unforgettable, even emotional, moment for all concerned, and proved how the natural, living beauty of this enchanted region of Scotland can be so enhanced by a glass of something golden, mystical and made only in the lands around where the Spey waters flow.

GLENFARCLAS

The south-west of Speyside has been blessed. Within it is the area known as The Glenlivet and the road to Grantown offers three detours in particular to places where great malt is waiting at the end of the trail. The first is to Glenfarclas. It is not, today, a name that people offer you automatically when asked to reel off the truly magnificent malts of Scotland. But they will.

It is found close to Tomfarclas woods where the hills that ripple out from Ben Rinnes seem finally to come to rest. And it is from springs on those hills above that the water for this sumptuous whisky comes. There has been a still on the site since 1835 and the distillery has remained in the Grant family for exactly a century now.

The current proprietor, John Grant, lives and breathes the distillery and his attention to detail has paid off. He has insisted on bringing in more sherry casks than a distillery this size would normally consider profitable – and the *oloroso* thread that runs through all his malts has vindicated his gameplan. I have tasted eight official Glenfarclas bottlings and, though the famous "cask strength" 105 is a bit too young for a malt of this depth to be seen in its best light, the 10-year-old is as complete a Speysider of that age as you are likely to find (with the possible exception of the 15-year-old!), with the long, nutty, malty finish almost refusing to make its exit. The 30-year-old is a masterpiece, too, though the first time I was handed a glass I spilt most of it ducking a couple of RAF fighters which screamed low over the distillery.

Once, the whisky was sold as Glenfarclas-Glenlivet. The suffix has been dropped as pointless and all distillery bottlings are simply called Glenfarclas. If you see an independent bottling, don't tell the Grants. Glenfarclas has been waging war on anyone who bottles a whisky under their name. Their stance is understandable and maybe not entirely without cause. Yet if Glenfarclas' aim is to wipe out the independent bottler, then I hope they fail because it was through the independents that I, and doubtless many others, first discovered what a gem Glenfarclas is. I hope their name carries far and wide; their malt should be experienced by anyone in search of liquid beauty.

CRAGGANMORE

While Glenfarclas is open to all and sundry, it is a more difficult task to get a peek at Cragganmore. This is the other great distillery in the Ballindalloch region and is located in a rural setting of farm buildings, forests and hills. When owners United Distillers announced their Classic Malts range, a fair number of bets were taken on which would be the choice for Speyside. Many thought Mortlach, others put their money on Linkwood and Glen Elgin. But it was Cragganmore which won the day; no enormous surprise when you know that manager Mike Gunn has, above his fireplace, the old A1 stencil plate. This is the original Scottish Malt Distillers' marking to show that their blenders regarded Cragganmore as the very finest of all their malts. Sales, though, have not been what they might: a shame as this is one of Scotland's most intricate whiskies, deserving of contemplation.

On the bottle of the 12-year-old you will make out a steam engine, marking the fact that Cragganmore was the first distillery to make use of the great iron road. Today the track has gone and its bed is the start, or finish, of a stretch of the Speyside Way, the path which now takes hikers through this gentle part of the Highlands.

The distillery is perhaps the neatest of all United Distillers' Speysiders. Its most impressive aspect is its stills which, like Dalmore's, have a sawn-off look about the top of them so they could fit into the low-slung stillhouse. Where neighbour Glenfarclas benefits from the use of sherry, 12-year-old Cragganmore is all the better for coming from ex-bourbon casks alone. This gives it a chance to buzz and bite at the tastebuds and for that most subtle hint of smoke to waft through uncloaked: A1 whisky, indeed.

Head back out of Ballindalloch, refuse the hairpin turn on the road back toward Aberlour and instead take an easier right and you are en route for not just the Highland town of Tomintoul, but undoubtedly the most famous malt whisky distillery of them all.

The great Cragganmore: *Situated to the west of Speyside, where distilleries are sparser.*

THE GLENLIVET

There has probably been more written about The Glenlivet Distillery than any other. Any connoisseur who knows his way round a tray of assorted malts will probably be able to trot off the story of The Glenlivet without too much fuss. Indeed, how the distillery acquired its name and the esteem in which it was held close on two centuries ago have almost been carved in stone and to question whether The Glenlivet still makes the last word in Speyside whisky is bordering on the sacrilegious. But, nevertheless, that question must be asked.

It would be ridiculous to think for a moment that the whisky served from its famous green bottle is anything like the whisky of 1824 when George Smith set up his first legal distillery. The area of The Glenlivet was 14 miles long and 6 miles wide and contained within it many bothies. Of all the whisky smuggled out of the Highlands, it was that from the Glenlivet area close by the River Livet which was in greatest demand for its fine quality. The name stuck and it was "Glenlivet" that was demanded by merchants buying the legal whisky from Speyside. For that reason, some distilleries in all directions, even, absurdly, Benromach to the north and Strathisla to the west, hijacked the Glenlivet title, attaching it to their name, and it took a legal battle for the Smith's Minmore Distillery to be the only one entitled to call itself The Glenlivet.

When, in 1924, the distillery issued a little booklet with a soft cloth cover to mark its 100th year, it made a point that the distillery lies where there was a plentiful supply of Faemussach moss, a peat used in the kilning of malt "free from all mineral impregnations". Today the malt brought into the distillery is very, very lightly peated. Also the stills have been steam-heated for the last decade or so, a fact that would bring deep, unremitting horror to Colonel George Smith Grant, the distillery's traditionalist owner at the turn of the century. He told the whisky commission that pot stills heated this way should not be allowed to call their make Scotch whisky! There is no doubt that the dram served now is a lighter relation to the whisky which then was hailed throughout the British Empire as Scotland's finest.

Whiskies do change, despite what the back of most labels will tell you. And I think The Glenlivet has gone through its shaky period. There was a time, according to my contemporary tasting notes, between 1988 and 1992 when The Glenlivet had become a rather tired dram, flat and uninspiring – maybe it was the casks it matured in. Certainly since then it has regained a lot of that flowery grassiness, that quintessential regional character which I first experienced 20 years back, and it is again a rather fine, distinguished malt, a kind of Cary Grant among whiskies. I adore the 12-year-old for its lilting, fruity tone which explodes all over the palate. The more sombre 18-year-old uses sherry just as it should, but the 21-year-old, showing not a jot of oak, is its champion, displaying delightful balance so the sherry and malt dance a rich *pas de deux* on the tastebuds. Better malts can be found on Speyside, but they are few and far between.

Connoisseur's Selection

THE GLENLIVET – AT 21 YEARS OLD, IT TRULY COMES OF AGE. MAGNIFICENT.

TOMINTOUL – FIND A 12-YEAR-OLD FOR A BIG BRUISING SPEYSIDER.

BRAEVAL – TRY TO FIND ONE FROM THE INDEPENDENTS.

TAMNAVULIN – PROBABLY BEST TRYING AT 14–15 YEARS OLD FROM AN INDEPENDENT BOTTLER.

Still, whenever passing the distillery, it is impossible not to remember the story of how a strong-willed man took on his once-fellow illicit distillers and, at the risk of death, turned legal. That was not on the site now occupied by the present sprawl of warehouses. His first site was a mile or so south which he called the Drummin Distillery. As poacher turned gamekeeper, he was on his guard against attack by smugglers and travelled everywhere with a pistol at his side. His son was the JG Smith you see with his name on every bottle and it was

The Glenlivet: *A utilitarian view of an ancient distillery.*

Tomintoul: *The distillery buildings may be new and purpose-built, but the whisky reflects the area's rugged beauty.*

JG who upped sticks and moved to the present location, with another site being used first. The distillery has now been altered beyond recognition from even its centenary year. But it is on a wild, high part of Speyside on a desolate road and captures the essence of the region in more ways than one.

ALLT-A-BHAINNE *(Alt-a-Bane)*

As lonely a place as The Glenlivet may be, there are a number of small roads to it. From Dufftown you would have passed Ben Rinnes very close to your right and where the summit appears to be nearest the road a cluster of small, reasonably tasteful buildings blocks the view. This is another Seagram distillery, Allt-a-Bhainne, built in 1975 solely to give malt for the company's blends, including Chivas Regal. Although never bottled by the company, it can be an alluring, sweet malt with just a hint of smoke and spice to complement the biscuity cerealness. The inside is a classic, late-twentieth-century, one-level design: a neat compact little distillery which suits this rarest of malts rather well.

TOMINTOUL *(Tom-in-towel)*

From The Glenlivet, you can now take a loop road that takes you to the three other distilleries in the true Glenlivet area. The first is Tomintoul, part of the Whyte & Mackay group – a newish structure a long way from the town and in operation since 1965, taking up a lovely spot selected perhaps because of springs fed by a subterranean reservoir. The outside jars a little with the area but its still-house forms an impressive sight and there's a nice touch with decorations of little thistle emblems. Its whisky is sold as a 12-year-old, arriving in the worst-shaped bottle on the market with a lip the size of a thermos flask cup. I just love the malt, though: big, strapping and raisiny with a hint of toasty nuttiness as it dries on the finish.

BRAEVAL *(Bray-val)*

As you head for Tomintoul, a left fork for Chapeltown takes you into a near-wilderness area called the Braes of Glenlivet. In medieval times monks lived here, and must have had a hard time of it. Where the road almost peters out there stands one of the most pleasingly designed new distilleries in Scotland. Built in 1972, it has a certain Spanishness to it which one sees to a greater degree in its sister distillery in Kentucky, Four Roses.

Of all Speyside's distilleries, this is the one which would have struggled to survive in a previous era: so remote is it that by the time the whisky reached the market, the spirit would have evaporated from old age. Beyond stillman Andy Watson's home there is no road at all, just forest and mountain. The distillery is attractive inside, too, with two large wash stills feeding the four smaller spirit ones.

When Seagram brought out Glen Keith and Benriach as single malts, I was surprised and disappointed that this beautiful whisky was not included. Yes, it is very light, but it is full of fruity and malty complexity with even the faintest tang of strawberries just before the dry finish. No longer is the distillery called Braes of Glenlivet. Seagram, wishing to see as few distilleries with the name Glenlivet as possible, has re-christened it Braeval. Curiously, there are floodlights trained on the building so that, complete with weather vane, it will glow in the night sky. Very pretty; it's just a shame there's nobody around to see it.

TAMNAVULIN *(Tamna-voolin)*

Passing through Tomintoul, you swing back north, but instead of heading for Grantown you take the country road back to The Glenlivet, and take in Tamnavulin-Glenlivet on the way. It was an Invergordon distillery, and was mothballed soon after the takeover. It is another new-ish distillery, not particularly attractive inside and even worse outside. In its concrete frame, it positively growls at you – and the whisky is not much friendlier either. It starts off sweet and attractive, but half-way through changes course to leave a strange, rather synthetic finish. Not great, but good enough to be working.

TORMORE

Compared to the next distillery, though, it is positive nectar. Having rejoined the road to Grantown at Ballindalloch, it's time to head out of Speyside. After passing the turn to Cragganmore, a vision arrives on your left so unexpected it could land you in a ditch. The Tormore Distillery bursts onto the scene, cathedral-like and without any warning, a strangely beautiful sight to behold, built in 1958 to the designs of the eminent architect Sir Albert Richardson. Sadly, its malt is barely a patch on Balmenach's close up the road; I have it on good authority that the man who masterminded the construction and design of Tormore was reduced to tears when he tasted the spirit which came off it. It was then under the auspices of Long John, who had a thing about stainless steel rather than copper. Since then successive managers have come and gone, all failing to bring it to heel. At the helm at the moment is John Black, a greatly respected manager. And still the new make I have tasted from there has been harsh and metallic: if he can't put it right no-one can. Why Allied have continued marketing it as a 10-year-old, I don't know. It has no give, no yield on the palate. I can't say it quite reduces me to tears, but I think I know what that poor chap meant. Back to the drawing board, boys.

BALMENACH

From Grantown there is a back road down to Glenlivet. But with no distilleries on the way, it is better to take the Charlestown of Aberlour road as if heading for Cragganmore or Glenfarclas. Just outside Grantown, as the road begins its pursuit of the Spey, there is a village called Cromdale and here is a distillery, Balmenach, which won the hearts of many when described so touchingly by Sir Robert Bruce Lockhart in his 1951 book *Scotch* – still, to my mind, the most readable book ever on whisky. The distillery was once owned by his family and he spent his formative years growing up around it. Lockhart's description of how the distillery came to be bears retelling:

Soon after the passing of the Act of 1823 he [Lockhart's great-grandfather James Macgregor] received a visit from the nearest Excise officer. Their talk was friendly and began with a generous dram of pure malt whisky. When these preliminaries were finished to the satisfaction of both men, the Excise officer mentioned shyly that he had his duty to perform and he had better look round. Out went the men to inspect the farm. All went well until they came to a rough stone building with a mill-wheel and a mill-lade by its side.

"What will that be?" asks the Excise officer.

"Oh," says my great-grandfather, "that'll just be the peat-shed."

Nothing more was said, and the two men went back to the house for another dram and talk about the crops and prospects for harvest. Then as the gauger took his leave, he said quietly:

"If I were you, Mr Macgregor, I'd just take out a licence for yon peat-shed."

Were he still alive, Lockhart would be saddened by the sight of the distillery now, silent after being mothballed a couple of years back. But he would be impressed with its grand demeanour inside and some of the quite excellent malt maturing with its name on. It can be astounding at 12 years old, one of the fattest, fullest-bodied drams in the whole of Speyside. This doesn't come through quite so well, though, on their own over-sherried bottling.

TOMATIN *(Tom-ar-tin)*

By-passing Grantown, it is back to the trusty A9, but, before heading south, a short journey northward will take you to the largest malt distillery in Scotland, Tomatin. I have passed it on the night train from Euston to Inverness and it looked prettier then. Up close the distillery looks what it is: somewhere where an awful lot of development has taken place in relatively recent times. Having said that, it is a fascinating place to visit, again in gorgeous countryside, though it's hard to spot its 1897 birthmark.

In 1986, Tomatin became the first distillery to be bought outright by the Japanese. It has struggled in recent years and no more than ticks over now, yet this is a vast improvement from before the Japanese intervention. But lately its enormity has worked to its advantage. Only half of the 23 stills are currently used. The others were in operation until the copper began wearing thin. Rather than spend needlessly to get them repaired, they switched over. This way the company spends at its own rate. While always accepting that it is a pretty decent blending malt, for years I could take or leave Tomatin, feeling it rather lacked character. Of late I have not been so sure: there is something about the languid maltiness of the 10-year-old which makes it quite an appealing dram for those quieter moments. A 12-year-old for the US market is actually quite lovely, with a fudgy, treacle-tart sweetness linking up with soft ginger and pepper spices. It is a fine malt to accompany their recently acquired Antiquary blend. On this evidence big, obviously, can be beautiful.

There again, the same applies to being small. Speyside has living, distilling proof of this fact further down the A9 at Kingussie. It is the last distillery in the region to find before heading toward Perthshire. And it is the newest. If you arrive in Kingussie, for a romantic touch try asking for directions at the local newspaper office, housed in the only surviving building of the town's previous distillery demolished after its closure in 1910.

SPEYSIDE

Even with directions and a map, it can still be Mission Impossible to find this new distillery, called appropriately enough Speyside. It can hardly be seen from any road and the gated entrance is little more than a track. But when you head down toward the banks of the River

> *Connoisseur's Selection*
>
> **Tormore** – Age does not matter. It is awful.
>
> **Tomatin** – At 12 years old, it does have a sweet, spicy say.
>
> **Balmenach** – At 12 years old, one of the fattest, full-bodied drams in Speyside.
>
> **Speyside** – Drumguish is inexpensive and very decent bottlings can be found.

Whisky gem: *Speyside, with its tiny pot-stills that hold a mere 18,000 litres between them, is one of the quaintest distilleries in the world.*

Tromie, there before you is a sight which stirs the heart. Built entirely of stone, low-slung, this barn built by a dry-stone dyker must be the closest thing in the region to a reincarnation of the distilleries of a couple of centuries ago. There are no warehouses – the spirit is tankered to Glasgow – and the manager's cottage is only yards from the distillery building: no manager in Scotland is more on top of his job than Richard Beattie. There is a third building, the oldest of them all: at the top is housed the office, below are the eighteenth-century workings of the original mill.

You would be forgiven for thinking the distillery old, too. But construction was started in 1962 and completed in 1976. The first spirit was run from the stills in January 1991. In all, it took the founding father George Christie, a Glasgow blender, 36 years to realize his dream of building his own distillery. It has even been shaped to follow the contour of the river which, in turn, has obliged the distillers by forming its own lake to supply them with all the water they need.

Most distilleries, as you have gathered by now, are set in stunning locations: Speyside's is truly awesome. In the far distance, in just about every direction, are mountains, the Cairngorms and Grampians, and not too distant is the 3,443-foot peak of Carn Bàn Mór, while forests stand out bold green against the snow caps of the hills. In mid-winter the Tromie gushes past, so cold it has been recorded below freezing. At times like that you escape inside the stillhouse, where the tiny stills, held aloft by tripods, hold just 11,000 and 7,000 litres respectively. And to add to the quaintness, the mash tun has a clock on it. Stainless steel washbacks apart, it is a near-faultless little operation.

Already the malt is out and about. It is being sold as Drumguish, the name of the hamlet nearby, and though it has been variable, with the worst displaying an unacceptable rubbery quality, the latest samples have been sweet and rich with an oiliness one might expect from a spirit still so small. Even as a four- or five-year-old it has taken on a delightful resonance and holds on the palate well with a hint of Brazil nut and apples.

If you are ever offered the chance to buy a cask from a distillery called Grandtully, in fact you are probably being offered Speyside. When they claim to be selling the only stocks from the Grandtully Distillery, it is worth asking them to explain what Drumguish is. I am nervous of claims being made about the potential profits of buying by the cask. The sooner Speyside call all their whisky by the distillery name the better. And if you want to buy Speyside whisky by the cask, I'd contact the company. Or go to the distillery in person. It is worth getting lost for.

EASTERN HIGHLANDS

The whisky industry has not been kind to the distilleries of the Eastern Highlands. Everywhere you go they seem to be closed, demolished, condemned to folklore. To the north, Banff has been flattened, Glendronach mothballed; down the coast the pink granite shell of Glenugie is still within sight of Peterhead prison but it's now an engineering plant; at Stonehaven, Glenury Royal has been closed; there is no future for Glen Esk and Lochside in Montrose; North Port, Brechin, even with its ornate interior, has also been demolished and back up north Glen Garioch is silent and up for sale with no-one beating down the door of owners Suntory to get their hands on it. When I asked a blender once why he thought all these distilleries had perished, he replied, "Well, perhaps because, basically, their whisky was crap." He had a point.

GLEN GARIOCH *(Glen Gear-ee)*

Not about Glen Garioch, though. Rumours regarding the fate of this lovely old distillery had been circulating for years, but David Morrison, while still head of Morrison Bowmore, told me there was nothing to them. The fact remained that the whisky had been changed beyond all recognition. Once, it was one of the peatiest drams made on mainland Scotland, even out-phenolizing Ardmore. But as a young spirit, it was raw and untamed and the peat didn't help. So to make it more acceptable to blenders, and therefore a better bet to break even at least, the peating was dropped considerably. The result was a new make that was raw and untamed, but lacked character. It seemed as if the owners couldn't win.

I have always loved this distillery. It stands in the village of Old Meldrum in Aberdeenshire and could pass off nicely as a quaint old schoolhouse, should you not be aware of its purpose in life. In fact it is/was a distillery which continued its own malting and creaked with history. Dating back to 1798, it has been part of the Morrison Bowmore portfolio since 1960. In that time they attracted visitors who were amused to find the waste heat from the distillery warming greenhouses in which tomatoes thrived. At its sister distillery, Bowmore on Islay, the heat is used to warm a swimming pool. Today the swimming pool attracts a community; the tomatoes were left to their own fate and forgotten long before the distillery was placed on the market.

A few years back I wrote that Glen Garioch (pronounced Glen Geeree) at 21 years old was one of the 10 finest malts I had ever tasted, full of enormous peaty depth, but without the pungent iodine character that frightens so many people off Islay whiskies. On reading the piece, a senior sales executive at another distiller rang me to say he thought I had gone mad and questions had to be asked regarding the reliability of my tastebuds. He was not speaking totally in jest. However, during the summer of 1996, a 1972 Glen Garioch won a coveted Gold Medal at the *Wine and Spirit* magazine Spirit Challenge. One fears, though, it is far too little, too late.

FETTERCAIRN

Why a distillery like Glen Garioch should be silent when another like Fettercairn survives is beyond me. This is a malt I simply dislike. There is a rubbery quality to it which I find impenetrable, and an aftertaste which I can remove only with toothpaste. Yet it sells as a single malt, and quite well, too. Amazing.

I love the distillery itself: it has a wonderful charm that convinces you good whisky is made there. Everything about the place – the faultless beauty of its inner workings, even the countryside with the snow-capped Grampians looming in the background – is right. It has even enjoyed links with one of Britain's greatest Prime Ministers, William Ewart Gladstone, whose grand family residence, Fasque, with its herd of deer grazing and rutting at the front, is just a mile or two down a country lane. But the whisky? I've tried the new make, at two years from the cask and at varying ages up to 20 years (there was an 18-year-old sample which was quite pleasant, actually). But for me this is malt which contrives to clog the tastebuds and what does get through is not very pretty at all. Whyte & Mackay's master blender, Richard Paterson, knows how to handle it, though. He uses it in a good number of his blends, which are usually first-rate. Indeed, the fact that he manages this perhaps goes to underline why he is considered one of the finest blenders of his generation.

Lovely distillery: *Shame about the malt.*

GLENCADAM

Much better, but still an occasionally feisty dram, is Glencadam, the sole surviving distillery in Brechin a few miles east of Fettercairn. The journey between the two distilleries on fine spring and summer mornings, with its gladed roadside and open, mildly undulating fields of fertility, is not how one might imagine the Highlands, but is none the less charming for that. Being part of the Allied group, Glencadam is broom-polished smart and the buildings, though slightly updated in the 1950s, leave no doubt the distillery dates back to 1825. But because it has two stills, there are many rumours buzzing about this distillery that it, too, could soon be sold off, or mothballed.

I hope not. Yes, I have had the occasional disappointing dram from here. But, when on form, Glencadam shows a delicious flair. The washbacks are made from metal but are still very attractive, and the stillroom is quite tiny and intimate with the lyne arms angled slightly upward, unusual but not unique. For this reason, it has been said that Glencadam's whisky is made uphill. What is unique is that from the distillery entrance you can watch Scottish senior football through the hedge that fences off Brechin City's Glebe Park ground.

Glencadam is not an easy malt to locate in the marketplace. Trusty Gordon & MacPhail oblige with something like a 20-year-old which, despite its juicy, honey nose, is a bit thin on the palate. Cadenhead sometimes come up with one of a similar age, the last I tried being inferior on the nose but firmer on the palate. Neither can be regarded as anything other than OK at best. Best to look out for younger samples, maybe between eight and 10 years.

Connoisseur's Selection

GLEN GARIOCH – THE 10-YEAR-OLD IS FULL OF ENORMOUS PEATY DEPTH, BUT NO IODINE.

FETTERCAIRN – NOT TO MY TASTE – BUT IT SELLS QUITE WELL AS A 10-YEAR-OLD.

GLENCADAM – JUICY, HONEY NOSE, BUT A BIT THIN ON THE PALATE – EVEN AT 20 YEARS OLD.

ROYAL LOCHNAGAR – LOTS OF SHERRY, GIVING A KIND OF HOT-CROSS-BUN NOSE, VERY CLEAN, WELL DEFINED AND LINKING EFFORTLESSLY WITH A TOFFEE-MALT-CHOCOLATENESS.

ROYAL LOCHNAGAR

The best of the working distilleries currently operating in the Eastern Highlands is Royal Lochnagar. The trek there from Fettercairn is one of the most dramatic offered by any route in Scotland. The meandering first leg to Strachan takes you over the western fringes of the Grampians and it is worth taking a stop at the Cairn o'Mount which, though only 1,500 feet above sea level, offers stunning views over the Howe of Mearns and Fettercairn to the sea in one direction, and the jutting masses of the Highland mountains to the other. If you are not driving, this is as good a time as any to partake of a wee snifter.

Lochnagar Distillery can be found by joining up with and staying on the south Deeside road to Ballater. It is a part of the world that has enchanted successive members of the royal family, except perhaps a princess who found it rather too boring. That was not how Queen Victoria saw it and the tale of how she patronized the little distillery a mile or so from her Balmoral home is pretty well worn, but one worth telling again.

On September 14, 1848 a rather younger and more beautiful Victoria than we usually remember her, accepted an invitation from the owner, John Begg, to see around his new distillery. Despite having sent the invite, John Begg was still taken aback to find his Queen at the front door with her husband Prince Albert and a couple of her children. Her Highness, a Highlandophile, was as enthralled with this aspect of traditional Scottish life as she was with most others and, at the end of the tour, accepted the offer to taste the whisky. Not only did she and Prince Albert sample the spirit as it tumbled from the still, but also some that had been matured for a few years. Even the children, so legend has it, got a taste as well. The distillery had been up and running only three years and was then called the New Lochnagar Distillery, as it had replaced one that

Royal Lochnagar: *A jewel in UD's crown.*

had previously burned down. Following Victoria's expedition, Begg became distiller to the Queen and was, by charter, allowed to used the "Royal" prefix, the "New" being hastily discarded.

These days Royal Lochnagar is little bigger than when Victoria popped in. It is by far the smallest in United Distillers' armoury and the 30,000 visitors who follow in her footsteps each year see a spotlessly clean distillery, the tiny stills and pipework highly polished on the orders of manager Alastair Skakles, and at the end of the tour sample a 12-year-old dram that is simply delicious. I enjoy it best when I am circling Loch Muick, close to the mountain of Lochnagar, whose waters still feed the distillery. On the hills surrounding Loch Muick are ring ouzels, and sitting watching them call while sipping from a hip flask filled with a soft, malty, gently honeyed dram made from the waters that run nearby is one of life's true pleasures.

There is also a Selected Reserve bottling with its regal gold and blue label. There is no age statement, but some pretty old stuff does find its way in there, apparently. However, it's the sherry which comes through most, giving a kind of hot-cross-bun nose: very clean, well defined and linking effortlessly with a toffee-malt-chocolateness. It is a fine dram, but never in a million years worth the £150-plus you have to pay for it.

PERTHSHIRE

Just the briefest mention of the Scottish Highlands conjures up visions of brooding mountains and hidden glens, rutting stags, snowdrifts and distilleries smoking dreamily away in remote passes. It is more than a little surprising to learn, then, that there is only one distillery which can be found in excess of 1,000 feet above sea level, and that is the one at Dalwhinnie.

DALWHINNIE

It could be argued that Dalwhinnie is a Speyside whisky, and there is some sort of a case to answer. But in truth Dalwhinnie is, well, Dalwhinnie. It is an accurate cliché to say that all malts are different. However, there really is no other malt in Scotland quite like this one. Yes, it sits by the River Truim which runs into the Spey and, to taste, there is a grassiness among its traits. But there is also a peaty heatheriness which is unmistakably northern Highland in character. The heather certainly reflects its mountainous location. But, perhaps most important of all, there is also a rich honey vein which is sheer Perthshire in style. It is surely no coincidence that the distillery, built some 100 years ago in a village which was formed at the confluence of old drovers' routes heading north, south and east, produces a malt of such diversity of style and character that it could almost be granted a status all its own.

This is a distillery which you just have to stop at and look around. The view it offers is awesome, whatever time of the year you go there. Being so high, it spends more time under snow than just about any other – the

The height of perfection: *Snowbound Dalwhinnie is Scotland's only distillery over 1,000 feet above sea level.*

manager's company car is a four-wheel-drive Range Rover – and, on a crisp winter's day, the Grampian Mountains to the southwest, opposite, sparkle spectacularly. In the late summer months the heather blooms a dark purple, and in the rain of all seasons the low cloud and the muscular presence of the nearby Monadhliath and Cairngorm mountain ranges, especially the Munro of Carn na Caim, induce a claustrophobic feeling.

Until very recently this oppressiveness carried on into the distillery itself. It was a dark, compact place and the stillhouse in particular clung to another age. But there have been many changes. Since the distillery attracted almost 50,000 visitors a year, its owners, United Distillers, felt that the home of one of their six Classic Malts should look reasonably spick and span without losing too much of its character and be able to cater for larger numbers, should they arrive. Well, the wonderful wooden washbacks are still there and the stills are polished for inspection. Those who have never been here before will not notice the difference. There are some of us, however, who lament the passing of its innocently grubby days. Nevertheless, the make is as good as ever and for that we should be grateful. And the local species of wild, jet-black rabbit also seems to have survived. Full marks, too, to UD for bucking the trend and using traditional worms which, sunk into new tubs on the outside of the stillhouse, give the distillery a back-to-front appearance. Moreover, a nice touch has been added by placing the mash tuns under the pagoda, so that the escaping steam gives the impression that malting is taking place. Dalwhinnie, a vital component of the Buchanan blends, surprised a lot of people by being chosen as one of UDs' Classic Malts. At one time their new make was affectionately known as "cabbage water" on account of its uncompromising sulphury heaviness, dissipated only by time. However, not only has it vindicated their choice, but the 15-year-old has proved the most versatile to be found on the whisky shelves today. Dalwhinnie may be a distillery among the mountains, but its whisky towers high above anything else around.

Safe and sound: *Blair Athol's new-make spirit gushes into a receiver.*

BLAIR ATHOL

Further down the A9 there is another distillery to be viewed and, being in the middle of the town of Pitlochry, it attracts even more tourists. Blair Athol is another ancient distillery, rapidly approaching its bicentenary. It was once a vital constituent of Bell's. Arthur Bell set up business in Perth and a later generation bought Blair Athol to guarantee a ready stock of decent malt, which it remained up to about 20 to 25 years ago. However, in the latter days of the company's history, prior to its takeover by Guinness, the whisky coming from the distillery was not of the highest grade. Like Inchgower and Dufftown, two other Bell's distilleries, insufficient funds and time were being made available for improving rapidly deteriorating distilling apparatus. The result was an off-key, harsh, fiery malt, sometimes bottled by Bell's, which did the distillery's reputation few favours.

In addition, there was an almost indecent haste to cash in on its potential as a tourist attraction. By the late 1980s and early 1990s it had lost much of its identity as an old Perthshire distillery and had become more of a festival of kitsch. Certain lessons have, however, been learnt and it is now a more pleasant place to visit. Those who decided not to enter on account of its appearance (and I have met them) might be rewarded by a second visit, if only to see the four delightful larch washbacks.

Anyone who has sampled the shuddering awfulness of the 12-year-old will be relieved to hear that the spirit tripping from the stills has improved markedly, shedding its unpleasant, all-masking griminess so that you can even detect a little peat. Much of this is due to former manager, Mike Nicholson, a quirky-humoured, mildly eccentric professor-of-whisky type, who made such an impact in turning things around. His reward was the plum posting to United Distillers' leading malt, Lagavulin. In the whisky world there really is such a thing as justice.

Connoisseur's Selection

DALWHINNIE – THE 15-YEAR-OLD CLASSIC MALT IS JUST THAT. A SPECTACULAR WHISKY WHICH APPEALS TO BOTH SEXES.

BLAIR ATHOL – WORTH LEAVING FOR A FEW YEARS UNTIL THE IMPROVED STUFF COMES ALONG.

Small is beautiful: *Especially in the case of Perthshire's Edradour, which is by far Scotland's smallest distillery.*

EDRADOUR *(Edra-dower)*

You don't have to be religious or to drink whisky religiously in order to make a pilgrimage. But there is one that is genuinely worth the trouble. Nestling in one of the many quiet glens whose burns swell the River Tummel as it circles Pitlochry to the west and south before disgorging into the Tay a few miles downstream at Balmacneil is the last surviving farm distillery in Britain, dating back to 1837, the year of Queen Victoria's accession. It is called Edradour after the rocky burn which runs through the site. The distillery is magnificent, having somehow escaped the onslaught of the twentieth century and enters the twenty-first stubbornly caught in a time warp which enables it to retain the art of making whisky as a cottage industry. Indeed, the tiny cluster of whitewashed buildings with red-painted doors are no more than a cottage in size, despite the fact they contain the stills, washbacks and even the barrels.

When you consider the hundreds of distilleries which have perished over the last century or so, stumbling across Edradour is not far off a miracle. Because it is so small, it should not take long to look round, but instead you find yourself engrossed by the pint-sized operation. These days it doesn't bother with a maltings or mill. Since 1983 the malt, all but unpeated, has been arriving in sacks ready crushed. The resplendently green and red cast-iron mashtun mashes 1.05 tons of grist five times a week. By contrast, at medium-sized Blair Athol three miles away, each of the 11 mashes contains 7.5 tons of malt.

Up until the 1950s Edradour sported two little washbacks made from larch. They were replaced with Oregon pine. Each is filled to 6,000 litres (1,320 gallons), about two-thirds of their capacity. At Blair Athol, in contrast, there are eight washbacks, four with a capacity of 20,000 litres, and another four double that at 8,799 gallons. Edradour's fermentation time is a relatively short 48, hours before the wash is pumped, via the last Morton's refrigerator in the business, into the double-bulbous low wines still, which holds 4,218 litres (947 gallons – 5,499 gallons at Blair Athol) and then the straighter spirit still which holds just 2,182 litres (480 gallons). This is easily the smallest in Scotland (Blair Athol's is 3,199 gallons) and the distillery's *pièce de résistance.* Ignore the perennial myth that the stills are "the smallest permissible under Customs and Excise regulations", as the distillery's own history puts it. In fact they

Connoisseur's Selection

EDRADOUR – THE 10-YEAR-OLD CAN BE OUTSTANDING. ITS OILY, HONEY FINISH IS LIKE A JAMAICAN POT STILL RUM.

ABERFELDY – FIND A 12-YEAR-OLD FROM INDEPENDENTS AND EXPERIENCE A RARE TREAT.

squeeze in with a comfortable 84 gallons to spare. But certainly they were quaint enough to entice BBC television to film *King's Royal* there in the 1980s, the only British period drama series about whisky that has ever been made.

Because the stills are so small, it would be reasonable to expect the eventual whisky to be rich, a touch oily and full of estery character. It is. But, since they can fill only six or seven butts a week, making their annual output roughly what an average distillery can produce in just one Monday to Friday period, Edradour's is not the easiest malt to find, though it can be obtained at the distillery's visitors' centre. Amazingly, some of the 300 casks stored in the single tiny warehouse will also find themselves adding a touch of class to the vatted malts occasionally launched by the company's owners, Pernod Ricard. But it is the single malt that deserves study, and where better than at the distillery itself. The surrounding countryside is nothing short of spectacular, with open views across the Tummel Glen to hills, forests and peaks beyond. This is the Scottish Highlands as all we romantics have imagined it and right in the middle, would you believe, is this enchanting distillery.

Tours are suspended during mid-winter but for me late January is the best time to go. The distillery is usually back in operation by then after its Christmas break and the Edradour burn, which supplies the water for the mash, is running at its fastest. If you are lucky, you might be treated to a sunset of pastel-shaded reds and purples, and the glass of 10-year-old will be at its sweetly honeyed best, the classic Perthshire malt which underlines the region's claim for an appellation all its own. But, because so little is distilled, quality can vary and if the dram strikes you as slightly thin, perhaps even bitter, when the honey has died, then you have no option. You will just have to make the terrible sacrifice of coming back another day and trying again.

ABERFELDY

The A9, that arterial road which picks and winds its way through the mountains of the Highlands often by clinging to the contours of whichever river happens to be at hand at the time, these days bypasses Pitlochry as it heads south toward Strath Tay. It is at the head of this region, where the Tay and Tummel meet, that prehistoric man has lived for thousands of years and has left countless stone circles, standing stones and tumuli to be visited as a mark of his culture. As a mark of ours, Perthshire is littered with distilleries.

And not all of them are remote. About a dozen miles southwest of Edradour you will come across another solid, central Highland town, Aberfeldy. On its very edge stands a distillery displaying typical late-Victorian confidence and with stills every bit as massive as Edradour's are tiny. Yet the distillery, which takes its name from the town, is barely heard of and settles instead for the praises of Scotland's blenders rather than the public. It has been so since Perth-based whisky baron Tommy Dewar built it in 1896, just a year after he became, reputedly, the third person in Britain to buy a motor car.

Aberfeldy does receive visitors, though they are more likely to go off wandering in search of the red squirrel population that manager Brian Bisset has been protecting in the distillery's expanding park and nature trail, part of a project with Scottish Natural Heritage. The planting of the traditional Caledonian pine is of special interest to whisky lovers like me, who happen also to be amateur ornithologists. With luck, it might attract Scotland's only indigenous bird, the rare and shy Scottish crossbill. If it did, Aberfeldy would gain an even higher place on my list of favourite distilleries. Aberfeldy is a good place for trainspotters, too. Recently, enthusiasts began working on the restoration of a "puggy", one of the small steam engines which pulled and shunted whisky-laden wagons through the Highlands to Glasgow. A hundred feet or so of track has even been relaid at the front of the distillery for the puggy to stand on.

It is a shame that the old Distillers Company decided to tack on a new stillhouse at the end of the original and quite substantial stone building, since the distillery does now have a slightly lopsided look. But inside the old quarter, four washbacks of larch stand proud in their original positions. The four

Aberfeldy: *All but a drop of the contents of these barrels is destined for blending.*

stills – two low wines, two spirit – are just about identical in shape, which is very bulbous. The spirit still is 10 times the size of Edradour's, holding 20,372 litres (4,482 gallons). But the matured whisky it makes, though lighter, is very fine indeed. The telltale Perthshire honeyness is there in a very unobtrusive way and, to add to its poise, there is a sprinkling of spice and peat and a bolstering of rich malt which makes for a dram that other distillers would be more than delighted to market as a mainstream single malt. As it is, UD produce limited stocks as a 15-year-old. Perhaps by then it has passed the heights it reaches at about 9 to 12, with the oak countering its sweeter tones, leaving the malt far more exposed at the finish. Nevertheless, it still makes for a near-perfect aperitif.

Like Edradour, Aberfeldy is set in stunning countryside. The last time I looked out the stillhouse, a large gathering in black was slowly making its way toward the cemetery opposite. One of the town's more cherished daughters was being laid to rest only yards from the banks of the River Tay. Overlooked by the kindly sculpted and forested Weem Hill and Cluny Rock to the north and Aberfeldy Distillery to its south, her final resting place was a form of heaven on earth.

TULLIBARDINE *(Tully-bard-een)*

Usually, whichever distillery you visit in Perthshire, you will find the stills hissing their merry song. However, there is always the exception. This region's is Tullibardine. It was mothballed in 1995 soon after Whyte & Mackay took over Invergordon Distillers, chiefly in order to get their hands on its grain plant. With Whyte & Mackay already the owners of three distilleries, taking Invergordon on board simply overloaded the system. Tullibardine became one of three to close.

Many Scottish distilleries which have been opened since the end of the Second World War have not enjoyed the happiest of fates and Tullibardine, a brewery until 1949, is a case in point. There is nothing wrong with the whisky which some describe as light – wrongly, I feel. I find it slightly fat, creamy-sweet and mealy. It has been available as a 10-year-old for a long time, but was never promoted by Invergordon with the same love and attention as Isle of Jura or Bruichladdich.

The distillery is situated in Blackford,

again on the A9, a village noted for its water and the home of Highland Spring bottled mineral water. The company gathers theirs by boring down into an artesian well. Tullibardine's is from the same source but is supplied to them naturally by springs which form the Danny Burn high in the Ochil Hills, and then tumble sweet and icy directly to the distillery to provide its mashing liquor.

GLENTURRET

To reach Tullibardine from Aberfeldy there is a wonderful cross-country journey that takes you through the Sma' Glen to Crieff via General Wade's old military road, built to keep the Scots in check after Culloden. So ancient is this route, that the Romans had been there some 1,500 years before him. On leaving Aberfeldy it is worth stopping before the road bends away, taking the town out of sight. There you have not only a viewpoint capturing the whole of Aberfeldy, but also the Pitillie Burn, whose waters feed the distillery. Once it fed a previous distillery, but this is long lost and no more than a few stones remain.

The distillery at Crieff, Glenturret, could also have been similarly lost had it not been for one man's passion. James Fairlie spent three years resurrecting a distillery that parish records show to date back to 1775, but which had been silent since 1929. Like many of Perthshire's farm distilleries, it reverted to farming use once the stills were removed, even though as long as a century ago it had grown beyond farm distillery status.

When the stills began running again for the first time, in June 1960, single-malt Scotch was virtually unknown outside the Highlands. The world was in the grip of blended Scotch fever and distillers were happy to keep it that way. James's initial vision was to bring a forgotten distillery back to life in order to add more malt to this river of blend. But later he decided to keep back some stock and eventually that was released as single malt.

Nearly 40 years on it would be safe to say that his enterprise has been a success. Each year 200,000 visitors come to see whisky being made there, thus providing one of Scotland's major tourist attractions, complete with exhibition, bar and restaurant. But, better still, the whisky can be rated among the very greatest the Highlands have to offer. It may have lost the family touch, being now part of the Highland Distilleries empire, following a period with Cointreau, but the family connection has not been entirely severed. James's son, Peter, remains within the group, though having just left Glenturret to take charge at The Macallan. However, there is now even a liqueur bearing the founder's name as well as celebrating the distillery's stillroom-born cat, Towser who, between 1963 and 1987, nabbed an estimated 28,899 mice, an achievement which entitled her to a place in the *Guinness Book of Records* and her

Connoisseur's Selection

TULLIBARDINE – A REAL SWEETIE WITH SOFT CREAM CENTRE AT 10-YEARS OLD.

GLENTURRET – FROM 12 YEARS ON THERE IS NO BAD AGE FOR THIS SOLID CLASSIC.

DEANSTON – FORGET ALL OLDER BOTTLINGS FOR NOW AND CONCENTRATE ON THE 12-YEAR-OLD.

Team spirit: *A century may have passed since these 16 men produced one of Perthshire's legendary malts – but little has changed.*

own statue at the distillery.

It would be reasonable to assume that any distillery so small and receiving such great numbers would look the worse for wear. In fact, Glenturret, beautifully situated on the banks of the temperamental Turret Burn, is a site to behold and at its most natural during the long winter months. It is located in the hamlet of Hosh, a couple of miles north of the old drovers' town of Crieff, and began life as Hosh Distillery before changing its name to Glenturret in 1875. Its charm lies not just in the fact it can be found in what Barnard so rightly described as "one of the prettiest glens in all Scotland", but also in the scale of the operation. The mashtun, into which water from Loch Turret is piped three miles to fill, is the same size as Edradour though, being of stainless steel rather than cast iron, is not so attractive. But the set of eight pocket-sized, dark-stained, black-ribbed washbacks in which the lightly peated Prisma barley ferments are stunning, as is the double-bulbed, brass-collared wash still which dominates the stillhouse. The much smaller spirit still is to be found in another chamber half a floor below and this gives a clue to how the distillery operates: by gravity, the oldest trick in the book. With the distillery now in the process of rebuilding an operational floor maltings, Glenturret is close to being run just as it was a century ago.

The excitement to add to the charm lies with the range of malts. There are 10 of them from the distillers alone, and they are a highly prized commodity among independent bottlers. Their most common incarnation is as a 12-year-old. Here the balance is about right: the obligatory Perthshire honey is there in force but with a fine backup of soft smoke and peat and a vanilla fruitiness. This is about as young as you can find. Glenturret is one of those rare malts that positively blossoms after its 15th birthday.

DEANSTON

Those on the lookout for unusual distilleries could do worse than Deanston. The building in which it is located is an historic landmark. Not for the making of whisky, which has been carried out there since only 1965, but for the milling of cotton. It stands aloof and set slightly back from the teaming River Teith. There is nothing remarkable about the distilling apparatus (except that it is about as traditional as you can find, with open mashtun, wooden washbacks and total lack of automation), the type of malt used (except, possibly that it is peat-free), the fermentation time or anything else. All are pretty standard. But nip down to warehouses 2A, 2B and 2C to see the spirit maturing and then you will soon discover what makes this distillery unlike any other.

There is no other way of putting it: Deanston is a cathedral to whisky maturation. In fact, with its gloriously vaulted ceiling built

Fill her up: *Another cask of Deanston is filled with new spirit before being warehoused.*

in 1785, you would swear you were in a crypt. This was once a weaving shed with grass growing above to keep the moisture in. Now it is the home of 14,000 casks, the hogsheads stacked no more than three high, all placed between a small number of columns which appear to be defying gravity by keeping the edifice aloft. When you are told that there is nowhere else like it in Britain, you can quite believe it. Nor is it any surprise to learn that this is a Grade I listed building.

To hold a conversation in the warehouse is a creepy business. Even the slightest whisper reverberates around the chamber as if the vaults were acting as amplifiers. It is a shame that the public does not have access to this or to any part of the distillery including the massive turbines. These are driven by waters from the Teith and produce so much electricity for the distillery that the excess is sold off to the national grid. Fortunately, the owners, Burn Stewart, are not so reserved about letting the public have access to their malt, which they make available as 12-, 17- and 25-year-olds.

I have yet to be impressed by the quarter centurion, despite its bourbon-like nose. And only lately have I begun to take to the 17-year-old. When it was first launched, I found it lifeless and dull. But the later bottlings have been pepped up by an injection of fruity spiciness, possibly thanks to sherry cask. To do Deanston justice, the rule tends to be: the younger the better. The 12-year-old is a belter, oozing with full-bodied zippy spiciness, remarkable for a whisky which uses peat-free malt. I have even tasted some eight-year-old which was full of mouthwatering, malty vitality. Burn Stewart might not be happy that I am so dismissive of their older bottlings, even though the 17-year-old is definitely pulling through. The compensation is that they are responsible only for the 12. The distillery had been closed by Invergordon before Burn Stewart saved it in 1982.

GLENGOYNE

The journey from the village of Deanston, near Doune, to the next distillery south, Glengoyne, is another foray into the ravined splendour of Perthshire. The Trossachs and Menteith Hills all parade their imposing beauty until a plain provides the opportunity for the Gargunnock and Fintry Hills to loom in the distance. At the farthest end you can see to the right is the 1,300-foot peak of Dumgoyne which starts its ascent a mere 40 feet above sea-level. Every year an entire platoon of masochists sets off from the base to see who can run up and down the near-vertical face the fastest. The winner's prize: a bottle of 17-year-old malt from the distillery where the race starts and finishes.

There are, however, easier ways to enjoy a dram of Glengoyne. Paying a small entry fee to look around the distillery is one. Unlike any other distillery I can think of, you get your measure of 10-year-old even before the tour starts. There is nothing like getting into the spirit of things as early as possible.

For a while, Glengoyne made much of the fact that its malt was the only one to be made from entirely unpeated barley. Of course, many distilleries had been doing this for some time, but never thought of boasting about it, or, because nearly all the make went into blending no one really cared. The whisky of Glengoyne is too good just to put down to a marketing point. It may not be located in Perthshire, but it enjoys all the trappings of the best things in the Perthshire style and comes up with a few tricks of its own.

Being just 14 miles from Glasgow, it is an easy distillery to find. And for those who are really in a hurry or who do not want to be part of the coach scene, there is even a helicopter firm which flies in tourists, the pad being down by the warehouses. It is, moreover, a very pretty distillery to visit. Artists rather over-elaborated its beauty during the nineteenth century, but it doesn't need any assistance. The waters, which in winter provide the liquor for the mash, make a spectacular entry to the distillery, crashing down Dumgoyne's volcanic basalt cliffs to provide a waterfall into a sandstone reservoir. Like the malt, the water tastes sweet at first, then dries: it is very soft, indeed.

The whisky-making process ends where it starts, with the modest-sized mashtun standing next to the stills. But elsewhere there are six Oregon pine washbacks frothing away before their contents are pumped to the large wash still. Glengoyne offers the only stillhouse with three stills in this part of Scotland, but it is not a triple-distillation system. The two others are spirit stills and both quite small, holding just 3,500 litres (770 gallons) each. No one will convince me that these tiny stills, allowing the spirit such regular contact with the copper, don't have a final say in the rich Glengoyne character.

It is one of the distillery's better-known idiosyncrasies that it is split in half by the imaginary line which divides the Highland and Lowland whisky regions. That line takes the road from Greenock, so the stillhouse looks directly out over it from the north and on to the warehouses. Thus, it is claimed that the whisky is distilled in the Highlands and matured, just a few feet away, in the Lowlands.

For years the people of Glengoyne have tried to convince me that the whisky made there was always unpeated. This is not a persuasive argument. The distillery was built in 1833 and retains its character from that date. Almost certainly they would have malted their own barley using peat: it was cheap and the accepted thing to do. But I need no persuading about the quality of the whisky, which is up among the front runners. At 10 years old, Glengoyne is such a delicate malt that you can often distinguish one vatting from another and, no matter what anyone tells you, that is not a bad thing. There is always a very clean maltiness. What varies is the degree of honey, the buttery flavour, the spice, the echoes of sherry and the crispness. But what you can guarantee is that it will be excellent. The intermediate 12-year-old is a silkier, more toffee-rich dram. Yet even when the 10-year-old is in top form it manages to give the 17-year-old a torrid time for complexity. The senior dram usually wins, though, which is a remarkable tribute to this whisky, because such a delicate malt usually cannot be kept for so long in a barrel. And if I didn't know better, I would say there was some peat in there somewhere, too.

Connoisseur's Selection

GLENGOYNE – BEAUTIFULLY CLEAN, MALTY AND SILKY AT 12 YEARS OLD.

INCHMURRIN (LOCH LOMOND) – A SWEET, SLIGHTLY MINTY AROMA AND LIGHT ON THE PALATE.

LOCH LOMOND

From Glengoyne, it is no great effort to head west toward the southern tip of Loch Lomond and find the Loch Lomond Distillery in Alexandria. To link this with the Perthshire malts is fanciful but, despite its southerly location, this is a Highland distillery, even though their silent sister Lowland distillery, Littlemill, is only a couple of miles south at Bowling. Really, Loch Lomond-style whisky does not fall into any one category: it is fast becoming an independent region of its own.

This is a distillery that makes a point of doing things its own way. Located in a former dye factory, its stills are extraordinary affairs with rectifiers attached to the heads so control can be kept over the type of malt made there. There are four stills in all, and at any one time the two sets could be making entirely different styles. A couple of times a year they even make a heavily peated malt spirit in the same way Springbank now make Longrow. The malt barley is brought in from the Port Ellen maltings on Islay, or sometimes Muir of Ord. The phenol level is a massive 40 ppm, bigger than anything on Islay, bar Ardbeg.

The company have their detractors, not least of all because they are putting their malts on the market at the same price for which you might find a decent blend. That said, there is nothing fundamentally wrong with their showcase whiskies, though it is unlikely they will ever be acknowledged as Scotland's finest. The two best-known are Inchmurrin and Old Rhosdhu. The former is named after the finger-shaped island nearby, the largest in Loch Lomond, and can sometimes be a very enjoyable dram. It has a light, sweet, slightly mentholly, minty aroma and a light, bubbly personality on the palate where the malt has a buttery feel to it: considering it has been distilled to round 86 per cent ABV, it is surprising it has that much character at all. Old Rhosdhu, distilled to a slightly lower strength, is more base and earthier on nose and palate and a more intriguing prospect with some heavy oils giving considerable weight.

There are four other whiskies made, but not marketed. One is Glen Douglas, slightly feinty and distilled to a more normal 68 per cent ABV, in a bid to produce a John Doe-type malt. The really peaty one, Croftengea, is certainly the densest dram made in Scotland, using 100 per cent heavily peated malt and distilled in the lead-heavy Rhosdhu style (it is their most challenging with a slight feintiness to the nose and bitterness to the finish, sandwiching the sweetest and oiliest peat attack in Scotland – well worthy of its own bottling one day). Inchmoan uses the same malt but is lighter as it is distilled in the Inchmurrin way; and there is a half-way house with Craiglodge, Rhosdhu in style, but with only half of the malt used being peated.

WEST AND ISLES

Once upon a time you could pay the fare and sail on a speed bonny boat like a bird on the wing over the sea to Skye. Today you get there by bridge. Britain's Department of Transport, with a road-building programme that seems to make a point of ruining the land's last unspoiled areas of beauty, has excelled itself this time. In 1995, this best-known and most historically romantic of all the Hebridean islands lost its true independence, and it is rare to hear a voice raised in favour of the suspended roadway. If the bridge at Kyleakin had been around in 1746, the Jacobite Prince Charles would have had to seek refuge elsewhere. There would have been no Flora Macdonald and we would probably now have the "Harris Boat Song", which doesn't have quite the same ring. At least the locals can seek solace in something that is pure Skye, that no bridge and its contamination with the mainland can take away: Talisker.

TALISKER

Islay has needed eight distilleries to put it on the whisky map. Skye requires only the one. Among the thousands of whiskies I have sampled from around the world, I can safely say there is nothing comparable to Talisker, despite the fact that it was at this distillery in 1975 that my search for the ultimate whisky began.

Located at Carbost on the craggy eastern coast (beware, there are two Carbosts on the island), it is not the prettiest distillery you will ever visit. It was gutted by fire early in 1960 when the stillman forgot to shut the manhole to one of the stills. The low wines bubbled over the side directly into the flames of the coal fires below. Many of the distillery's ancient features were consumed in the inferno that followed. The maltings survived, but only until 1972 when someone at DCL decided to knock it down as it was no longer being used – probably the same person who razed Caol Ila to the ground on Islay. But its location, on the shores of the seawater Loch Harport, is grand, as are the views of the almost permanently snow-capped Cuillin Hills, with three peaks of over 3,000 feet (1,000 metres) – a veritable Himalaya in British terms.

The distillery dates back to 1831 and could easily have failed many times over because of the laird's refusal to allow the distiller to build a pier. Instead, casks had to be floated out to ships. On occasions it resulted in the loss of barrels, and sometimes put lives at risk. In 1892 the situation became so frustrating to the owner, Roderick Kemp, that he sold out his stake in the company to his business partner, Alexander Allan, and invested his money in The Macallan Distillery on Speyside.

It was about this time that a liqueur made at Broadford Hotel on the other side of the island by the proprietor, John Ross, was beginning to gain in popularity. On April 24, 1893, Ross applied for and obtained from the Patent Office in London the trade mark for a liqueur which he called "Drambuie" at the suggestion of one of his customers (in Gaelic it means "the dram that satisfies"). In 1965 a relation of Ross recalled in her unpublished memoirs: "I remember helping to peel the lemons and he [Ross] used loaf sugar – pure cane sugar and Talisker whisky and saffron."

Talisker became linked with the then largest malt distillery in Scotland, Dailuaine, before being swallowed up by the expanding DCL. One of their biggest blends, Johnnie Walker, began to depend on Talisker as a vital flavouring constituent and even as late as the 1980s, bottles of Talisker single malt bore the Johnnie Walker logo.

Until 1928, Talisker was a triple-distilled whisky although, with its heavy peating, it was never likely to be as light as a Lowland or Irish whisky. Today there are five stills, two wash and three spirit, all served by old-fashioned exterior wooden worm tubs. Talisker matures rapidly. The old DCL company used to bottle it as an eight-year-old and even United Distillers, who prefer to allow their

Skye line: *The rugged mountains envelop Talisker.*

Big Ben: *The distillery can now make a whisky as imposing as the mountain which overlooks it.*

malts to mature to great ages, have settled on 10 years for their Classic Malt range. What they have not altered is the strength: it is bottled at 45.8 per cent ABV. It was given this unusual strength because it was considered perfect for warming you up on brisk outdoor days. And they are right.

To reduce it to any less or to drink it watered down is sacrilege. You do not sip this whisky. It is one you warm to body temperature and then take by the mouthful. The definitive description of this phenomenon came some years back from another whisky writer and broadcaster, Derek Cooper, a good friend, who resides part-time on the island: "The pungent, slightly oily, peaty ruggedness of the bouquet mounts into my nostrils. The corpus of the drink advances like the lava of the Cuillins down my throat. Then vroom! Steam rises from the temples, a seismic shock rocks the building, my eyes are seen to water, cheeks aflame I steady myself against the chair. Talisker is not a drink, it is an interior explosion, distilled central heating; it depth-charges the parts, bangs doors and slams windows. There's nothing genteel about Talisker."

Why is it so different? The peating is around the 25 parts per million (ppm) phenol level, less than the Ardbegs, Lagavulins and Laphroaigs of this world. The water, though, from Cnoc-nan-Speireig is unbelievably peaty. Former Johnnie Walker and Talisker blender Dick Freeson is convinced that it is the peculiar angle of the lyne arm which allows extra reflux back into the wash still, so that the spirit stills work from purer low wines. Who knows?

One thing is certain. No matter how much you love whisky or think you know about it, your education is woefully incomplete until you try Talisker, unquestionably one of the greatest whiskies in the world. You see, this is not so much a drink as an experience.

Connoisseur's Selection

TALISKER – IF YOU HAVE ONLY ONE MALT YOU COULD EVER BUY, THE EXPLOSIVE 10-YEAR-OLD IS IT.

BEN NEVIS – THE 19-YEAR-OLD IS AS RARE AS IT IS LUSH AND THE RICHNESS CLINGS FOREVER.

BEN NEVIS

Fort William may be a bit of a tourist trap. But at least it offers the most northern distillery on Scotland's mainland west coast. Actually, until 1983 that honour was held (by a few hundred yards) by Glenlochy, always the smarter of the two distillers, but that has closed never to re-open.

Ben Nevis Distillery has every right to call itself just that, tapping into the waters which run over red and grey granite from the Allt-a-Mhullin Burn high on Britain's tallest mountain. The distillery has been in operation since 1825 when a mountain of a man called "Long" John MacDonald built the distillery and obtained an operating licence. After great success in selling his Dew of Ben Nevis whisky, his name became one of the most famous in whisky. The company which traded on his name and the distillery which made it famous went their separate ways sometime in the 1920s. But as these things have a habit of doing in the whisky world, they caught up with one another again when Long John International bought the distillery from another larger-than-life character, Canadian millionaire Joseph Hobbs. He owned a cattle ranch in the area, and introduced both Coffey stills – for a short-lived venture in the grain-distilling business – and concrete which he poured over the outside walls of the distillery, and from which he even made two washbacks. The distillery looks particularly attractive today: the washbacks have gone.

Now the number plate on the distillery manager's Jaguar tells you who the current owners are: NIKKA. And after an uncertain time with Long John, those enormous, almost stainless-steel-shaped, copper-pot stills are in operation again. This is probably the only distillery where you can walk in and, on request, the manager will fill up a cask or two with new make for you, charging the same rate at which he sells to the industry: something to bear in mind if you are looking for the ultimate 18th birthday present.

Virtually all the whisky you see with the Ben Nevis name is blended. Even though there is much stock available, Ben Nevis as a single malt is criminally hard to find. It's a great shame; some samples of 12-year-old I've happened across have been magnificent with a chewy toffee and nut middle; others have been oilier yet lighter at the same time, with orange-marzipan nose and buttercream middle – quite delicious. There is, however, a 19-year-old at full cask strength of 60 per cent ABV produced by the distillery, and, though it's not cheap and maybe lacks a touch of fruit for perfect balance, whiskies like this just don't turn up every day. From the soft, Ancient Agey, bourbon-style nose, through the milky-fat start on the palate, the intense, sweet malt middle (plus just a background hint of smoke) and the drying finish with a benign oak vanilla finale, this is a malt to end the day with, forgetting all your troubles and woes, and concentrating on what will be happening to your palate next. A mountain of a malt, in fact.

OBAN

One of the great mysteries of Scotch whisky is why so few legal distilleries ever operated in the rugged Western Highlands. There has always been a generous supply of peat or clean water and countless illicit distillers have made good use of this. Some have said that it's an area incapable of producing good whisky and use Glenlochy to underpin their argument. But it is a pretty thin case and one which can be contemptuously dismissed with a single glass of the sublime Oban.

This is the 14-year-old fruit of a very small malt distillery and one of the last to operate in the centre of a town. Indeed, walk through this neat yet characterful port with its sturdy, extensive Victorian buildings and you will have to look twice to find it, its old brick chimney marking the spot. But, in fact, its place at the very heart of Oban is quite fitting, since it was the distillery, or brewery as it began life, around which the town grew. And this may be a clue as to why the west coast is so ill served by distilleries. A feature of island distilleries is that, as a rule, they face out to sea, enabling their merchandise to be easily collected and shipped off to market. Inland communications from the Western Highlands are still pretty basic. Two centuries ago they were appalling. Oban, some 100 miles from Glasgow by road, provided an excellent harbour. Thus, not only was it a perfect place to build a distillery, but the family behind the project, the Stevensons, took advantage of the location to establish a community complete with hotels.

Oban Distillery dates back to 1794, which makes it one of the world's oldest continuously working distilleries, the vicissitudes of the industry apart, which saw it silenced in the early nineteenth century, in the 1930s and again in the late 1960s. Oban was a rather insignificant fishing village when the first stones were laid. Evidence uncovered in the mid-1990s suggests that the distilling was carried out very slightly (and we are talking about a few yards) nearer the sea than it is today. The distillery was granted a licence in 1797 and the money injected by the Stevensons made sure that it was as well equipped as any in Scotland. Although the distillery thrived and still does, it is a remarkable fact that the single pair of stills that were first installed may have been repaired and from time to time replaced, but they have never been added to, ensuring that its output was among the lowest in the Highlands.

The stillhouse was rebuilt in the late 1960s but, like the rest of the distillery, it remains a pretty cramped affair. There had been much expansion in the 1880s with the building of warehouses, though space was at a premium. The distillery backs into a cliff face and it was while an old cave was being excavated for the construction of a warehouse that the remains of eight prehistoric people – four adults and four children – were discovered. That immediate area of the west coast has long been known to archaeologists as one of outstanding importance in the piecing together of the history of the people who first populated the northern British isles, the Scoti. Some 5,000 years ago they used caves on raised beaches, just like those at Oban, to afford basic comfort and protection.

Above the cave is another remarkable

Connoisseur's Selection

OBAN – THE OZONE-FRESH 19-YEAR-OLD IS ONE OF NATURE'S GREAT RESTORATIVES.

TOBERMORY – LOOK FOR OLD BOTTLES MARKED 'LEDAIG'. THEN IT IS POT-LUCK BETWEEN PEATY PERFECTION OR BIG DISAPPOINTMENT.

A Colossus and a Colosseum: *Oban's magnificent malt is matched by its magnificent location.*

Mulling it over: *The Tobermory whisky XI of distillers and maltsters line up for the 1928 season.*

piece of local history, McCaig's Tower. This, Scotland's rendition of Rome's Colosseum, is one of the more extraordinary sights you will discover around the world's distilleries. Do not refer to it as a Victorian folly, though. Even today, the locals regard it with fondness since McCaig, a wealthy man at the outset of its construction, used the project to give work to impoverished stonemasons in the area. Funds, however, dried up and it stands today not as a folly, Obanites will tell you, but as the mark of a very caring and Christian soul.

Until the 14-year-old was launched, you could toast McCaig with a 12-year-old Oban. It was a pleasant enough whisky, but you always had the feeling that there was more to come. Now the distillery possesses in Ian Williams one of the few managers who genuinely feels that his whisky is bottled at its optimum age. Fourteen is absolutely right for Oban. It has opened up and come alive with the peat from the waters of Loch Gleann a' Bhearraidh, continuing the tradition of this smoky dram and working in unison with delicate oak. When it was first launched by United Distillers as one of their six Classic Malts, it was an inspired choice. The bottlings for the first few years were almost abrasive in their light, spicy, ozone freshness. That is still the leading trait of the whisky, but I fancy it has been toned down a little in recent years by the softest hint of sherry and caramel, although this is more likely to be through evolution than design.

It remains, however, a superb dram and one I find irresistible after a frustrating or gruelling day. At its best, it gives the feel of the cool sea breeze slapping you across the face with the peat smoke of the cottages on the wind. All imagination, of course. There is only one warehouse left in the town and the likelihood is that the casks used for the malt have come from inland, well away from the sea. Just another little mystery from the Western Highlands.

TOBERMORY *(Tober-moree)*

From Oban, the island of Mull is just a short ferry journey away. On a blazing summer's day it becomes a glorious expedition to the island's only distillery, Tobermory, or Ledaig as it is sometimes called. The town in which it is located is about as quaint as any in the Hebrides, with the shop fronts painted in delicate blues, pinks and yellows. Beyond the pier, under silt and sea, lie the remains of a Spanish galleon from the Armada. Beyond the distillery, just inland, is an impressive waterfall. If ever there was an enchanted place for a distillery to be built, this is it.

The town of Tobermory was developed by the same Stevensons who made such a good job of Oban. However, they had nothing to do with the distillery which was built at more or less the same time. That, and the fact that it was once owned by the same John Hopkin that Oban is still licensed to, is about all the two distilleries have ever had in common. Where Oban has been in almost continuous use, Ledaig has had a less certain career and, when it was reopened in 1972, it had been silent for 42 years. The new owners ran the plant for only three years and distilling was intermittent. Some of their make, which can still be found today, was truly spectacular and remains among the best Scotch still to be had. When the owners ran short of cash, inferior casks were used and the quality of the matured spirit is markedly poorer. Sometimes the whisky from this vintage can be full-bodied and enormously peaty, at other times lighter and off-key.

Poor old Tobermory remained silent for four more years until, in 1979, a Yorkshire entrepreneur decided to invest in the Scotch industry and made Ledaig his. His firm, Kirkleavington Property Company of Cleckheaton, had no other interest in whisky and immediately ran into difficulties. If you make a whisky, the chances are that you will not find an enormous number of people who will pay cash for it. The idea is to exchange some for others to help with a blend. All Kirkleavington had was Tobermory Distillery, so they brought out a whisky by that name which contained a little old Ledaig, but consisted chiefly of vatted malts from other companies. It was not enough to keep the concern going, despite the best efforts of Joe Hughes, the man brought in to kick-start the distillery back into production.

Extra funds were brought in by the selling of warehouses for flats, which meant that all the make had to be tankered to the mainland for maturation, and by opening up a visitors' centre, one of the first in Scotland to charge for admission. Even a local dairyman was permitted to rent space among the washbacks to allow his cheese to mature. The sight of rows of festering, yellowing, pungent milk curds, a veritable breeding ground for wild yeasts, among the resplendent pine remains one of the most surreal visions of whisky making that I have personally encountered.

It was inevitable that the distillery would go up for sale and today it is in pretty safe hands, with Burn Stewart, owners of Deanston, as the new masters. They spent time and money bringing the place up to scratch before distilling again. The cheese was the first to go. Kirkleavington's malt was gently peated. Burn Stewart currently operate only two of the four stills available at any one time, boast elegant Oregon pine washbacks and use an unpeated malt, but have plans to make occasional distillations in the heavy peat style to cater for connoisseurs who quite rightly rate 1970s Ledaig among the all-time greats. Future single malt from unpeated barley will be called Tobermory; the heavily peated variety will keep the name Ledaig.

The current Tobermory in bottle is a reasonable dram, a bit flat and spoilt a little by an indifferent finish. Younger, maturing stocks seem to have a lot more pizzazz and are coconut-sweet with a slightly fatter malt richness. The current new make is not entirely smoke-free thanks to local water, but even sweeter still and quite rich, expansive and buttery, rather than cheesy. As ever, the forthcoming bottlings of Tobermory – or Ledaig – over the next dozen years are going to be full of surprises.

ISLE OF JURA

"The least islandy of all Scotland's island malts", a mainland distillery manager once told me about Isle of Jura. "Whenever I've tasted it, I've always thought it was from Speyside, or maybe even the Lowlands." This was a put-down, a dismissive squirt into the spittoon from a man who had spent years on Islay and was convinced that island whiskies had their place in the scheme of things. Jura was the round peg in the square hole. It had let the team down and no amount of advocacy on my part, however respectfully received, was going to persuade him otherwise.

His is not the only voice that I have heard raised against Jura, though one of the very few from someone who has actually been there. "Bland", "austere", "tart" – these are among the adjectives I have seen heaped upon it. But not by me. It is a dram that has been patchy, certainly. But catch Jura right, like the glint of the sun in a diamond, and you are in

On a roll: *Jura Distillery is being pushed around the world by distillers Whyte & Mackay.*

for a sparkling performance.

Yes, the nose does catch the breath with a slight trace of ammonia. But forget all that. Taste this one slowly and you will be rewarded. Furthermore, it is worth celebrating the fact that there is a distillery on Jura at all. There are barely more than 200 hardy souls living on the island; there is only one road, a lone hotel in the solitary village and a single, tiny ferry serving Jura from Port Askaig on Islay. Yet it is rich in wooded and scree-dashed mountains, lochs, golden eagles, deer, midges and poisonous snakes.

Look at the official distillery's bottling label and you will see a teardrop-shaped island surrounded by nothing but sea, with no sign of other land. The reality is that on two sides it is shadowed by solid land. To the south-west, Islay is almost within touching distance and to the northeast, where the road runs out, the Scottish mainland around Crinan is only three or four miles away. Still, it was remote enough for George Orwell to find the necessary solitude he required to write his famous novel, *1984*, though it is unlikely that he had any Jura malt to keep him company and provide inspiration, since the distillery by then had been closed for 48 years.

The Isle of Jura Distillery had begun life more than a century before Orwell's stay. Originally, like the sites of so many other island distilleries, it was in the late eighteenth century a place of illicit distilling. It is thought that the smuggler turned honest on a modest scale around 1810. By the time the indefatigable Barnard reached the distillery, a matter of 75 years later, there had been great changes: "It is one of the handsomest we have seen, and from the bay looks more like a castle than a distillery." Only 10 years earlier it had been rebuilt and there were three stills of contrasting sizes, but a match for anything on neighbouring Islay, with one wash, two spirit.

By the time the First World War ended the distillery was silent. The population dropped as work was sought elsewhere and the distillery fell into ruin. It was a major surprise, then, when the blenders Charles Mackinlay decided to rebuild the distillery from scratch in 1960, a three-year task. In 1978 the stills were doubled from two to four and it became one of the main malts for Invergordon and, following the absorption of the company by Whyte & Mackay, the 10-year-old has enjoyed even greater marketing prestige.

However, the best Jura I have ever tasted, even better than their splendid, occasional 26-year-old: a softly peated, almost syrupy heavyweight, came from a private bottling from the hotel opposite. The owner was a director of the distillery and had the pick of the warehouse. It is a full-mouthed dram, as near faultless as you will find. It had an altogether different feel from the present-day Jura which bristles, in a strangely non-peaty way, on the palate.

ISLE OF ARRAN

There is now one other island which boasts its own distillery: the Isle of Arran. Once, the island, located at the head of the Firth of Clyde, was a by-word for smuggled whisky – "Arran Water". There were also two or three legal distilleries that lived briefly in the south, though the last one fell silent in the 1830s.

Yet the distillery operating today is to be located in the rugged north of the island, on the outskirts of Lochranza. Although this village looks out to sea, and is offered stunning views of Kintyre, the distillery itself shares with Highland Park the distinction of being one of only two off the mainland which is not surrounded by surf. Instead, the distillery sits at the bottom of a hollow bordered on three sides by mountains. Loch na Davie, the source of the peaty water which supplies the distillery, begins life as a spring that feeds the tiniest lake you are ever likely to find. It was this constant supply which led to the distillery being built in 1995 at such a superb location.

The building of the distillery was held up while first a pair of rare golden eagles decided upon their nesting site and then a protected species of dragonfly were also safely out of the way. These were expensive delays for a company which had advertised to the public to get the distillery started. It was the brainchild of former Seagram managing director Harold Curry, who was determined to return to the whisky world. To gather funds he sold bonds in which investors were repaid at intervals with matured whisky from the distillery.

Those investors are likely to be happy with their return. I was fortunate enough to be the first ever person to taste the spirit out of the safe when it distilled for the very first time. It was at 2.29 p.m. on Thursday, 29 June 1995 that I made a footnote in history when legal Arran spirit was experienced for the first time in exactly 160 years; a sweet malty dram with hints of peat and late, lilting, cocoa notes. Subsequent samples I have tasted have been, as one might expect, fractionally less lively but have retained a recognizable charm and richness which augers extremely well for the future: my money is on it being one of Scotland's finer whiskies. The workings of the distillery are superb: a pair of small Forsyth-made stills working in tandem with equally diminutive wooden washbacks and stainless steel mashtun, from which the aromatic sweetness of the barely-peated malt spills. The beauty of the place is not lost on distillery manager Gordon Mitchell, a veteran of the start-up of the somewhat less graceful Cooley Distillery in Ireland.

Connoisseur's Selection

JURA – SOME VERY OLD INDEPENDENT BOTTLINGS SHOW UNUSUAL SPICE.

ISLE OF ARRAN – THE SINGLE MALT WILL NOT BE AVAILABLE UNTIL 2001. PREPARE FOR A WHISKY ODYSSEY.

ISLAY

Islay whisky is so much its own master that it is more than just a region of Scotch. As a style, it is as different from other Scotch single malt as Bourbon or Irish or Canadian. In its purest, peaty form, it is a style that allows no compromise: either you are for or you are agin'.

BUNNAHABHAIN *(Bunna-harv'n)*

Not all the distilleries on the island make a malt so thick in peat that you could stand a spoon in it. The lightest Islay has to offer is Bunnahabhain (pronounced by locals as either "Bunna-harv'n" or "Boona-harv'n") which uses malt that is all but unpeated, at around 2 ppm phenols compared to Lagavulin's 35 ppm, and pipes water in from a small loch so that it has no chance to pick up nutrients from the bogs which abound in the area.

To reach Bunnahabhain direct from the mainland, you take the ferry to Port Askaig rather than to Port Ellen. This tiny harbour is served by a hotel (which has not changed since being a backdrop in the 1950s Ealing comedy, *The Maggie*) and a shop-cum-post office, and is a dead end if you don't count the ferry which negotiates the torrid currents between Islay and Jura. The steep, twisting road inland offers a right-hand turn and that takes you to Bunnahabhain. It is a glorious, single-width track through farmsteads, offering delightful views of Jura opposite, though you have to keep your eyes on the road to avoid some nasty bends, kamikaze sheep or whisky lorries coming in the opposite direction.

Until 1891, there was no village of Bunnahabhain or distillery. It was a wilderness area, but one that prospectors realized was perfect for making liquid gold – whisky. The natural bay was deep enough for small steamboats to load up with whisky, and plenty of local peat and water were available for the making and distilling of malt. As the distillery was built, the village grew around it (though, oddly, acquiring an extra "n" in its suffix).

There were two rows of cottages where the workers could live, and larger houses for the manager and excise officer. At the end of the top tier of cottages was a school for the children. These cottages still stand today and, until the early 1990s, the daughter of one of the original workers at the distillery lived in the very cottage in which she was born, who, sadly, recently passed away.

The malt is a vital component in the make-up of Famous Grouse. No one is quite sure when Bunnahabhain became an unpeated whisky. It happened longer ago than anyone can remember, although it did not start out that way and from time to time gives a fair impression of being a peaty one again. Two American whisky lovers, James Harris and Mark Waymack, earned the derision of some within the industry as well as of connoisseurs when they included a number of inaccuracies in their book *Single Malt Whiskies of Scotland*, especially the statement that Bunnahabhain was "a decent Islay malt, well peated ... has a light touch of the iodine taste which can be found in many of the Islay malts". One can understand that particular error. Their book was written in 1992, which happened to be the year in which a rogue batch of Bunnahabhain was in circulation. I was staying at one of the cottages and first noticed the unusual flavour in a bottle I opened. Then at the "Islay Whisky Nosing Championships" I managed to correctly identify six out of the eight whiskies poured, but wrote on the answer card that I could not distinguish between X and Y but guessed: "X is a highly peated Bunnahabhain, Y is a lowly peated Bowmore". In fact, X was Bowmore and Y the Bunnahabhain. No one at the distillery could account for the smokiness. The most likely explanation was that 12 years previously the distillery might have run short of malt and acquired some from the Port Ellen maltings which was mixed in with the last of their own unpeated grain. On Islay everybody helps everybody else, irrespective of the fact that they may be rival companies.

The distillery is unique in that the malt is still brought to it by boats which land at the long pier. That the pier is still intact is a small miracle. Just a few hundred feet from it a large ship lies rusting on the rocks, the most accessible of all the hundreds of wrecks to be found in the seas surrounding the island. Instead of plotting a safe route between Islay and Jura, it veered off course and missed the distillery's pier by only inches before running aground. Ironically, the captain and first mate were drunk, though it is unlikely that Bunnahabhain was the errant seamen's tipple.

I have yet to come across a malt which improves by being drunk somewhere other than where it is made. Tasting Bunnahabhain outside the cottage on a balmy summer's

Connoisseur's Selection

BUNNAHABHAIN – THE ORDINARY DISTILLERY BOTTLING IS AS GOOD AS YOU'LL FIND.

CAOL ILA – VIGOROUSLY PEATY WITH PEPPERY SPICE ON THE NOSE AND BIG, SWEET MALTINESS.

Scotch on the rocks: *Bunnahabhain offers the whisky connoisseur one of the most spectacular views in Scotland.*

evening, with the sun setting but with Colonsay and even Mull still visible in the far distance and the Paps almost luminous thanks to their chalky scree, is one of life's more intimate moments, especially if you are liberally doused in insect repellent. Bunnahabhain is the most northerly outpost on the island and the engulfing beauty is timeless. Although unpeated, the malt as a 12-year-old usually has a beautiful briny edge amid soft honey and a jagged maltiness. One or two tastings of late have suggested that they are introducing more sherry into the vatting and I wish they wouldn't. Bunnahabhain is such a delicate malt that it should be left alone: it simply cannot defend itself against the intrusive grape. Just like the courtyarded distillery, it should remain rugged, wild and at peace.

CAOL ILA *(Cole-eela)*

The journey back toward Port Askaig also takes you to Caol Ila. From the track road there is no sign of the distillery, just a few of the workmen's houses. A new approach road has been built, navigable with care by car, lorry or bicycle. When Barnard made the same trek things were slightly different: "We soon came in sight of the Distillery lying directly beneath us and we wonder for a moment how we are going to get down to it. Our driver, however, knew the road well... But the way is so steep, and our nerves none of the best, that we insist on doing the remainder on foot, much to the disgust of the driver, who muttered strange words in Gaelic."

The view that would have greeted him at the bottom of these cliffs is one of the most rewarding on the island. The buildings were set into the rock face and only yards from the burbling Sound of Islay, the narrow strait of water separating Jura and Islay, whose Gaelic name is Caol Ila. This was unquestionably the most attractive of the island's distilleries, dating back to 1846 with extensions and modernization 33 years later in classic Victorian Gothic. Now only a warehouse survives. If the current distillery looks familiar, it is because you might have seen it at Clynelish or perhaps Teaninich: an off-the-shelf box design as devoid of character as the old one was full of it. The distillery's output was tripled to make it a workhorse blending malt.

The whisky has changed, too, although there is nothing wrong with the malt produced from the massive stills. Indeed, in many ways it is equally as good. The old spirit, the product of only two stills, was just as vigorously peaty, but had a little more peppery spice on the nose and was more relaxed about the malt coming through for an earlier, bigger and sweeter say. It was oilier than the other malts on the island, but nothing like as clingingly oily as the present make. This holds on the palate longer and only allows in the malt and other constituent parts close to the finish. For a blending whisky this is useful: it means you do not need quite so much Islay, but it hangs around longer, adding weight. Perhaps the easiest way to describe the difference in the two malts is to emphasize that the old Caol Ila was much more impressive on the start, with slight cedarwood and pine adding to the fatty complexity, while the new Caol Ila wins hands down on the longer,

A sound whisky: *Translated from Gaelic, Caol Ila means "Sound of Islay".*

stronger, oilier finish. But the old-style Caol Ila was a sad loss and its closest relation on the island in terms of style was its sister distillery, Port Ellen. How ironic then that this, too, should die in order to allow the new Caol Ila to live.

BRUICHLADDICH

(Brew-ick-laddie)

The road to Bridgend cuts across some of Islay's more fertile lands. Now and again, small roads break off and head to farmhouses and keepers' lodges and even ruins of ancient inland distilleries which once worked under the names of Lossitt, Daill and Newton. These died out in the early to mid-nineteenth century as the bigger distillers on the island found it easier to sell their make by being at the edge of the sea. Even Octomore, just inland from Port Charlotte, perished. Every distillery on the island now faces out to sea, enabling them to receive their casks directly from vessels and send out their whisky the same way. The roads on the island in Victorian times were poor and transporting whisky to the coast would not have been an easy task: just one cask falling off a wagon and smashing would have proved a costly business.

Islay whisky had become popular at the turn of the nineteenth century, thanks partly to government legislation which decreed that the island was the only area of Scotland where revenue officers were not employed, the collection of taxes being the responsibility of the laird. Under this lax regime, smuggling flourished and, with the peaty water adding to the richness of turf used in the malting process, the whisky of Islay became famed for its powerful, pungent character.

Blending companies looked to set up distilleries on the island and in 1881, while Bunnahabhain was being built on the north-eastern shore, on the road to Port Charlotte another distillery was being constructed, Bruichladdich. Apart from a period in the 1920s and 1930s, when the distillery was silent, it has had an unremarkable career, churning out its malt for countless blenders but never gaining a reputation beyond the island for its fine make as a self whisky.

Like Bunnahabhain, at some time after the Second World War it became a virtually unpeated malt, although this may have been gradual since its magnificently weird, cognac-like, limited-edition 21-year-old has some distinct peat traces, despite the sherry. But the standard 10-year-old's creamy texture and slightly sweet, nutty character has made it by far the most popular malt sold on the island in recent times. Ask an islander what his dram will be: if it's not a blend, the chances are that Bruichladdich (pronounced "Broo-ick-laddie)" will be his choice. Even so, its local popularity has failed to save it from the threat of extinction. In 1983 it was closed for a short period but in 1995, after Whyte & Mackay's takeover of Bruichladdich's owner, Invergordon, the distillery was mothballed, the new masters deciding to make Jura their showcase for island whisky.

Compared to the other period distilleries on the island, the appearance of Bruichladdich and its terrain may be a bit ordinary. But once you go through the lovely gates and archway and enter the buildings themselves, then you are taken back in time. Some years ago one of the distillery workers proudly showed me around. It was probably the third or fourth time that I had been there but it is a place of which you could never tire. He pointed to the mashtun which had the date 1881 and told me that it had been there since the distillery was built. Not quite. In fact, it was the original tun from Bunnahabhain. It is curious to speculate which Islay distillery it might be serving 100 years on. Bruichladdich, I hope.

BOWMORE

A few miles on are the remains of Port Charlotte's Lochindaal Distillery, once a massive concern but silent since its centenary in 1929. Its remaining buildings are used for a variety of purposes and, until the 1980s, some were utilized by another distiller for warehousing. The next working distillery is in the opposite direction, back through Bruichladdich and the gladed village of Bridgend and then southwest a few miles to Bowmore. This is the island's capital, a planned village dominated at the top end by the round church, designed so the devil has nowhere to hide, and at the bottom by the shores of Loch Indaal, Bowmore Distillery, where some might say the devil would feel most at home.

This is not only the oldest distillery on the island (it has been in existence since 1779) but the one which goes out of its way to cater both for the tourist and the connoisseur. It may receive fewer than 10,000 visitors a year, but Islay can hold only so many extra folk and those who do not want to look around the distillery can always enter the old No. 3 warehouse and go swimming in a pool warmed by the waste heat from the distilling process.

It is marvellous to see a distillery so comfortable in the midst of its community. The Lowland classic, Rosebank, became the target of complaints by people moving into newly built homes next door. Other distilleries have had to close because of effluent problems. Here, however, two industries, whisky-making and tourism, combine to provide extra revenue for a fragile island economy which always feels the pinch when a distillery is put on a short working week or closed down altogether.

The distillery's former manager, now ambassador, James McEwen, is one of the most vibrant whisky men in the industry and his enthusiasm for his subject is contagious. He was also unique among managers in being the only one in the world who actually bottled his own spring water to add to whisky, though the project is part of his desire to give employment to the disabled in the community. It is no coincidence that Bowmore is the only distillery in Scotland which also has a rampway so that the wheelchair-bound tourist can inspect every single part of the distilling process in as much detail as the able-bodied.

Connoisseur's Selection

BRUICHLADDDICH – VELVETY AND UNPEATED, THE 10-YEAR-OLD IS THE ISLANDER'S FAVOURITE MALT.

BOWMORE – THERE ARE SOME TEMPTING 21-YEAR-OLDS, BUT THE CHOCOLATE-RICH 17-YEAR-OLD IS MAJESTIC.

Since 1963, when the company was bought by Stanley P. Morrison, after he overheard a conversation to the effect that the distillery was up for sale, it has been the flagship distillery of the company, to the point of being renamed Morrison Bowmore. The Japanese distillers, Suntory, began to acquire a stake in Morrison who did a lot of business in the Far East. Then, amid long-standing rumours about Morrison Bowmore's struggle to keep on a profitable course, in 1994 the company became part of the Suntory group.

All this was not before an extensive programme of demodernizing within the

Just capital: *On the shores of Loch Indaal, Bowmore is one of the most tourist-friendly distilleries in Scotland.*

distillery had been carried out. The most remarkable achievement was the reversion from the characterless, stainless-steel washbacks to beautiful Oregon pine. With the distillery still carrying out floor malting, this move in the direction of traditionalism was seen as one that could only further improve the quality of a very good whisky.

Of all Islay's peated malts, this is the lightest, although weighing in with a robust 20–25 ppm phenols. For that reason it is called medium-peated. The number of styles of Bowmore that the whisky lover has to choose from is startling. The company has made a younger malt available, with the peat smashing against the tastebuds in the same haphazard manner that waves sometimes pound the distillery walls. Its 12-year-old continues to be its usual attractive, slightly sweet dram and it also boasts an extraordinary range of 21-year-old-plus whiskies, including the uncompromising Black Bowmore, a £100-a-bottle malt which has an extraordinary *oloroso* fruit cake richness on top of the heavy peat. It is a connoisseur's malt for those with a healthy purse, steady nerves and a palate that can look after itself. The lightly sherried old 'uns are also truly stunning and offer enormous complexity. But I would happily make do with something a little younger and leave the sherry cask in Jerez. The best of the Bowmore pack comes as a 17-year-old. Every distillery has its optimum age. For Bowmore, this is it: a richly peated whisky with dollops of malt, chocolate and even honey that I have weaned many an Islay-hater on to.

As you head out of Bowmore towards Port Ellen, the next stopping place, you will find a number of warehouses on the edge of the town away from the hubbub of the distillery, but still close enough to the sea to catch the tang of brine in the wind which envelops the entire island. You will also find a tree with a number of old dents and scars on its trunk, caused by a former Bowmore manager and good friend of mine who somehow, and at regular intervals, managed to wrap his car around it. Because of this tree's uncanny, magnetic effect on the manager's car bumper and headlights, it was eventually named after him.

Islay may be an island with a violent past, where tales are recounted of the Lords of the Isles and bloody battles on windswept moors, but there is many a story still untold about those responsible for the noble dram that is called Islay whisky. And some are better left that way.

PORT ELLEN

The journey from Bowmore to Port Ellen is about the most tedious on any of the Scottish isles. There are miles and miles of flat peat muir although, if you are lucky, you might spot a short-eared owl quartering by day or dusk. To the right, beyond the plain, is the broad expanse of beach which absorbs the waves that sometimes lap and sometimes crash into the sweep of Laggan Bay. So flat is this area, where much of the island's whisky-making peat is cut, that the little airport is located here, too. On entering the town, the pagodas of Port Ellen come into view, which can be seen just as well from the ferry as its approaches the dock.

Unfortunately Port Ellen now no longer makes whisky. It is dwarfed by an industrial-scale maltings owned by United Distillers, but the distillery has not been used since 1984. It could be put into service again: the stills remain in place and the buildings are not too tarnished by time. Since parts of its workings are being cannibalized from within the group, new equipment would be needed.

The chances of its ever distilling again, however, are slight. United Distillers also own Lagavulin, which makes all the company requires for marketing an Islay single malt, and Caol Ila the fodder for blended. Port Ellen was not closed because its make was inferior. In fact, I would say that it was the cleanest, most easily enjoyed peat whisky that has been made in Scotland for the last 20 years, and if you get the chance to buy any, do not hesitate. It simply became surplus to requirements. Caol Ila was state of the art in 1974 and built for minimum maintenance. Port Ellen dates back to the early 1880s. It has seen hardship before: it was silent between 1929 and 1966, so it, too, had undergone extensive refurbishment. But unless someone comes up with an offer that United Distillers simply cannot refuse, the chances of another revival look slight.

Poignant pose: *Redundant pagodas of Port Ellen are overshadowed by new industrial maltings.*

Charlie's Angel: *Prince Charles regards Laphroaig as his favourite whisky – and there are legions who agree.*

LAPHROAIG *(La-froyg)*

However, the outlook for its neighbour, Laphroaig, is anything but bleak. This distillery above all others, managed to put Islay on the connoisseur's map long before the extraordinary Lagavulin 16-year-old arrived on the scene. It is the flagship single malt of Allied Domecq who acquired the distillery in 1967, by which time its name was enjoying international renown, not least of all in the United States where its intense Islay iodine "medicinal" character allowed it to be prescribed by doctors during the period of Prohibition.

Like Lagavulin, the ground on which Laphroaig currently operates is a site where two distilleries once worked side by side and, like both its neighbours, Ardbeg and Lagavulin, one that was previously favoured by illicit distillers and smugglers. Between the 1830s and the 1860s the Ardenistiel Distillery weathered a number of crises until it was mismanaged into oblivion. Only a short distance away Laphroaig, which had been around since about 1820, gained in reputation and even during Victorian times became a byword for very heavily peated whisky. It also flourished, despite years of bickering and fighting among its owners over land, water rights and shares.

It is a curious fact that this rugged, remote part of Scotland became something of a haven for women whisky owners at a time when the industry was very much a male preserve. Over at Port Ellen the widow Lucy Ramsay ran the distillery between 1892 and 1905 following her husband's death, while at Ardbeg the sisters Margaret and Flora MacDougall had been in charge during the 1850s. At Laphroaig, however, there have been two periods of female rule. For a considerable period at the turn of the century Catherine Johnson was manager and then, quite remarkably and more recently, a former secretary inherited the distillery as reward for her devotion.

This is probably one of the most remarkable tales to be told in whisky. In the early 1930s, Bessie Williamson left her native Glasgow, where she had been teaching, to take up a temporary position as shorthand typist to the owner, Ian Hunter, a friend of her father. So impressed was he with her and so enchanted was she with the island that he offered her the position full-time. It was not

Connoisseur's Selection

Port Ellen – Just get hold of any bottle you can. Brilliant.

Laphroaig – The cask-strength Duty Free version is better than all other Laphroaig put together.

long before she became his personal assistant, helping out not only with the day-to-day running of the business but with production as well. When Hunter died – heirless – in 1954, he left his entire estate, including the distillery, to his trusted friend and secretary. Firmly at the helm, she became an enormously respected, almost legendary figure on the island and steered the company toward greater success. In 1967 she sold the distillery to Long John Distillers, but stayed on as managing director until retiring in 1972, by which time she was known as Bessie Campbell, after marrying very late in life.

Today Laphroaig is the best-selling malt in the Allied Domecq armoury, having acquired a cult status. Its greatest-known advocate is Prince Charles who has bestowed his royal seal upon the distillery. Is it any great surprise, then, that when he was unfortunate enough to crash-land his plane on Islay in 1994 by approaching the runway too fast, he just happened to be on his way to the distillery?

Yet, despite Laphroaig's almost mystical reputation, I had not been too impressed with its standard bottlings since the late 1980s. Some 20 years ago you could almost chew the peat. Until quite lately, however, the 10-year-old and even the 15-year-old have lacked that characteristic turfiness and have been, by Laphroaig's own high standards, quite bland. It could not have been anything to do with an experiment in the distillery's early days under Long John management when the lower section of one of the wash stills was replaced with stainless steel and painted copper on the outside. That foolishness lasted just six months before nerves frayed and those responsible came to their senses, perhaps with the thought: "If it ain't broke...". For years I have been telling anyone who cared to listen, especially at Allied Domecq, that it is likely that Laphroaig suffers more than most from chill-filtration, the process by which certain microscopic solids and congeners are removed in order to render the bottled spirit clear when in cold temperatures and reduced to 40 per cent ABV. It is noticeable that the samples I have encountered direct from the cask have been much more enjoyable. Thankfully, Allied themselves have produced a new 10-year-old 57 per cent "cask-strength" bottling for duty-free which is not only back to its superb best, but by far the best malt newcomer to be released in 1995. And guess what? It's not chill-filtered.

LAGAVULIN

Up the road at Lagavulin there are no such debates about quality: this is the most distinguished mainstream malt found today. The distillery stands on an even more beautiful spot than Laphroaig and the area's historical pedigree is brought into sharp focus by the crumbling remains of Dunyveg Castle, once the home of the Lord of the Isles, which casts an eerie shadow over the white-painted distillery. One of the great charms of Islay distilleries is the way they are painted white with their name displayed on the walls of warehouses in massive black capitals, so that from the ferry a quick twiddle on the binoculars soon tells you which great house you are passing. Somehow Lagavulin always seems to be the one that beams the brightest towards the Irish mountains of Antrim which on a clear day can be seen 20 miles away.

From a malt which is so broodingly big, you would somehow expect the distillery to be large in size, but it is not. There are four stills, but they are smallish and fat. At Lagavulin it is not so much the quantity but the quality. This is a distillery which has always enjoyed a high reputation since its somewhat confused origins. There seems little doubt that whisky was being made on the site as far back as the 1740s, when 10 illicit stills were manned in close proximity, the spirit perhaps pooled in the style of a co-operative before being smuggled to the mainland. In 1816 and 1817 two legal distilleries were built side by side although, by the 1840s, one had absorbed the other. History was to repeat itself when Peter Mackie built the Malt Mill Distillery within the Lagavulin complex in 1905 as part of his expanding White Horse empire. The distillery ran until 1960, using Lagavulin's mashtun (as Kininvie today uses Balvenie's) but with its own washbacks and stills. The one glass of it I ever tasted was more intensely peaty than any other whisky I have ever encountered, and that was Mackie's intention. Eventually that distillery, too, was swallowed up by Lagavulin and, to my knowledge, not a single cask of it remains.

Above Craigellachie in Speyside (which he built) and Hazelburn in Campbeltown (which he bought), Lagavulin (which he inherited) was Mackie's true gem and retains its connections with White Horse to this day. Scottish Malt Distillers made a fine job of introducing it to the world as a 12-year-old malt, with its distinctive, almost powdery, iodine and cocoa peatiness. When United Distillers launched their Classic Malt range, Lagavulin became the big daddy of the pack. As a 16-year-old it not only added gentle oak to the multi-layered peat, but a fair proportion of sherry casks were included in the vatting to add an extra fruit-like intensity. So successful was it that demand for this glorious dram soon outstripped supply and for months there was no 16-year-old Lagavulin available at all. Now extra casks are laid down to ensure that the public are never so cruelly deprived again, since Lagavulin remains the biggest seller among the Classic Malts. It will subtly change in style, though, in about 2010. An experiment in upping the peating to the 50 ppm phenols which you can taste now has ended. It has reverted to its original 35 ppm, which is still a hefty portion of peat, enough to give the tastebuds a real jolt. And I do not think that the sherry now has quite the same influence that it had back in 1987.

But do not let any of this lull you into complacency. This is not a big whisky: it's

Classic malt: *The heavily peated 16-year-old from the ancient Lagavulin Distillery is a world favourite.*

massive. For the beginner it is one to approach with caution, not to mention reverence. It has style and tenacity. It has class. It starts sweet but boasts a subtle dryness. The peat is not simple, as with Brora, but multifaceted. It does not offer the complexity of an Ardbeg but extra weight instead. So be warned. It is not a malt you simply sip: it devours you.

ARDBEG

Thanks to the strange, horseshoe-like shape of Islay, the length of coastline is quite out of proportion to the land mass. A narrow strip of bird sanctuary is all that stands between Lochs Indaal and Gruinart splitting the island in two. Islay is also remarkable for the varied horizons it offers, although the Paps of another island – Jura – often dominate, since Islay is much less mountainous than other islands in the Hebrides. To the west, at The Oa, a place once cherished by illicit distillers, cliffs jut some 600 feet into the air, so aircraft sometimes fly below the promontory on which you may be standing. Beyond Port Charlotte is the delightful village of Portnahaven where time seemingly stands still, and seals sunbathe off small islands a short distance from the tip of the Rinns Peninsula. In the northeast, a track from Bunnahabhain takes you to a remote lighthouse and hidden beaches below the fern and bracken. Further south is a no-man's-land of tiny mountains and gentle glens accessible only on foot. All these places are suffused in an aura of romance and beauty which sets Islay apart from any other island I have visited, and this aura is magnified when you visit them with a peaty dram close at hand.

However, it is that stretch of Islay from Port Ellen towards Kildalton where the romance and beauty are joined by another ethereal quality: mystique. I have never been able to quite explain it, but the further you travel up that road the greater the sense of unease until finally you reach the church and cross at Kildalton. The church is a ruin and the cross, over 1,000 years old, is the only complete Celtic high cross surviving in the whole of Scotland. I always thought the eerie presence I felt there was my own imagination, until on one occasion the person I was with said she sensed it before I even mentioned it to her. We both left smartly.

Heading back down to Port Ellen, you soon reach the first of the cluster of three distilleries which are sometimes called the Kildalton distilleries. This is Ardbeg. If the mystique of Kildalton is nothing more than an over-active imagination, then there is no doubt about the mysticism surrounding Ardbeg.

For me, this is unquestionably the greatest distillery to be found on earth. My view has not changed since I was poured a dram of this

> *Connoisseur's Selection*
>
> **LAGAVULIN** – THE ENORMOUS 16-YEAR-OLD IS PROBABLY THE ULTIMATE CHALLENGE TO THE WHISKY LOVER.
>
> **ARDBEG** – TRY TO MAKE SURE IT'S PRE-1977 AND YOU CAN HAVE A MASTERPIECE.

Perfection! *For years Ardbeg Distillery made the greatest whisky on earth. Hopefully, under Glenmorangie, it will do so again.*

incredible stuff in Port Ellen in the early 1980s. Countless thousands of tastings of other whiskies worldwide have only confirmed my initial reaction. Ardbeg produces a malt which can be flawless. A glass of this, first warmed in the hand and then slowly taken around the mouth, just has to be the reason we were given tastebuds. The former Bell's blender, Ian Grieve, is fond of using the analogy of malts as being the individual instruments in the orchestra of a blend. If this is so, I can only say that Ardbeg is a harpsichord plucking at the tastebuds, while the Laphroaigs and Lagavulins are the hammered bass notes of the pianoforte.

It naturally goes without saying that, because Ardbeg is such a truly breath-taking malt, it is near impossible to find. The distillery was closed for eight terrible years between 1981 and 1989, with well-founded fears that it would never distil again. The irony is that the man who made the decision to mothball it, Allied's Alistair Cunningham, also regards Ardbeg as the finest malt he has ever encountered. When I first "discovered" the distillery, it had not long been silent. It was proud, freshly painted and its three pagodas glinted in the sun. Today the distillery reeks not so much of peat as of decay. Warehouses 4, 5 and 7, only yards from the sea and dating back well into the last century with their perfect gravel floors, have gone, bulldozed rather than repaired. The same fate befell the former owner's elegant house.

In a previous age this was a favoured haunt of smugglers, like Lagavulin a mile or two down the coast. It was a difficult place for revenue cutters to visit, with myriad jagged rocks protruding toothlike out of the sea, waiting to bite into the hulls of any ship that came near. From 1815 distilling was carried out legally after a false start in the 1790s. The distiller who got it up and running was John MacDougall, a man so proud of his clan that he once paid the court fine of a MacDougall he had never known, claiming that anyone by that name could do no wrong. He ended his days confined to a wheelchair and badly treated by his servants. His fate was not so wretched, however, as that of the hapless Donald Johnson, founder of Laphroaig, who died a couple of days after falling into a vat of his own burnt ale.

The distillery remained in the hands of the MacDougalls, one way or another, until 1976 when it was taken over by Hiram Walker, now Allied Domecq. It was at this time that things began to change at this most traditional of distilleries. Until the takeover, the floor maltings of Ardbeg had worked flat out seven days a week to produce all the malt it needed. Within a year of the takeover it was down to about 35 per cent, a very lightly peated malt from Kirkcaldy being mixed in with it, lightening the flavour of the spirit. In December 1980 the famous old floor maltings were closed altogether and heavily peated malt was brought over from Port Ellen. In March 1981 the distillery itself was shut down. With Laphroaig forming part of the package with Long John, Allied now had two heavily peated Islay malts. Since the blenders were turning away from rugged peatiness, it was Ardbeg, with its limited output from single-wash and single-spirit stills, which inevitably drew the short straw. The fact that it made the best whisky on the island did little to save it from years of silence. Since coming back on stream it continued distilling uninterruptedly, until closing again in 1996, but never near full capacity and with only four warehouses – numbers 3, 9, 10 and 11 – still operating.

There is little doubt that the whisky made there now is different from what it was before 1977, and it has not improved. When the maltings were in operation, peat only was burned over a 24- to 30-hour period before being finished with anthracite coal. If you nose the steam rising from the mash now, you will notice a distinct difference. The last malt brought to Ardbeg was still peated to a phenol level of 40 to 50 ppm, averaging in the high 40s, just a fraction lower than of old. But the industrial maltings at Port Ellen use a different peat. For years Ardbeg cut their peat from Duich Lotts, reaching a depth of around eight feet (2.5 metres) where the peat was black and endowed with extremely dense vegetation which imparted untold riches to the malt as it roasted in the kiln loft. Now it is cut by machine from another part of the island, to a depth of only about three and half feet (1.1 metres) and the composition is lighter and less complex.

This is not all that has changed. Some of the last new make which I nosed and tasted was lacking a degree of body. That is partly due to the peat, but there could be other reasons. For example, the running time of the distilling has been cut fractionally so that fewer congener-carrying rich oils are present. This would make it a more attractive proposition to potential blending customers. And, since Allied were not apparently putting Ardbeg in direct competition with their own Laphroaig (although, cleverly, they were putting it in a twin-pack with Laphroaig in duty-free), under Allied, blending remained the principal task of Ardbeg malt. But the distillery no longer figured in Allied's plans. After mothballing it once more, they eventually sold it in February 1997, to Glenmorangie, for £7 million – after outbidding eight other rival distilleries – such is Ardbeg's Celtic charisma.

So just what is so special about Ardbeg? It is a near impossible whisky to describe – so tantalizing on the nose, so natural on the tastebuds. Lagavulin was for many years peated to 50 ppm phenols before reverting to 35, but that is an entirely different dram. Ardbeg does not carry the same weight. It has the uncanny ability to allow the malt free reign amid the smoke, so that the taste pings around the palate in no particular order, from bitter marmalade to intense malt, to dark chocolate, to gentle malt, to earthy peat, a hint of Java coffee, flakes of oak and a twist of demerara sweetness, Talisker-esque spice but without the fire. All this random flitting around the palate like a butterfly, never settling anywhere for more than a few

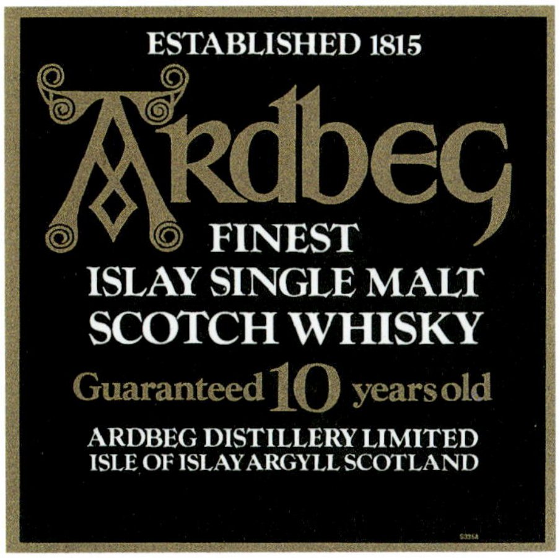

moments before landing somewhere else – if perfection on the palate exists, this is it.

If anybody should hand me a blank cheque and say: "Go and buy yourself a distillery", I might think of Edradour in Perthshire; Kentucky's Wild Turkey would flit across my mind, as would Dickel in Tennessee; but such consideration would last a mere nanosecond. Ardbeg is really the only choice. More would have to be spent on restoring the wonderful floor maltings back to working life. And the greatest warehouse of them all, No. 1, where for decades the very finest whisky always seemed to mature, would return to its former duty, rather than go to waste as a cask store. No need to worry, though, about the larch washbacks or the cast-iron mashtun. Nor would I have to concern myself about the water: that precious stuff still makes its four- or five-mile trek from Loch Uigeadail to Loch Iarnan (itself once an area where Ardbeg's peats were cut), all the time picking up flavours from the turf before flowing into the distillery. But I would resume peat-cutting at the Lotts. Thus, the pagodas would, day in day out, emit the light-blue haze, once more signalling that Ardbeg had been restored to its former and truly unique glory.

Recently connoisseurs have begun to seek Ardbeg with great fervour. As soon as the independent bottlers put a consignment of their rare stocks on sale it disappears, even though the very best casks seem to have vanished now. It would take 10 years to put right, but I would make sure that the world could always find a bottle of the ultimate dram.

CAMPBELTOWN

Since Ardbeg's big problem is that you can't find their malt on the shelves, I often have to advise people to go out and locate what I consider Scotland's second-best dram. That is Springbank which, with Glen Scotia, remains one of the last two distilleries to be found in the erstwhile whisky capital of Scotland, Campbeltown.

This small, compact, ancient burgh, close to the tip of the Kintyre peninsula, is the sort of place where an industrial archaeologist, a whisky lover and, ideally, a whisky-loving, industrial archaeologist can have a fascinating time. Just a century ago there were 21 distilleries operating in a town with fewer than 2,000 inhabitants. It meant that, per capita, Campbeltown was the wealthiest outpost of the British Empire and one where distillery owners tried to outdo each other by building their villa, the status symbol of the age, a fraction larger than their neighbour's. In the adjoining streets, the children of those who worked the distilleries or in the fishing fleets, ran barefoot outside their tiny, damp, cramped homes.

That fleet which filled Campbeltown Loch with mizzen masts and sail has long since vanished, along with the schools of herring. And so, too, have the distilleries, which belched smoke over the town and waste into the evil-smelling loch. While the music hall crooners sang "Campbeltown Loch, I wish you were whisky", unbeknown to them, to a degree it already was. The loch, save for a few massive jellyfish, is as clean now as it has been for the last two centuries. But this means that, whichever street or close you seem to turn into, there are the rotting or demolished remains of an old distillery or its warehouses. Shells of distilleries are now factories, bus depots, garages, creameries. Yet, in many ways it is the skyline which has changed most dramatically, with the forest of chimneys now felled.

Campbeltown has expanded a little since those days but its whisky-making has suffered the biggest decline in the world, even outstripping Kentucky, Canada and the Scottish Lowlands in this respect. Moreover, one of the two survivors, Glen Scotia, is teetering on the brink and is again silent and up for sale. The demise has been particularly sad because Campbeltown is believed by some to have been the cradle of Scotch whisky. If it is true that it was the Irish who brought the art to Scotland, then Islay and Kintyre would have been the first stopping-off places. After all, when St Columba first introduced Christianity to these lands from Ireland, it was in Kintyre he made his home before moving on to Iona.

There is no question that the town and the area immediately around it had been a hotbed of illicit distilling and smuggling long before Archibald Galbraith, Matthew Harvey and James Elder were running their distilleries in 1798. At the same time as those three noble men upheld the law, some 31 others made their spirit in a more underhand manner. But it was in the 1820s and 1830s that Campbeltown went whisky crazy: 26 of the 35 known distilleries began life in that period, a great many undoubtedly originating with those who kept their illegal stills. Both Springbank and Glen Scotia were among them.

The clock stops: *Time had run out on all but two of Campbeltown's distilleries by the 1990s.*

There are a number of reasons why the distillers of Campbeltown had this sudden urge to become law-abiding businessmen. The first was the Act of 1823, the second perhaps the availability of cheap coal which was being mined with industrial-age efficiency. Moreover, since Campbeltown possessed such a fine harbour, it was easy to transport the whisky to nearby Glasgow and markets beyond. Just as there was a run of good fortune in the 1820s, so a similar vein of bad luck meant that things fell apart almost exactly a century later. Coal became more expensive and one of Campbeltown's most important markets, the United States, was in the grip of Prohibition. One by one, distilleries had no option but to close. For years they had alienated Scottish blenders. At one time their quite heavily peated malt had been of the highest class and greatly prized, but now they were turning out some pretty poor stuff as they tried to undercut one another and took money-saving shortcuts in the distilling processes. By the 1920s the biggest and oldest distillery in the town, Hazelburn, had tried to distance itself from its neighbours by writing to tell its customers that it no longer made Campbeltown whisky, now a byword for inferior muck – "stinking fish" it was called – but Kintyre whisky. Likewise, Glen Nevis, during its final days in 1923 – and even Springbank – was calling its make "West Highland".

In 1934 Riechlachan, a distillery with as fine a reputation at the time as any that had made Campbeltown malt, closed leaving just Springbank and Glen Scotia to carry the region's flag. Around that time both distilleries were emerging from long periods without production. There have been no further fatalities and, while the reputation of Glen Scotia has ebbed and flowed like the tide on the shores of Campbeltown Loch, the name Springbank has now become synonymous with style and complexity.

SPRINGBANK

Springbank does not encourage visitors, more's the pity, because they would find, in the backstreets of Campbeltown, something of a time warp – a working museum of whisky where old values and time-honoured traditions are not just something to write about on the back of a label, but are built into the infrastructure of the distillery itself.

This is no doubt due to the fact that the distillery has remained in the hands of the same Mitchell family who built it in 1828. Members of the family had started Riechlachan in 1825, but Springbank was built on the site of Archibald Mitchell's illegal still. This Archibald was the great-great-grandfather of the distillery's current managing director, Hedley Wright, whose idiosyncratic personality has ensured that his particular operation has always been just a little detached from the rest of the distilling industry. Hedley is the kind of man who would cross the street and walk in the opposite direction rather than speak to someone he has no wish to see (which is probably why he and I and have never met after all these years). Yet his nephew, Gordon Wright, until recently, the marketing director, would catch a plane to a far-flung corner of the globe and battle down rapids single-handed in a barrel in order to get his worthy message across to someone who had not yet tasted Springbank whisky.

Their styles may vary but their objective was the same: keep Springbank different and a cut above anything else in the market and never allow standards to drop. The distillery operates a partial triple-distillation system which, theory insists, should make a lighter spirit but this happily turns out not to be the case. The mashtun dates back nearly to the distillery's foundation. The most traditional of traditional boatskin larch washbacks are resplendent in their livery of red. The company has quite recently even rebuilt their own floor maltings, so now every drop of spirit which gushes from the still was made from first to last at Springbank. To cap it all, they actually have their own bottling plant and here they make sure that the minimum strength of their malt will be 46 per cent ABV. The reason for this is that they refuse to chill-filter or add caramel. Thus, every bottle of Springbank is whisky in its purest form. And just to be different, once a year they clean out their distilling apparatus and make the most heavily peated malt they can muster, which they call Longrow after the distillery which was once just across the yard from them and into which Springbank has expanded. Not content with that, in early 1997, they decided that, by the end of the year, they will have produced their first ever fully triple distilled whisky – making them the only malt distillery in Scotland that double and triple distil.

Springbank possess probably the best collection of old, low-roofed, dirt-floored warehouses in Scotland. In these perfect conditions stocks mature to great ages and in a variety of different casks, sometimes even rum. There is a row of casks different from anything else in the world: they contain organic whisky. They were filled in 1992 by the Welsh organic farmer, John Onstwedder, who wanted to create for the millennium a whisky made from barley grown free from chemicals and produced in the most natural way he could find. Springbank was the only distillery which could match his exacting criteria.

Hedley's strained relationship with the rest of the industry, not helped by the practice of his subsidiary company, Cadenhead, of bottling other distilleries' single malts, has gone some way to explaining why Springbank rarely, if ever, fill for other blend-

Connoisseur's Selection

SPRINGBANK – IF YOU EVER SEE A LONGROW, BUY IT.

Triple tipple: *Springbank is Scotland's only distillery that makes peated, unpeated and limited-edition triple-distilled malt.*

ing companies. For this reason all Springbank ends up as single malt or in the company's own small-run blends. That is something we should be thankful for. This is a malt whose salty, dry, slightly oily character guarantees a complexity which confounds, especially in the heavy, earthy and truly miraculous 21-year-old where the use of sherry cask has been kept to a minimum. The 15-year-old is more malt-rich and complex still, while the 25-year-old has a frisky life of its own. Even the Longrow, with all its glorious peat, still manages to maintain a briny character. Each individual one is simply stupendous.

GLEN SCOTIA

Poor Glen Scotia, silent again, boasts only a fraction of Springbank's complexity, yet when it has aged to around 13 and 14 years old can display a wonderful honey character alongside the Campbeltown saltiness and becomes a fine malt in its own right. In operation since 1832, it spent much of the 1980s in silence, and is now owned by Glen Catrine. It is sim-

ply too good a distillery to be allowed to die, though some of the whisky made there in the last decade will not do its reputation much good. But now even the term "Campbeltown Whisky" is under threat. When in 1994 the Scotch Whisky Association sent out maps of their distilleries to mark the 500th anniversary of the great spirit, the owners of Springbank and Glen Scotia were stunned to discover that they had been lumped in with the Highland region. Speyside was now regarded as its own appellation, but Campbeltown had vanished. When Springbank asked for the "error" to be corrected, the SWA wrote back to say that because there were only two distilleries remaining, Campbeltown could no longer be regarded as a region. With only three Lowland distilleries surviving, there is a dangerous and flawed logic in the SWA's stance. Of course, the fact that neither Springbank nor Glen Scotia were owned by companies who are part of the SWA had nothing to do with the decision. Perhaps they just had not had the chance to taste these two briny malts for a long time and thus realize that they were uniquely different. Both distilleries are stubbornly remaining Campbeltown malts, upholding a great Scottish tradition. And in every map of every book on the subject I ever write Campbeltown shall remain a region all its own – even if Springbank becomes the only distillery to occupy it. What is beyond dispute, however, is that this old town, where the court of Dalruadhain crowned Scotland's first kings on the great Stone of Destiny, still has in its midst a monarch among distilleries.

Connoisseur's Selection

GLEN SCOTIA – HANDLE WITH CARE.
AT 14, THOUGH, IT CAN BE SUPERB.

THE LOWLANDS

Where Scotland's many whisky regions – Highland, Speyside, Perthshire, Islay, even Campbeltown – manage effortlessly to conjure up visions of a land at its most romantic or historic, the Lowlands has always struggled to win a similar place of affection in people's hearts.

Yet parts of the Lowland region, that vast area south of an imaginary line between Greenock and Dundee, are as inspiring as many found in and around Speyside. As the rapidly improving A74 cuts a swathe through this region from Carlisle to Glasgow, it passes some breathtaking country, much of which, at one time or another, was the scene of whisky-making, either legally or illegally. There have been at various times well over 300 distilleries legally operating in the Lowlands. Unlike Campbeltown, where the majority thrived until well into the 1920s, many of these survived for a decade or two in the early nineteenth century before failing. The fact that they started in the first place is hardly surprising. Many were in urban developments and even those in rural areas were relatively close to large towns and cities in a part of Scotland much more heavily populated than the Highlands. Most failed either because their quality was simply not good enough or because there was too much competition. Yet, it might have been expected that more than the current four distilleries would survive the slaughter – and a question mark hangs over the future of two of these. Just like the mid-nineteenth century, the period of the 1970s, 1980s and 1990s has been a particularly brutal time.

Connoisseur's Selection

Bladnoch – Don't bother if older than 15 years old.

BLADNOCH

One victim during this period was Bladnoch, easily the most aesthetic of all Lowland distilleries. This has been officially mothballed but with virtually no chance of restarting. Until 1993 it was Scotland's southernmost distillery, located near Wigtown, Galloway. Lying on the serene banks of the Bladnoch river, it was unquestionably one of the most attractive traditional malt distilleries in Scotland and, when given the chance, made an exceptionally delicate, delicious, citrus-tart malt. Since it had been neglected somewhat by Bell's, the new owners, United Distillers, were reluctant to spend too much money in sorting out effluent and other problems. Moreover, being such a long way from anywhere in particular, it was an expensive plant to run. So it was closed.

One of the traditions of Lowland whisky was triple distillation, where the wash was distilled in a first still, the weak spirit being distilled in the second, intermediate still with the feints (impure spirit) of the third still. That third still acted as a normal spirit still.

Land of the Sassenachs: *Yet the Lowlands often matches the Highlands for beauty.*

Theoretically, the end product would be stronger in alcoholic content and lighter in character, since some of the heavier traits would have been distilled out. But, if Barnard's accounts of his visits to the Lowland distilleries are to be believed, it was the attempt by some distilleries to distil more than twice which could have led to their downfall.

As far as I can ascertain, during the mid-1880s Barnard visited 28 Lowland distilleries which made malt whisky. One, Glen Mavis, made theirs from a Coffey continuous still. Cameron Bridge made some using a one-pot still working in tandem with a continuous still, while the other 26 used pot stills. The number employed ranged between two and 18, with six using three stills. He specifically mentions two distilleries performing triple distillation, though one of those used five stills. That was Greenock, where he talks of the distillery having wash stills holding 4,491 gallons, a low-wines still holding 1,007 gallons and two more stills "containing 879 and 776 gallons respectively". He claims that: "the product is really distilled three times". But the distillation method he illustrates actually means that it was distilled four times, since it was passed through the last two stills twice. Although he called the end result "malt whisky", which it was, it appears that the fourth distillation would have been carried out to produce a spirit with an extremely high alcohol content, something in the high 80s or low 90s perhaps. If other distilleries carried out their operation in this manner – and it's hard to believe that Greenock would have been alone – it explains why Lowland whisky was considered so inferior in quality to Highland malt. Moreover, the prohibitive cost of making whisky this way would have left distilleries like Greenock working on borderline profit margins. The fact that Greenock failed during the first year of the First World War could hardly be seen as a surprise. It is amazing that it survived so long.

AUCHENTOSHAN *(Ocken-toshen)*

Now only one distillery, Auchentoshan, continues to triple-distil. When it was built, around the turn of the nineteenth century at Old Kilpatrick, it was some distance from Glasgow, close to the River Clyde and deep in open country. Today the outskirts of the city have crept up and surrounded it, a council housing estate lying cheek-by-jowl with the warehouses. The views from the distillery over the river were once spectacular. Now a massive motorway, the Erskine Bridge, fords the watercourse and, overhead, planes drone wearily during their descent toward Glasgow airport. At least the distillery has somehow managed to remain quite pretty externally, and inside has retained something of a natural, old-world character.

Remarkably little is known of its early history, but its more recent record is interesting enough. It is now Japanese-owned, being part of Suntory's Morrison Bowmore group. When Barnard paid his visit, there were only two stills. For as long as anyone can remember there have been three and they work in true triple-distillation, rather than partial as is the case at Springbank, Benrinnes and Mortlach. At Auchentoshan, when the spirit emerges from the wash still it is 18 per cent ABV, 54 per cent from the intermediate still and 81 per cent from the final, spirit still. The quality of make had long enjoyed a healthy reputation, but, even so, for a few years output at the distillery was reduced almost to stalling level. Thankfully, for the last two years, the picture has been a lot brighter.

However, the 10-year-old malt, which I once cherished for

Auchentoshan: *Among one of the last of the Lowlanders.*

its remarkable sparkle on the palate, has not been quite so boisterous of late and even, by comparison, a little dull, with a bigger malty say. Likewise, the new make had been noticeably lacking in its trademark, zestiness. However, the wash still was replaced during 1995. Apparently it had worn pretty thin and insufficient amounts of copper were being extracted during the distilling process. Things are looking better and perhaps just a little more care with the vatting will enable that wonderful lemon-sherbet buzz to be reintroduced.

LITTLEMILL

It will need more than careful vatting to bring the nearest distillery to Auchentoshan, Littlemill, into line. This is another ancient one, dating back to 1772. But I have not found a decent bottling of this since probably the late 1970s. Its problems have been an intense fieriness, which occasionally incinerates the tastebuds, but with very little flavour to compensate. Situated on the Glasgow–Dumbarton road at Bowling, it is an attractive distillery but the new owners, Glen Catrine, know that they will have the greatest difficulty in transforming this into a top-line malt and have put the distillery up for sale.

Whether it will ever distil again is debatable. Considering that triple-distillation was carried out here until the 1930s, one can only shudder at the thought of what that is like. The pot stills responsible for the present Littlemill are peculiar, though not unique, in that they are also attached to a rectifier. The idea was to give greater control to the spirit. It also meant that they made two other types of experimental malt during the 1970s, one called Dumbuck, a heavily peated dram which did little to impress the blenders, and Dunglass, an oilier, unpeated malt, which did little to impress me. By coincidence, the new owners, Glen Catrine, also operate an adjustable rectifier at their original distillery, Loch Lomond, just up the road and across the Highland line north of Dumbarton. Only there they do it much better.

While old, established Lowland distilleries died off, some distillers tried to hold back the tide by building new ones which were theoretically much cheaper to operate. The master plan was to make full use of their grain distilleries by incorporating malt distilleries within them. There was one in the Highlands at the Invergordon Distillery called Ben Wyvis, built in 1965. But that lasted only as long as the majority of the Lowlanders, which was next to no time at all. In short, the plan was a flop.

KINCLAITH

The first of the new-wave distilleries was Kinclaith which, from 1957 until its demolition in 1975, was part of the Strathclyde grain distillery in Glasgow. In 1965 Glen Flagler was built at the Inver House grain distillery at Airdrie, boasting the biggest mashtun in Scotland. Curiously, Glen Flagler ran traditional pot stills between 1965 and 1969, before moving to a "bourbon" style of malt whisky in which the wash ran through a continuous beer still and then a pot still. And, until 1970, two other types of malt were made there: Islebrae, a peaty Lowlander at 15 ppm phenols which was phased out, owing to its inability to match an Islay heaviness of body; and Killyloch. All malt distilling finally ceased there in 1982. Next, in 1966, and finally, came Ladyburn, part of the William Grant Girvan complex. Those four stills became silent in 1974, though not before gaining some sort of fame by appearing on the cover of Ross Wilson's 1970 book *Scotch: The Formative Years.*

INVERLEVEN

It was the very first Lowland of them all, Inverleven, which made the best whisky and is the only one, officially at least, still alive and with its distilling equipment intact. Inverleven was built at exactly the same time as the massive Dumbarton grain plant was erected on the banks of the Clyde in 1938. In its striking red brick, this is the most imposing of distilling sites in Scotland, and Inverleven, itself built in the same material, is dwarfed beside it. The whole distillery has a cramped, claustrophobic feel to it, as if the imposing distillery next door were about to crush it out of existence. Indeed, it has not distilled since 1992, though not because its make is not good enough. It is part of Allied Domecq and, having only the two stills, is one of their least important plants. At one time the malt complex was split into two separate distilleries. One was Inverleven, the second was Lomond, with its squat "Lomond" still, named after the distillery, producing a much heavier, oilier malt. On the same principle Mosstowie was made at Miltonduff and Glenburgie was the home to Glencraig.

Inverleven is a soft malt in the recent Lowland style and considered by most to have been much better than any of the other grain distillery malts. But if you talk to any of the blenders involved with the now dismantled distilleries they will tell you that these whiskies were never given the chance to prove themselves. There is hardly any Ladyburn surviving and what remains is pretty oaky. Some decent Kinclaith can be found here and there, sometimes with a faint, cognac-like sweetness and "spirityness". However, although it never gained great praise as a new make, the few remaining casks of Glenflagler are simply wonderful. At 13 years old, it has a very attractive honeycomb and spice nose and just a hint of wood. The taste is impressive: an enormous blast-off of biscuity malt, very slightly fat, a delicate sweetness which blends well with a very light spice. Nevertheless, it is the vigorous malt which impresses most of all. The finish is a touch oaky and is inclined toward a burnt-toast bitterness, but that sweet edge keeps it in balance. What is certain is that it does not require any more time in the cask.

GLENKINCHIE

The other working Lowlands distillery is Glenkinchie and, being one of the United Distillers' Classic Malts, its future is the rosiest of them all. This distillery, which dates back to the 1830s and has never suffered the ignominy of sharing its grounds with a grain distillery, is situated at Pencaitland, far removed from anything approaching an industrial complex, in the heart of the undulating barley-growing farmland south of Edinburgh. The villages around there have almost an Englishness about them, and it is easy to imagine, especially when entering Pencaitland, that you are somewhere in the

Connoisseur's Selection

BLADNOCH – DON'T BOTHER IF OLDER THAN 15-YEARS-OLD.

AUCHENTOSHAN – TRY TO FIND SOME OLDER BOTTLINGS, IF YOU CAN.

LITTLEMILL – PERFECT FOR THE PERSON IN YOUR LIFE YOU LOATHE.

KINCLAITH – HIT AND MISS FROM THE INDEPENDENTS. KEEP YOUR FINGERS CROSSED.

INTERLEVEN – GORDON & MCPHAIL HAVE DONE THIS DISTILLERY PROUD.

GLENKINCHIE – THE CLASSIC MALT ISN'T, BUT PLEASANT ENOUGH.

Glenkinchie: *A chunky distillery that produces a light Lowland malt.*

Cotswolds rather than travelling toward the Lowlands' most productive distillery.

Although the land surrounding the distillery is pleasing to the eye, the squarish, functional appearance of Glenkinchie itself is a bit jarring. Its aspect is, however, softened by a bowling green for the workers, just as the Caledonian brewery in Edinburgh has one for theirs. But once you are inside the distillery, things take a turn for the better. A former manager decided to put together a number of fine artefacts to create a museum, one of the most popular being a working model of a distillery which was displayed at the Empire Exhibition at Wembley, London, in 1925, and is still able to make whisky. However, my favourites are the distillery workers' "dogs". Made from copper, these were designed to be sunk into the cask when no one was looking, siphon off some of the precious spirit and then be hidden away down the trouser leg.

The whisky of Glenkinchie is worth spiriting away. It is exceptionally malty with a smokier hue than most Lowland malts. The Classic Malt is a 10-year-old and for the first few years a pretty temperamental dram which, from bottle to bottle, could be sweet and chewy or dry and flighty. It has settled down into a light- to medium-bodied fellow, untaxing and maltily pleasant. The lightness probably comes from the size of the stills which are almost bloated in their enormity.

ST MAGDALENE *(Saint Magdalinn)*

Edinburgh once had its own malt distilleries but they have all gone now. Another distillery in the area was St Magdalene at Linlithgow. That was closed by Scottish Malt Distillers in 1983 and a friend of mine lives in one of the flats into which part of the complex has been converted. It was never a particularly great dram when young for blenders, although, like Glenkinchie, it was double-distilled. Be that as it may, United Distillers are currently marketing a 23-year-old which has buckled slightly under the weight of the oak, but has by no means given way, with a delightful, lemony nip adding to the malt and liquorice. I think, though, that I preferred the malt when it reached about 10 years. At that age, it still held a whiff of smoke and the maltiness was rich and oily, with a bold toffee finish which hung on and on. Its secret was to keep you guessing whether it was a sweet or dry malt. After an age of battling on the palate you would decide it was either, neither – or both. The best 10-year-old I tasted from there was distilled in 1982, a year before it was closed, and at a time when brewer George White had just switched his water supply and thought he was making something rather good.

Connoisseur's Selection

ST MAGDALENE – HOLDS UP WELL UNTIL ABOUT 12 YEARS OLD.

ROSEBANK – IF YOU CAN EVER FIND ONE AGED 8, RE-MORTGAGE THE HOUSE FOR IT.

ROSEBANK

Ten years later he was at another Lowland distillery just as the plug was pulled on it, this time by United Distillers. Perhaps I shouldn't say "another" but "the". This was Rosebank. I am not someone to criticize other writers when it comes to whisky: every person is entitled to their opinion. But when Brian Murphy in his *World Book of Whisky* (1978) wrote: "...it must be admitted that none of them [Lowland malts] approaches the sunny majesty of the greatest Highland malts...", I was unable to take the book seriously again. I know of one blender who, against his better judgement, had agreed to take part in a blind whisky tasting on the radio. When he heard that Rosebank had been chosen as the Lowlander he all but pleaded not to go on air as he knew he would never spot it among the top Highlanders on show.

For me Rosebank is the classic Lowland malt. And while I believe that United Distillers' choice for their Classic Malt range has been truly inspired, I feel that their Achilles heel is Glenkinchie. Rosebank is the superior Lowlander by a mile. In the days of Scottish Malt Distillers it was bottled as an eight-year-old and was a great success in Japan. Someone knew what they were doing, since this is the optimum age for this malt when everything – citrus fruits and apples, honey, malt and the very gentlest of spices – comes together for a veritable crackerjack of display on the palate. United Distillers currently bottle it as a 12-year-old, still a magnificent dram but one in which the oak has taken a toll on the more exuberant notes. At its best, Rosebank must be ranked in the top five of all Scotland's malts for its sheer charm.

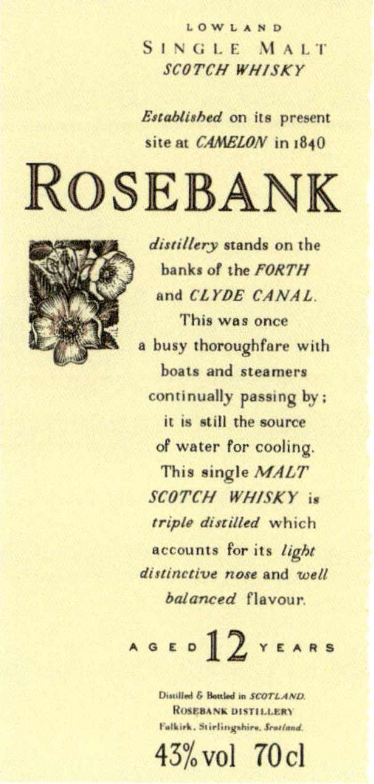

And yet the distillery has been closed. Why? Well, for a start, it is situated close to the town centre of Falkirk, squeezed between the A9 and the Forth-Clyde canal. It originally acquired its name because of the roses which grew on the canal bank. The roses have long since withered away, the canal is redundant and stagnant, and the run-down distillery, where a partial-triple distillation system similar to Springbank once operated, has gone three long years without producing and hopes are fading fast that it will ever be saved. More than £2 million would have to be spent on building and plant and on bringing the distillery's effluent treatment up to European standard. During the last days of its operation, I witnessed the death throes of a working museum, The malt mill was as old as any I had seen, the cast iron mashtun looked as if it had been new when the distillery was opened 130 years before, and all around the stillhouse was a feeling of age and tradition.

However, tradition does not always count for much when corporate finance is involved. Nor does quality. But I suppose, at the end of the day, shareholders have to be paid and profits made: without that philosophy no distillery would exist at all. And so a great distillery has ceased to be. Both the Lowlands and the whisky lover are so much the poorer for it.

Out of lock: *The Forth-Clyde canal is still used by tourists, but Rosebank's future appears to be well and truly sunk.*

THE LOST DISTILLERIES OF SCOTLAND

It is often a trait of human nature to speak better of the dead than when they were alive. We will tell tales about old so-and-so and others, laugh at some of the funnier stories concerning them and reflect on their kindnesses. As a mark of respect, their failings and the less favourable side of their nature will not be dwelt on. In many ways, the same can be said about Scotland's lost distilleries. When one more closes, it is as if another piece of the country's fabric has been picked bare, the further erosion of a nation's heritage in the name of commerce.

This, of course, is true. But what is sometimes forgotten as time passes is one of the reasons why distilleries close: some were simply not good enough.

A couple of years back I was looking through the shelves of a large, high-class wine and spirit shop. On these shelves were whiskies from over a dozen distilleries which had joined the great stillhouse in the sky and the man serving me eulogized long and hard over each one. If what he said was true, every single malt (and a single grain) was nothing short of marvellous, the bottles contained some of the finest spirit ever seen and would soon be seen no more, and so on. It was a wearying speech and I did not have the energy, or the inclination, at the end to put a slightly different slant on his story.

For instance, he had some North Port from Brechin there. If there was indeed really top-grade stuff in those bottles, it would have been the first I had tasted in my life. Likewise his Coleburn and Banff were masterpieces, or some such adjective, though the samples I have tasted over the years point in another direction.

The plain, sometimes unpalatable, fact is many distilleries died simply because their make was not good enough. Blenders didn't want to use it – not just those who worked for the company which owned it, but also those from other companies whose patronage would have led to reciprocal arrangements for that whisky to be swapped for another.

That said, there are distilleries gone now which should never have been allowed to die. Their quality, heritage and importance to a local community outweighed the relative pittance that would have had to be spent on them to keep them in shape. Here one thinks of the three Inverness distilleries, Glen Mhor, Glen Albyn and Millburn, all of which perished in the blood-letting purges of Distillers Company Limited in the disastrous mid-1980s. Perhaps Glen Albyn was suspect, always miserly thin with a kind of off-balance feintiness hanging onto it like nicotine impregnates the clothes of a 40-a-day man. But Millburn and Glen Mhor, in particular, were something else. Millburn was honey-yoghurt sweet and fat, malty and solid as a rock; Glen Mhor also had a touch of honey but a much smokier persona, giving it extra depth and an enormous finish. Both should still be in operation; a bottle of both is essential for any whisky lover.

We have already looked at the pointless loss of the classics Rosebank and Port Ellen in their prime – both these distilleries were making as good a spirit as they had ever done. They are just two of around 25 malts and grains you might spot in whisky shops where stocks are finite. There might soon be more: the fate of distilleries like Glenglassaugh and Glen Scotia hangs in the balance, only time telling what their future holds.

The question is, is it worth going out to buy bottles of these whiskies which are disappearing daily? In many ways the answer must be yes if you regard yourself a true whisky connoisseur. I would be tempted to get two bottles if I could afford them: one to keep, the other to experience. Or perhaps they could be split into two 35cl bottles: again one to keep, never to be re-opened, the other in which to indulge and keep the memory up to date from year to year.

Some whiskies are perhaps drinking better now than at any time when they were alive. That is because a number, like Glenesk (maltier and less abrasive) and Glenlochy (sweeter and less cloying), have actually improved with age, though the former is still pretty poor stuff. Others, though, are past their peak and are in decline. Ladyburn is

River of no return: *Cambus, once Scotland's smallest grain distilllery, made a great whisky.*

almost impossible to find now and oak has taken a hefty toll; some pretty old Glenury has been doing the rounds which, for all its salty oakiness, is not a patch on a younger, ozone-fresh, vibrant 10-year-old. Lochside are bottling their own 10-year-old which is actually an attractive, cereally dram; Gordon and MacPhail have a 1966 version full of prunes and stewed gooseberries, a veritable fruit cocktail of a malt that is well worth taking the time to investigate.

The lost grains are also whiskies worth seeking out. Many independent bottlers specialize in bringing them to us at great age and cask strength. Some are glorious, but have little in common with the spirit that rushed from the continuous or Coffey still a generation back.

Almost impossible to find is Garnheath, a solid grain from Moffat which has not been made since the mid-1980s. This was fine stuff with a great mouth-feel, being both soft and firm in equal measures. For me, though, the greatest grain of all was Cambus. Only recently lost, it was Scotland's smallest grain distillery with a wonderful tradition dating back to 1836. Even the brand-new spirit of the stills would sit on the palate, so silky-soft it would mould itself into the shape of every tastebud and quietly sing lullabies. On five years it had none of the harshness or rigidity of other grains and at 10 showed deftness of texture and complexity which left many malts in its wake.

Flower of Scotland: *Perhaps not unsurprisingly some Scotch displays a heathery quality.*

The other two United Distillers grain plants to go were Carsebridge and Caledonian. The former, a neighbour of Cambus at Alloa, was also a characterful chap, though the maize was oilier and rigid in a rye-grain kind of way. The latter, from Edinburgh, was sweeter and more yielding, but with an inferior, less controlled finish. Both are well served with excellent bottlings by the independent, Signatory.

A 27-year-old Lochside grain released by James MacArthur is spirity beyond expectation and has taken on an oaky persona, as one might expect. What is a bit of a shock is the slight fieriness of it. But this is tempered by a delicious molasses-type sweetness which guarantees a long, enjoyable finale. At the moment, though, the pick of the grain bunch must be Ben Nevis. This is sold at least 25 years old now and then, usually sweet and almost identical in nose and body to a decent nine-year-old bourbon. These are exceptional whiskies and well worth a small investment, especially another Ben Nevis by MacArthur, also 27 years old.

That is the easy way to visit the lost distilleries of Scotland. The harder way is to go there and find the locations personally. Some have completely vanished, others stand silent and sad, others have been converted into homes, offices and, at Glenlochy, even a guest house. Whenever I visit these memorials to the past I cannot help feeling a sense of loss, even if the whisky made there was less than perfect. Yet at the same time I feel a slight exhilaration as I try to imagine what life must have been like there in its formative days; how the founder probably invested all the time, capital and energy he had to make his venture come good; I try to imagine the dreams and aspirations he must once have had.

Those dreams in many cases came true. But dreams do not last forever. Neither will the whiskies these distilleries made, which are becoming rarer day by day. Eventually, they will be only a number at an auction filled with collectors talking fondly about such-and-such a distillery and its great old days, but never really speaking of the failings that brought it to such a pass.

3  SCOTTISH GRAIN WHISKY

Scotch grain whisky has been pretty hard done-by over the years. Usually, it is referred to as a "neutral spirit" which, as the implication goes, is insidiously mixed with malts to make blended whisky. Over the last decade or two it has taken on the mantle of the arch-villain, the piece of rough that brings the sophisticated Perthshires, Speysiders and Islanders back to earth with a thump. I suppose at one time I was guilty of dismissing Scotch grains as neutral myself, the lazy way of explaining to people how blended whisky is made.

But be sure about one thing: there is nothing at all neutral about the spirit made from wheat or maize. Therefore, this chapter will be the first ever to treat Scotland's grain distilleries with the same respect as their pot-still alter egos. Certainly, because the distillation method is continuous rather than batch and therefore cheaper, grain distilleries are pretty hard-pressed to engender anything like the charm of a malt distillery. The stills are massive great things, storeys high, sometimes without a single piece of gleaming copper to be seen anywhere, and there is little of the mysticism or personal touch that is so common among the Balblairs, Inchgowers and Edradours of this world. Yet each distillery has its own distinct character and history. Just as there are no two malt whiskies alike, so there are no two grain whiskies alike, either, even though theory dictates that anything that has been distilled to 94.4 per cent ABV should nose and taste pretty similar. It is worth remembering that 95 per cent of all the Scotch drunk in the world is blended; and, in that blend, something in the region of 65–75 per cent will be grain whisky.

Because of the striking difference between these grains, some blenders use them very carefully. Without doubt the most flavoursome grain whiskies will have been distilled using maize. For that reason, at least one distilling company has made a point of continuing to distil with this cereal, even though its price rocketed against that of wheat. In the mid-1980s, most grain distilleries converted to using wheat to cut costs and the character of their make duly changed. Ten to a dozen years on, those prices have levelled out, thanks mostly to a European Community set-aside programme that has seen the reduction of wheat farming, and one or two distilleries have looked at the possibility of reverting to maize. Blenders are convinced, though, that when the spirit has had sufficient time in the barrel the differences in character are ironed out. That may be true for grains that have reached 12 years or more, by which time – depending on the age of the cask they are matured in – they are beginning to take on a distinct bourbon character, but for those aged around three to eight years I have still to be convinced.

Conversely, other blenders use grains on their availability only, paying little regard to the character but safe in the knowledge that a significant portion of peaty whisky or fruity, dry sherry will keep any inferior grains (inferior amongst grain whiskies, that is) safely under control. Where the blender has to be on his guard is with the Cutty Sarks, J&Bs and Chivas Regals which thrive on a grassy, Speyside character and have to be blended with quality characterful grain. Oddly, it is these whiskies which often benefit from the sturdier, maize grains to give extra firmness. Whatever, all blends go a long way toward achieving balance by using quite a number of different grains to even things out.

Over the last decade, single grain whiskies have been bursting out all over the market-place, with new, smart distillery bottlings acting as "official" versions of the, often single, casks occasionally on the lists of independent bottlers such as Cadenheads and Signatory. The most well-established grain distillery is Cameronbridge and in the "Kingdom" of Fife, which lies to the north of Edinburgh, particularly around the town of Kirkcaldy, it is drunk in the region's pubs in preference to malts or blends. Invergordon have also been trying to establish their 10-year-old, and the vattings are certainly more impressive now than when it was first launched. William Grant, of Glenfiddich fame, have launched their Girvan grain (in mainland Europe to start) under the name of Black Barrel. This is a toffee-soft experience that deserves success. However, marketing people tell me it's an innovation – which, of course it isn't. Back in 1906 the owners of the late, great Cambus Distillery made a point of bottling their own seven-year-old single grain as part of their battle against malt distillers who were trying

Ready to launch: *The grain whisky from Girvan's state-of-the-art distillery is now available in bottle form.*

to win over the Whisky Commission to their case that grain whisky did not have the right to be called whisky at all. One of the things that a Cambus advert of the time claimed was that not only did their grain whisky not affect the liver but there was 'not a head-ache in a gallon'. Having sampled a fair bit of grain over the years, I respectfully beg to differ…

Something else grain distilleries have in common with malt distilleries is mortality. As the 1980s approached, there were 13 working grain distilleries. Of those only seven now survive, although a new one is now up and functioning.

GIRVAN

Once, the most southern point of Scotland, west of Dumfries, the town of Robert Burns' death, was the home to a small family of distilleries. One by one they died off until only one remained: Bladnoch. To all intents and purposes that has now gone, a beautiful slate-roofed effigy to distilling by the banks of the river of the same name lapping only feet away. Still owned by United Distillers, the whisky made there was a riot of delicate citrus fruits and in full bloom at between eight and 10 years old. But being so far away from the main rural areas of malt distilling, it was deemed expendable. So now you have to travel still further west, and to the north, to find Scotland's southernmost distillery.

The journey from Glasgow takes you down the east coast, passing a satisfying array of derelict medieval castles and abbeys; the journey from the south takes you across wild, undulating country and the spectacular Nith Valley which, had you not known better, you might have mistaken for somewhere in the Highlands. The distillery is to be found on the northern outskirts of Girvan, a town which looks better at night than during the day, thanks to some clever use of lighting to focus attention on the more ancient aspects of its architecture. From a distance, the distillery appears to have an outer wall, giving the semblance of an enclosed establishment. Closer inspection reveals those 'walls' to be a complex of warehousing. And just as the owners William Grant have managed to make their Dufftown distilleries a veritable whiskyopolis to malt, then so – with the grain silos, the tall column stillhouse, acres of warehouses – Girvan looks every bit the shrine to mass-produced grain whisky it really is.

The distillery dates back to 1963 and some of the builders who helped erect the plant in an astonishing eight months were

Connoisseur's Selection

GIRVAN BLACK BARREL– SWEET, ALMOST CANADIAN IN STYLE, AND QUITE DELICIOUS.

Against the grain: *Girvan's single grain whisky is attempting to win converts.*

invited to join the distillery and continue to work there today. Indeed I cannot think of any other distillery where the workforce have been together so long; even the gateman was the stillman of the now-defunct Ladyburn grain distillery which ended its short life back in the 1980s.

It is a strange-looking distillery, to be sure. The washbacks may be only four years old, but being outside and exposed to the ferocious winds and lashing rains driven off the sea just a few hundred yards away, they look 10 times older. Even the stills are exposed to the elements and at Christmas 1995 they froze during one of the coldest snaps the country had ever experienced. Two days' production was missed until they could be thawed sufficiently to safely start again. If you take the long walk to the top of the columns you can understand why: even on a relatively mild day the winds whipped up by the Gulf Stream would make it a no-go area for those with hairpieces, though the reward for the long walk is a fabulous view, not only of the town but of the dome-shaped Ailsa Craig beyond and to the right, jutting surreally from the sea.

Yet, despite this apparent conspiracy to test the skills of the stillman, Girvan produces as soft a grain whisky as you will find today. Not since 1985 have they used maize; 90 per cent wheat and 10 per cent malt is the recipe here. It is since Girvan has come to terms with using wheat, and a third column still, that its stock among blenders has risen considerably. Girvan for a time did not enjoy the best of reputations, and samples I have, displaying a rough, unwieldy spirit, show why. Some from the early 1980s, however, are full-bodied, oily, almost sensual in their mouth feel: quite fabulous. Blenders have been wary of inconsistency.

Ailsa Craig: *A dramatic Ayrshire feature.*

Today, though, Girvan enjoys perhaps the healthiest reputation among Scotland's grains, and deservedly so. You can try for yourself with a single grain whisky called Black Barrel. The blurb on the back claims the whisky has been 'triple distilled', which is stretching a point almost to breaking. But it is a very good example of what this distillery is capable of making and what it can achieve by filling into brand-new American oak. Its most endearing aspect is its cushion-soft landing on the palate and then the slow dissemination of its sweet cereal across the palate without a single hard or bitter facet making itself visible. With the new wood, it tastes like a 10-year-old, but is more likely to be only half that: at once astonishing and magnificent. This quality can be detected in some of the Grant blends, but comes into its own with the lush Gordon Highlanders, where the grain is evident but only as a silky platform to some rich malts.

The standard William Grant's Family Reserve, for generations previously known as 'Standfast' (a title now considered too old-hat), is delicious because the grain comes out so well on both nose and palate. As the blend gets older, the malt takes a heftier share of the character, but there is another Grant's blend, the 100 US proof version for duty-free, which allows the grain, in tandem with others, to have a healthy run of the mouth. Peppery, grainy and malty in equal measures, it is irresistible stuff.

INVERGORDON

Scotland's grain distilleries have traditionally been found in the central belt that takes in Glasgow and Edinburgh. Where Girvan is the exception to the south, so Invergordon is the exception to the north. Their geographical polarization apart, these two grain distilleries have other things in common. Both are comparative latecomers, Girvan being built in 1963, Invergordon, 1959. Both also built malt distilleries within their complex, only to discontinue and dismantle them in the 1980s. And both have become very highly respected by blenders after periods of doubt.

Indeed, Invergordon's grain became so prized that it was for the control of this distillery that Whyte and Mackay launched its protracted, and eventually expensive, takeover of the Invergordon company. Apart from its desirability, Invergordon's other claim to fame is that it is the only grain distillery in the Highlands; and just a mile or two away from one of the greatest and most historic of all Scotland's malt distilleries, Dalmore. Since the Whyte and Mackay takeover, the two distilleries have been operated by the same firm.

However, where Girvan stands detached amid expanses of farmland, Invergordon, despite its Highland address, is squeezed beside houses in a port town built on the head of land which juts out to pincer the Cromarty Firth against Newhall Point, a mile or so away on the other bank. From the outside, the distillery looks much the same as any grain plant built since the Second World War, more of a factory than a distillery. Once inside, though, it becomes a much more interesting proposition.

The manager, Ian Palmer, was born in Invergordon and takes an obvious pride in the employment the distillery gives the area. As he points out, the oil industry gives jobs for a short while and takes them away again. Invergordon, though run efficiently, brings a degree of security and hard currency to a corner of Scotland where work opportunities are limited. He also takes pride in the spirit he produces there.

Connoisseur's Selection

INVERGORDON – THEIR 10-YEAR-OLD IS SOFT, UNCOMPLICATED AND TOFFEE-RICH.

There is nothing particularly startling about the way the whisky is made. The mash consists of about 90 per cent wheat to 10 per cent malted barley, cooked to 145 degrees in batch pressure cookers, then fermented in 22 washbacks, of which four are open-air to cope with expansion. The method of distilling is curious, though. The first still, the analyzer, is made from 100 per cent stainless steel. The second still, the rectifier, is 100 per cent copper, including copper plates. It may be this which leads to the spirit being one of the sweetest that blenders can choose to work with, yet the spirit is not powder-puff stuff; there is a definite rigidity to it as well, especially toward the middle.

There is an Invergordon 10-year-old grain available. That sweetness is still evident, but all those years in wood have melted the steeliness somewhat and there are big toffee notes very similar to some Canadian whiskies; you should hold it long on the palate to extract the maximum sweetness. I thought this was a pretty insignificant dram when first launched in the early 1990s: either better casks to choose from or a more assiduous selection has improved it significantly. But the grain was meant for blending and is an important constituent part in most of the Whyte and Mackay brands. Their blender, Richard Paterson, reckons he has not had to alter the recipe particularly of any of his blends now the

Prize catch: *Invergordon Distillery whose grain whisky was long battled over by Whyte & Mackay.*

The perfect blend: *Edinburgh's North British Distillery mixes tradition with new technology.*

Invergordon Distillery is part of the group: they were using it heavily anyway – hence the takeover bid.

It is, unquestionably, a fine grain, quite befitting its Highland appellation.

NORTH BRITISH

There is something reassuringly anachronistic about the North British Grain Distillery. Even its name, North Britain being a Victorian, imperialistic, patronizing term for Scotland, points toward a starched past and, on entering the offices, you are faced with wooden panels, a carved staircase and not a painting in sight to alleviate the gloom. Without any question, North British is a throwback. And at a time of change and high technology, you are glad to find a distillery like this still around.

That doesn't mean to say that North British is a dusty old plant living in the past. The apparatus to make the whisky is every bit as up-to-date as any other Scottish grain distillery. It is located in Edinburgh and the tale of how it came to be founded goes back to the very roots of the blended whisky industry.

The man who was acknowledged as 'inventing' blended whisky, the mixing of grain and malt whiskies to produce a light yet characterful product, was one Andrew Usher, famed for his Green Stripe brand. Holding onto his frockcoat of success, other companies began blending, and eventually large concerns began to evolve. In a bid to control the market, distilleries began fixing prices together, much to the annoyance of the blending companies which did not have their own grain distilleries. So in 1885, a group of them got together to invest in their own distillery, with no single company being able to hold a controlling interest. Another benefit was that they could control the quality of the grain whisky they made and would know what to expect from one delivery to the next. When you see that the first board of directors included John Crabbie of Crabbie's, William Sanderson with his VAT 69 brand and George Robertson of Robertson and Baxter, it is obvious that here was a formidable company and it was no surprise when the grain whisky giants, the Distillers Company, tried to merge with them. The board of North British was not the slightest bit interested.

At the time there was already the well-established and respected Caledonian Distillery in Edinburgh, which the founders had tried to buy with no success. There was also a Caledonian railway. The land chosen to build the new distillery was next door to the North British railway line. Perhaps that is the reason for the distillery and company name.

The distillery remained fiercely and very strictly independent until the mid-1990s. Now it is owned jointly by IDV, whose J&B brand used a hefty 50 per cent of North British in its grain make-up, and Robertson and Baxter. Neither has a controlling interest. But that apart, nothing has really changed. It is the only grain distillery with its own maltings, though it doesn't use a kiln. Green malt is used for two reasons: it is cheaper to produce and is more enzyme friendly. Also, more malt

Connoisseur's Selection

NORTH BRITISH – RICH AND RIPE WHEN AROUND 12 YEARS OLD.

LOCH LOMOND – WHEN IT COMES ON THE MARKET YOU WILL FIND IT SURPRISINGLY SWEET.

is used here than any other grain distillery. Most use 10 per cent malt, 9 per cent if they can get away with it. Here they use much nearer 20 per cent, again a throwback: a century ago nearly all Scottish grain distillers used a minimum 25 per cent malted barley. And just like the old days, North British's malt is not mixed with wheats, but with maize, usually brought in from France. Sticking with maize when all but one other distillery turned to wheat in many ways sums this distillery up. They did have a very brief flirtation with wheat many years back, but when J&B and Robertson and Baxter, oddly enough, made their objections known, they returned to the hallowed maize in double-quick time.

While the entrance may be featureless, the army of 37 steel washbacks, even those which are 40 years old, make amends. Their uniform is metallic: gold on top and silver underneath. Fermentation here is a slow process, 72 hours minimum. And to guarantee that the spirit will be full-bodied and weighty to the end, the wash is sent into one of three gleaming new Coffey stills, also unusually gleaming with a diamond-shaped marking to the stainless steel. The analyzer is stainless steel throughout, but inside the rectifier the spirit makes contact with a fair chunk of copper, including the plates.

The new make is as oily and rich as you might suspect and remains full-bodied as it matures. Some grains take on a Canadian-style toffeeness as they get older; this one undoubtedly moves toward a bourbon character, with the maize-malt recipe obviously having a strong input.

While some distilleries are compact, this one is spread over quite a large area. The former, turretted offices in Slateford Road, near the charming old Caledonian brewery, are now the (cramped) headquarters of Pentlands, the whisky industry's independent research laboratories, and directly behind them are old warehouses with their giveaway black mould on the stonework, which at street level gives a beautiful smell of maturing spirit to anyone passing by. The distilling part is some distance away, once overlooking and now overlooked by the impressive and historic Heart of Midlothian football ground.

For a whisky writer, it is a dream come true to visit a distillery where tradition goes hand in hand with the newest distilling technology. And there is a sense of relief when you have done so. For the first one to try it was a certain Alfred Barnard, nearly a century ago. It was the only distillery which refused him entry...

LOCH LOMOND

Over toward the west coast, beyond Glasgow and just as you reach the southernmost shores of Loch Lomond, is Scotland's newest grain distillery. Just like North British, it was constructed with a similar "nuts to the rest of the

Still waters: *Loch Lomond gave its name to a distillery – and even a type of still.*

industry" attitude. And that is about all you can say they have in common.

North British was built by a consortium of big players, almost as a co-op. Loch Lomond has been built from the finances of a small distilling and blending company. Just as with the malt it makes in its pot-still distillery next door, the philosophy has been to pile it high, sell it cheap. For that reason, today's major distillers seem to regard those who operate Loch Lomond with quiet disdain and, while there was no whooping for joy when they heard that the first spirit coming from those brand new stills was pretty poor, there were few tears of sorrow, either, or teams of troubleshooters running to their rescue. A year on into the grain-making process and Scotland's whisky major-leaguers are having to take some notice. After a painful learning curve, the grain spirit coming from those stills is pretty decent stuff.

Remarkably, the £8.5 million required to build the distillery came from cash funds. Not a single penny has been borrowed from the bank. The distillery is found in Alexandria, a small town you stumble across as you head out of Dumbarton toward the Highlands. The malt distillery is located in what remains of an old dye works. The grain plant has been constructed on waste ground beside it and inside is a mass of stainless steel all at the end of a master computer. It came on-stream with the first fermentation on February 7, 1994; "the first faltering steps," as manager John Peterson, a veteran of Strathclyde grain distillery, succinctly put it.

Being so close to Loch Lomond means the land around the distillery has a high water table. The distillery uses half a dozen bore holes to find the calcium-rich water needed to run the plant. Wheat is used with the obligatory 10 per cent malt to aid fermentation in the 10 mash tuns. There is a single set of stills, the rectifier being all copper, but trying to get the apparatus to work in harmony proved more difficult than had been hoped. It was stop-start, stop-start with just 100,000 litres of alcohol produced in 1994. However, after months of fine-tuning: bingo. Now over 800,000 litres is being produced each month

Echoes of Ontario: *Dumbarton is a mirror image of the Walkerville Distillery in Canada.*

and some will be going into the firm's High Commissioner blend. The spirit being made in the summer of 1996 was remarkably soft and sweet with a distinctive fruit-sweet and bubble-gum aroma. It is the kind of grain small blenders needing high grain content for cheaper blends have been praying for. The hardest thing to achieve with budget whisky is to bring sweetness into it from young spirit. If Loch Lomond can keep this quality up, both they and the small blenders will be mightily relieved.

DUMBARTON

Heading back from the Loch Lomond Distillery, on the return journey to Glasgow, the road swings round to offer a view of a substantial red-brick building in the distance. This is not just a distillery, but for sheer weight of presence, *the* distillery in Scotland. From this distance it looks remarkably similar to the Seagram's plant at Lawrenceburg, Indiana.

This is Dumbarton Distillery, built in 1938 on the site of an old shipyard. It makes colossal seem small, and its dimensions appear all the larger by an exterior consisting of nothing other than red brick. It was designed by the same architects – Smith, Hinchman and Grills – who a few years earlier re-shaped the Hiram Walker Distillery on the banks of the St Clair River, Walkerville, Canada.

Dumbarton was Hiram Walker's first major foray into the Scotch whisky market and they intended to arrive in style. They had already taken over two Speyside distilleries, Miltonduff and Glenburgie, but that was pretty loose change to what was happening on the banks of the Clyde. Not only was this the largest distillery ever built in Scotland, but a Lowlands malt distillery, Inverleven, was also erected, though it was dwarfed in size by the grain plant and barely noticeable. With this never-ending supply of grain, they were now fully prepared to push their Ballantine brands, which they had also recently secured.

Just like Walkerville, the distilling plant is today up and running with some of the same apparatus that was installed at the time. And like Walkerville, the enormous matching brick warehouses are now redundant as far as the whisky is concerned. As you enter through the main gates you are not met by the smell

Connoisseur's Selection

DUMBARTON – AT ITS BEST AT 12-PLUS – AND ALWAYS TRY TO FIND THE WHISKY MADE FROM CORN.

STRATHCLYDE– TEMPERAMENTAL, SOME AT 15 HAS CALMED DOWN THANKS TO AN INJECTION OF OAK.

of maturing spirit or mashing grains. Instead, the enticing aroma of roasting coffee hangs in the air: in one of the warehouses the Kahlua coffee liqueur is made.

It is not only the distillery which is impressive. Opposite is Dumbarton Rock, a mile in circumference and protruding 260 feet out of the sea. In the late Middle Ages it was a kind of Alcatraz to out-of-favour royalty and nobility. Today, if one executive is to be believed, it is where sales directors end up if they don't meet targets. It must be getting pretty crowded…

Inside, the distillery is similar again to Walkerville. They make Canadian Club in an atmosphere of the old and new, but essentially the old. Same again for Dumbarton which positively glows in its aura of fading state-of-the-art. The cookers are relics, but work brilliantly, I am told. Unusually for a grain distillery, they separate the solids from the wort and the stills work on pure wash only. Most other distilleries apply the North American method of distilling through solids.

The end product is a top-notch new make grain, probably the fattest currently made in Scotland. Significantly, it has a cocoa-chocolate bitter-sweetness even before it enters the barrel; it is a grain that laughs in the face of neutrality. A £7.5 million modernization programme cannot really be seen, except that the distillery now has the ability to make from wheat as well, should it want to. That new make isn't a patch on the original maize formula.

Dumbarton remains a vital input to the Ballantine character. Blender Robert Hick, personally taught by the legendary Jack Goudy, uses it cleverly: such a hefty grain could easily over-egg the recipe. These days there is a veritable rash of Ballantines, from the standard Ballantine's Finest through to the 30-year-old via the 12, 15, 17, 18, 19, 21 and Special Reserve. The Finest is pretty weighty in the grand Allied tradition, yet bristling with complexity, and the grain doesn't come in until the very end – and pleasingly so. By contrast, the 30-year-old is lighter despite its years and has the most tantalizing of bourbon traits on the nose and finish: no prizes for guessing where that may have come from. A word about the 21-year-old in particular, though: glorious. The grain is in there, somewhere, but it is so fleeting and flitting it merges brilliantly with the enormous malt diversity.

As the Ballantine blends reveal, it's one thing being able to make a fine grain. The real magic is in putting it to best use.

STRATHCLYDE

Allied Domecq have a second grain distillery, Strathclyde, this one being at the very heart of Glasgow in the famous, or infamous, Gorbals. Sitting on the south bank of a particularly narrow stretch of the Clyde, and dating back to 1929, the distillery is shoe-horned onto just a one-acre site, and to the locals it is not known by its distillery name, Strathclyde, but by the proprietorial brand that once owned it, Long John. Because of the crowded environment there are no warehouses on site and the spirit is tankered out to Allied's maturation plant near Dumbarton. Yet it was still big enough to house a tiny malt distillery called Kinclaith. That was ripped down in the days of Whitbread ownership when they rebuilt the distillery and turned the site of Kinclaith into a water tank.

The grain made at Strathclyde is… well, interesting. It is certainly unlike any other of Scotland's grains, and the boiled cabbage aroma to the new spirit gives some idea why: there is precious little copper in them thar stills.

For that reason don't expect it ever to be launched as a single grain. But for blending purposes, after it has had time to smooth out some rough edges after a few years in wood, it can do a decent job. Most blenders, however, treat it with care and some I know refuse ever to allow their brands to carry more than 10 per cent of it.

Strathclyde is nothing if not efficient and produces its make not only using wheat, but also just 9 per cent malted barley. Around a third of its output goes toward Beefeater Gin, another third is produced for other companies, and the final third finds its way into the Allied brands, including, naturally enough, Long John. For 24 hours a day, seven days a week,

Crushed grain: *The Strathclyde Distillery is shoe-horned into just one acre of the Gorbals.*

42 weeks a year the distillery works flat out. For 10 weeks the staff take their holidays and the machinery is repaired.

The washbacks are exposed to the Gorbals air, while the housed continuous stills which have replaced the old Coffey stills there contain copper only in the plates and a bed of nails on the head of the analyzer and rectifying columns. It's not great spirit, but probably better, one suspects, than manager Richard Russell might expect to get from what he has available. I just wonder what it would be like if a coppersmith were brought in to give that rectifier an overhaul. Still, while Allied have never really got their act together regarding their malts, their blends are near-faultless, so Strathclyde must be making some sort of positive contribution. There is always room for improvement, though...

PORT DUNDAS

There is one other grain distillery in Glasgow. As the crow flies, it is just a mile or two from Strathclyde and north of the river. Its location defies logic, and if you have ever driven along the main M8 motorway which passes through the city, heading east to west, you may have spotted it on your right without really noticing. As a rule, distilleries are found on low-lying ground on account of having to be near a source of water. Port Dundas is actually atop a hill that overlooks the city, its impressive old chimney a landmark for miles around, including the nearby motorway.

Yet, in fact, it does sit by water, the Forth-and-Clyde Canal, and when two malt distilleries were built here in the late eighteenth century doubtless it was used to ferry the barley to the distillery and the whisky away to its markets. The distilleries merged in the 1860s, but not before they had also begun making grain whisky on the site with the employment of Coffey stills. In 1877 it became part of the Distillers Company and, though there has been rebuilding, it remains a rather special distillery to look at, a celebration of an age that pleases the eye.

That's outside the distillery. Inside is quite something else. I can think of no other distillery in the world where so much paint has been used to brighten the apparatus. It is as though Joseph's coat was used as the colour coder. If it could be moved, it would probably fetch a small fortune at a gallery somewhere. Should you go to Port Dundas, ask them to make whisky for you, certainly. But never let them design the interior of your house. The display in the fermenting room is particularly eye-catching. While the wash charger is Ferrari red, the buffer tank next to it is Trabant green with psychedelic yellow underneath. The 19 washbacks have to make do with a mere eggshell green top and canary/custard yellow bottom. The first time this multi-coloured vision met my gaze, the person taking me around the distillery was telling me all about fermentation times and yeasts. I don't think I took in a single word of it.

Even the lovely Coffey stills could not escape. They are red and gold...

Some blenders once tried to avoid Port Dundas' grain. It was thought far too rich and full-bodied for something which was supposed to just make up the numbers. Since United Distillers' other grain plants at Cambus, Carsebridge and Caledonian all closed so Port Dundas could survive with Cameronbridge, there has been a big effort

Starting point: *Alfred Barnard began his epic whisky tour of Britain from Port Dundas.*

made to make the two grains very similar. Certainly it is lighter than how I first remember sampling it a dozen years ago. Old Port Dundas that sometimes comes my way reaffirms my belief that it has calmed down a little, possibly with the advent of wheat. Some made from maize is just bursting with energy and would give zest to any blend rather than just meekly make up the numbers.

Yet the new make is still different to Cameronbridge and long may it stay so. Blenders at United Distillers use it for availability purposes rather than character, anyway. Seeing that the majority of the better blends they produce have real peaty backbone, it is a grain that naturally gets on well in good company.

Outside the distillery, I am admiring the fabulous old buildings. The manager, Jim Wilson looks at what I am purring over, and tells me with great delight that there are plans afoot to knock it all down and rebuild. It jarred me, and if he heard the comment, there is an old man probably still spinning in his grave. Port Dundas was where Alfred Barnard began his epic journey around all Britain's distilleries. When he arrived at Port Dundas in around 1885 that dignified old building was probably the first thing he clapped eyes on. Is nothing sacred?

CAMERONBRIDGE

North of Edinburgh, in the ancient kingdom of Fife, there is a brig which fords the River Leven by the village of Windygates. In summer, swallows and house martins dart under its arches while lorries rumble over them. It is a pretty piece of stonework, though a narrow safety walkway that's been added to it spoils the old-world charm a little. Nonetheless, it is the only bridge I can think of which has given its name to a distillery: Cameronbridge.

Of Scotland's eight working grain distilleries, none quite enjoys the history or reputation of this one. As a grain whisky distillery, it is the oldest in the world, dating all the way back to 1822 when a young man passed over the bridge on horseback. It has become a part of public relations within the Scotch whisky industry these days to link distilleries with blends. But at Cameronbridge, no such convolutions are necessary. That young man was John Haig, his father was a distiller and his family's history in whisky could be traced as far back as January 1655, when one Robert Haig living near Alloa was charged with distilling on the Sabbath.

The bridge was beside the old Cameron Mill and young John, fresh out of university, was keen to strike out on his own. Yet, being so young, he needed his father's backing to secure the tenancy for the lands on which the distillery was built and in operation by 1823. The Haig family had by this time spread far and wide and one of his cousins was the same Alexander Stein who invented the first continuous still in 1826. Keen on innovation, John Haig had no second thoughts about immediately installing one, paying 1d a gallon distilled to his relative. Equally, he had no qualms about removing it a few years later when Aeneas Coffey came along with a much more efficient still on the same theme. Haig was no relation of Irishman Coffey, but he was of the Jameson family who had emigrated to Dublin to begin distilling there. Those involved in the early days of Cameronbridge read like a Who's Who in the evolution of whisky.

Eventually the distillery expanded to become the most adaptable in the whole of Scotland. By the time Barnard got there, its output included grain whisky, "Pot Still Irish", "Silent Malt", presumably malt distilled in a Coffey still, and "Flavoured Malt".

Some of the buildings from that period still survive, though thankfully the last three types of whisky haven't. Green malt is used in the mashing process and tall, round continuous stills have replaced the Coffeys. However, a link with its past has been maintained: the shop where the distillery workers buy their whisky at staff rates has been whimsically called the "Coffey Shop".

The ordinary, single grain called Cameron Brig is a popular seller. It is drunk as the first-choice whisky for miles around. However, there is now a 12-year-old which is easily the best single grain on the market today. The label quotes Barnard as saying that the whisky of Cameronbridge had no equal in the world; certainly as a bottled grain, this one is out on its own and surpasses in its coy charm a number of single malts I could mention.

Local hero: *Cameronbridge is popular in Fife.*

But Cameronbridge is a blending whisky and serves all United Distillers' brands, including Bell's, White Horse, Black and White, Dewar's and the wonderful Johnnie Walker stable. Strange to relate, the nearest malt distillery to Cameronbridge was a Lowlander distilling in a Highland manner, Auchtertool. It vanished many years ago, but a cask or two turned up recently, and some of its contents have been added, probably by pipette, to Johnnie Walker Blue. This Auchtertool noses of sweet spearmint with hints of oak and smoke, and to taste is soft, dry and malty with a slow crescendo of almost chalky vanillins. It would be a bit of nothing whisky really, except for the minor detail that it was distilled in 1923... which just happened to be the centenary of Cameronbridge distillery.

Connoisseur's Selection

PORT DUNDAS – AT AROUND 14 YEARS, IT IS HEAVY, A LITTLE SPICY AND FULL BODIED.

CAMERONBRIDGE – THE 12-YEAR-OLD IS A BEAUTY, A MELT-IN-THE-MOUTH MASTERPIECE.

4 IRISH WHISKEY

Every nation needs its own identity. In its whiskey, Ireland has something that is both genuinely unique and almost timeless. No other nation makes a spirit so recognizable, so invigorating, as pure Irish pot-still whiskey. There are malt and blended whiskies made outside Scotland that you would swear were Scotch. There are grain whiskies from Scotland matured for a great many years in oak which have all the characteristics one might expect from a fine bourbon or Canadian. No one, though, has ever been able to re-create by accident or design the extraordinary, mouth-watering qualities of traditional Irish.

But just what is Irish pot-still whiskey? I have greatly offended the Republic's green-shoot distillers, Cooley, by saying that they were wrong to call their pure malt whiskey Irish pot still. Look, their heated argument went, we make whiskey, in Ireland, using a pot still: QED. Ah, yes, came my reply, but not by using unmalted barley. And it is this unmalted barley which provides the "y" in the equation which is Irish whiskey.

If Irish distillers have a problem, it is getting the public to recognize that Irish whiskey is a whisky category all of its own. For years after their formation in the 1960s, Irish Distillers spun the tale that to be Irish whiskey it had to be (a) made in Ireland, (b) triple-distilled, (c) entirely unpeated. Obviously there is no dispute with point (a) but the others were patent nonsense. When Barnard visited Ireland in the 1880s, quite a few distillers worked off a double distillation system. And while at the time it had become the done thing for the larger Irish distillers, especially those based in Dublin, to substitute coal for peat when the barley was being kilned, much Irish whiskey was once as peaty as Scotch. A chemist who visited an illicit still in Donegal or Inishowen during the mid-nineteenth century, reported that about 25 per cent of the barley used was unmalted and turf was used in the kilning of the malt, which also picked up some smokiness in its flavour from the bog-water it had been steeped in.

It was this kind of whiskey, made from some 2,000 little distilleries dotted all over Ireland, which every Irishman would have instantly recognized; the style made in Dublin with its access to coal would have been lighter by comparison. But it was the lighter whiskey which gained a market beyond the island's shores and became more common as the little distillers, illicit and otherwise, closed down.

So the advent in 1989 of Cooley Distillery has been a boon to Ireland beyond all expectation. With their heavily peated Connemara pure single malt, they have re-introduced a style of whiskey back into Ireland that had been too long away. It deserves success – and the gold medal it has already received in its short life. But it is not, whatever they claim, true Irish pot-still whiskey. If it were, how would one be able to identify the only two brands which fit that title: Green Spot and Redbreast? Both are made from a mixture of malted and unmalted barley and neither has grain whiskey added. A blend with a remarkable amount of Irish pot-still is Powers, one of the most endearing blends in the world, and certainly the most enigmatic. Another is Jameson Gold, a brand new blend designed for duty free but proud of its unmistakable, mouth-watering Irishness.

The great pity is that it is hard to find most of these whiskeys outside Ireland. The choice, usually, is between Jameson, a gentle blend that has improved the sturdiness of its character in recent years, and Bushmills, a pleasant but unexceptional malt. Oddly, it is a malt which actually improves by having good quality grain blended into it, as the magnificent Black Bush proves. Irish Distillers are fighting hard to improve their Jameson range so people might get a better insight into the beauties of Irish whiskey: one launched in 1996 and Jameson Gold is already a world classic.

Everyone should find a week in their life to explore Irish whiskey and it should start with a ferry or a plane journey to that greenest of isles itself. There are superb distilleries to visit in the north and south; a relic of a long-lost distillery, Kilbeggan, in the centre of the country; visitor centres and pubs-cum-village stores. And there are the locals, proud, warm-natured and knowledgeable when it comes to good whiskey. For that reason

Irish heritage: *In praise of pot-still whiskey.*

Powers remains understandably the most sought-after whiskey in the land, while a generous gulp of Connemara, Redbreast or Green Spot when walking through the hills of Donegal is something that will firmly replant any Irish roots you may have.

Hoops heaven: *Kilbeggan's resident cooper, John Neilly, maintains the barrels that are used to mature the spirit from Cooley.*

THE HISTORY OF IRISH WHISKEY

Dublin: *Jamesons Distillery in its heyday.*

The legends which surround Irish whiskey are fantastic and manifold. It was, so many books tell us, the early messengers of the Christian faith who brought to Ireland the art of distilling from grain, before moving on to the Scottish islands and beyond, taking their alchemy with them. Over the years, St Patrick has sometimes been accorded the distinction of bringing distilling to the British Isles, stopping off in Ireland first; others prefer to credit St Columba. Apparently, when Henry II invaded Ireland in 1174 the natives were already happily making and drinking the stuff. We are told, in the *Annals of the Four Masters*, that in "AD 1405 Richard Magrenell, chieftain of Moyntyrolas, died at Christmas by taking a surfeit of *aqua vitae* ... it was not *aqua vitae* to him but *aqua mortis*". All such tales are told as evidence to prove it was the Irish and not the Scots who invented whisk(e)y.

Sad to say, then, but legend is all these stories remain. There is not a shred of hard fact or proof anywhere. This is not a defence of the Scots: the fact is, no one has yet discovered beyond doubt just where whisky was first made, and tales of Irish whiskey pre-dating Scotch – and vice versa – should be taken with so much salt. Yes, there is evidence of a beer-like drink being made long, long ago in Erin. Jonus wrote between 589 and 640 AD: "When the hour of refreshment approached, the minister endeavoured to serve about the ale which is bruised from the juice of wheat and barley." And yes, it may have been distilled. Yet ancient Irish Brehon law does not recognize distilling and there is no word in the old language to cover the practice. The truth is, no one has a clue.

Jamesons: *These buildings still stand but the whiskey is now made many miles away.*

Like in Scotland, the earliest *aqua vitae* was made from distilled wine, which is where some of the confusion may arise. The first written mention of distilling from barley doesn't arrive in Ireland until 1556 with an Act of Parliament passed in Drogheda.

What is beyond dispute is that, by the end of the eighteenth century, there were around 2,000 distilleries operating in Ireland, very few of them legally and nearly all of them employing barley. Most were simple bothies, as in Scotland, hidden far away from the tracks which criss-crossed the country and close to peat and cold, clear water. Queen Elizabeth I is said to have taken to Irish whiskey, as she did to another future staple of this land, the potato. So it was left to a later ruler and government to impose tax.

In those days the whole of Ireland was subject to the crown and obeyed laws passed in London. Like Scotland, it saw a revolution in its whiskey-distilling practices with the Act of 1823, making lawful distilling easier with the payment of a £10 licence, but with stills having to be of a minimum size of 40 gallons. Just as in Scotland, a number of well-established distillers became even better established, especially in the larger cities of Dublin and Cork.

It is hard to consider Irish whiskey and not wonder what might have been. Its lighter, fruitier style, often brought about by the use of unmalted barley, made it at first a more popular beverage than Scotch outside Scotland. So why did it never gain the same eminence? Well, first came a well-intentioned mistake. A Scotsman working in Ireland, Robert Stein, invented a continuous distilling process which

Blessèd Isle: *Ireland has many superb pubs.*

horrified the Irish but which gained great support in his native Scottish Lowlands. A much improved model was made by Aeneas Coffey, an Irishman who was forced to do business outside his own land as Irish distillers would initially have none of this tampering with their flavoursome spirit. It was a decision they were later to regret.

Next came the Capuchin Friar, Father Matthew who swept through the country on a tidal wave of anti-alcohol fervour. When he began his crusade in 1838, there were 21,000 drinking places in Ireland. By 1844, that was down to 13,000 and an enormous number of distilleries went with them, unable to find a market for their make. In two rallies in Dublin alone, his Total Abstinence Movement claimed to have signed up 75,000 converts. That may have been propaganda; what was beyond dispute was that the distillers of Ireland had taken an awful pounding.

As Ireland's larger distillers began looking for markets elsewhere, they discovered that a new lighter Scotch which included a patent-still whisky had appeared on the market. It may not have tasted as good as Irish, but it was a lot cheaper.

Still, the big Dublin distillers continued to thrive. They had the entire British Empire in which to expand their market ... until 1916 and the outbreak of the Irish War of Independence. Then came partition and civil war between 1919 and 1921. When the Irish Free State was formed, the distillers of Cork and Dublin suddenly discovered that the massive markets of the British Empire, including Canada, Australia, South Africa and New Zealand, as well as Great Britain itself, were beyond their grasp. A trade embargo saw to that. They would still have had the United States, but in 1920 that country began its 13 year nightmare experience with Prohibition. Within six years of that coming to an end, the Second World War descended upon Europe and distillers had little or no grain to work with. Whoever it was that first brought whiskey to Ireland must have cracked a lot of mirrors and walked under numerous ladders in his time.

Strangely enough, the Belfast distillers who were still part of the British Empire fared little better than their southern cousins, who were dying off one by one as they began running into debt. In Belfast distillers tended to make malt and spelt their whisky without an "e" in the Protestant manner. In a way they missed the thrust that the Jameson and Power distilleries, which were then supplying only home markets, had put into Irish whiskey as a genre. Against Scotch whisky, Irish was perceived as inferior, though it wasn't, and some distillers, like Coleraine, produced a blended product before dying off in the 1960s. Comber, Kilbeggan and Tullamore had perished a decade earlier. In some ways, serving a country of just a few million, it was a minor miracle that they had survived that long.

By 1966 the sorry handful of operating Irish distillers, the beleaguered survivors of the once proud 2,000, decided something radical and drastic had to be done to ensure their survival. Jameson, Power and Cork Distillers, proprietors of the famous Paddy brand, agreed to merge. The two Dublin distilleries were closed and a new purpose-built distillery was built next door to Cork Distillers' existing but ageing Midleton plant. Only Bushmills in Ulster remained outside the umbrella, but not for long. They joined forces in the early 1970s and Irish Distillers meant just that.

Since then, only the Bushmills and Midleton distilleries have operated within the group, with the Jameson and Bushmills brands being pushed internationally and the Paddy and Power's labels spearheading the old brands fighting the home front. However, a third distillery popped up near Dundalk, with the emergence in 1989 of the independent and Irish-owned Cooley Distillery. Irish Distillers, by now a subsidiary of the French-owned Pernod Ricard group, tried to take them over, only to be thwarted by the Irish government, and since then the new distillers have launched a number of high-quality malt and blended whiskies ... much to Irish Distillers' annoyance. After the rejection of Irish Distillers' bid, Cooley were in poor financial shape. Only a $1.6 million investment by the Kentucky distillers Heaven Hill, who bought stocks of Cooley's whiskey to market in North America, kept them alive. Things are still tight at Cooley, but a lot healthier than in the days of 1994, the year they were too broke to distil.

Some people within Irish Distillers, though, privately admit that the advent of Cooley has been one of the best things that could happen to the industry. There is competition again amongst Irish distillers; the market is more open to innovation, and every other month, it seems, a new brand is popping on to the market from either Cooley or Irish Distillers. What had been the most staid and predictable of whiskey styles has exploded over the last couple of years into easily the most exciting.

Cheers! *An example of early advertising art from John Jameson's (above).*

MIDLETON

There are still parts of the British Isles which can surprise and delight, and with its many bridges and churches, Cork in the south-west of Ireland is a city overlooked at the traveller's cost. Discover this on a business mission and you will think, yes – I must come back here for a weekend and share its splendour with the one I love.

Or you could just spend a weekend with the whiskeys you will learn to love. Cork and whiskey are synonymous. There is none made in the city itself anymore, though at the old North Mall Distillery – typically located on an island marooned by the twin spurs of the River Lee, and once the site of an ancient friary – some very fine whiskeys are married together before being bottled there. But once, the aroma of malting and mashing barley hung deliciously over the city as Daly's, The Watercourse and The Green distilleries all vied with North Mall for supremacy. By 1867 they realized they were producing too much whiskey for too few customers and two days before Christmas that year they merged to form the Cork Distillers Company. Oddly, though, the idea had initially been mooted by distillers that were not based in Cork City at all.

On the pretty road that takes you out of Cork and east to Youghal, the half-way point in the journey is marked by a small town called, appropriately, Midleton. This was the home of the James Murphy Distillery, owned by the same family which spawned the Murphy brewery in Cork. James Murphy became a guiding light in the Cork Distillers' empire and Midleton remained, with North Mall, one of only two distilleries that continued to operate. In 1920 North Mall was wrecked by fire, leaving Midleton to go it alone.

Enter the little town of Midleton today and at first glance it is much as any other. Without any pretensions to beauty, it retains a charm peculiar to Ireland; it is how British towns used to look before the 1960s and the arrival of property developers, blinkered councillors and blind architects. Yet as you enter the town from the south, almost immediately to the right you are faced by something grand and obviously exceptional. It is the solid body of the old buildings that were once Midleton Distillery and, just in case you weren't sure, a brightly burnished copper pot still has been planted outside the entrance for confirmation.

Connoisseur's Selection

MIDLETON GREEN SPOT 40% – A SUBLIME POT-STILL MALT OF EXTRAORDINARY CHARACTER.

The output of Midleton Distillery is exceptional. Yet the visitor will never be able to see it made. The new distillery, despite its size, is hidden from view by a fortification of trees. These ensure the ancient charisma of the old distillery is not diminished by its juxtaposition to a new-fangled Canadian or Scottish grain-looking plant. It's a pity really, because the present Midleton Distillery must represent one of the great wonders of the whisky world and deserves pilgrimage and worship in its own right. However, the visitor must make do with the original buildings of Midleton – a handsome trade-off as this, too, is an extraordinary place to visit.

Its centrepiece is the largest pot still in the world. Its riveted form reveals its great age, its peculiar bulbousness accentuating its Irish origin. When working, it held 31,648 gallons and required a room more or less of its own. Everything at this distillery appears on a grand scale. Perhaps this is because it was built at the tail-end of the eighteenth century not as a distillery but as a textile mill. However, that venture foundered and soon it became a barracks, before in 1825 being bought by the Murphys who recognized its position by the River Dungourney as a prime site for making whiskey. At the distillery there is still a massive metal water wheel which replaced the original wooden one and was efficient enough to give the plant the power it needed.

But as soon as Midleton became part of the new Irish Distillers group, the old distillery's days were numbered. It lasted for nine years after the 1966 merger, but in July 1975 the new plant was ready and the proud old distillery abandoned. For people like the current distillery manager, Barry Crocket, it was a day of mixed emotion: the excitement of entering the new custom-built home, with its giant fermenters forming part of the building's fabric, together with the pain of leaving the place in which he was actually born.

One thing is certain: the whiskey made at the present Midleton Distillery is vastly different from that which came from the old pot stills. And as magnificent as the old whiskey was, there is nothing wrong with the Irish made there today and the distillery is solely responsible for some of the best spirit made on God's earth. Old Midleton had also been the home of a column still for grain spirit used in blending. At the new distillery, the pot stills and patent stills were placed facing each other in the same, temple-like stillhouse. Where the pots at Old Midleton had been dumpy in that peculiarly Irish manner, these are tall and graceful, easily the biggest anywhere in the world. Consequently the spirit they make is lighter but, because of the strange wizardry used in the running of the stills and the endless permutations of distillations and type of grain used, some well-weighted spirit does emerge from time to time.

Until Cooley popped up on the scene, every drop of Irish whiskey consumed, bar the obvious Bushmills' brands, came from Midleton. That was quite a remarkable achievement: anyone who has tasted a Paddy, Powers and Jameson 1780 one after the other will testify to their total diversity of taste and style. But that was exactly what Midleton set

Dublin's River: *The River Liffey bisects the city and once divided the famous Jameson and Power's Distilleries.*

out to achieve. I think it fair and correct to say that no other single distillery in the world is quite so able to produce such an enormous range of very high-quality spirit.

The old Midleton Distillery was particularly famous for a single brand: Paddy. It was named after Cork Distillers' top salesman Paddy Flaherty who would buy everyone a glass of their Old Irish Whisky. In those days, and until quite recently, it was the only brand sold in southern Ireland with the whisky spelt without an "e". When publicans used to phone or write to re-order stocks of the whisky, rather than asking for Old Irish, they asked for "Paddy Flaherty's whisky". So the brand was re-named after the genial salesman. Once it was quite a heavy whisky. Today it represents a much lighter style of Irish. The pure malt used in it is the very lightest of the three types of malt made at Midleton. That, in turn, quietens down the pure pot-still and allows the grain to have a more important say in the character.

There are a number of other light whiskeys which Midleton produces, and all for small, traditional markets. Although the brand is now owned by Allied Domecq, Tullamore Dew is a Midleton product. This is a mean, thin, frustrating and ultimately characterless whiskey. A 12-year-old version has subsequently been launched for duty-free and this is a much better proposition which, despite a sluggish start, actually takes off very pleasantly with a certain pot-still richness arriving.

Three other light blends produced there are also curios. One you will never taste on its own goes directly into Bailey's Irish Cream liqueur. With such a wonderfully rich-textured spirit to give it backbone, it is hardly surprising that Bailey's is head and shoulders above other liqueurs of its genre. The blend has far greater complexity than Dunphy's, a brand designed for Irish coffee, though the very best of that style is found in the unlikely but charming setting of Fisherman's Wharf, San Francisco. Take any trolley to the wharf and you can be dropped outside the Buena Vista café. They have their own Irish whiskey named after the café, blended exclusively for them by the same Barry Walsh who blends every other whiskey out of Midleton. This is a pretty delicious whiskey on its own, with just the right amount of pot and pure malt to give a pleasing balance. But at the Buena Vista you can stand transfixed as it is poured liberally, at a dozen cups at a time, into probably the tastiest Irish coffee made in the world; demand is so great that they get through some 36,000 bottles of Buena Vista whiskey every year.

Another light Irish is the recently launched and even more recently re-labelled Old Dublin. Designed for the "economy" end of the market, it does at least have an unmistakable aura of Irishness and is enjoyable enough, despite some obvious deficiencies. It is not a patch, though, on Hewitt's, a rare blend of malt from Midleton and Bushmills. It is the kind of whiskey which you ignore at your peril. But there again, with Irish whiskey, that is often the case anyway.

The single brand name Midleton Distillery is known for the world over is Jameson. Irish Distillers deny it, yet I'm certain that it has picked up just a little extra body and sweetness over the last year or two. Either way, it has an overall constitution of pandering affability which the distillers see as representing an Irish character, but which doesn't really challenge the drinker. Being, by world standards, only a small to medium-sized company fighting amongst giants, Irish Distillers felt it a better bet to put their eggs into that basket rather than show the enormous diversity and challenge of Irish whiskey. Their decision is understandable, but sad nonetheless with gloriously superior whiskeys like Powers and Redbreast waiting in the wings. Of late, though, drinkers in the USA have been able to find Powers at an enticing price as part of a battle against a rival brand.

Even so, Irish Distillers have made a much better effort over the last two years to give the whiskey-lover a wider choice. For some time now there has been the gloriously crafted and complex Jameson Crested 10 (the drink I choose if no Powers is around), the much heavier but subtly sherried 1780 and the *oloroso*-thick Distillery Reserve – this one available only from Midleton's visitor centre. These three whiskeys are not just good, they are magnificent, and leave the palate in no doubt just how subtle yet forceful Irish whiskey can be.

Super coopers: *Barrel-makers from Jameson's Bow Street Distillery, Dublin, in the 1920s.*

The best, though, is yet to come. The company have at last given their excellent blender Barry Walsh the chance to work on some high-quality new brands and he has not let them down. He has just completed putting together a new one called Jameson Gold, the first to have rich strands of honey on the palate amid a riot of pot-still freshness and very sweet and gentle grain. It is a masterpiece. His new Jameson 12, more sherry-dependent and therefore less glittering on the palate, is also a very chewable and big whiskey of considerable class and substance. The odd thing about the launch of Jameson 12 means that, with 1780 and Reserve, there are now three Jameson brands boasting the 12-year-old tag – a unique situation, I think, for any brand. Tasting them side by side for the last six months has been intriguing and it is hard to decide which is the superior.

These are mood whiskies: the 1780 (named after the year the Scotsman John Jameson is believed to have landed in Dublin to start his distilling empire) has the more flitting, perhaps more complex, nose and, though no slouch on the palate, allows the very fine grains through to give a lighter feel. The Jameson 12, meanwhile, with its fuller yet more intricate body, is for those quieter moments either after dinner or before bed and revels in a fatness on the palate which is unusual for Irish whiskey. The Distillery Reserve, with its enormous sherry-spice richness, was designed for contemplation. All three whiskeys excel in their pot-still character as well. These are very fine Irish whiskeys indeed, and if you mix equal proportions of them together (maybe with an extra tad of 1780) the result is your own blend which will launch your tastebuds into orbit.

Yet the best to come from Midleton are different in style again. There are three whiskeys which are not only examples of Irish pot-still magnificence, but are really the last bastions of the style in its truest form. The most easily obtainable is a blend called Powers. Value-for-

Midleton: *This proud old distillery is no longer used, but it remains an impressive museum piece.*

money-wise, it is probably the best deal offered in the world: it sells at the price of a decent blend, yet contains something in the region of 70 per cent pure pot-still whiskey of which 60 per cent is unmalted barley. It all adds up to the ripest, most flavoursome blend you are ever likely to find; something as uniquely Irish as the Blarney Stone and Guinness.

Once upon a time, most Irish whiskey was sold by merchants buying the casks from the distillery and bottling it themselves. Today only one such merchant has been able to keep its name on a label, Mitchel of Dublin. They still produce, via Midleton, a 100 per cent pure pot-still whiskey called Green Spot. Any trip to Ireland must be deemed a failure if you do not return with a bottle of it. Hard to find away from their old store in Kildare Street, Green Spot represents Irish pot-still at its finest: brittle hard, tangy, menthol-cool, yet spicy. This eight-year-old has a touch of everything that is great about Irish whiskey. Slightly easier to find is Redbreast, a 12-year-old pure pot-still re-launched by Irish Distillers: it is not, however, anything like as easy to find as it should be. When Gilbey Vintners ran out of their last-ever stocks of their famous brand they were using some 25-year-old pot-still from the old Jameson Distillery in Dublin. Irish whiskey does not keep so well in the cask as Scotch and it was pretty tired stuff. This is much, much better, with a nose promising a lot and a palate that's happy to oblige. Assertive and full of honey, fudge and spice, a lovely touch of sherry sparks off the rigid pot-still surge. Marvellous stuff.

But what of those looking for some original Midleton to compare with the current make? Well, there is some around. While the Midleton Very Rare, a fine and ever-improving but seriously overpriced vintage blend, originally contained traces of the redundant Midleton, it doesn't now. Instead Irish Distillers launched a one-off called Dungourney from a 1964 cask of Midleton. It is stunning: the acacia honey, pot-still and evocative ripe cornfield nose is reflected in the clean and crisp palate with virtually no oak to spoil the party. A heavier, more accessible Old Midleton (which they correctly call "whisky") was bottled in 1995 by the owners of the excellent Toucan Irish pub in London's Soho. It was distilled before 1960 and consequently has more oak displayed in a eucalyptus and mint nose, but the sweetness and oily riches of the pot still are truly glorious. These two stupendous pot-still bottlings represent probably the last of one of the most drinkable links with a bygone age.

Connoisseur's Selection

JAMESON GOLD 43% – THEIR NEWEST RECRUIT TO THE RANGE AND A WHISKEY OF AMAZING BEAUTY.

POWERS 40% – A CLASSIC IRISH WHISKEY, BRIMMING WITH MOUTH-WATERING POT-STILL.

GREEN SPOT 40% – A PURE POT-STILL WHISKEY FOUND MAINLY IN DUBLIN BUT GAINING FAME FOR ITS ASTONISHING CHARM AND SOPHISTICATION.

COOLEY

For more years than was healthy, the only Irish that could be found around the world's bars was Jameson and Bushmills. Lately, though, some strange names have been appearing in the most unlikely places: one called The Tyrconnell which I spotted in Illinois, and another called Millar's Special Reserve in Germany. And, what is more, they have been very, very drinkable Irish whiskeys. It is amazing what a little competition can do. These brands from Cooley Distillery have set Irish Distillers twitching. They are not part of the great scheme of things, yet in many ways they have done great national service in focusing people's minds on the pleasant surprises that Irish whiskey can bring.

John Locke's: *The old distillery at Kilbeggan in Westmeath is now a whiskey museum.*

The Cooley Distillery itself is one of the hardest to find in the British Isles. It is north-east of Dundalk in a corner of County Louth, just a mile or two away from the border with Northern Ireland and is in just as politically sensitive an area of the Republic as the old Dunville Distillery was, close to the Grosvenor Road in Belfast. Fitting, then, that it produces a Dunville blend. Its official address is Riverstown but you have to work hard to find it on any map, as Riverstown is an area rather than a municipality. It is found on a dwarf peninsula jutting chinlessly between Dundalk Bay and Carlingford Lough, the head being called Cooley Point.

Cooley Distillery offers quite a visual shock in its setting; a beached battleship is not an inaccurate description, though even this is not unique. Driving through the most forsaken area of Inishowen, close to Malin Head, I stumbled across a building of identical design. And, so I discovered, it was designed by the same Czech architect for the same purpose: to distil alcohol from potatoes. The distillery may not win awards for aesthetics, but it is at least painted green which blends in to some degree with the easy-on-the-eye foothills of the Cooley Mountains which eventually lead, after the interruption of the lough, to the truly romantic Mountains of Mourne. It has to be said that what is being made at Cooley today cannot be compared with the industrial alcohol for which it was originally designed. The whiskey of Cooley is, quite simply, superb.

This is the only Irish distillery that uses double distillation. The stills arrived via Northern Ireland where it was hoped they would bring the old Comber Distillery back to life. When that venture was aborted, Cooley gladly took them in hand. They were united with locally made stainless steel washbacks and a mash tun which had seen active service at the now dismantled Inver House Distillery in Scotland. There is, as yet, no official whiskey called Cooley on the market. Some feel it is not a name that inspires. Instead, they have tended toward resurrecting famous old brands and celebrating the wildest area of their country. One brand that has done both is The Tyrconnell, which is both a region and a famous, almost-forgotten, old brand. This is Cooley's stock single malt. As malt production there began only in 1989, it was launched as a mixture of three- and four-year-olds which had matured very quickly; today it is a vatting of fives and sixes. As time goes on, it will get older.

The original label shows three stars, the present one five. Don't be fooled. This has nothing to do with age, it was just felt that it looked better! Some of the very first bottlings of The Tyrconnell were not that great – there were some poor casks around at the time. But the vattings became ironed out and, amazingly, the old three-star is actually superior on the nose to the current five-star, with heaps more sweet malt pounding through. Yet it is the current blend which delivers on the palate, extremely malt-rich, confident and faintly spicy against the first bottling, which died off after a lovely start because of a youthful imbalance with the oak. Cooley single malt is also cropping up around the world under the guise of various own-labels.

If The Tyrconnell already seems a lot older than its five or six years, and boasts excellent weight and balance along with the delicious malt, where does that put the sublime Connemara? Ireland already has some hefty whiskeys, thanks to the older and sherried Jameson brands. But there is nothing else

quite like this. They have used copious amounts of heavily peated malt, becalmed slightly by a small addition of unpeated. The result is a must for those with a bent for the finer Islay malts; though it has none of the oiliness of some of those great distilleries, it is a match in complexity and muscle tone.

Like Midleton, Cooley makes some very high-quality grain whiskey, theirs being slightly more viscous and sweet, so there is also a full array of blends. At first there were just the two, Locke's and Kilbeggan. Originally, there was not a great difference between them, with Locke's edging ahead by virtue of its superior malt ratio. These days they seem to be poles apart in a three-tiered blending portfolio. Top of the range are Inishowen and Millar's Special Reserve. This began life as Millar's Gold Label, but changed name to avoid the wrath of a certain Scotch blender. This is full and lush on the palate and attractively sweet; the Inishowen is reliant on a degree of peated malt to give a unique depth to an Irish blend. Below these, just, and some way ahead of the next two, is Kilbeggan, sweet and well-balanced. On its label is a line drawing of the old Locke's Distillery at Kilbeggan, now the most beautiful museum to whiskey anywhere in the world, but whose warehouses are used to mature Cooley's spirit. Propping up their blends are O'Hara's, a not unpleasant whiskey but very grain-reliant, and Locke's which is disappointingly lacking in charm and complexity by comparison with its earlier form.

Yet, considering the company have only a single malt and single grain to work from, they have done exceptionally well to arrive at these. They have in common a very soft style and a lovely more-ishness. And the really good news is that, provided the company can continue to thrive, the best is still to come.

Connoisseur's Selection

CONNEMARA 40% – EXTRAORDINARY, RICHLY PEATED MALT, CONFIRMS COOLEY'S GREATNESS.

KILBEGGAN 40% – THE FINEST OF THEIR BLENDS, EXCEPTIONALLY WELL BEHAVED AND MALTY.

BUSHMILLS

Travelling around Ireland and finding the remnants of what used to be, from the old distillery at Kilbeggan, the thick-walled and roofless remains of Jameson of Dublin, across the Liffey to the massive, open-aired pot stills of Powers which sit far from the surviving entrance; the crumbling warehouses of Tullamore; and finally to the mass of the old Midleton plant, it becomes obvious that on every one of those sites the making of whiskey was carried out on a far grander scale than in Scotland. This, in part, may have led to their eventual demise.

But at least one distillery remains in Ireland which would not look out of place in

Scotland, be it by the shores of Islay's Loch Indaal, overlooking the Cromarty Firth, or even on a riverbank somewhere in Keith. Old Bushmills Distillery, to give it its full title, is the last surviving in Northern Ireland and really looks the part. It has twin pagodas which exude late-Victorian, or perhaps Edwardian, charm with their fish-scaled tiling. The stone walls are old and solid and it retains that feeling of tradition and splendour. It is set in the awesome beauty of County Antrim with its eye-soothing hills and mountains accentuating the wide and deep-carved valleys; its numerous little hidden beaches and quaint harbours; and the extraordinary geological freak that is the Giant's Causeway, a series of basalt columns formed by a lava flow at the time when these glorious lands were still being shaped.

Bushmills, enjoying its own relative agelessness, remains something of an enigma. It is a distillery which makes malt whiskey yet, truth to tell, it is currently a better blending whiskey than it is a single. It makes single malt now, though that was not always the case: when Barnard arrived there in the 1880s he watched them distil traditional Irish pot-still, that mixture of malted and unmalted barley. The change-over, though, was not long in coming. In my home I have a Bushmills bottle, empty alas, that has been identified as being from just this side of the turn of the last century. Interestingly, the glass moulding shows a traditional, bulbous-type pot and etched on that are the words "pure malt". One of Bushmills' other little quirks is the knack of having strange and maybe misleading stories told about it.

One such story was told to me by a friend in the USA. Apparently people he knew were tipping bottles of Bushmills down the sink and vowing never to buy it again after reports filtered through alleging that the distillery carried out strict sectarian practices, namely refusing to employ Catholic staff. Not working at the distillery, obviously I have no idea what goes on at job interviews. But it was a story I found difficult to believe. Certainly, just yards from the distillery there is a housing estate so fiercely Protestant that the kerb stones are painted loyalist red, white and blue. But against that, Bushmills is part of Dublin-based Irish Distillers, which is in turn owned by the French drinks company Pernod Ricard, so there are two strong Catholic cultures acting as a possible counterbalance to Protestant sectarianism, should one be needed. Also, the town of Bushmills has one of the lowest Catholic populations in Northern Ireland. It sounds as though an awful lot of decent whiskey has been pointlessly wasted but it all serves to remind us of the tensions in the province.

A much harder story to swallow is Irish Distillers' claim that Bushmills is the oldest distillery in the world. It isn't. It is certainly quite an aged place and my tell-tale old bottle says, just as the trademark application did a century ago, that it was "Established 1784". Illicit distilling is said to have been carried out on the site for some half a century before. Yet obviously such antiquity is not enough for some because every bottle today makes a point of the year 1608 (there is never any mention of 1784 at all) and claims it is "from the world's oldest whiskey distillery".

The reason for the claim is that in 1608 a licence was granted to Sir Thomas Phillips, King James I's deputy for the plantation of Ulster, for whiskey to be made "within the countie of Colrane, otherwise called O Cahanes country or within the territorie called the Rowte in Co. Antrim". Now that is a pretty big tract of land and indeed, until 1978, whiskey was being made by Coleraine Distillery, though they did not make such audacious claims regarding the age of their distillery. The simple fact is that Bushmills Distillery did not begin life until 1784; it is the oldest whiskey distillery in Ireland, but not the world. Just to underline the point, if you or I set up a distillery in the same area, although established 1996 or 1997, we would share the same dubious right as Bushmills to claim to be the oldest distillery in the world. Or maybe I could set up in the same part of Scotland from which Friar John Cor operated, and date my new company 1494: that is the kind of madness that these marketing follies encourage. For the serious

Bushmills Distillery: *Founded in 1784, a distillery whose malt just gets better and better.*

whisky-drinker there is nothing quite so frustrating or irritating as seeing a marketing wheeze over time become carved on a tablet of stone as false "history".

It is for such reasons that I take very little notice of what is claimed on the outside of whisk(e)y bottles and look inside instead. In the case of Bushmills, I am usually pretty impressed with what I find and, of late, have become increasingly so. Although the standard 10-year-old single malt leaves me pretty unexcited, the malt, when given just a few more years to develop, appears to build up in style and intensity. The Italians get the chance to taste it as a five-year-old, and an attractively, malty, sweet and oily drop it is, too. Yet by the time it has doubled its age it has thinned out in character.

Perhaps this is partly down to the fact that at Bushmills the malt is triple-distilled, which generates a lighter spirit character. To bolster things up a bit, Bushmills add some fresh sherry cask to their vattings to instil some extra body and fruit. This can be tasted at its fullest in an 11-year-old Bushmills called Distiller's Reserve sold exclusively from Heathrow Airport in the Allders Whiskies of the World series. Here the sherry hangs heavy, though not so heavy as to prevent an initial first-rate sweetness and then a chocolate maltiness seeping through to add excellent balance. Yet, even with all this weight about, the ethereal notes are the most dominant. To a lesser degree the same can also be said of Bushmills' Downtown Radio, a 10-year-old brought out to mark the Belfast station's 20th anniversary, though the second-fill sherry casks used still add a certain voluptuousness. The pick, however, of the Bushmills' malts is Distillery Reserve, a quite outstanding 12-year-old. The slightly oily, toffee-cream nose is nothing less than superb. This cream toffee explodes on the palate too to help form the sweetest and most distinguished Bushmills' malt I've ever come across. I'd be astonished if they could transfer such quality to a standard 12-year-old, but it might be fun trying.

But where Bushmills is already established for undoubted high standards is in its blends. Black Bush remains the most majestic, despite a late and vigorous challenge by another duty-free-only blend called 1608. Black Bush is the silkiest of all Ireland's blends. There is a remarkable malt content of 75 per cent and this seven-year-old is mixed with some very good six-year-old grain from Midleton. It's a wonderful marriage; it may be beaten for complexity and sheer mouth-watering bliss by Powers, but Black Bush clings assiduously to its obvious intention of singing lullabies to the tastebuds. By contrast, the 1608 does all it can to shake some life back into the palate. Since just 10 per cent of its make-up is grain whiskey, it is only just a blend. And the addition of a barrel or two of 14-year-old to the predominant 12 helps underline the fizzing spiciness amid the colourful sherry tones. It is a whiskey that is just too easy to drink – just as well you can only stock up with a litre when travelling around the world: there are insufficient reserves to make this a mainstream blend on the more easily accessible shelves.

A couple of other blends are not anything like so good, but now both better than they have been. A brand made exclusively for the Northern Irish market is Coleraine, grain-dominant and one which you simply don't bother to sit down and savour. The other is considerably less obscure – Bushmills' Original, or White Bush, as it is sometimes known. This really was a pretty awful blend a couple of years back, totally devoid of charm. Stung into action by criticism (of which mine was probably the loudest), the blenders at Bushmills have done something about it and changed certain aspects of this whiskey, including the age. The result is still not a classic, but for the first time in memory I can taste this stuff now and not grimace while doing so. In fact, it can be almost pleasant.

For years nothing new came out of Bushmills, but things are changing. The launch of 1608 in the early 1990s was a major, and pleasant, surprise. But over the last year there has been enormous experimentation with different cask use. At some stage it is likely we will be seeing a malt finished off in port pipes, as is done with Glenmorangie. They have bought 54 of them and have just launched a 16-year-old. I managed to taste the whiskey after it had spent five months rounding off in a port pipe and it was not, it has to be said, overly impressive, being very confused and fizzy on the palate. Their experimentation has taken Bushmills into the unknown and blender Barry Walsh has kept his nerve to witness the contrasting wood styles marry into something that seduces the nose if not the tastebuds. The aroma is extraordinarily subtle with orange and marzipan linked to praline. Some pepperiness on the nose explodes on the palate with unusual winey notes. This is something glorious and different with panache. There is something very exciting about a distillery as traditional as Bushmills being prepared to rewrite the textbooks as far as Irish whiskey is concerned.

Connoisseur's Selection

Bushmills Distiller's Reserve: Cask Strength – Always an excellent choice.

5  BOURBON & OTHER AMERICAN WHISKEYS

For the best part of a century now Scottish and Irish distillers have been happily receiving the plaudits. Screeds have been written in countless books and articles about how the ancient art of distilling was practised and perfected in those beautiful, wild lands. By contrast, very little has ever been said about American whiskey, which is rather a shame, because, of all the distilling nations, no spirit is so closely interwoven into a nation's fabric as bourbon is with the USA.

Cumberland Gap: *Grey brooding skies guarantee lush pastures and reflect the character of Kentucky's deep and extraordinary whiskeys.*

George Washington made whiskey. Abraham Lincoln's father worked in a Kentucky distillery and even sold his house for a mixture of cash and whiskey. It has provoked wars and offered up legendary characters. And the irony is that it was brought to the country by the Scottish and the Irish as they headed west through the Cumberland Gap from Virginia with their meagre resources.

Of those resources, one of the most important was their ability to distil: the extra money they received for their spirit could mean the difference between success and failure during those barren, inhospitable winters. Two centuries ago, Kentucky was perceived as the promised land: the Indians had called it "Ken-tah-teh", "the land where we will live". Yet, despite its natural wealth, some of its inhabitants are among the poorest in America and whose illicit moonshine whiskey to this day brings in much-needed revenue.

Though there have been hundreds of distilleries in America, the production of bourbon, from the very first mash to the final distillation, today can be found only in Kentucky and Indiana. The industry has vanished in Maryland and Pennsylvania and hangs on by the slenderest of threads in Virginia. A sub-species of bourbon, Tennessee whiskey, is produced by just two distilleries and, while vastly different to each other in style, are often served outside the USA when a bourbon is asked for.

This is perhaps the key to bourbon's image problem. Despite its extensive history, it has failed to cash in on the romance of its past and grab the attention like Scotch. Ask anyone on the street what bourbon is and they will stare blankly at you and at best mouth something about Kentucky. Ask them to name a bourbon and Jack Daniel's, a Tennessee whiskey, will probably be the one.

Yet the distillers of Kentucky and Tennessee have so much to beat their chests about. In many ways this region of the world surpasses Scotland and Ireland for natural beauty. It cannot compete for rugged coasts – the closest thing it has to one is the northern state line of Kentucky which follows the Ohio river. And there are no sleepy distilleries set beside snow-capped mountains. Yet the distilleries of Kentucky are found in deepest bluegrass country famous for its song and horses. There are enormous barns where the locally grown tobacco dries. And for miles as far as you can see there are gentle undulating pastures and forested hills. There are also impressive mountains to negotiate on the way to Tennessee, another state whose beauty has been extolled by a myriad of passing writers.

Perhaps, though, the most striking thing about the region is its enormity. These are big lands with small populations and people who will always think of doing you a good turn before a bad one. It is a land I have come to love and, for part of the year now, have made my home. In it is made a whiskey which is not so much good as glorious. Because, if any good has come from the terrible numbers of closures the industry has had to endure thanks to a downturn in demand, it is that the average glass of bourbon from any Kentucky distillery is of better quality than its counterparts anywhere else in the world. Frankly, it has to be to survive.

Hopefully the world will finally wake up and discover just what magnificence can be found in these bottles with often dowdy, old-fashioned labels.

Spoilt for choice: *America's fine whiskeys.*

THE HISTORY OF BOURBON

Whiskey may not have been the first spirit distilled on the North American continent, but it has certainly become the most important. Indeed, whiskey came low down the list of spirits which the very first settlers of New England imbibed. Brandies made from the local fruits were their first source of fortification. Apple trees abounded and cider brandy – applejack they called it – was popular, as were brandies made from peaches, plums and cherries. However, in the winter months, the fruit gave way to potatoes and turnips. Rarely, spare grain was used but in such minute amounts that it is unlikely the spirit was consumed by any other than the family which made it.

It was rum that was to become the regular tipple of the New World inhabitants, with stills working the molasses which were brought up in the sugar-cane ships from the West Indies. Contemporary reports of the time claim the rums of New York were on a par with those of the Caribbean and represented the most important single industry of North America.

Only when members of the Celtic race began to flood into America to avoid starvation and religious persecution in Great Britain, did distilling with grain become a common occurrence. But the Scots-Irish found their religious beliefs no more tolerated in the established settlements of the new continent than they had been in their homeland. Understandably, they were keen to move further west into Pennsylvania and Virginia to find land of their own, away from political and religious interference, despite the near-certain hardships they would face. But go they did, and with them they took the art of making whiskey.

Those who settled in Pennsylvania discovered a land where rye grew abundantly, so they made their whiskey from that. In 1779 there was even a law passed forbidding whiskey to be made from any grain other than rye and barley. The further west settlers moved, the harder it became to cultivate small grains such as rye, barley, wheat and oats. So another type of grain, maize, which grew naturally in that part of the world – Indian Corn as it came to be known – was used instead. Today, by law, bourbon whiskey, to qualify as such, must contain 51 per cent of that Indian corn. The early settlers had chosen wisely.

Daniel Morgan: *Whiskey warrior.*

However, even after those earliest families had bedded down in their new Pennsylvanian lands, they were still not beyond the ever-lengthening reach of government interference. The British Government had passed the first Excise law there as far back as 1684. But, as the gaugers of Scotland and Ireland discovered on their much smaller patches, the implementation of such laws was far from straightforward. Thus, at first, Pennsylvanians managed to ignore government edicts. Things changed, though, as the eighteenth century drew to a close and it all came to a head after a law, that all stills had to be registered, was passed on March 3, 1791.

It had been ten years since the cessation of the American War of Independence, when in 1794, fighting broke out again after three years of smouldering tension. This time it was between Pennsylvanian farmers and the militia, brought in to collect payments for whiskey. The locals were outraged at having to pay a tax on something they grew themselves which, had they eaten it, they would have had to pay no tax on at all. Many had escaped the British Isles for precisely this reason. They were further angered at the hardships that the fines caused. Unlike similar unrest in Scotland and Ireland, where the battle was between small, localized pockets of distillers and smugglers against Excise men and limited army support, in Pennsylvania the farmers decided to join forces and fight together: the Whiskey Rebellion had begun. During the ensuing unrest there were deaths on both sides, but it was the government which won in the end, with no little thanks to the 15,000 men Washington, himself a distiller, sent in to put down the country's first civil war. Amazingly, it took him more men to defeat the whiskey army than the British one.

By the time the whiskey wars were over, the first bourbon distillers were already operating and well-established in Kentucky, many having ventured west through the Cumberland Gap from Maryland and Virginia. The name bourbon derives from a county within Kentucky, which had become the ninth state of the USA in 1792. Before becoming a fully fledged state of its own, Kentucky had been the western-most county of Virginia. It was then split into five, of which one enormous county was Bourbon. Today, having been divided in two, it is quite tiny by comparison and its capital, Paris, is a liquor-shop-free zone, though contrary to common belief you can drink there in a couple of bars and restaurants. Over 200 years ago old Bourbon county was well stocked with whiskey-makers. Already the whiskey of Kentucky was regarded by some as the most prized in America; and the best of all was said to come from Bourbon.

Any number of whiskey labels or books will tell you who the first Bourbon distiller was. The favourites for the honour seem to be Elijah Craig, Evan Williams, James Ritchie, Daniel Boone's cousin, Wattie, and others. But the unromantic truth is no one really knows for sure, or ever will. Certainly these gentlemen were among the front-runners but to name a single person is purely fanciful.

What is beyond doubt is that, as the nineteenth century progressed, the march of commercial whiskey-making in the USA gathered pace. In 1838 Morewood reported, without stipulating just what was being made, that there were 3,594 stills in Pennsylvania, 2,000 in Kentucky, 591 in New York (many for making rum and brandy), 560 in Connecticut, 343 in Ohio and 126 in Georgia. The number of stills in Tennessee was unknown, but 801,000 gallons of spirit was produced there, roughly a third of the output of Kentucky and Virginia.

The early commercial distilleries of America were crude affairs. Most buildings were made from timber and, though pot stills were prevalent early on, as the century progressed they eventually gave way to continuous stills. Fermentation would have been a particularly extraordinary sight, with barrels often preferred to large vats. At the Daviess County Distillery in Owensboro in 1883, for instance, the stills were fed by no less than 720 mash tubs. And it was around that time that distillers began to use a sour-mash method of distillation in preference to sweet mash.

Sweet mash is the traditional form of fermentation used by Scottish and Irish distillers, where fresh grain is used in each fermentation. Sour mash uses a portion of the previous fermentation, already stripped of all its sugars and therefore "sour". The idea of this was that the acids within the sour mash were able to keep certain natural bacteria under control in the hot, humid temperatures in which the distillery operated and thus prevented the mash from spoiling. The character of bourbon whiskey as we know it today was slowly but surely taking shape.

As the growth of these distilleries continued, so did a number of movements designed to put them out of business. The Temperance issue became a major one, with organizations often closely associated with churches whipping up choruses of disapproval. The priggish attitude toward the whiskey industry can still be seen today, with many histories of states and counties which were written at that time refusing to acknowledge the existence of the whiskey industry, despite it being, in some places, among the most vital they had. Yet the movement against distillers was such that even the mountain people of Kentucky, who had once left the moonshiners to go about their business – and were occasionally known to have their homes or barns burnt down if they didn't – began to inform on their distilling neighbours in increasing numbers.

County by county, state by state, the distillation of whiskey and the drinking of alcoholic beverages in general was being stopped. The Prohibition period of 1919 to 1933 is one of the best-known periods of American social history. From it arose a whole new language and system of black-market racketeering. It was a period when vote-winning, bible-thumping and knee-jerk extremism defeated common sense and intellectualism at a price, i.e. organized crime. The country still pays today. Yet it is not commonly understood that Prohibition had arrived in the USA long before the Volsted Act came into being. Tennessee, for instance, had been dry since 1910, with its distilleries being forced north into Kentucky and beyond.

By the time the Act had been repealed, the damage done to the bourbon industry was almost incalculable. Much of the stock made prior to 1919 had been used for "medicinal" purposes, stolen by gangs or was too old and woody to drink. Most distillers had insufficient capital to start all over again. Worse still, perhaps, American drinkers had become used to lighter-flavoured whiskey smuggled in from Canada, Scotland and Ireland. Bourbon was pretty heavy stuff by comparison, and remains so today. Rye was heavier still and it has all but disappeared. Subsequently, the once-thriving industries in

Dram busters: *Smug-looking Federal Agents show off their latest seizure.*

Maryland, Pennsylvania and Missouri vanished and even across Kentucky can be seen the stricken carcases of literally dozens of once-famous, but sadly now-forgotten distilleries.

If there is a movement against bourbon today, and with ever-shrinking sales on the home market it certainly seems that way, the reasons are to do with health. There has been a move away from strong alcohol by those worried that the inside of a whiskey bottle is injurious to their well-being. Oddly, those who appear not to agree are doctors, for whom I have given many a tasting. Instead, quality rather than quantity appears to be the in-thing, and probably rightly so. Kentucky, Tennessee and now even Californian distillers are happy to oblige by providing high-strength, high-price and invariably high-quality whiskeys which are to be savoured rather than guzzled.

With only 11 working distilleries in Kentucky and two in Tennessee, we can now only pray that the shrinkage within the industry has stopped. At least the moonshiners are still hard at work in the mountains of Georgia, Tennessee and Kentucky. But it is about time that the nation became re-acquainted with the spirit that their forebears once actually took up arms to protect: rye and bourbon – in moderation, of course. Because along that route lies happiness. And rediscovery.

KENTUCKY

Frankfort

From the hilltop grave of frontiersman par excellence, Daniel Boone, much of the downtown of the city of Frankfort can be admired. The view is how you imagine every American town to be: neat, homely buildings in linear formation, the streets easily identified; elegant, larger establishments dotted here and there; and crowning it all the state capital – St Paul's without the grime. All this against a backdrop of heavily wooded, steeply climbing hills and the deep running waters of the Kentucky river, offering a sometimes clear blue, but often murky brown, natural border. It was the river which indirectly gave the settlement its name. Stephen Frank was an early explorer killed by Indians after he had camped overnight by a cave on the river bank. The crossing and settlement that followed remember him, and Frankfort was born.

Daniel Boone would have been happy to view this panorama of 200 years of tasteful growth: you cannot see the shopping malls from here.

Boone's relatives later became leading Kentucky distillers, so it may irk him somewhat that another thing you cannot see from his resting place is a distillery. There is one in Frankfort – well, two really, but both follow the water trail away from town. The nearest is at Leestown, itself a one-time, tiny, frontier community which has now been nibbled at, though not swallowed up, by the expansion of Kentucky's capital. The distillery is an old one and these days goes by the name of the Leestown Distilling Company. None of their whiskeys is known under that title, but if you live in the USA, the name Ancient Age might ring a bell.

Daniel Boone: *Pioneer spirit.*

Ageless: *The differing styles of the Ancient Age distillery architecture.*

ANCIENT AGE

Certain American whiskeys are very well known, banging the drum of tradition and pride. Others do a very quiet job and yet still make quite exquisite whiskey. Without any doubt, the bourbon of the Ancient Age Distillery represents some of the world's finest whiskey. To my taste there is only one other Kentucky distillery which outshines it in terms of class.

Had Ancient Age been part of a major world spirit producer, it would by now have received the international recognition it deserves. At the moment it has to make do with regular Gold and Silver medals for its single-barrel bourbons. The time for its wonderful AAA 10-year-old, probably the most complex standard bourbon on the market, will come.

The distillery itself is about as impressive as anything of its ilk on the North American continent. It shares a similarity with the now-deceased Gooderham and Worts Distillery in Toronto, Canada, in that its buildings reflect many years of change and expansion. Like Gooderham and Worts, Ancient Age was built on the waterside and the steps which led down to the boats which once serviced the distillery can still be made out. Distilling here dates back to the 1860s under the auspices of the Blanton family. A decade or two later it was in the hands of Edmund Haynes Taylor, who sold the distillery to Captain George T. Stagg so he could concentrate on the building of a newer plant on Glenns Creek, now known as the Old Taylor Distillery. Taylor had already called the Leestown distillery the Old Fashioned Copper Distillery, and from it the OFC brand became famous for the best part of a century. As the Stagg Distillery, it was one of only six in Kentucky to be granted a licence to distil during Prohibition, the others being Glenmore at Owensboro, and the Old Forester, Stitzel Weller, National and Frankfort distilleries in Louisville. Perhaps because it was for small-scale, prescription-only demand, the management at Stagg did not take up their option and the plant remained silent through that grim period.

Ancient Age Distillery is an architectural historian's – as well as a whiskey historian's – dream. Some of the buildings, especially those where the old Dickel Distillery was housed when it moved north following Tennessee's early move into Prohibition, display the same limestone materials favoured by the distillery builders who preferred nearby Glenns Creek as their distilling base. The company recently brought in a specialist who studied the Ancient Age site and repainted sections of it in the same salmon pink/brick red livery he discovered the first builders had used. Rounded off with dark green window frames, the distillery can give a bit of a jolt to the visitor seeing it for the first time.

The distillery is best viewed in winter or early spring. From the other side of the bank of the Kentucky, close to the sewage works, the distillery with its A–Z of building styles can be seen in full, capped by an elaborate water tower with Ancient Age written massively in white on a background of red which, when dusk falls, shines like a beacon for miles around. With steam rising into the cold air, this is quite a picture, and one that cannot be seen during the summer months because of thick foliage. However, there are other compensations then. Children can come and play in gloriously lawned and wooded gardens,

As you were: *Colonel Blanton who is immortalized by a full-size statue within the distillery grounds.*

through which a small stream runs, liberally forded by delightful wooden bridges. By night, the gravestone-white, sculpted figure of Colonel Blanton, the legendary Master Distiller, casts a ghostly figure. In the morning a blue heron might be seen breakfasting on the goldfish, and the figure of the Colonel casts a lengthy, more benevolent shadow.

Inside those buildings will be found a straightforward distillery sprinkled with typical Kentucky good humour. Up one flight of steps there is a warning: "Quiet! Tasters at Work". A doubler stands sentry by the stillhouse door and one flight up a beer still works at only a third its capacity. The fermenting room is unforgettable: 12 iron-alloy giants each holding 92,000 gallons. Sometimes the strange, doughy aroma of fermenting pure un-malted barley, for the Japanese market, might be spotted.

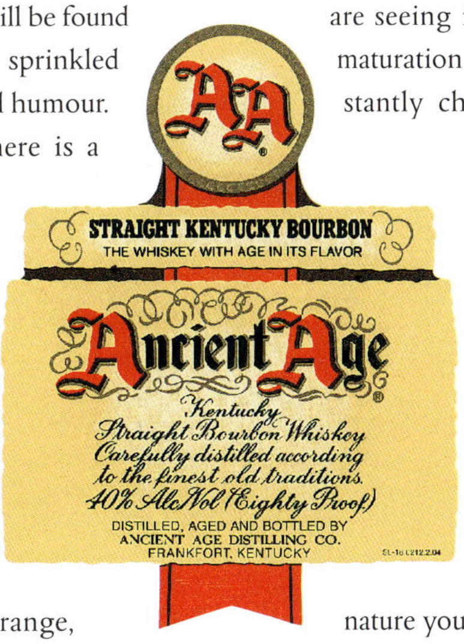

Things tend to tick over rather than hum at Ancient Age. But there is no shortage of staff. Few distilleries have such labour-intensive bottling practices. In the single-barrel bottling hall, or room, really, there are about 25 people unpacking, gluing, twisting and re-packing things. But the company takes enormous pride in its single-barrel brands and considers the expense well justified.

They are trying ways of saving money in other directions, though. At the moment they are seeing if they can speed up the maturation of their whiskey by constantly changing the temperature within their heated warehouses. If it doesn't work within two years, the experiment will be abandoned. The company's main driving force, vice-president Joe Darmond, is philosophical about the chances of success, saying: "Usually, when you try to hurry nature you screw it up."

Mondays are an interesting day to visit Ancient Age. Then you might get a glimpse of a small, avuncular-looking man, sometimes wearing a cap, usually a smile, who likes to make sure that things are running as they should. He is Elmer T. Lee, one of only four

Connoisseur's Selection

Hancock's Reserve – Bad malt character and startling coffee and honey finish. Brilliant.

A living legend: *Elmer T. Lee, one of only four men alive to have a bourbon named after him.*

distillery managers at Leestown since 1912. His stint came between 1952 and 1980 and, though retired, it is still his responsibility to taste and approve every barrel which goes on to provide the whiskey which carries his name. He is one of only three men living to have a whiskey named after him. Perhaps, with no less than three Elmer Lees listed in the Frankfort phone book, the label includes the middle initial T to save any confusion. Elmer's knowledge of bourbon-making is encyclopedic. And not only could he make good whiskey, he knew how to spot it in the warehouse. A single taste of his Elmer T. Lee brand is all that is required to show that he still does.

On the international stage it is the distillery's single-barrel whiskeys which are earning them the spotlight. For sheer oomph only Wild Turkey is their peer. Ancient Age single-barrel or barrel-proof whiskeys are classic bourbons, all variations on a theme. There is no doubting their pedigree. To nose, at least, Elmer T. Lee is the leader. The complexity is awesome and somehow shows gracefulness and full body in harmony. To taste, it starts delicately with butterfly notes of corn and rye with strong oak-vanilla. These single barrel whiskeys range between six and eight years but always retain that same character. The next best to nose is another with which Elmer is closely associated, Blanton's Single Barrel; though being a bigger seller he does not inspect each and every cask used. This, the first single-barrel bourbon, has been on the market over a decade now. It is much more powerful and fruity than the Elmer T. Lee, though not as sweet and grainy as the effervescent Rock Hill Farms single-barrel. Benchmark is the softest, least clear-cut Ancient-Age style but exudes enormous generic bourbon quality. It's a clever piece of work in the hands of present-day Master Distiller Gary Gayheart who has proved his right to follow in the revered footsteps of Colonel Blanton and Elmer T. Lee. Gary's own masterpiece is Hancock's Reserve which, though left behind by the Elmer T. Lee nose, catches up with a toffee-malt-corn complexity on the palate that lingers forever. The late coffee and honey rounds it off beautifully. Drink any of these whiskeys and you will be spoiled for life.

If you are ever in Kentucky look out for another magnificent Leestown bourbon, the 10-year-old Ancient Ancient Age. This is perhaps the one I drink most when in the state, not least because Kentucky is the only place you can find it. It is difficult to say exactly why AAA is so good. Very often a decade of Kentucky summers in the wood can mean the kiss of death for a bourbon: very few can comfortably negotiate so much oak and none of the single barrels dare age that long. Yet barely an acorn can be detected in the AAA. The nose is pretty basic. It is only when it arrives on the palate that you realize that your tastebuds are in for a rare treat. The gentle spices refuse to go away, as does the finish which begins a liquorice attack before backing down and going in with intense cream toffee. Even at 86 proof it provides a finale of beguiling length.

It is encouraging to know that not all Ancient Age whiskeys border on the exotic. There are a number which are simply old-fashioned whiskeys, too young to impress with anything more than a bludgeoning beauty. Some don't quite make it that far. For the home market there is a 38-month-old as green as an unripened orange and nearly as sharp. Nothing other than caramel makes it out of this one. One-dimensional and unsophisticated are its good points and, though the metallic hardness does have some attractions, the finish is unforgiving. But it just goes to show what an extra 10 months in those warehouses can do. The standard Ancient Age, a four-year-old, which is marketed outside the USA and sometimes called Bullitt, is much fatter and sweeter with an oiliness which softens everything considerably. While the 38-month-old is geared, even by the distillers, to be nothing more special than the foil for ice and a splash on a very warm day, its slightly older brother keeps good company on its own, especially the sweeter still, even nuttier, 100 proof version.

There are other versions, like a six-year-old, which is confusingly called 10-star. This doesn't quite have the same charm as a four- or a 10-year-old, though now we're being picky: it is still superb but with a cream-toffee quality one normally associates with only the very finest Canadian whiskies. And there is another one called Barrel 107, a 10-year-old of matching proof which is a colossus on the palate with big notes of violets and dark cherry. Astounding.

It is when you have learned to admire and love every aspect of these bourbons, and as you sit on the wooden veranda gazing at the hallowed image of Colonel Blanton reflected in the sparkling stream, that the realization suddenly hits you: Ancient Age is not so much a distillery but an institution. A keeper of the very finest bourbon traditions.

There is no sadder sight in the whole of the whiskey industry than a dead distillery – except maybe three dead distilleries all in a row. And until the summer of 1996 that was what you would find on the squeezed-in backroad due south out of Frankfort, following the picturesque Glenns Creek.

What made the sight all the worse was the fact that this was right in the heart of Kentucky. Yet, miraculously, it seems, one distillery has risen from the grave so that the aroma of mashing corn drifts down the narrow valley once more.

As the Old Crow Distillery was in operation as recently as 1987, and all its plant is still in working order, you would be forgiven for thinking it would be that one. Or maybe the Old Taylor Distillery a mile away which, though pretty weather-beaten after two decades of inactivity, could run again if the money was forthcoming. No, it is neither of these. Instead, the 25th anniversary of the closure of the Labrot and Graham Distillery three miles or so south, the other side of Millville, has been marked in 1996 by its re-opening.

LABROT AND GRAHAM

Of all Kentucky's distilleries this has always been the one I loved most from an aesthetic and maybe purely romantic point of view. I never managed to taste its old whiskey, but it seems inconceivable that such a place was capable of producing anything other than great bourbon. Until the spring of 1995, the distillery was little more than a shell, hanging grimly yet successfully on to the last vestiges of honour and tradition. Above a door a millstone had been inscribed in badly faded black paint: "Old Oscar Pepper Distillery Est. 1838 Labrot and Graham Est. 1878".

Yet still it retained an extraordinary beauty, its rich-textured, chunky limestone walls in striking contrast to the blue waters and deep green pastures which surround it. It looked especially glorious from the road above. A house stood on the top of the hill and, looking down from there, the distillery appeared to defy nature by continuing to stand. Some smaller buildings had already given up the fight and tumbled into ruin or near-ruin, though the warehouses, some of stone, others of light-red brick, looked as sturdy as the barrels they once housed.

The distillery was patrolled cheerfully by a stray dog called Bourbon, which my young son, James, befriended, and who would take us for walks around the empty acres beside the river close by the distillery's dam. In a tree overlooking the distillery a Red Cardinal would make its guttural, hollow call as it watched us play and occasionally a Goatsucker swooped down nearby. If there was a heaven on earth, this was it.

It does not seem that long ago, yet now the distillery has been restored and a visitor's centre to accommodate an expected 100,000 tourists a year has been erected where the old house used to be.

And, when it is ready, this will be no ordinary whiskey, either. Unlike any other bourbon currently produced in Kentucky, this is being made exclusively in copper pot stills. When Brown-Forman decided that they wanted to make a very special small batch whiskey, they decided not to stint in the process. Part of the $10 million-plus budget includes buying back a distillery they closed and lands they sold off in the 1970s and three stills made and shipped over from Forsyths, the famous coppersmiths in the Scottish Highlands.

As I was told when things were still in the planning stage: "We want to go a long way back to re-creating how the first distillers made their whiskey in Kentucky."

It is unlikely that those hardy families who left Ireland and Scotland to battle their

Connoisseur's Selection

WOODFORD RESERVE – A CLASSY SWEET BOURBON WITH LASHINGS OF CARAMEL TOFFEE (DISTILLED AT EARLY TIMES).

Spirited revival: *Three brand-new pot-stills mark the return to life of the Labrot & Graham Distillery.*

way through the Cumberland Gap and into Kentucky would have used triple distillation on quite the same scale as it is being used here and, if they did, they would have used stills considerably smaller than those at Labrot and Graham. But you can only admire the sentiment.

It was decided to make the mashbill identical to Old Forester: 72 per cent corn, 18 rye, 10 malted barley, but what will arrive from those barrels in 2001 will not be remotely like that style of whiskey. The pot stills will ensure that. They have eschewed the temptation to produce Kentucky's one and only malt whiskey, and rightly so: Labrot and Graham made bourbon, not malt. They have already launched one brand, Woodford Reserve, named after the up-market county in which it is situated. It's from the same recipe and distilled at Early Times. Master Blender Lincoln Henderson picked a number of barrels much sweeter than the normal Old Forester style and put them into Labrot and Graham's H Warehouse. The result is a classy, sweet, truly sumptuous seven-year-old bourbon with lashings of melt-in-the-mouth caramel toffee.

The owners have even made the first of the three pot stills different to anything else on earth. It looks the same as any other pot still from the top, though from the bottom it takes the shape of a spinning-top. As a safety measure against losing too much bourbon character, the team who designed the distillery decided it was sensible to run solid wash through the first still, using steam to meet the beer on a similar principal as a continuous still, but since it was in a pot the spirit came out with much lower alcohol and more flavour, thanks to its contact with so much copper.

The previously untested system caused a few hearts in mouths: the process created a vortex inside the still which made the thing shudder, but they have countered that now. Making life a lot simpler, the high wines still (or intermediate, as they would call it in Scotland or Ireland) and spirit still both distill from clear liquid.

After these experiments, including some using different mashbills, the stills were placed in the old building side by side. In place of the old steel fermenters are two tiny beauties, holding just 7,500 gallons each, both made from cypress wood. Two cooling coils stand like skeletal ribs to show where two more will be going.

In the spring of 1995 I had taken from the corroding pipes of the old fermenters some grain solids of the last-ever beer to run from it. These, like the cookers which were at the back of the distillery, had now gone. During the previous week the first new beer had been worked through stills one and two. At 12.40 the spirit still was heated. And so it was that at 1.56 p.m., Kentucky time, I was honoured, almost a year to the day as at Isle of Arran, to be the first person to taste the first potable spirit from a new distillery.

After he had turned the swivel spout into the spirit receiver, Brown-Forman's prodigy Master Blender Steve Hughes filled a glass and sniffed. I filled a glass and tasted. We had been monitoring the spirit's progress up until that point. Considering it had undergone three distillations and considering the mash had consisted of mainly corn rather than barley, it was remarkably rich. There was very soft spice but the sweetness was fruity and maybe a little nutty, thanks to the rye which had lasted the journey well. The finale had distinct shades of cocoa powder, starting slightly sweet but finishing pleasingly bitter. Lincoln Henderson later thought of the exact way to describe it: praline.

For many people the high quality of the spirit came as an enormous relief. They had already run the stills and made tests over at the Early Times Distillery in Louisville with Glen Moray's manager, Edwin Dodson, being brought over from the Highlands to show the way. So they were confident. But that training did not allow for the surprise of a steam valve blowing as the spirit still began warming up and a workman accidentally leaning against the still's emergency shut-off button in mid-distillation.

These were frustrating incidents at the time, but will soon be another story to tell in the already long and marvellous history of Labrot and Graham. It was here that a distillery manager decided to overcome pilfering of the whiskey by tainting a few barrels. Those who were off work sick the next day ended up in jail. And a stonemason working on the restoration of the building pointed to the weighbridge and said: "See that? That's where my uncle dropped dead on the spot."

This really is the most colourful whiskey country in Kentucky. At the Old Taylor Distillery, where I have a tiny home, my landlord Cecil now plans to try to resurrect distilling at the plant, perhaps by the introduction of very small pot stills. The Old Crow plant was started by the same Pepper family which began the Oscar Pepper Distillery before it was sold to Mr Labrot and Mr Graham. The Peppers are said to have begun distilling in the vicinity of the Old Crow Distillery as far back as the 1780s. And there was legal distillation going on there in 1812 before the distillery was formally established. On the other bank opposite the distillery an ancient stone pathway takes you toward the Peppers' old home, which is inside the building that now stands there.

There is no more enchanting a distillery than this one, as forthcoming generations of tourists will doubtless discover with immense pleasure.

No longer will my son or I be able to spend quiet evenings in its grounds alone with nature, a whistle or a call bringing four light and nimble legs scampering fast and affectionately toward us. Bourbon has gone. But, thank heavens, the whiskey is back.

Blossoming distillery: *Labrot & Graham's pot-still whiskey will not be ready for bottling until 2001.*

Lawrenceburg

WILD TURKEY

You do not have to travel very far in Kentucky before something about the place makes your jaw drop. Usually, it is related to the scenery. Often, it is the whiskey. Now and again, it is a combination of the two. At Wild Turkey, the sound of jaws clattering to the ground can be heard many miles distant.

The etched beauty of Kentucky, where for hundreds of thousands of years rivers have cut their single-minded way through yielding limestone strata, makes for the most spectacular of backdrops. And when the Ripy brothers followed in their father's footsteps by building a distillery further up the cliff-face from his at Tyrone, a short cart-ride from Lawrenceburg, they seemed to know what they were doing.

A contemporary photo of E.F's, J.C's and Forest Ripy's investment could have been taken on top of an inhospitable Yorkshire moor. Characterless buildings with a tell-tale chimney are cloaked in what seems to be mist. Today those buildings appear just as dowdy, the unusual brown livery peeling by the foot having been baked, frozen and blown away because of where they sit above a gorge with the Kentucky river, alive with bass and turtles, 259 feet below.

Wild and wonderful: *Cypress wood fermenter.*

Beside the distillery the rusting frame of a railroad bridge spans a third of a mile from one cliff to the other. The track is still there, slightly buckled and rough and brown from neglect. Once the grains were brought to the distillery via that construction, but no train would dare test its strength now. Only the occasional film company makes any use of it, when a scene of high drama is required. Or the odd thrill-seeker. The bridge is single-track width and there are no supports on the outside. The drop from the sleepers is unrestricted and sheer.

The line carries on into Lawrenceburg and a small loco does make the journey from there: it cannot be a large one as another wobbly trestle bridge has to be negotiated. Having unloaded its cargo, the train stands so close to the entrance of the stillhouse you almost have to breathe in to get past it.

Sometimes I drop into the stillhouse at night-time. The hum of the all-copper beer still is all the more acute then. The highly polished doubler, also an all-copper affair, virtually glows in the dark as it stands in its gloomy surroundings right next to the outside door beside the railtrack. Already, you feel you can almost taste the whiskey to be.

The best time to watch the fermentation, though, is during the day. That's when you will find distillery manager Jimmy Russell overseeing every aspect of the whiskey-making process. I have been privileged over the years to meet legendary distillers the world over, many of whom, I hope, have taught me a lot, though just fractions of what they know. But with respect to them all, I doubt if any I have met have such a feel and extraordinary affinity for whiskey as Jimmy. When he began working there in 1954, there was still a Ripy there, the son of Ernest Ripy who began the distillery.

Once, we were gazing into the aged cypress fermenter. Neither of us said a word as we soaked up its soporific qualities. I noticed that the patterns from the bubbles were changing shape. That, he informed me, was one way he could tell just how long fermentation had been taking place. He studied the peanut-shaped bubbles for a moment, thought and announced the number of hours. On checking with an attendant, we found he was on the button. Jimmy is a man who goes about his business with the quiet, unruffled air of someone who knows exactly what they are doing. The distillery owners, Pernod Ricard, occasionally send him to Europe to educate the uneducated, trips which he enjoys immensely. But he always looks his best, his most comfortable and his happiest in a ramshackle pile of buildings above the Kentucky river.

Jimmy is also one of the few distillers I have ever met who shares my view that whiskey is at its best at around 100 proof. 101 is his magic number. Needless to say, of Wild Turkey's eight styles of bourbon, four are to be found at that strength and two more stronger still. Even the exceptional straight rye is a 101!

Is it sheer coincidence that a man who has devoted a lifetime to whiskey, having learned from those who had done likewise, happens to run the distillery which, it would not be unreasonable to argue, makes the best whiskey in the world? I think not. But I am sure the tons of copper the spirit comes into contact with has a big say. It might also be the apparently endless supply of water they tap from in an area which abounds in springs. Down the hill, toward the near-vanished city of Tyrone, there are the remains of at least three distilleries to be seen, the biggest being the first Ripy Distillery, in the 1880s reputed to be the biggest in Kentucky, its remains are now under fields of Burley tobacco.

So what about those two banks of fermenters to be found just beyond the stillroom? The second tier is of nine stainless steel fermenters, each containing 30,000 gallons each. The first tier includes two rows of five which fit in exactly with the original outline of the fermenting room. Nine of those are made from cypress wood, and each is twice the size of those at Labrot and Graham, though there is no uniformity to their height. Such

Gorge-ous: *The Kentucky River, straddled by a railroad bridge that once fed the Wild Turkey Distillery.*

fermenters look jaded, but the round-toothed tops have an immeasurable beauty.

Those stainless steel fermenters are a clue to how things are going down at Wild Turkey. While sales of bourbon, like other brown spirits, have been spiralling downward for decades, Wild Turkey's sales have continued to climb. At one stage it was 14 per cent year-on-year, which put enormous pressure on the distillery to produce sufficient stocks. In short, they failed. But the problem of filling bottles meant the brand returned to its roots.

The Austin Nichol Company dates back to 1855 as importers of groceries and spirits. During the Second World War, at a time when Scotch and Irish stocks were low, owner Thomas McCarthy concentrated harder on his bourbon, which he personally preferred as a whiskey style anyway. His company's speciality was an eight-year-old 101 which he bought from an undisclosed distillery. In 1942 he named the brand Wild Turkey. By that time the Ripy Distillery had become the JTS Brown Distillery and they were one of a number of distilleries which supplied Austin Nichol. When the company decided to buy a distillery to make Wild Turkey themselves, it was JTS Brown they chose. In 1971, it became the Wild Turkey Distillery.

With such enormous demand for Wild Turkey, from time to time specific brands would contain the whiskey from more than one distillery, though these days this is becoming quite rare. I have one bottle of six-year-old 86.8 proof which I once mistook for Ancient Age. Little surprise there because Ancient Age (my second favourite bourbon whiskey) is what Wild Turkey prefers above all else to augment stocks. Their last vatting was 4,000 barrels with 20,000 Wild Turkey, but it still showed. Rye-recipe bourbon from Stitzel Weller has also been used in the past, but it has been some four years now since they bought from anybody.

People may regard such practices as undesirable, but those that do may not fully appreciate the traditions of bourbon-making. For me it adds a little colour and keeps connoisseurs on their toes. It is unlikely any Wild Turkey sold in the USA, under any label, will contain anything other than that which originally ran through their doubler. And their premium and single-barrel brands are also the real McCoy. Put a Kentucky Spirit and a Blanton side-by-side and see what I mean. While some may struggle to pick which they prefer, there is no mistaking the difference in their origin.

That is why I am convinced Wild Turkey is the best single-distillery whiskey to be commercially available in the world today. Ardbeg on Islay is without doubt the finest of all, but it is nearly impossible to find and, because of its rarity, can change dramatically from bottle to bottle.

Certainly the Wild Turkey 86.8 can be a little temperamental for reasons we all now know, and the standard, brown-labelled four-year-old is simply too young for a Grand Cru whiskey and sits uncomfortably on the palate. But as soon as you start tasting the 101, which enjoys the company of eight-year-olds, you are beginning to discover just what delights eventually await you. For the first time genuine honey richness begins to emerge; this is confirmed by two full eight-year-olds, Traditional and barrel-proof Kentucky Legend, which positively revel in the 75 per cent corn-12 malt-13 rye mashbill. By the time you progress to the eight-year-old, single-barrel Kentucky Spirit, the realization that you are tasting great whiskey will have hit you. There is a 12-year-old, a bourbon I simply adore for its uncanny ability to remain delicate and complex despite its firm oaky start. Its nose, with freshly peeled orange, acacia honey, raisins, molasses, rye and so much more, has to be experienced to be believed. Sometimes I think it is my favourite. It isn't, really.

Because, for all-round perfection, Rare Breed must have it. This bourbon, known as 1855 Reserve in duty-free, seems to benefit from being a mixture of six-, eight- and 12-year-old Wild Turkey, though not on the nose in comparison to the 12. Again there is oak, once more the honey, you welcome back the corn and rye, yet all are intermingled in a way that is peculiar to Wild Turkey. This time, though, the complexity reaches new heights. It may occasionally be out-pointed by a single barrel, especially Kentucky Spirit, but that is rare.

In three years' time Jimmy Russell may have to retire. He'll be 65 then. He could have gone at 60, but didn't want to. For a man who even on his days off drives around the distillery just to get his daily fix of its extraordinary aura, it is unlikely he will be willing to go when the government says it's time. But go one day he must. And there waiting in the wings is his son fully trained by his father, the master of all Master Distillers.

Connoisseur's Selection

RARE BREED (AKA 1855 RESERVE) – OAK, HONEY, CORN AND RYE YET ALL INTERMINGLED IN A WAY THAT MAKES COMPLEXITY REACH NEW HEIGHTS. ALL ROUND PERFECTION.

FOUR ROSES

All around the world, distilleries come in all shapes and sizes. There is quite an assortment in Kentucky and Tennessee, but nothing quite prepares you for the beautiful and extraordinary outlines of a veritable cathedral to whiskey found to the right of the small road that spins off Route 127 just before the Blue Grass Parkway ramp.

Once it was called Old Joe's. These days it's known throughout the state as Four Roses. Looking at its unique Spanish facade it could have been called Old Jose's. Painted a startling off-lemon yellow and complete with bell tower, the distillery looks as if it's been wheeled directly from the dusty Mexican sierras of Chihuahua to this delightful, lushly-grassed, undulating site near Lawrenceburg, right in the heart of Anderson County, central Kentucky.

A peculiarity of the distillery is that its straight whiskey is these days tasted by bourbon drinkers the world over, with the exception of the USA itself. Its owners, Seagram, decided to withdraw the whiskey from the home market, certainly as far as straight bourbon is concerned, and concentrate on the blended variety, instead. The Four Roses name is well enough known in the States, but just how it tastes straight is but a fading memory to its 250-million population.

Despite the exquisite charm of the distillery, entering its office is pretty sobering stuff. On the left is an ancient, wooden, barrel-weighing mechanism and on it are distillery tags showing the plants once owned by the Seagram empire but now closed: Athertonville, Cynthiana, Midway, Lawrenceburg, Fairfield, Louisville. There was even one called Frankfort that was located in Louisville. That, too, has gone.

Another famous old name has vanished, but at least the distillery survives to this day. Indeed, I first knew the place as the Old Prentice Distillery until around 1986 when it was decided to give the plant a brand profile and re-christen it Four Roses. There had been a Four Roses Distillery at Shively, near Louisville, and just around the corner from Early Times. But that, too, has closed.

How the Four Roses name began is a peculiarly all-American affair. No other distilling nation has traded famous names around so many distilleries. Scotch distillers always, with just a handful of exceptions, sell their single malts under the name of the distillery. Blended brands may change hands between distilling companies, but often what goes into them remains largely unaltered or at least adheres to a particular style.

In the case of bourbon, proprietorial brands are sold off, often as distilleries close, and although sometimes the mashbill and/or yeast remains the same, the taste may be quite different on account of having been made at a different distillery.

Obviously I have no idea just how Four Roses tasted when Paul Jones brought the brand from his native Georgia to Kentucky in 1888, except that it would have little in common with its present-day, feather-light style. Just how the brand, and therefore the distillery, got its name is open to debate. Seagram themselves are hedging their bets and, bizarrely, on different bottles over the last few years I have read two different accounts. According to one version, it was named after four sisters whose surname was Rose; according to the other, it was named after the fiancée of Paul Jones who wore four roses as a mark of her betrothal. It is unlikely that anybody will discover the true reason now.

Whichever, the Four Roses name has its detractors. There are those who reckon it to be counter to bourbon's macho image and therefore it misses out on a certain chunk of the market. The call at the bar: "Hey bud! Four Roses … and put it in a dirty glass" doesn't quit have the right ring to it. And the character of the whiskey is not particularly brawny, either, preferring a much more ethereal character.

A walk through the distillery is an enjoyable exercise. Everything is as you would expect until you reach the fermenting room which, when the sun catches it right through the windows, gives a strange feeling of timelessness. Some fermenters here are extremely old, and at the top in an even worse state of erosion than those at Wild Turkey. Open-topped fermenters made from a natural, non-processed material offer a sight which quickens the heart. One of the beauties of good whiskey is that there is nothing synthetic about it. Such a sight only sharpens the expectation.

When Joe Peyton set up his original distillery some time after arriving in 1818, that same sight would have been recognized by him, except in his day fermentation would have been carried out in a barrel, not an enormous vat. Old Joe's log-cabin distillery was eventually replaced by a rock construction, and if you stroll across the shady lawns at the rear of the Four Roses Distillery you will soon enter a small wooded area where its remains stand, moss-covered and proud, like an ancient Roman wall. As with the numerous remains of lost distilleries to be found around the Lawrenceburg area, it is best to go exploring them in the winter rather than in spring or summer. Then there is less foliage to cut through and fewer copperhead snakes to tread on: old rocky distilleries are very much their territory.

Although the present working distillery, built in 1910, has been owned by Seagram since the 1940s, the distillery is now under new management. In 1995 Ova Haney retired as manager there after 13 years. Had such a retirement happened at a Scottish or Irish distillery, there would have been a visit from one of the parent company's big-wigs, a few speeches and a gold medal. Ova's final day ended on a Friday lunchtime with a feast with all his fellow workers (no bourbon, though,

Bell of Kentucky: *The striking outlines of the Four Roses Distillery would not look out of place for a tequila-maker.*

as they are not allowed to drink on duty) as well as three guys from the Fox's Creek warehouse complex near Bardstown strumming their guitars with a farewell song they had written for him. Nearly two years on, I still can't get the catchy little tune out of my mind.

There are warehouses to be seen opposite the Four Roses Distillery. But those are used by Wild Turkey. Instead, new manager Jim Rutlege needs only to concentrate on matters within the distilling complex. For a period in 1996, with the temporary halting of production at the Seagram Distillery at Lawrenceburg, Indiana, they supplied all the company's bourbon needs. Unlike most Kentucky distillers, who prefer to work with a tried and tested (or just plain economic) mashbill, at Four Roses different styles of bourbon are produced. Then they are blended together to produce certain brands. Indeed, single-barrel apart, Four Roses whiskey is the most complex of all Kentucky's bourbons as far as structure is concerned.

These days, Seagram have only the four brands, all somewhere bearing the Four Roses name. The standard straight bourbon is the Yellow Label. That alone contains 11 different styles of bourbon, once you have taken yeast types, distilling strengths and mashbill recipes into account. At its heart will be a bourbon made predominantly from a 75 per cent corn, 21 per cent rye and 4 per cent malt specification. That is a lot of rye, yet the yeast keeps things light and in control, perhaps too well, as I feel that there are one or two dead spots on this one, a little like a stalling engine.

By far my favourite is the Black Label version, where not only older whiskeys are used, but around 60 per cent of the blend will originate from a mashbill of 60 per cent corn, 36 per cent rye and 4 per cent malt. You don't have to be aware of these facts to know that Black Label is swimming in a hard, yet fruity rye character. It comes through on the nose and eventually on the palate, though not before the corn has first blood. A spicy treacle finish shows that this is a bourbon of substance. Black Label is a deeply satisfying whiskey, one that confidently rams home the point that bourbon can be a lot more than one-dimensional and wholly-oak dependent, a view mistakenly held until maybe 15 years ago.

The Platinum brand is also pretty rye-intense but, as lovely as it is, for me it just fails to match the complexity of Black Label. The single barrel obviously changes from batch to batch, though the Four Roses blending style really shows here because, even for all its rye and toffee, rarely can it ever be described as complex.

It's a pity, though, that Four Roses is not available as a straight in its native country, or even state. It represents a different style of bourbon from any other. For Black Label, certainly, deserves to stand shoulder to shoulder with Kentucky's finest.

Connoisseur's Selection

BLACK LABEL – FRUITY RYE CHARACTER ON THE NOSE AND PALATE; THE SPICY TREACLE FINISH SHOWS A BOURBON OF SUBSTANCE.

Clermont and Boston

JIM BEAM

Just a few hundred yards from Interstate 65, as it winds its way down to Nashville from Louisville, the little town of Belmont spreads itself over a small area of iron-ore rich land. It is a remarkably unremarkable place at first sight, the houses modest and low-slung, and there is little or no sign of industry. Taking dogs for a walk and gardening appear to be the community's favourite activities. Little indication, then, that no other town in the world is surrounded in all directions by so much gold. That is until you head west out of Belmont and in no time at all the road peters out as you hit a military no-go area. To enter it would be a foolhardy thing to do because further on is Fort Knox, the grand safe of the Federal Bank where the bullion reserves of the USA are housed under the double security of camera and cartridge.

Head 12 minutes by car south to Boston and there is more gold: liquid gold, as tens of thousands of casks of Jim Beam mature in 35 enormous warehouses. For the casual visitor it is probably just as easy to find their way into Fort Knox as it is Jim Beam's Boston Distillery: this is the one they don't talk about. Every bottle of Jim Beam mentions Clermont. That's a little place even nearer Belmont, to its north-west which dominates the community in the same way The Glenlivet does in the remotest part of Speyside.

Arriving at the distillery can be eventful. Sometimes locomotives are noisily shunting wagons of grain, honking forlornly as they do so. With the coming and going of tourists and trucks, it makes for the busiest distillery in Kentucky. This is the whiskey wing of the enormous American Brands empire and they make the kind of fuss of their bourbon as Jack Daniel's do of their Tennessee. And with some good reason. In some quarters, especially outside the USA, Jim Beam's whiskey has attracted its critics. And it is criticism I have long felt to be unjust. Because there is no age statement, because also of its ubiquitous nature, Jim Beam has been an easy target for those who work on the principal: "Oh, there is a lot of it about, *ergo* it must be inferior." I wonder just how many other bourbons these critics have tasted, and just how wide a sample of Jim Beam they have drawn from. For me, Jim Beam makes light but excellent whiskey.

Also, and somewhat against the odds, it has managed to maintain a family feel at the distillery. At other distilleries, such as George

 Boston swamp: *Beam's Boston Distillery becomes an island during the flood of March 1997.*

Dickel and Jack Daniel's, the family connection vanished long ago. But there has not been a day in its 203-year history that a Jim Beam Distillery has operated without its founder Jacob Beam or one of his direct descendants. Working within its walls at the moment, on the production side naturally, is the more than ample form of Booker (Fred) Noe. He is the son of the biggest name in Kentucky whiskey, Booker Noe, grandson of Jim Beam (who resurrected the distillery after Prohibition in 1934), himself great-grandson of the founder.

It must have been in the late 1970s or early 1980s when I speculatively called a distillery to find out something about the making of bourbon, a spirit whose beauty I had just begun to recognize as being on a par with Scotch. From a distance of 15 years or so I can't recall which one it was now, and I remember the manager was away on vacation or at a conference. But the man at the other end reckoned himself unworthy of passing on too much information. His words were: "Wharl, sir, if yer really interested in bourbon, ring the big man at Jim Beam, Booker Noe. What he don't know about whiskey-making and its history just ain't worth a spit." I think he said "spit", anyway. And it's true. With Jimmy Russell over at Wild Turkey and Elmer T. Lee at Ancient Age, Booker accounts for one-third of Kentucky's finest distilling heritage still living and about half in physical presence.

He has retired now from the daily grind of making whiskey and is used as a larger-than-life ambassador, a position to which he was born and excels in. Things have changed a lot since his family began distilling in 1794. Now they have 19 fermenters, each taking three lots of mash, and a five-foot diameter column still to accommodate. The still is stainless steel except for the head of copper and this produces low wines of 125 proof (62.5 per cent ABV) which are sent downstairs into a copper-screened doubler which pumps the alcoholic strength up another five per cent, standard Kentucky practice. At the very top of the stillhouse is a supplementary part of the still which acts as a filter to reduce the ethyl carbonate, a chemical compound frowned

Mr Beam: *Jim, great-grandson of Jacob.*

upon by certain government regulatory bodies, especially those in the USA. Beam had long been troubled with pretty high ethyl carbonate figures, but thanks to the filter they are not any more.

From the very top of Beam's Clermont stillhouse the green, undulating expanse of Bernheim Forest can be seen. Even this was given to the people by a prominent distiller and for whiskey writers like me, who happen to be keen birdwatchers, this is as close to paradise as you might find. On lower ground than the hill-top pine forests where there is a turtle-friendly lake, any number of woodpecker species are to be spotted, along with Eastern Bluebirds, Carolina Chickadees, White-breasted Nuthatches and many more. And further south, past the forest, you will spot Boston Distillery.

This is located on much flatter land than its northern neighbour. It is also the only distillery in living memory to have been pummelled by a tornado. There are men still working there who remember that terrifying day, April 3, 1974, when the twister appeared from the north-west as if out of nowhere, without warning and, spinning round directly into the plant, missed the distillery itself by yards, but stripped the roof and four walls off one warehouse, while sucking whiskey-laden oak barrels off their racks as if they were balsa-made empties. Other warehouses nearby were clipped as it tottered off to cause devastation elsewhere. Miraculously, no-one was hurt, although an awful lot of bourbon perished and the worst-hit warehouse, of which only barrel-laden racking remained, was eventually torn down to be rebuilt. Photos on the office wall show the grim aftermath of nature's most awesome show.

It's just as well the distillery, dating back to 1953, was not wrecked. For me, it makes a better spirit than Clermont, beautifully balanced and crisp on the nose and sweeter with more evident rye. And spicier, too. It all just goes to prove that though you may have exactly the same equipment, as the stills certainly are, and two distilleries which share ingredients, but you can never make an identical whiskey. The water is different, certainly. Clermont's comes from Long Lick Creek and Bernheim and Sportsman lakes, while Boston's comes from Wilson Creek. There are 19 fermenters here, too, maybe a fraction larger and in a different configuration, being very close to each other. The doubler is positioned differently as well. But the idea has always been to make two bourbons as similar to each other that the difference cannot be told. Well perhaps after a vatting maybe they are close, but *vive la différence!*

Only one of Jim Beam's bourbons actually comes exclusively from the Boston stills. That, ironically, is Booker's, something of a Kentucky mould-breaker. This was the first bourbon to be brought on to the market direct from the cask without being chill-filtered. It is aged anything between six and eight years and the sample I have at seven years and eight months and 126 proof is a gentle giant, a bit like Booker himself. Yet, strangely, as mango-nosed, nut-sweet and richly delicious as it is, it plays second fiddle to Beam's finest bourbon, Knob Creek – a 100 proof batch whiskey from Clermont. This is a nine-year-old, which though sweet is drier by comparison and finishes with the bitterness of dark chocolate. But its rye-rich hardness for me makes for a crisper, more precise whiskey of the very top flight. Another Clermont batch whiskey, Baker's – named after retired Master Distiller Baker Beam, Jim Beam's great nephew and Booker's third cousin – is beautiful for all its honey, yet not quite in the same league.

Apart from the small batch boys, there are other Jim Beam brands without the Beam name. In 1987 American Brands swallowed up National Distillers, which owned some old distilleries, namely Old Crow, Old Taylor and Old Grand-Dad.

Advertising art: *Jim Beam poster.*

All three distilleries were situated around Frankfort and, in keeping with the grand tradition of takeovers, closed down. But, in keeping with another Kentucky tradition, the names have been kept and so too have three distinctly different whiskies with the last yeasts and recipes of the doomed distilleries being kept alive to ensure some continuity. Old Crow, unbelievably a four-year-old, is the pick of the bunch, a near classic. This is the crispest, cleanest, maltiest and most citrus-fruity of all Beam's whiskeys, with a lovely rye backbone; Old Taylor, a fine six-year-old with a bitter rye sub-plot, also gets the tastebuds moving. The brand whose mashbill holds most rye is Old Grand-Dad. This is a four-year-old, and a bit younger than the days when the lovely old distillery on the banks

Twist and shout: *The aftermath of the terrifying tornado that wrecked a warehouse in April 1974.*

Well and good: *Owner Cecil Withrow has plans to revive distilling activity at the 90-year-old Spring House at the Old Taylor Distillery.*

of the Elkhorn River north of Frankfort was strutting its stuff. With the exception of the delightful 101, this is a generally disappointing bourbon. I have some Old Grand-Dad circa 1995 in a litre bottle which is charming and more-ish, yet I have other up-to-date stock which is hard and almost impenetrable: this is a whiskey which I am watching closely.

The Beam brands themselves have the lowest rye content in Kentucky and are made up from approximately half and half Boston and Clermont whiskey, though depending on the availability of certain aged stocks there could be up to a 20 per cent swing either way. Ordinary Jim Beam White Label averages at about four and a half years old and is a fine, elegant introductory bourbon, though perhaps not quite as fruity and cut-grassy as it once was. Beam's Choice can show just what a difference six months or so can make; not a great deal of complexity, but loads of silk. The Beam Seven-Year-Old sometimes shows characteristics of having bourbons even older than that in there and is very corn-fat. The Australian market enjoys Beam Gold Label, an eight-year-old which has surprising crispness for a 100-proofer. It is meant to be almost identical to the pick of the Jim Beam brands, Black Label. This is 90 proof and is the most complex of them all, being lush and combining an aged toastiness with a rich corn softness.

Also from either plant is Basil Heyden, a small-batch bourbon named after one of Kentucky's pioneering distillers who, it is said, began making whiskey in 1796. Distilling remained in the Heyden family and it is thought they created the Old Grand-Dad brand in honour of old Basil. This is delicious stuff, rye-crisp yet delicate and gentle. To add anything to this other than branch water would be sacrilege. Beam may be proud of their own heritage, but it's good to see they are big enough to celebrate so majestically the memory of others who blazed the still-uncharted whiskey-maker's trail.

Connoisseur's Selection

KNOB CREEK – EXCELLENT, SWEET-DRY BALANCE AND DARK, BITTER CHOCOLATE FINISH. STUPENDOUS.

BLACK LABEL – THE MOST COMPLEX OF THE JIM BEAM RANGE: LUSH, AND COMBINING AN AGED TOASTINESS WITH RICH CORN SOFTNESS.

OLD CROW – CRISP, CLEAN, MALTY AND CITRUS FRUITY, WITH A LOVELY RYE BACKBONE.

Loretto

MAKER'S MARK

According to the road map, the Maker's Mark Star Hill Distillery is not that far away from Beam's Boston plant. Yet in reality, the twisting back roads of Kentucky make for something of an adventure and, of all the Commonwealth's distilleries, it is this small, lonesome one on the fringes of the modest township of Loretto which gives the biggest feel of the great outdoors; that pioneering spirit – in more ways than one – which conquered the West. Actually, to be precise, Maker's Mark is not Kentucky's westernmost distillery. But you will certainly not find any further south.

Maker's Mark prides itself on its diminutive size, its neatness and compactness, its spotlessness and above all, its whisky. I say whisky here as it is one of two Kentucky distilleries to spell it the Scottish rather than the Irish way. But, whichever way you spell it, what is beyond any doubt is the quality of the bourbon.

Just as the tiny distilleries of Scotland, such as Edradour and Speyside, belie their size to produce blockbusting, full-bodied whiskies, then so too does Maker's Mark in no small measure. And just like those two distilleries, a creek runs through the site. At Maker's Mark, though, as the summer temperatures hit the 100s, figures practically unheard of in the Highlands, that creek is more likely to dry up than in Scotland. For that reason, the water to meet the distillery's tiny output of 36 barrels a day is fed to the distillery from a lake a quarter of a mile from the distillery.

Bill Samuels: *Whiskey revivalist.*

Even from my own old Kentucky home near Frankfort, it is a long journey to Loretto, but one of my favourites. Sunrise there can gladden the heart, but sunset at Star Hill will for anyone be an abiding memory, the warehouses silhouetted on high ground against the receding gold, the stillhouse black against the darkening sky. A raptor circles around on the dying thermals on one last reconnaissance before the day ends and the stillness which envelops the meadows and forests is disturbed only by the aroma of mashing grain.

With a location like this you half expect Daniel Boone to pop out to say "howdy"; instead you get Bill Samuels who has done his best to oblige by marry-ing into the Boone family. Not that his own family line is short of pioneering credentials. In that truly stunning part of Kentucky that runs north-west of Boston to Frankfort, where the undulations mean that you cannot go 100 yards without being stopped in your tracks by yet another view of outstanding beauty, there is, just west of Bernheim Forest, a small settlement called Samuels, named after his forefathers. Next door is Deatsville, where the remains of the original Samuels' family distillery rusts away beside some railroad track. The warehouses still stand high and are used to mature Maker's Mark whisky. Until 1894 the settlement was known as Samuels' Depot after William Samuels who, in the early eighteenth or late nineteenth century, like many others, left his native Virginia and supplemented his income from the gristmill by attaching a distillery to his enterprise, the first in that part of Nelson County. And if that doesn't impress you enough, the Samuels were also related by marriage to Jesse and Frank James, and a pistol of theirs hangs fully loaded with Western legend in the boardroom at the distillery.

The charismatic Bill Samuels, who has probably covered more air miles than any other distiller to preach the gospel of bourbon, now represents the seventh generation of that proud family to continue the distilling tradition, though these days the company is owned by the giant Allied-Domecq group. Until 1953 the Star Hill plant was a run-down silent distillery under the not-so-fitting name of Happy Hollow Distillery. But Bill's father, William, spotted its potential for making high-quality, small-batch whisky and put

Distillery of distinction: *The red and black livery means this can only be Maker's Mark.*

enormous energy behind creating the Maker's Mark brand and matching distillery. His hunch was right and Maker's really is different in style to anything else around.

It holds a special place in the hearts of Kentuckians and many distillers rate it in their top two or three, if only because loyalty to their own brand comes first. Older distillers, now retired, remember the first bottles of Maker's with a bit of a shudder. But it was only a matter of years before the distillery hit the kind of consistency for which today it is famous and even envied.

Needless to say, they do things slightly differently at Star Hill. It was Bill's father who decided to make an unusual recipe for the mashbill and it has remained more or less the same ever since. Ideally there are 70 parts of corn to 14 of wheat and 16 malted barley, though the corn percentage may rise sometimes as high as 75, with the small grains being brought down in equal measure. But it is the winter wheat which the folks at Maker's feel separates their whisky from the rest. Any whiskey you find from the Stitzel Weller Distillery is also a wheat recipe, but with none of the softness which Maker's Mark has managed to achieve.

So there must be other reasons. Well, their whisky spends a lot of time in the wood and, because they use so few barrels compared to other distilleries, they have figured it's worth the investment to pay over the odds for oak casks which have been seasoned in the open air, making them the last Kentucky distillers to keep to this expensive tradition. It could be the fermenters. The first eight "official" fermenters in Fermenting Room 1 are all made of cypress wood and hold 9,658 gallons each. Off-limits for those outside the whisky industry are six more added to Fermenting Room 2 and made from stainless steel, each holding 10,488 gallons, and in the small ante-room which comprises Fermenting Room 3, directly overlooking Hardin's Creek, there are three more steel fermenters, each holding 10,300 gallons. As regards the debate over the pros and cons of wooden fermenters against stainless steel ones, it is the whisky now being bottled which would show any differences. As yet, none have been spotted.

Connoisseur's Selection

Black Seal – Wheat on the nose; taste wallows in a dry cream texture and richness.

The wooden fermenters, mistakenly thought by some to be the only ones the distillery possesses, are a real picture. Surrounded as they are by wooden walls, floors and ceiling they seem a triumph of nature. But it is not just what they are made of that counts. What goes into them also make an important contribution and here again Maker's Mark takes a different route to the rest of Kentucky's distillers.

Usually in Kentucky the bubbling, toffee-brown cauldron of frothing mash consists of 25 per cent backset, the spent beer which has been separated from the solids during distillation (indeed, law dictates that for it to be called bourbon it cannot contain anything less). It is this backset, removed of all its sugars during the previous fermentation, which puts the sour in sour mash. It serves two purposes: first its high pH level helps kill off any unwanted organisms within the wash, and second it helps provide consistency, for each fermentation contains some of the last. At Maker's Mark the backset is higher at about 33 per cent.

And, apart from Labrot and Graham, it is unlikely any other distillery ensures that its spirit has quite so much contact with copper than Maker's Mark. The column still is a relatively tiny affair standing close by the mill, of all things. Even here, the Star Hill Distillery is meticulous, rolling the grain rather than pounding it, the thinking being that a slightly lower yield is an acceptable trade-off for a more flavoursome one. And then, of course, there is Maker's Mark's famous doubler, a gleaming, domed, copper pot which gently boosts the spirit percentage up.

The white dog which exits from there is pretty distinct stuff, as you might expect, with a green quality to the nose unlike any other Kentucky spirit and a delicious dryness on the palate. Other distillers have long been curious about Maker's Mark's filtration method for this new spirit: charcoal is passed through before it is filled into the virgin barrel to extract some of the heavier components. In order to make sure nothing more is lost, there is no chill-filtration of the fully matured whisky and the strengths at which it is normally bottled makes the exercise a near-pointless one anyway.

The finishing touch: *The seal of Maker's Mark.*

Sadly, there is not an enormous amount of Maker's Mark to be found around the world, a position which a company like Allied-Domecq find hard to accept. Yet, those additional fermenters apart, Bill Samuels has done a great job in fending off head-office demands for greater output. The general shortage of distilling water to work from has been both a pain and ultimately a blessing.

So the most common Maker's Mark brand is its Red Seal (hand-dipped in red plastic wax) which is a thumping 90 proof and five-and-a-half-years old. This is enigmatic stuff: quite weighty in body, yet light in character with enormous longevity on the finish, displaying just the right amount of spice one expects from a wheat mashbill and, just to show it can do no wrong, very sweet as well. There is also a 101 version, Gold Sealed, supremely balanced and with even more fizz and intensity. But the pick of the bunch is the woefully rare Black Seal, a 95 proof celebration of bourbon. The wheat lifts off on the nose, hand-in-hand with soft oak, while on the palate there is a drier, cream-textured richness, an intriguing cross-style of the very best of bourbon and the finest of Canadian. This is not just because of the extra two-and-a-half to three years spent in the barrel. A lot has to do with where those barrels have spent their time. At Star Hill they have been kept in zone three, an area designated by the distillery in the bottom, cooler half of the warehouses where the whisky matures more slowly. The result is a lighter, more vanillin-dominant whisky without the powerful, toasty liquorice tones that are often part and parcel of older bourbons. There is a, yet, even rarer 95 proof Maker's Mark, the elusive 1983 Vintage – last seen at Allders Heathrow – and possibly outpoints the Black simply because of its easy balance and stupendous honey richness.

I cannot say it is my very favourite bourbon – two other distilleries show much more complexity in their character – but this is clever, highly impressive stuff which hits the tastebuds with the accuracy of Jesse James's pistol. Maker's Mark, a great whisky of which there is little, but what little there is, the distillers make sure it counts.

Bardstown

Jesse James's gun may be hung safely on the wall at the Maker's Mark Distillery in Loretto, but a place where his bullets had bitten in either fun or anger can still be seen to this day on another wall a few miles north. In the Talbot Inn there are, on a second floor landing, indentations in the brickwork that show what the combination of whiskey and gunslinging can do.

Bardstown is that kind of place. There are porched residences designed in the style one associates with the Deep South, a magnificent whiskey museum which it is the duty of any true whiskey connoisseur to visit and a couple of very busy distilleries within its city limits and two or three just outside. A funny thing about Jim Beam's whiskey is that from reading the label you would think their bourbon is from the Frankfort region: "Beam Clermont Frankfort Kentucky" it confusingly announces. Clermont is four times nearer Bardstown than the state capital and Beam's Boston Distillery is nearer still. Since it is such a hive of whiskey activity little surprise then that, when the annual Bourbon Festival is held, beautiful Bardstown is its venue.

HEAVEN HILL

Most people who have drunk Kentucky whiskey will have experienced Bardstown bourbon, though few will be aware of that fact. The Heaven Hill Distillery probably supplies more whiskey to private customers than the rest of the bourbon industry put together and the number of labels it can be found under around the world, from once-famous but now localized American brands to own-label supermarket bottlings, is as bewildering as it is staggering. Even they admit they can't give a figure.

Yet for one afternoon of indescribable horror, it looked as if a great Kentucky institution would be lost. In mid-afternoon on 7 November 1996, as a storm passed over central Kentucky skies, flames were seen dancing from warehouse "J". Before anyone had a chance to react, the building was an inferno. With powerful, gusting winds fanning the flames, it was just minutes before warehouse "I" was engulfed and then another and then another.

Eye-witnesses I have spoken to described a scene that almost defies imagination: barrels shooting into the air and exploding, rivers of burning whiskey, a blue-flamed torrent out of control as some 90,000 barrels of whiskey were consumed: a vision of hell at Heaven Hill. The burning whiskey flooded into the distillery, and that too was destroyed. As the distillery and warehouses perished, another distiller a mile or two away prayed the wind would change direction. Luckily for him, it did.

I for one, had a lump in my throat when the old Heaven Hill distillery perished. It was one of my favourite places in the world. Yet when I spoke to its owner Max Shapira just a matter of weeks later, there was not a sound of sorrow: "Look, Jim. It's business as usual. We haven't lost a single brand or failed to meet a single order." Distillery fires have been common in Kentucky for two centuries and Max was treating the matter as an everyday occurrence, despite no-one having seen anything like this one in living memory.

Production has been temporarily switched to Early Times Distillery in Louisville, where they are taking advantage of spare capacity and are distilling to their own specific mashbill. And in the meantime the irrepressible Max is planning the rebuilding of the new Heaven Hill Distillery.

But I will always miss the old one. Like Ancient Age, there was a feel to the distillery which gave the whiskey classic status even before you had tasted a drop of it. Things were old and traditional; nothing was done to impress the tourist, just the drinker. And while younger Heaven Hill whiskeys are sometimes pleasant, though usually unexceptional, find the stuff at six years and onward and you are talking classic whiskey from a classic distillery.

There were those who criticized the likes of the original Heaven Hill plant in Kentucky, Alberta Distillery in Canada and Scotland's Girvan Distillery for not being the tidiest, most well-scrubbed in the world. These are people who prefer sterile distilleries. For me, Heaven Hill was of that breed that have that wonderful lived-in look, a Walter Matthau of a distillery; a genuine character in an industry where personality is so important.

In the case of Heaven Hill, its Hopper Scale Floor was among the most atmospheric distillery compartment in the entire state,

Connoisseur's Selection

ELIJAH CRAIG – OAKY ON THE NOSE, NUTTY ON THE PALATE WHICH SWEETENS TO A LINGERING, OILY FINISH.

Tragedy: *Another Heaven Hill warehouse becomes an inferno and thousands more casks are lost.*

where little had changed since it was built. It was a distillery where you are got back to basics and, as the quality of the whiskey proves, the result was outstanding. On this floor there was a railroad track 60 feet long on which there were steel hoppers carrying precise amounts of crushed Indiana corn and barley and rye from North and South Dakota. The train, which lived on this tiny upper floor railroad, sat above holes in the wooden floor and dropped the respective grains into the cooker so they could be carefully mashed: as elsewhere in Kentucky the corn entered first at 140°F, then was heated up to 168°F when the rye was added, and then cooled to 149°F when the malted barley was finally introduced so as not to be damaged. All around this floor was a layer of flour, which was not so usual.

Because Heaven Hill supplies so many own-label customers the world over, their output was, and still is, enormous, between 400 and 500 barrels a day. This was evidenced by the two fermenting rooms which between them held 31 fermenters, six of which were 50,000 gallon giants. The prettiest were numbers 2, 3, 5 and 14 which were gnarled cypress wood originals, though with limescale attached to the ancient planks. The yeast gave the first hint of a Beam connection here: hops are used to act as preservative rather than add flavour (which they probably do anyway), something unknown to distilleries in Scotland, for example, but around Bardstown pretty standard practice. And, indeed, Beams are to be found here in abundance. The Master Distiller is Parker Beam (whose father Earl was previous Master Distiller and brought the yeast to Heaven Hill) and second-in-command is son Craig, whose enthusiasm is contagious even to those of us with the bug. Craig is great-great-great-great grandson of the same Jacob Beam who started the dynasty: in this part of the whiskey world Beams get everywhere. And they are proud of it, too.

The stillhouse was no less an impressive sight, with all-copper beer stills and a doubler, and the close configuration of the stills just yards from the cookers makes for about the warmest in Kentucky – even before the fire. Up the hill from the distillery heading toward downtown Bardstown was an estate of 25 warehouses, now reduced by half a dozen or so, some with strange, stepped gables. However, Heaven Hill requires the capacity to hold half a million barrels of whiskey at any one time, so they also have 19 more over at the old Samuels' Distillery at Deatsville and Chapin and Gore Distillery actually in Bardstown itself.

Both those were early Kentucky distilleries, now lost. And although Heaven Hill sat exactly where any ancient distillery should be found, in a pretty hollow by a river, it actually dated back to only 1935. Remarkable. If money were being wagered, you would have taken one look at the darkened brickwork and placed your dollar that it was turn of the century at the earliest, and the dust from the grist which seemed to have become part of the structure only added to the illusion of antiquity. Although the final plans for the new distillery are far from complete, Max admits he would dearly love the facade of the building, which survived the inferno, to be incorporated in the new structure.

Looking at its location, it is hard to believe that distilling was not carried out there when Kentucky was first conquered. However, had it not been for a careless attorney, the distillery would have been known as Heavenhill, all one word, after the farmer, William Heavenhill, who owned the property in the late eighteenth century. When a family of Kentucky businessmen, the Shapira brothers, decided to branch out into distilling shortly after the end of Prohibition, they picked this prime site on the Loretto road close to two lakes from which the distilling water was brought. They were going to called it the Heavenhill Distillery; the documents came back as Heaven Hill, a title they appeared to prefer.

The distillery still remains within the Shapira family, thus making it Kentucky's last remaining independent distillery, and where the forest of warehouses end at the quiet country road entering Bardstown, there are new single-storey offices which house Max Shapira, the current executive vice-president and his staff. His good-humoured nature, complete with staccato delivery, somehow reflects the throughput of business the distillery enjoys. While half a mile down the road at the distillery, in the pre-fire days, those in it were typically laid-back and relaxed, Max was the perfect antithesis, answering a seemingly endless line of phone calls with machine-gun replies and decisions. For this part of the world, he is a one-man tornado, who seems to have gathered speed following the disaster.

One of the things Max sometimes has to do is buy in whiskeys from other distilleries to eke out stocks, 500,000 barrels or not. Until the fire, it didn't happen that often but it might hit any brand at any time, though not his straights: the Heaven Hill style can be spotted a mile off.

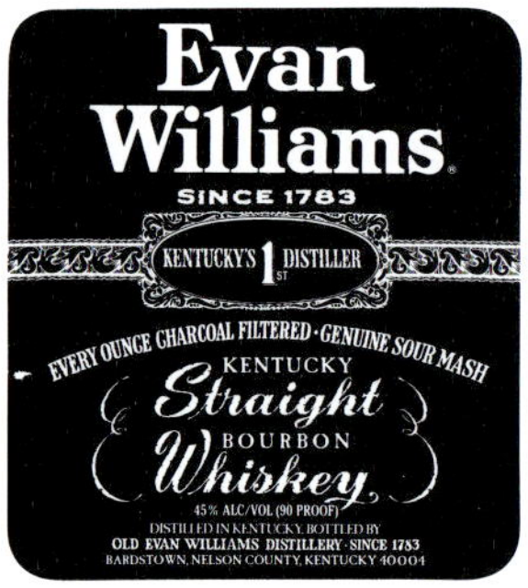

There are any number of four-years-olds which they happily confess to bottling as their own brands rather than someone else's. These include Heaven Hill and Dant; neither, it must be said, at that age struggle much past the fiery tag. There appears to be more than one style of four-year-old, and eventually Max admits to this. One has slightly higher malt to rye, the other vice versa. Both, however, adhere to the same small-grain content. Some can be tidy though uncomplicated, others a little off-key. All display a rawness which suggests that this is a whiskey which prefers time to get to know the oak. Those I detect with the greater rye are the ones I feel have just a little more character.

The company hit upon the idea of brand-naming famous pioneer bourbon distillers like Elijah Craig and Evan Williams, and the whiskeys used for these brands are uniformly superb. The latter, as a seven-year-old, is one I particularly cherish, with sweet toffee and balancing cinnamon on the palate following an alluringly spicy nose. Elijah Craig is aged a further five years during which time it becomes twice as rich and complex, with the small grains showing to great effect. There is a simmering oak presence on the nose and toasty, nutty qualities on the palate which sweetens further as the long, oily finish lingers. This is truly great whiskey, the pick of a fine bunch.

Beyond the four-year-olds there are also some finely tuned bourbons in the Heaven Hill range worth investigating. The six-year-old has some pleasing orange-peel notes with gentle toffee, and a 10-year-old carries on with the caramel theme, though this one has a kind of minty-milky-yeasty edge, too, with a delicious, bold rye hardness. In some ways the fruit has broadened out, but the vanillins are much more sturdy. All these are solid whiskeys, each confident enough to carry hefty toffee and fruit complexity.

Without doubt Heaven Hill represents a style unmistakably bourbon yet defiantly different to anything else around. If you see a bottle with "Distilled in Bardstown" on it, chances are it came from Heaven Hill and demands exploring; if it says "Distilled in Bardstown Aged 6 Years", you're in for one heck of a Kentucky treat...

WILLETT

Not every barrel of Heaven Hill ends up in bottles around the world. Just a mile or so up the Loretto road a narrow trail runs off to the left and along it you will find the rebuilt Willett Distillery. On occasions you will see Heaven Hill whiskey dumped into troughs there, presumably for one or two of their own brands. But for the connoisseur there are two brands from here which are musts, the super heavyweights Johnny Drum and Noah's Mill. Both were distilled at the old Willett Distillery which closed in the early 1980s. The Johnny Drum 15-year-old has the nose of an old Irish pot-still whiskey with the hard, small grains flying in all directions on the nose. It also has a ripeness which one associates with unmalted barley: odd but seriously delicious stuff. The even older Noah's Mill tastes a little as if it were made by the Biblical character, with oak from his ark aplenty. Now past its best, some bottles still hold a fine grainy sweetness.

For the last eight years the Willetts, under Even Kulsveen, have been slowly rebuilding their distillery which is overlooked by Heaven Hill's warehouses. They are hoping to begin distilling again during 1997, using a traditional Kentucky beer still in conjunction with a pot still. Experimental whiskey made under lab conditions has been quite good: one prays, with their liberal use of rye and barley, that it will be again. If another Johnny Drum 15-year-old is on the market in 2011 half as mouth-watering as their present one, then they will have succeeded.

Like most museums, the whiskey museum at Bardstown has a startling inclination to act as an iceberg. That doesn't mean that the welcome you get will be frosty – far from it: the genuine hospitality for which Kentucky is renowned is here by the warehouseful. It is just that what is on show to the public is only a fraction of what the curators have under their auspices. Thwarted by lack of space, even in a building of generous proportions like that at Spalding Hall, they do a remarkable job and there never seems to be quite enough time to take in the old labels, bottles and apparatus that is on show. Particularly impressive are the tiny pot stills dating back to well into the last century.

The museum was the brainchild of the late Oscar Getz, one-time owner of a distillery in the town. Indeed, the museum was once located within a cramped section of the distillery itself, at the end of what is now a row of offices. It has been at its present site since the 1980s.

BARTON

It is particularly ironic that the distillery Getz owned is the Barton Distillery. Of all those currently working in Kentucky and Tennessee this is the one the casual passer-by, or even enthusiast, would have greatest difficulty in getting in to see without making prior arrangements. Without being unkind, it is also the one distillery outside Louisville which will entwine itself around the bourbon-lover's heart with the loosest of grips.

Had Scotty beamed me down (there are those Beams again!), I would have reported back to the captain that I appeared to have landed in a Canadian distillery or a Scottish grain whisky plant. And if it was a central Kentucky bourbon distillery, it was not as we know it. Only the single-storey offices adjacent to the distillery building offer anything in the way of age, though given that the present distillery dates back to only 1946 that is hardly surprising. The distillery buildings themselves are functional, as is the stainless steel equipment inside. It also follows the late-twentieth-century design of having fermenters on the outside which saves the cost of building walls. Strict temperature control means that the beer inside is not entirely at the mercy of sub-zero winters and 90–100° summers. Even the bottles show little sign of romance: "Distilled and Bottled by Barton Distilling Company ... Distilled Spirits Plant – Kentucky – 12".

Another irony is that the museum should have been established at Barton, which is easily the most disinclined to go into specific details about the way it goes about making its whiskey. Certainly, the man responsible for the rare receiving of writers, Jerry Dalton, was the most gracious of hosts before he recently left, good-natured and with a disarmingly dry sense of humour; a man, I must say, I like very much. But ask any questions which may reveal some detail of why the whiskey has the character(s) it has and Jerry soon put the Fifth Amendment into practice.

That doesn't mean to say there was any big deal about me seeing the stuff being made. They have two wash tubs, each holding 15,390 gallons of grist made of hammer-milled corn, rye and malted barley in that order and water drawn from the 31-acre Teurs Lake, fed by limestone springs and siphoned off from there into their own holding ponds. There are 13 enormous fermenters each holding 49,470.54 gallons and fermentation time will vary between 74 and 78 hours, with a fraction less than 25 per cent backset being used. Taking into account the background of the company, there were no prizes for discovering that the 55 ft-high, 6 ft-wide beer still was made chiefly from stainless steel with copper at the head. Outside the building is the 6,000-gallon doubler which boosts the spirit from 125 proof to 135 proof. This is made entirely of copper, though this cannot be seen because of the lagging.

It is at this point that things start to get hazy and Jerry begins to "sandbag", as he aptly puts it. Making up almost its own district in the town, Barton has 30 seven-floor warehouses, each capable of holding 20,000 barrels. Now it's regarding what's in them that Jerry and I worked out the perfect understanding: I asked the questions, he refused to answer.

What is the oldest whiskey in there, Jerry? Fifth Amendment. Do you have whiskeys from other now-lost distilleries? Fifth Amendment. Do you take barrels from different parts of the warehouse to achieve contrasting characters for your whiskey brands? Fifth Amendment. Are there bourbons in there made by you that are of different mashbills? Fifth Amendment. Actually, not quite – I got a begrudging "possibly" on that one. I have suspected for some time that they have just too many different styles of whiskey (beyond the standard 75–15–10 ratio) for one distillery that makes a point of bringing out so many four-year-olds. Only the Very Old Barton is older, a six-year-old with sprinklings of even more aged whiskeys to keep the style in shape

The peculiar thing about this silence is the fact that Barton's whiskeys are, well, different. Not just in comparison to other distilleries, but even among themselves. Some, like Colonel Lee, either as an 80 proof or BIB (Bottled in Bond), I find almost impossible to find good words to say about. He was obviously an officer who never took prisoners. Others, like Kentucky Gentleman, have a certain rye brutishness about them that appeals to my baser instincts. None, though, even bother to pretend that elegance is on the agenda. But some can certainly claim that complexity is amongst their character traits. These are whiskeys designed for a certain price range in the market and they do a great job. They are also whiskeys which just now and then you have to slip into a liquor store to pick up. One can take only so much smooth, honey-silk perfection. Sometimes a man's gotta do what a man's gotta do. And that means finding a bourbon that has no second thought about ripping the lining out of your tastebuds.

Unlike with any other distillery in the world, I have no idea what something older

Connoisseur's Selection

JOHNNY DRUM (WILLETT) – THE NOSE OF AN OLD IRISH POT-STILL WITH LOTS OF SMALL GRAIN. ODD BUT SERIOUSLY DELICIOUS.

KENTUCKY GENTLEMAN (BARTON) – A RYE BRUTISHNESS THAT APPEALS TO THE BASER INSTINCTS. THE FINISH IS EXCEPTIONAL.

than six years tastes like at Barton. Or why the marketing people there don't bring out a bourbon that gives the house character time to be tamed in the barrel.

The best shot you get is Very Old Barton. There are whiskeys in there over six years old and certainly no younger. And it comes in a variety of strengths within the narrow band of 80 proof to Barton's favoured BIB 100 proof. Strange to relate, however, VOB is not the best whiskey produced by the company. Of the range, the BIB wins by a nose, quite literally. There is a pleasing delicacy about them all, with the 80 proof showing sweet malt and rye and the BIB weighing in with a shovel-full of ripe oak. This is great, late-night fare on a cold winter's night. But, for taste alone, the weakest of them all is hugely entertaining and soothing.

Internationally, the best-known brand is Ten High, once on the Hiram Walker team and similar, in floral style, to a Jim Beam from just down the highway. Again there is a maltiness to this that almost propels your nose back into the Scottish Highlands, something akin to a Benriach. And it's their blandest brand by far. Far better than Colonel Lee, yet refusing to show any form of complexity, it is a whiskey which tries to do as little as possible yet still has sufficient vanilla and caramel to let you know it is a bourbon you are drinking. It is not a patch on the old Hiram Walker style which was heavier, rye-richer, oilier and altogether more satisfying. Kentucky Tavern can be a confusing brand: the whiskey will have been distilled either at Glenmore, or more likely these days Barton, depending on how old the stocks are. The easiest way of telling the difference is that The Glenmore is much sweeter in its early signature and after a promising malt-corn introduction falls away dramatically with an off-balance, frankly unpleasant finish. You can't miss it. That distilled at Barton is a BIB 100 proof. It has a healthier, maltier nose, a crisp rye start and then another weak, rather characterless and slightly green finish.

Their one bourbon which gives some clue to the distillery's past is Tom Moore. It was he who set up the first distillery on the site now occupied by Barton way back in 1879, though none of it survives. In many ways this whiskey represents the house style: lots of small grains force their way into the early reckoning, but the nose and initial taste are quite low-key, except for that familiar buzzing of complex and fluctuating characters. It is the ripe cherry and dark chocolate finale which grabs the attention. The odour of the drying glass offers, believe it or not, fried rice. Not the kind of whiskey which may first set you purring, but it certainly rewards longer study.

My favourite, however, just has to be Kentucky Gentleman. There is more rye character leaping out of a glass of this than perhaps any other bourbon. The finish, also, is exceptional, with plummy fruitiness and big corn-vanilla, cocoa and even coffee. Even this, though, is well capable of singeing the hairs on your chest. If it didn't, it wouldn't be Barton.

Thus, such is the high quality of whiskey in Kentucky, even a distillery like Barton that produces something pretty base is quite capable of conjuring up something truly magnificent. For that, stand up Master Distiller Bill Friel, renowned locally as the maker of "Willy's Whiskey", who stands beside an avowed intention not to change a single thing in the character of Barton whiskey – be it good, be it bad.

 Whiskey and water: *The Ohio River has been associated with the distilling and the ferrying of whiskey for over two centuries.*

Louisville

Louisville was once awash with whiskey. Kentucky's largest city by far is bounded to the north and west by the Ohio river on whose opposite banks lies Indiana. There was a healthy whiskey industry there, too, though that has now vanished bar the slender presence of Seagram. Even before the arrival of the railroad, Louisville was a great place for commercial distilling. The Ohio, as it was such a wide and navigable river, was perfect for bringing materials in to the distillers and shipping out their wares.

With a swelling downtown, then state, then national population to cater for, these small distilleries grew until they became quite massive. Sadly, many became too big, producing too much whiskey. As takeovers within the industry gathered momentum, and with it the vigorous tightening of commercial belts that inevitably followed, most of those distilleries were considered too unwieldy to operate. Today, like some Kentuckian Campbeltown, Louisville is littered with redundant, decaying warehouses, rusting water towers and darkened chimney stacks showing just where the city's distilleries, once the heart and life-blood of the town, had been.

EARLY TIMES

Exactly a century ago there were 21 distilleries within the city limits. Today there are just two (provided you count the satellite town of Shively), almost identical in failure proportions to the little Scottish town on the Kintyre peninsula. The distillery in Shively to have survived the onslaught is Early Times. Of course, in keeping with Kentuckian tradition, that was not the name it was born with. It was built in 1935 and was christened, inappropriately enough, the Old Kentucky Distillery. Much of the distillery has been rebuilt since even then, having been bought in 1940 by Brown-Forman, and during the summer of 1995 I watched as the last original warehouse was razed to the ground. Today not a single brick of it can be seen.

For a city distillery, Early Times enjoys a remarkably rural aspect, but then it is only a short canter away from Churchill Downs, home of the Kentucky Derby. A glorious lawned avenue heads out toward Louisville's city centre and has more of a feel of a park than a distillery. Even the small wooden cottages which surround the entrance to the distillery have a country-clean, grimeless, healthy feel to them. No wonder: the distillery's owners clean them, and even the trees, from the natural black fungus which grows relentlessly wherever whisky matures that can be seen at every other warehouse-owning distillery around the world.

Close to where the avenue ends, a rusting water tower in the same eggshell green as Early Times' fermenters shows where the old National Distillery once did its stuff. From the roof of the distillery can be seen, in the opposite direction, an enormous brick warehouse that belonged to the Four Roses Distillery, once of Louisville. Beyond the railroad tracks and the new warehousing is the road which takes you to where the formerly ubiquitous Yellowstone used to be made. A couple of miles north, closer to the city's heart, is the redundant Old Forester Distillery.

While Early Times hides behind the curtain of freshly scrubbed trees, Old Forester with its outrageous whisky-bottle-shaped water tower was, and still is, a city landmark. Old Forester is made at Early Times these days. And, truth to tell, that is the better of the two types of whiskey made there. Actually, it's whisky. Like Maker's Mark, Old Forester has never gained an "e" in its spelling of the spirit. Early Times did, but has lost it somewhere along the way.

Connoisseur's Selection

OLD FORESTER BONDED – AN EARLY MIXTURE OF HONEY AND SPICE GIVES WAY TO AN IMPRESSIVE ROASTINESS. BIG AND COMPLEX.

For me, the reason for Old Forester's superiority is that it enjoys a healthy 18 per cent rye in its recipe. Early Times is now down to 11 per cent, the balance spent on corn, and it shows. As a straight bourbon, Old Forester wins hands-down for depth and complexity every time. But most Americans will not know what Early Times bourbon tastes like. In the 50 states that brand is now fashioned as "Old Style Kentucky Whisky". That is Brown-Forman's way of saying that the whisky inside the bottle was matured not in virgin oak casks which signifies bourbonship, but used oak casks which signifies something altogether inferior. It is a whisky that has its pleasant moments, occasionally, but if you are looking for a touch of class it may be one worth skipping. To find Early Times, the straight bourbon, you must go to Japan. Again, you may not find the journey worth it. Early Times is full of playful character and does have certain attributes, but sadly, charm and intricacy are not among them, though I must admit I find a large gulp of it a bracing, liquoricey and pretty enjoyable restorative when I'm feeling dead-headed.

Old Forester is a different proposition. It has long been the major bourbon brand for the Brown-Forman company which first marketed it and is well endowed with style and delicious liquorice, roasty depth, boasting much more complexity than its softer, lazier stable mate. Old Forester comes in 86 proof and a Bonded 100 proof, the former spicy and sweet, despite its comparative weakness, the latter really piling on the roastiness. Both are big, complex and hellish good whiskies. Whichever strength, every bottle of Old

Forester attests: "There is nothing better on the market." This claim is made in the hand of George Gavin Brown, whose signature every bottle carries. He began selling the brand in the 1870s, a century or so after his forefathers had left Scotland to begin life afresh in America. At first it was a vatted bourbon, with bourbons from more than one distillery being mixed together the bottle being sealed to guarantee it was not tampered with, a not uncommon problem of that era. It is thought that Old Forester was the first brand to do this and one can easily imagine George Gavin Brown insisting on his spelling of whisky as a mark of his Scottish background, though the idea is not one wholly accepted within the company.

The pedigree of Early Times goes back even further. It began life as a far-flung wing of the Beam empire and its first distillery was founded in Nelson County near Bardstown at a lonely location called Beam's Station. It had been operating for some years as a small-time operation before registering the Early Times trademark in 1893 as whiskEy. By the onset of Prohibition, the Early Times Distillery had grown enormously and occasionally moved house. Since 1979 it has shared premises with Old Forester, though this time it was Early Times which stayed at home.

Even so, some 80 per cent of all bourbon being made there is to the Early Times mashbill of 79 corn, 11 rye and 10 malt, in comparison to Old Forester's more hardy 72–18–10. Not only does Early Times have to serve its "Old Fashioned" brand and its straight bourbon, but also Canada, where it is used as a flavouring whisky. Whichever style is being made, the distillery has recently switched over to a system of virtual triple-distillation: beer still to thumper to doubler, the doubler having been converted from a redundant thumper. The idea of this system is to take out some of the heavier notes to end up with a cleaner spirit. It is certainly that, yet has retained a full character, though in the case of Old Forester the corn shouts louder than you might expect. Once a year or so some very decent rye is made there, too.

It is just as well the distillery sticks to making whisky. Not that long ago it went into the fish-farming business with a new warehouse converted into a water tank. The idea was to fatten them up on the solid wastes from the whiskey-making process. A long time ago it was discovered on both sides of the Atlantic which creatures benefited from consuming this high-protein waste product … and fish didn't. They started to die off at alarming rates.

The warehouse was put to much better use when it became the testing site of the triple-distillation pot-still apparatus built for the Labrot and Graham Distillery. After some tinkering here and there, it began to work perfectly – with no fatalities. Maybe this was divine intervention to remind whisky people that distilleries were put on this earth for the making of whisky.

Bernheim bricks: *Kentucky's new-built distillery is overshadowed by its massive warehouses.*

BERNHEIM

This distillery may be new, but all around it are the trappings of a distiller's heritage. Bernheim is pretty state-of-the-art, as it should be, having opened as recently as 1992. Yet its surroundings give the feel that nothing is out of place and tradition is being followed.

Perhaps it's those 13 enormous all-brick warehouses, one towering as many floors high. On the ground a metal track follows them – not for a railway, but for barrels, just like at Labrot and Graham. Those warehouses are something else, even by Louisville standards, and walking around admiring them can result in a cricked neck. They are absolutely huge, each capable of holding between 20,000 and 25,000 barrels, but since they are so high those lower floors can remain relatively cool: the ability to control the speed of maturation is quite striking and gives blenders an above-average choice of materials to work with.

Bernheim's neighbourhood is not quite as enchanting as those of Kentucky's other working distilleries. Around here are homes which have seen better days and roads along which you may prefer not to walk alone at night. Even so, the feeling of whiskey history runs deep. It is not only the warehouses which tower above the distillery. To the back of it is an old chimney stack which belonged to the famous Belmont Distillery, handsome bottles of whose make can still from time to time be found in auctions. Apart from the warehouses, that is all that remains of a distillery dating back to 1881, a cornerstone of bourbon distilling in Jefferson County. Soon after being built it was only one of tens of distilleries competing for local and outside markets. Its closest rival was the Astor Distillery, only yards away. Both distilleries were latterly owned by United Distillers and, as the buildings and apparatus became more enfeebled, the

> *Connoisseur's Selection*
>
> **PRESIDENT'S RESERVE** – AN ORANGE-TOFFEE NOSE IN WONDROUS HARMONY WITH WARMING PEPPER AND AN OLD HICKORY FINISH.

decision was made to close both and make way for a twenty-first-century affair. There must have been contingency plans afoot, because within a year or so of Bernheim's opening the Stitzel Weller Distillery was silenced, its wheat bourbon-making operation being transferred across the city. That, though, was almost certainly not why Bernheim was constructed.

From late in 1996 it will be possible to taste the whiskey of Astor once more. United Distillers are taking the welcome step of producing rare whiskeys from distilleries now lost. One of the first two to be launched will be under the famous old brand title Henry Clay, a 16-year-old distilled at Astor in 1980. Despite the enormity of its age in bourbon terms, the nose shows little over-cooking and although oak is there, so is honeycomb to counter-balance it. At 119 proof it is about as full-bodied a bourbon you can hope for, but miraculously it has not been tainted with over-ageing. The spice mingles beautifully with the vanilla and the rye also pushes itself into the frame. Great stuff for the connoisseur and old Astor lover alike. Even taking the many years of maturation into account, it is markedly different in style to anything produced at Bernheim today.

Before taking on board the needs of the Stitzel Weller Distillery, Bernheim got on with making its own brands quite happily. These are I.W. Harper and Old Charter, both of which are produced on one stainless-steel based beer still. Next to it stands another, likewise including copper in the head and condensers, which makes the wheated bourbons of the Weller, Old Fitzgerald and Rebel Yell families.

Whether of the wheat or rye type, stainless steel mashtuns are used, as is a thumper to complete the process. The yeast strain varies, but the method of distillation is the same. There is a policy of bringing these whiskeys off the still at slightly lower proofs than is the norm in Kentucky and filling into barrel at lower strength too – around 112 proof instead of 125. It is argued that the whiskey, by not having to be reduced down quite so much for bottlings, keeps more of its original style and flavour. There is a counter-argument that by putting into cask at a lower strength, there is less active alcohol to leach and interact with the wood. Doubtless there are pros and cons on both sides.

Where there is certainly a difference is in the warehousing. The rye whiskeys invariably end up achieving adulthood in those mighty brick warehouses. At Stitzel Weller the lovely, easier-on-the-eye, old ironclad warehouses, which retain the heat longer, are preferred for the wheated bourbon.

The rye-recipe brands have enjoyed a long history. I.W. Harper was a name personally chosen by the distillery's founder Isaac "Ike" Bernheim, a Pennsylvanian Jew who migrated to Kentucky and with brother Bernard started a whiskey business with the purchase of a single barrel of bourbon. So successful were the brothers that soon after the turn of the century they built their first distillery, and so rich did they become that they were eventually able to hand over to the people of the Commonwealth of Kentucky one of its most beautiful natural treasures, Bernheim Forest, which sits between the two Jim Beam distilleries, straddling Bullitt and Nelson Counties.

The name I.W. Harper, with which the Bernstein family made much of their wealth, has a curious history. Not particularly happy about using their own surname to promote their whiskey, they borrowed the name of a horse-owning friend of theirs and prefixed it with Ike's initials I.W. Sounds strange, but this was a pretty usual way of doing business at the time: if the name sounded good, use it, however peripheral it may be to the whiskey itself. And here, for devotees of both bourbon and the Wild West, is another tenuous whiskey link with the notorious James brothers. Harper owned the Black Horse Tavern near Lexington, which was the birthplace of Zerelda Cole, mother of Frank and Jesse.

Today the whiskey is still pretty sound stuff. Where wheat whiskey prefers a few more years to find its feet, the rye-recipe brands can run from an early age. The standard I.W. Harper Gold Medal is a good example of this: youthful with plenty of small-grain involvement, making for a bourbon that

Old Master: *The diminutive Ike Bernheim peers over his nineteenth-century office furniture.*

Distiller's dozen: *Thirteen Stitzel Weller employees from the early 1930s.*

pounds the tastebuds. The 101 is much bigger and fatter, with the corn this time having the bigger say. But these pale in comparison to the President's Reserve. An orange toffee nose works wondrously with the warming pepper and then you are bowled over by the subtlety and delicacy on the palate and hickory finish. The nose, however, really impresses: one of those where you hurry downstairs the next morning just to experience the sweet, lingering traces in the empty glass.

The Old Charter brands also enjoy noses way above the average, but since the youngest is an eight-year-old that is hardly surprising. Lots of honey dominates the 80 proof eight-year-old, at least on the nose and very early assault on the palate, but after the rye arrives in the middle, the finish fails to carry on the good work. The same can be said for the 10-year-old, whose finale in no way matches the fine build-up of corn and oak. Two extra years do the trick, though. Old Charter Classic is a 12-year-old bourbon that takes you by surprise from first to last. The small grains present a crisp, enticing body, absolutely full-flavoured and finished with a superb cocoa bitterness. It also helps by being a confident 90 proof, allowing those bullet-sharp grains to clatter into the tastebuds at full-pelt. A year on, the 13-year-old Proprietor's Reserve with its cinnamon and toast is even better: the most complex of the range.

These bourbons go a long way toward telling you about whiskey maturation in Kentucky. Even at more than a dozen years old, the oak doesn't hint at being on the heavy side. Those elegant old brick warehouses are not just a pretty facade.

STITZEL WELLER

I have seen some sad moments in the world's whisky industry over the last decade. Few, though, were sadder than when my phone rang and a voice with a deep Kentucky drawl told me that Stitzel Weller was being closed. When a distillery like this has to shut its doors you do begin to wonder ... .

Back in the early 1990s, the advertising posters displayed on London's Underground network were enlivened by a campaign for Rebel Yell. The marketing people had recognized that younger drinkers were turning their backs on anything which might even remotely be construed as middle-aged. Therefore, brands with the name of old this and old that were regarded as old-hat. For years Rebel Yell had been a bourbon sold exclusively in the Confederate states. Now that United Distillers had bought into the bourbon industry they had a number of brand names to choose from to hit the international stage. A name like Rebel Yell had a sure-fire appeal, it was reasoned, to drinkers not ready for the shackles of middle age.

To meet the projected demand the Stitzel Weller Distillery produced flat-out. Despite the hopes, despite the test tastings, despite the advertising, the converts did not come forward in great numbers. The warehouses filled with wheated bourbon as supply outstripped demand. Inevitably the stills were shut off, the distillery closed.

For once I cannot blame the marketing people. Their logic made sense, the label with its Confederate flag was stylishly done and, had I been a gambling man, I would have bet heavily on the brand's success. Significantly, there was absolutely no way you could fault the whiskey. I loved it then, I love it now. Rebel Yell is as individual and characterful as any in Kentucky. And maybe that was its downfall. Perhaps it needed to taste of nothing. It had none of the heaviness one associates with some American whiskeys, which one might have considered a plus. There was an enticing, malty, minty, spicy-pepperiness on the nose enhanced by a gradual sprawling of delicate complexity.

Today the distillery remains silent. All the work required for its brands is easily managed four miles away over at Bernheim. The distillery could work again and various plans have been put forward within the company to see if that is possible, but so far without any result. The chances of those magnificent copper beer stills producing as they did before are virtually nil. Certainly those 28 fermenters will never again be full of wash of varying degrees of liveliness and sweetness all at once, and the two white-painted, cast-iron mashtuns each holding over 11,000 gallons would be pointless. If anything is ever to work there again, it would have to be on a very much smaller scale.

The distillery in its present form dates back to around 1935, though its roots with W. R. Weller date right back to 1849. The Weller company merged during Prohibition with the Stitzel distillers, who themselves date back to 1870. It has a chimney with the post-Prohibition trademark lettering to show the brand, as was the case at the La Salle Distillery in Montreal and at Glenmore at Owensboro, until it was unceremoniously blown up by new owners Barton during late 1995. At Stitzel Weller the legend "Old Fitzgerald" reaches high into the sky, making the distillery easier to locate than might otherwise be possible in the maze of narrow roads which criss-cross this part of Louisville.

The distillery is set in the kind of lawned and wooded grounds that also makes Early Times so attractive to the American robin, blue jay and whiskey-minded person alike. Although bricked, the buildings are wonderfully neat, and azaleas and magnolias soften their aspect. At the original, wood-slatted entrance to the distillery a warning can still be seen from Pappy Van Winkle, a president of the distillery just after the turn of the century: "No Chemists Allowed". This was a declaration of his abhorrence of those who considered making bourbon in any other than the good old-fashioned way.

The name on the chimney stack is an impressive reminder of the Old Fitzgerald brand which made the distillery tick. The most straightforward example of the brand itself fails to match the stack's impressive demeanour, though. The 86 proof at four years old shows just why wheat-recipe bourbon needs those extra years, though the Bottled in Bond 100 proof version, while by no means perfect, enjoys a richer sweetness which helps mask one or two inadequacies. The Very Old Fitz, a 12-year-old at 90 proof, is one for those who prefer complexities in

Opening time: *The windows of the old ironclad warehouses at Stitzel Weller.*

Sign of the times: *A century ago, Stitzel Weller's President, Pappy Van Winkle, banned all chemists from his distillery. He would not be sleeping soundly now!*

their life: well, in their glass anyway. There is caramel and custard to follow the apple brandy and still unripe nose. This is the kind of teasing bourbon I love.

The Weller range follows a similar pattern. The younger Special Reserve goes nowhere on the nose and palate, yet the Centennial 10-year-old and Antique have you howling with delight. The former is again a complex wheat bourbon that combines delicacy with a build-up of increasingly peppery, warming notes. The Antique dispenses with all that: no pitter-pattering around of small grains, just an enormous vanilla statement which cloaks the palate, though cleverly allowing in the corn to give depth and the wheat and malt to gave shape and complexity. Both are lovely whiskeys worth hunting for. However, one can only hope that the stills at Bernheim will do just as good a job.

The immediate question, though, is what to do with all that wheat whiskey in those warehouses which was intended for Rebel Yell. One imaginative solution the distillers have come up with is to launch an entirely new brand: the Dickel label. During Prohibition, when Stitzel Weller was one of six distilleries in the state allowed to make whiskey for medicinal purposes, they also produced for two of the others licensed in Louisville, Old Forester and Frankfort. Ironically, they didn't produce for Stag in Frankfort, who at that time housed the Dickel Distillery, then a refugee from Tennessee. So to make amends belatedly, they are intending to launch George Dickel RX Cascade Prohibition whiskey. This is something else: heaps of soft caramel, nothing even remotely complex, but just the easiest bourbon you will find to drink. It has been designed for the younger market, hence its simplicity. And it has been achieved by putting charcoal chips into the whiskey prior to bottling as part of a Tennessee-style mellowing process. The result is a one-off hybrid: half Kentucky, half Tennessee, wholly delicious.

Connoisseur's Selection

VERY OLD FITZGERALD – A 12-YEAR-OLD FOR THOSE WHO PREFER COMPLEXITY. CARAMEL AND CUSTARD FOLLOW THE APPLE BRANDY AND UNRIPE NOSE.

At least the extra warehouse space that has been created by the railroad tracks has meant that the first serious archive of Kentucky distilling has been set up. While the museum at Bardstown gives the whiskey-lover the chance to look back at bygone days, the records kept at Stitzel Weller give one of the greatest insights into the industry any student could wish to find. The archive is maintained by resident historian Mike Veach. The company is also blessed by having within its marketing team someone who not only knows how to sell whiskey, but comes from a bourbon family and has also married into one, Chris Morris. He is in the forefront of the next generation of true bourbon men.

MISSOURI, ILLINOIS AND INDIANA

WESTON

You can travel for a whole day west of Louisville, as straight as an arrow flies, and still find yourself in what was once bourbon country. After such an arduous journey, where for 500-plus miles the road continues unflinching across flatter and flatter lands, through St Louis and Kansas City, you can relax in the very same cast-iron, semi-ornate tub belonging to the man who, a century before, owned a distillery as far from the east as safe trading would allow.

This distillery still stands today, its buildings in keeping with elegant residences nearby, its still and fermenters in pristine condition despite a decade and a half of inactivity, the focal point of curious tourists. Those tourists may well have stayed at Benner House, now a period bed and breakfast home in Main Street, Weston, the charming Missouri (or Miz-zor-a, as locals pronounce the state) town on the edge of the famous old river. This was the home built by George Shawhan in 1898 and, just to remind you, within the house can be seen bottles of Shawhan's "Four Generations Bourbon" and "Peer and Pioneer American Whiskey". After all these years the corks have remained intact, but there is no sign of the whiskey – which absolutely sums up the state of play in Weston: the distillery is still there but not a drop of its original whiskey is to be found.

How the town acquired its name was a pun on its location, then the most westerly settlement in that part of America, and on the name of a founding father, Tom Weston, whose job it was to design the town. A distillery was not long in arriving: fitting really, seeing that the land on which it was built was purchased in the 1830s from an Indian trader in exchange for a single barrel of whiskey. The distillery dates from 1844, initially built, with the aid of slave labour, as a refrigeration plant. Twelve years later it became a commercial distillery to serve the thirsty mid-west. Since then it has been known as Blue Springs Distillery, Holladay Distillery, Shawhan Distillery, Old Weston Distillery and, finally, McCormick's which closed in 1985.

All the bourbon made at Weston has long since disappeared, though at a lovely Irish pub nearby – itself a former brewery – I managed to get hold of some original Weston Corn Whiskey, which turned out to be sweeter, fuller and more complex than that which replaced it, indicative of the heavier Missouri whiskey. The McCormick company are still trading. And, irony of ironies, they have been using another non-Kentucky bourbon, from the 1920s red-brick Pekin Distillery near Peoria, Illinois, which itself ceased whiskey-making in 1991 but which continues to produce ethanol. Both distilleries were once owned by the Mid West Grain Company before the McCormick operation was taken over by outside investors. This is probably the sweetest-tasting bourbon to be found anywhere in the USA. And the softest. It was made to a 74.5 per cent corn/15 per cent rye/10.5 per cent malt mashbill and passed just the once through the beer still at very high strength, around 159 proof, without the aid of a doubler or thumper. So here's a tip: if you see the McCormick or Stillbrook labels with "Distilled in Illinois", get them now as they are being phased out as stocks dwindle (Heaven Hill's Kentucky whiskey is being used instead). Both the Illinois whiskeys are officially 36 months old, though the Stillbrook tastes and feels a lot older and displays delicacy and explodes on the palate, a bit like a young Ancient Age or George Dickel. The McCormick is considerably flatter, though the rye comes through more clearly.

It's a real shame a Missouri distillery is dispensing with Illinois bourbon. During 1995 McCormick had a close look at reopening but decided against. On the other hand, with the increase in demand for small-batch bourbon, one can only pray that one day whiskey may be made once again 500 miles west of Louisville. I for one will celebrate in a 100-year-old, cast-iron tub – soap in one hand, a glass of Weston's finest in the other.

> *Connoisseur's Selection*
>
> **SAM COUGAR (SEAGRAM, INDIANA)** – A STUPENDOUS BOURBON, BRIMMING WITH ENORMOUS RYE HARDNESS AND SPICE. A REAL MOUTH-WATERING BOURBON FROM THE TOP DRAWER.

SEAGRAM, LAWRENCEBURG

On June 2 1996 bourbon whiskey appeared to lose a little of its sheen when the stills at the Lawrenceburg Distillery ran for what was believed to be the very last time. The order had been given by those on high within Seagram.

This was not the Four Roses distillery near Lawrenceburg, Kentucky, but the one to the west of Cincinnati, Ohio, in an Indiana town, coincidentally and confusingly bearing the same name as its sister distillery in Kentucky. The distillery would not close *per se*, because the company's gin and vodka are made there on their state-of-the-art apparatus. But the apparent ending of whiskey production struck a sad note and goes to show, at a time when new distilleries have started in Kentucky and California, just what a delicate industry this is. Whiskey-making in Indiana seemed to be no more. And I thought Seagram had made a monster of a mistake: there is no other whiskey in the world made

Back on stream: *Seagram's Indiana distillery is again making bourbon and rye.*

with such brittle richness. The goose that laid their golden egg had been slaughtered. Or so it seemed. Because just a few months later, the Seagram blenders were convinced all was not lost. A few days further on, manager Larry Ebersold rang me to say they were back in business. Indiana whiskey had been saved.

Some 110 years earlier the ending of the state's whiskey industry would not have been considered much of a loss by those outside it. There was overproduction on both sides of the Ohio river, and Kentucky distillers kept themselves to themselves, not wishing to be linked with the inferior whiskeys of Indiana. Even the Kentucky whiskey made at Covington, on the outskirts of Cincinnati south of the Ohio, was tainted by association. All stuff made north of the river was regarded as whiskey to be drunk days, weeks, at best months old. Kentucky distillers prided themselves on allowing their whiskey to mature a minimum of three or four years, which was another reason why Kentucky bourbon gained such a high reputation. Also, the corn content of Kentucky bourbon was around 70 per cent; that of Indiana and Ohio was very much higher. The dismissive view of prominent distiller John Atherton in 1888 was typical of his time: "Those houses along the Ohio river ... make some whiskey which I presume they call high grade, but which is not intended to be aged and which does not come into the market as Kentucky whiskey." There is a certain irony that Seagram closed down the Athertonville Distillery a decade or two before the curtain briefly came down on their own distillery north of the Ohio.

Viewed from afar, the Lawrenceburg Distillery stands tall and solid, overlooking uncharacteristically fertile plains, in the same red-bricked, box-shaped way Dumbarton and Walkerville tower above their watery domains in Scotland and Canada respectively. Except that now, around the distillery, there is the visible debris of a lost industry. Just yards from the Seagram Distillery is the abandoned Schenley plant, a building I once walked through, treading over smashed glass and rotting floors. Scattered around were some old documents pertaining to the spent beer.

It is unlikely the Seagram Distillery will reach that state, though only by the grace of its gin and vodka business. The distilling of whiskey was set to return once the rye arrived from the frozen north, perhaps in February 1997, with some 97 days of distilling before the summer's end. What happens after that, no one is entirely sure. Yet for all the scorn heaped upon whiskey from this region, for me it was nothing short of magnificent. Using 14, 25,000-gallon fermenters dating back to the distillery's cen-tenary in 1965, it made the many types of whiskey which eventually found their way into 7 Crown, including a beautifully fruity and lush barley whiskey; and two types of bourbon, one with an unbelievable 35 per cent rye content to just 60 per cent corn, easily the most full-flavoured, steel-riveted bourbon it has ever been my good fortune to find (though one never made available as a straight). Their 75 per cent corn bourbon is a much softer proposition; and there were three ryes, too. One was an exquisite sweet-spiced, all-malted barley, another was just 52 per cent rye and the other was 95 per cent rye to 5 per cent malted rye. The reason why all these whiskeys were of such high quality might have been the water, the hardest in North America. Or that the beer still was a small affair, just four feet in diameter, while the doubler was a monster, easily the largest in the USA. Both stills were, significantly, made entirely from copper.

With such a high-class background, Indiana whiskey can be spotted a mile off. At the moment the one straight whiskey it features in is Sam Cougar Black, for the Antipodean market. Of all Seagram's bourbons this is my favourite: a class act with top hat and cane. Averaging six years old and made entirely from the 75 per cent corn/20 per cent rye recipe, Sam is a whiskey which takes hold of the tastebuds and bombards them with so many flavours, it's hard to know just what is happening. It's as mouth-watering as any whiskey you will find in the world, even including pure pot-still Irish, and the rye is glorious and uncompromising.

Unfortunately the marketing people have compromised. Once again, no pride is taken in its Indiana origin: this one is called "Authentic Kentucky Style". The mud has stuck and, so the marketers say, the bourbon drinkers in Australia and New Zealand want the real thing, i.e. Kentucky bourbon. But Indiana is gamely fighting back and surely, sooner or later, someone will at last appreciate its real worth.

VIRGINIA AND PENNSYLVANIA

VIRGINIA GENTLEMAN

If it weren't for a single, small, peculiarly shaped copper pot still, things would not be right in the world. That piece of gleaming apparatus is all that remains of Virginia's once enormous whiskey-distilling heritage. It stands alone, stubbornly defying the course of history which has witnessed the disappearance of America's greatest tradition.

When you consider that Kentucky was no more than a county in an enormous land stretching into the unknown named after the virgin Queen Elizabeth of England; and that it was here and in the more northern lands of Pennsylvania that migrants from Celtic lands began distilling from grain rather than the already established molasses, you begin to understand why Virginia's place in world whiskey is one that cannot be forgotten. In 1838 Morewood gave details of distilling practices in the United States. He could not name the number of legal distilleries in Virginia, but its production of alcoholic spirit put it into third place, ahead of Kentucky. Almost certainly, most of that spirit would have been whiskey.

Today, just a single Virginia whiskey brand can be found: Virginia Gentleman. If you look carefully at the label you will find two types: the older, plainer ones should be snapped up if you see them. Or if you find a dust-covered bottle sitting half-empty and forgotten in a third layer of whiskeys at the back of a bar somewhere, see if you can persuade the bartender to sell it to you. Because this is a dying breed: Virginia whiskey cooked, fermented and distilled in the Old Dominion State. When I was last at the distillery in April 1995, I visited a warehouse where there was still half a length of barrels distilled at the original distillery. They have gone now, each and every one of them. Each bottle of Virginia Gentleman sent out now is distilled twice at Heaven Hill before the white dog, the raw spirit which has tumbled from the second distillation, is tankered by railroad over to Fredericksburg for a third and final distillation in the copper pot.

This does not mean the Virginia Gentleman you will find today is a souped-up simple Kentucky bourbon: far from it. It will have been made to a high, small-grain specification: 65 per cent corn, 20 per cent rye and 15 per cent malt, the same recipe as the old Virginia Gentleman. Also, it will have had contact with the strangest pot still in the States, one that, thanks to a worm-like design, generates a light spirit which, in tandem with those small grains and the extra contact with copper, ensures a degree of complexity.

Although the making of whiskey in Virginia spans two centuries, the original Virginia Gentleman Distillery was a post-Prohibition concern. It was situated in what is now Reston. Sixty years ago it was built on wide-open farmland; today the outer environs of Washington DC have encroached. There is nothing left of the original distillery which was closed in 1987. Jay Adams, related by marriage to the distillery's founder, A. Smith Bowman, ended production there when the economics made it near-impossible to break even, producing a whiskey from scratch. Consequently he moved the company downstate where, halfway between Washington DC and Richmond, can be found the genuinely historic and captivating town of Fredericksburg. Strolling around in the downtown area of Fredericksburg is like being in a time-warp. The white slatted houses have not changed in a century and here and there are still the visible scars of internecine tragedy. That the American Civil War came so close to the country's capital is evidenced by musket shot and cannon ball holes left unrepaired after nearly a century and half of peace.

Fredericksburg is probably the most attractive town I have found in America, similar to Frankfort but on a grander and prettier scale. The making of whiskey now offers an additional attraction to the town and the distillery is housed in what was once a cellophane factory, but for all the world looks as though it was built as an early twentieth century distillery, complete with warehousing. The dismantled beer still from Reston is housed in one of these warehouses and could be used again if need be, though the chances of that are almost nil.

Jay Adams is not only a man who has the history of Virginia coursing through his veins, being related to three early American presi-

Cracking good whiskey: *(Above) A. Smith Bowman, Virginia Gentleman's founder.*

Still going: *Virginia Gentleman's large new premises contains just a single still.*

dents, but he is a pragmatist, too. By using a single final distillation he has managed to keep Virginia whiskey alive. And, to his own amazement, when the switch was made in 1996 from original Reston Virginian whiskey to the Fredericksburg variety, not a single complaint was heard from his customers.

There is no doubt the Reston whiskey is the finer, being heavier, more full-bodied and unbelievably complex with the small grains generating enormous flavour – in fact, a world classic. Fredericksburg whiskey is much lighter, moderately complex and with a flavour profile that is attractive, though nothing like so mouth-watering. It is a good whiskey, deliciously easy to drink with enough small-grain character to keep the tastebuds fully occupied. What's more, it's Virginian. And for that we should be thankful.

MICHTER'S DISTILLERY

Such are the ironies and vagaries which beset the whiskey world that there is only one Pennsylvanian whiskey that can be bought today – and though, because of its location, it should be rye, in fact it's a bourbon. But what a bourbon!

The small town of Scheaferstown is set in the green-pastured, rolling countryside between the sprawl of Philadelphia and the river-bisected city of Harrisburg. It is close to the Amish community and in the background, to the north, sit the low-slung Blue Mountains. These now-gentle lands. which America's earliest settlers cherished after taming their wildness, later became the home to a magnificent style of whiskey, now ridiculously difficult to find: rye.

Indeed, the Michter's Distillery in Scheaferstown was once a rye distillery. Records show that the making of whiskey there had been carried out since 1753 when, like possibly thousands of others in the state, the Shenk farming family built a distillery to help maximise the full potential of their fertile land and gristmill. No one can be entirely sure what they made there, but almost certainly rye would have been an important crop, grown either by themselves or by neighbours who used their mill. The distillery had been in operation for 40 years when the Whiskey Rebellion flared in the west of the state, but none of the government's taxation demands seemed to end legal whiskey-making on the site. By the turn of the 19th century, the distillery was operating purely on commercial lines and by 1861 it had passed, through inheritance and sale, to Abe Bomberger who gave his name to the plant and the rye whiskey it certainly by then produced. Like so many others, it fell into disuse during Prohibition but found a new lease of life after the Second World War. A member of the Beam family was shipped in to get the distillery back on its feet and from the mid-1950s a rich new bourbon called Michter's Pot Still became available. There was, indeed, a pot still used in the old-fashioned way for a second distillation after the traditional American beer still had been used.

Despite the whiskey's high quality, the distillers did not have the marketing strength to guarantee its success and in 1988 the distillery finally limped to its closure. A whiskey man, Adolf Hirsch, bought some 1974 stocks of the whiskey and brought it out as very old bourbon under the Hirsch name. That whiskey is now owned by the Hue family who run the Cork 'n' Bottle liquor stores in Covington, Kentucky; they seem, single-handedly, to be attempting to give their town a name for fine whiskey which it never enjoyed during its production days of a century ago.

To prevent further ageing, the bourbon is now kept in stainless steel tanks. The 16-year-old Hirsch is the better of the two. While the 20-year-old (and old bottles of 19-year-old) is attractively oaky, minty, spiced and lush, there is a certain flatness which underlines its age and detracts from its greatness. Its younger brother has not yet crossed the fine line of old age. It is still lively with honey deliciously evident on the nose and palate, and a youthful corn-oiliness mingling well with the sweetness. This is big, confident, high-class whiskey. Strangely, however, if you spot this whiskey on the shelves you would never know its Pennsylvanian origins. There is no mention of the state or of Michter's Distillery anywhere on the stark, claret-style label. Perhaps it is just an oversight or maybe the snobbery about the alleged quality of bourbon produced outside Kentucky is in evidence again. But it is rather remarkable.

A shred of consolation is that at least the old distillery is protected by law because of its historical value to the nation. It's a pity the same protection wasn't offered to its whiskey: in early 1996 all the remaining stocks of bourbon maturing in its warehouses were destroyed by court order. People had continued to break into the warehouses and help themselves to stocks. There were also questions about its quality. It is a tragedy for the last whiskey made by this distillery to suffer such an ignominious end. The chances of the distillery ever operating again, however, are almost nil. But, there again, the loss of such a glorious piece of heritage as Pennsylvanian rye was a tragedy in the first place. One can only hope that the entrepreneurial skills that have caused the opening of new distilleries in California and Kentucky spread further west.

Connoisseur's Selection

VIRGINIA GENTLEMAN – LIGHT IN BODY WITH DECENT SMALL GRAIN CHARACTER.

HIRSCH 16-YEAR-OLD (MICHTER'S) – DELICIOUS HONEY ON NOSE AND PALATE WITH YOUTHFUL CORN OILINESS MINGLING WELL WITH THE SWEETNESS.

TENNESSEE

Once, Tennessee was a bourbon-making state like any other. There was no great difference between the whiskeys from the numerous stills found all over its territory, and that from Virginia and Kentucky to its north. And there was no reason why there should have been.

The limestone shelf beneath the rich waters which feed the Kentucky distilleries extends far under the Tennessee soil to fertile land in a warmer climate. The settlers who flowed west through the Cumberland Gap headed further north into deepest Kentucky, or south into what is now Tennessee. Whichever direction they took, their distilling skills travelled with them. And so whiskey became the natural spirit of the Volunteer State, just as it had of the Bluegrass State, although being further south, it was not a place where rye and barley crops flourished so readily. So it was that Pennsylvania and Maryland perfected the art of making rye-based whiskey, while Kentucky and Tennessee concentrated on corn.

Tennessee is a state whose beauty fair sucks the air from your lungs. If Kentucky is my favourite place on earth, then its southern neighbour cannot be far behind. But two centuries ago, the journey there for settlers was an arduous affair through mountains and forests and across deep, wide rivers, like the meandering Cumberland. Today, to reach there from the bourbon counties of Kentucky you can rock and roll all the way down Interstate 65 with wall-to-wall Lynyrd Skynyrd and Elton John. Or, if the Nashville bug has bitten you, you can line-dance on every other station with Garth Brooks. And if that sounds like too much fun, you can tweak the knob and seek salvation as a hillbilly Bible-thumper threatens you with eternal damnation in staccato, machine-gun delivery. This is a colourful country.

Before you reach the border you will pass Mammoth Cave National Park on your right, a place which gave its name to a distillery that once made quite excellent whiskey. I was lucky enough to taste some 18-year-old, distilled in 1909 and 85 years on it showed firm sweet toffee and rye amid the strong oak. It would be interesting to find a Tennessee whiskey of the same vintage: a year later the state felt the first effects of Prohibition. It was another nine years before Prohibition became law across the entire nation.

This was a blow to a thriving industry. A little more than a century ago there were close on 700 distilleries going about their legal business in Tennessee and probably twice that number to be found illicitly operating in the mountainous regions near the Kentucky and Georgia borders. You can still find plenty of moonshine, but only two legal distilleries – Jack Daniel and George Dickel – remain alive and kicking, and they had moved out of Tennessee to continue their operations elsewhere. It was a wise and, ultimately, life-saving move for both.

It wasn't until 1941, though, that Tennessee was granted its very own category of whiskey, quite distinct from bourbon and rye. Some people think the fact that Tennessee makes sour mash whiskey sets it apart. Actually, so does every bourbon distillery in Kentucky – it is merely the addition of the sour-tasting, sugar-free spent grains from the previous distillation, the backset, into the next mash to help prevent bacteria thriving in the warm fermentation rooms. The real reason we shall discover later.

The strange thing is, although there are two distilleries operating here, their products could not be further apart in style: one is heavy and oily, the other lighter and flighty; one calls itself whiskey and the other whisky. What they do have in common, though, is that both have won the right to sell whiskey at their distillery, something Kentucky has at last fallen in line with. And that means that it's easier to get a true taste of Tennessee whisk(e)y where it is made, something that always adds to a whisky's beauty.

People are used to making the pilgrimage to Tennessee to visit the shrine of Elvis Presley or Nashville. They can also pay homage to Dickel and Daniel by visiting the two distilleries which, for entirely different reasons, have to be counted among the greats of the whiskey world.

JACK DANIEL

You would be forgiven for thinking that if any distillery in the world were to suffer from an identity crisis, Jack Daniel would be it. Ask for a bourbon anywhere outside the USA, Canada included, and the odds are that the first whiskey to be thrust at you will be a trusty bottle of black-labelled Jack. Yet Jack is not bourbon but Tennessee whiskey.

The strange fact is that between the American Civil War and the Second World War, Jack Daniel did make bourbon. And not just Tennessee bourbon. When Prohibition struck the state in 1910, the distilling operation was moved to St Louis. For 23 years Jack Daniel's name was renowned for its Missouri bourbon!

Now it is established as a Tennessee whiskey-maker, the fact that Jack Daniel's springs so readily to mind when bourbon is thought of does not upset those in the small, smart town of Lynchburg. They will feign hurt ("Hell, we ain't a bourbon – no bourbon is as good as Tennessee") but naturally they are delighted because, of all America's spirits, Jack Daniel's has developed a worldwide appeal of its own. And owners Brown-Forman have on their hands a sure-fire international winner, the most easily identified whiskey, irrespective of its genre, in the world.

Why Jack has done quite so well is open to debate. Every marketing guy and gal in the whiskey trade will tell you it's a nasty old world out there, and nastiest of all are the younger drinkers, turning their backs on dark spirits in droves and finding a tasteless substitute in vodka instead. With the exception of one whiskey, that is: Jack Daniel. The beleaguered marketers will tell you how younger people don't want to know anything about how things used to be: they want things that matter now. And, perhaps more importantly, they want something they can't taste. On both counts, Jack Daniel's fails the test.

Stern sentinel: *Jack Daniel founded his whiskey empire during the American Civil War.*

On every billboard, in every magazine and newspaper it seems, is an advert featuring old men leaning back in rocking chairs keeping a traditional, deep-southern watch on ageing barrels of whiskey. It's as home-spun and old-fashioned as apple pie. Yet it works. And the whiskey itself is as rich, oily and uncompromising in character as a peated Islay. Still the youngsters come back for more. And wear the T-shirts to pledge their fashionable allegiance to the world of Jack.

One reason for this fashion is simply that Jack is often mixed with something else, so the full force is not experienced head-on. But sometimes it is drunk as nature intended, and with gusto. People are still realising there is nothing else in the world quite like a Jack Daniel's. The whiskey purists rarely have much to say about it that is complimentary. It falls into the same category as Jim Beam: too common and therefore beyond serious consideration. The enormous liquorice wall the palate hits is described as rough and unsubtle. Perhaps the connoisseurs are right, but that in itself does not mean that Jack is not a good whiskey. Taste some of the rarer bottlings specially selected by master blender Lincoln Henderson and even the most hostile of purists would have to take note. And if those purists would actually sit and drink neat JD at 80 or 86 proof at room temperature and take note of its charisma, they might actually start to enjoy themselves.

The Buzzard's Roost: *Barrel House No. 1 is the Tennessee whiskey lover's holy of holies.*

Connoisseur's Selection

BARREL HOUSE I – A MASSIVE WHISKEY WITH LOADS OF MALT BATTLING TRHOUGH TO JOIN THE TRADEMARK LIQUORICE AND HINTS OF GUYANAN POT-STILL RUM. AN ABSOLUTE CLASSIC.

The distillery, little more than an hour's drive from the Alabama border, is a great one to visit. Every bottle of Jack makes a point of where it is made: Lynchburg, population 361, which was the case when a little man with enormous self-confidence decided to set the distillery up in 1884. The population today is many times greater, though the lovely town centre with its old-fashioned stores is pure ancient Tennessee. The whiskey is made nearby and, although it is located in a town, the creeping ivy and trees help give the distillery a semi-rural feel.

Just wandering through the place makes you wonder just what it is about Tennessee whiskey which sets it apart from bourbon. After all, bourbon is still made in Virginia and Indiana and, until the last decade or so, in Pennsylvania, Illinois, Missouri and elsewhere. It's certainly not the fact that the distillery has recently set up a micro-brewery in the old bottling hall which makes an appropriately roasty lager. So it must be the whiskey.

Well, the mashbill which enters the cooker is an unexciting and totally normal 80 per cent corn, 12 per cent rye and 8 per cent malt; the methods of cooking are the same as anywhere else; the fermenters look the same as elsewhere, even if there are a lot of them. The four 64-inch-diameter beer stills are also pretty standard, if well represented. Maybe it's the fact that Jack Daniel is only single-distilled that makes it Tennessee. No, it's not that, either, though that does guarantee its richness. There is a doubler below the beer stills, but that only re-distils the vapour from the beer heater, which makes it pretty well unique not just in the USA but the world. It also accounts for the heaviness the whiskey enjoys: nothing else in the USA is half as weighty as a JD.

Yet it would be weightier still had not the single thing that makes Tennessee whiskey Tennessee whiskey been implemented: charcoal filtration. This is what they like to call a "mellowing" process where 12-foot-high tanks packed full of maple charcoal pick out the stronger congeners. The spirit off the stills passes through these vats, a journey that takes around four days to complete. Only when the spirit runs out through the bottom is it then filled into cask.

As well as having taken out the excesses of the Jack Daniel character, the charcoal will have added something, too. The maple has been fired in stacks at the distillery but in a way some sugars will have been retained, some of which will have been passed on to the spirit. In recognition of the peculiar results of

Mister Jack: *It always causes quite a stir.*

this charcoal filtering, in 1941 the US Government officially granted Tennessee whiskey its own generic status beyond bourbon, which until then Jack Daniel had been called, and rye. And as for the discarded charcoal: make sure you have a space in your trunk to bring some back – it gives a special piquancy to any barbecue it is used in!

Much is made of the legend of Jack Daniel, and rightly so. Though only 5 feet 2 inches tall, he has now achieved the stature of a giant. He had barely reached his teens when he learnt how to distil, and found a market during those years of the American Civil War … and a vocation. When the war ended and the country returned to a state of normality, he found it easier to find custom and had no hesitation in setting up his own distillery. This he located next door to a source of water he had discovered, called Cave Spring. In this area of Lynchburg, known as the hollow, he set up in full production in 1866. Oddly enough, Jack's big chance had come at an early age because at the first distillery where he worked, he had taken over from a preacher compromised by the encroaching tide of temperance.

The Jack Daniel story has an unusual, and sad, end as well. One day he was unable to get into his safe and in a fit of temper decided to give it a good kick. The result was a broken bone in his foot which never properly healed. The pain grew worse as the infection slowly took hold and he died several weeks later.

It was Jack's death in 1911 that brought about the famous Black Label. Until then the Old No. 7 brand was in vivid green. That Tennessee brand still exists in the southeast states of the USA and in very small pockets elsewhere in the country. As a straight four-year-old it is younger than the Black Label version by at least 18 months, but some Americans refuse to drink any other: the drier, lighter character is markedly different to anything else the distillery makes. There is another light whiskey, Gentleman Jack, which retains many of the same traits, except that it is very much sweeter and the liquorice, though still there in force, is nothing like so lumpy in texture. This is as smooth as it gets, because the whiskey has undergone a second mellowing programme, this time with the matured spirit being sent through those charcoal-filled vats before bottling. A peculiarity of this whiskey is that, while it shares the same liquorice depth as the Black Label, it is actually the same age as the Green Label. There is nothing straightforward about whiskey, wherever in the world it's made.

Over the last couple of years two other new Jack Daniel brands have been launched, both on the ultra-high-quality side: one for the Far East and duty-free markets, the other to be sold at the distillery. In contrast, the whiskey they have withdrawn was a super little 12-month-old with wonderful character, called Lem Motlow. He was Jack Daniel's right-hand man who took over the distillery after JD's death and spent many years after Prohibition trying to save the business by negotiating with various prospective buyers including

Fire raiser: *The time-honoured tradition of lighting the maple wood stacks at the Jack Daniel Distillery.*

Schenley. At the United Distillers archives at Stitzel Weller I once held a letter written in his own flawed hand, asking – almost begging – to be taken over. The offer was declined: probably the biggest mistake in American distilling history. Any spirits company would today give its right hand to have this distillery in its armoury.

Apart from the money-spinning success of the Black Label brand, from a sheer quality point of view, the best of all are two small-batch beauties. Master Distiller is a six-year-old, the whiskeys drawn from the top of the southern warehouses: it tastes twice its age. It is the sweetest of all the Jack Daniel brands and the one which shows most rye, though not before the corn has had its say. This is marvellous whiskey showing great finesse. Yet there is even better to come when you come to Barrel House 1.

I've been lucky enough to climb to the top of the inside of Barrel House 1, the Buzzard's Roost as it is colloquially known, and taste the whiskey direct from the cask as it cooked in the barrel under the inverted frying-pan roof of the ironclad building. Selected barrels spend a year rounding off there after five years in other parts of the warehouse. From the bottle, not to mention the cask, you will find a whiskey of stunning deliciousness. It is hefty stuff with only a fraction of Master Distiller's silky nature. But the complexity is on another plane. This is not a big whiskey, but a massive one, with loads of malt battling through, and helped along with the heaviness not just of the trademark liquorice but by a Guyanan pot still effect as well. With the rye making a late entrance, this is magical stuff, an absolute classic. Again, if, like me, you adore peaty Islay whiskies, this should be just up your street.

But what of Jack Daniel's Old Time No. 7 brand? It may not be a patch on either of those two glorious whiskeys, yet it is an any-time-of-day whiskey which proves that you don't have to be devoid of character to be enormously popular, and that the bigger, full-flavoured whisk(e)ys of Scotland, Ireland and the USA cannot only be enjoyed by the connoisseur but by new drinkers too. In many ways it is not so much a beacon as a flare, a whiskey that explodes on the palate yet throws light on just how great big, bruising whiskeys can be. For everyone.

DICKEL

Anyone confronted with a glass of George Dickel, irrespective of its age or strength, may have to concede that the laws of distilling are

Southern charm: *Jack Daniel's advertising strategy is steeped in rural nostalgia.*

neither linear nor doctrinal. Because George Dickel's Cascade Hollow Distillery is an eye-opener, a revelation to connoisseur and whiskey-drinker alike, especially those who like to pigeon-hole distillery styles. It even spits in the eye of those who claim Tennessee whiskey is spelt with an "e". George Dickel makes whisky.

Indeed, not only is it proud to make whisky but without question its stills are responsible, with Wild Turkey, for the most complex and sophisticated whisky to be found anywhere in the USA. If it were a Bordeaux, it would be a Lafite.

Why is it, then, that so few people have ever heard of it? It may make arguably America's best whisky, but it trails behind Jack Daniel's and Jim Beam in the advertising stakes by a mile and has always done. Every year 300,000 visitors go to see how Jack Daniel's is made, some sporting faded, black T-shirts like soccer or basketball fans bearing their team's favours. Yet just 7,000 make it the extra 16 miles to Cascade Hollow and there is rarely a Dickel shirt in sight.

It is the tourists' loss: the distillery is situated in a valley more delightful than any in Scotland, which is another quite remarkable feature. The hills that surround it are not as austere as at Dalwhinnie in the Scottish Highlands, or as soft and weatherbeaten as those in Speyside or as heavily forested as those in Japan. Rather, Cascade Hollow is overlooked by boldly sloped, lush, tree-framed pastures of a kind more usually found in Switzerland, Liechtenstein, Austria or perhaps even England's Lake District.

Maybe that is the key to Cascade Hollow's special attraction: it is so hard to find, and when you do there is the overwhelming realisation that you must be one of life's fortunates. Where Daniel's has a town location which is easier to find than miss, to track down Dickel you must be in possession of a very good map and the ability to follow confusing signs. Despite the distillery being allowed, since January 1, 1995, to sell its whisky from its shop, Cascade Hollow is still very much in a dry county and farmers refuse to allow signs showing the way to the distillery on their land: even now the signs can be spotted lying fallen and smashed by the wayside, torn down by those claiming to be the glove of the hand of God. They argue that no amount of money will entice them to help folk along the path to damnation.

Hidden classic: *The George Dickel Distillery is obscure by JD's standards but makes sublime whisky.*

In fact, drinking a generously filled glass or two of Dickel on the veranda, with the crimson, early-autumn glow of a Tennessee sunset silhouetting the cottonwood trees laden with restless red-wing blackbirds, is about as close to the promised land as you may find on earth.

If you do visit, hotels are rarely licensed to sell the whisky, so some accommodating folk, like the Underwoods at the nearby Parish Patch Inn – part farm, part hotel – will gladly allow you to bring and drink your own. And with Dickel's rural location, a town stay would be entirely inappropriate.

Surprisingly, the nearest town, Tullahoma, is only a short drive away. Its main street presents quite a sight: two wide roads and slap between them an equally broad railroad track. It was with the advent of the railroad that Tullahoma was founded, as it was a stopping-off point for both crew and, occasionally, passengers of the Chattanooga Choo Choo that ran to Nashville. Even today, it is an unusual occurrence to be standing in Tullahoma and not hear or see a loco clank and toot its way through the town ahead of a seemingly endless procession of wagons. It was these strong railway links that saw the town double in size during the Second World War as soldiers were posted there for training, with a number of them setting up home for good when hostilities ended.

Yet within 10 minutes of leaving the city limits you are crossing a railroad track at Normandy. This is deepest, darkest Tennessee, and just a mile or so on from there hidden away is the Dickel Distillery.

Just to underline Dickel's rural pedigree, a few hundred yards up a cart track from the distillery can be found the remains of the original establishment. It consisted of little more than a shack, as was usually the case in those early post-frontier days of the mid-nineteenth century. Some of its long-fallen walls can still be made out amid the thick growth and rotting branches. Set beside the Cascade just a few yards further on, a

George Dickel: *The distillery's German founder.*

waterfall allows the water to gulp air and breath. Old George evidently knew how to pick his spot.

But just who was this George Dickel, the man with the unlikely-sounding whisky name? Most Kentucky or Tennessee distillers gave their distillery the name of the location where it was founded, or the source from which the all-important water came. Those who gave their surnames were often of Irish or Scottish extraction. Dickel was German, born near Frankfurt am Main in 1818, and is known to have reached the United States by at least 1844. The fact that his parents were millers probably led to him eventually becoming a distiller. He had already entered the whiskey trade by 1870, and from selling wholesale he went one better by setting up his own distillery in 1879. At first he took the water route, calling his brand Cascade Whisky.

For those who visit the distillery, though, there is something worth looking out for. There is an ancient bottle, complete with a century-old label, and on it the contents are clearly marked as "Tennessee Whisky". This was a bold move because, at that time, Jack Daniel was still describing his whiskey as bourbon, possibly to appeal to a greater market. It was Daniel, though, who went to the trouble of persuading the US Government to grant Tennessee whiskey its own status. That was in 1941 when Dickel, ironically, was being produced in Kentucky.

The original site was abandoned in 1910, over a century after it was originally built as a grist mill, when Tennessee was stricken with Prohibition. The first move was to the Stitzel Weller plant in Louisville which made Dickel whisky under licence until 1937. Then Schenley bought the name entirely and moved the operation to the Stagg, now Ancient Age, Distillery. The Dickel circle was now complete: from Frankfurt to Frankfort.

The present distillery was purpose-built in 1958, to a rather squarish, red-bricked design. Although hardly as atmospheric as George's old shack, somehow it managed not to jar against the outstanding natural beauty of its locale.

Distillery manager David Backus has been doing his bit by encouraging creepers to grow against the walls of the distillery to soften the building's impact, but it is the log-built stores across the creek which really catch the eye. This is the distillery shop and at first glance looks as though it could have been erected by George himself.

Dickel No. 12 brand: *Liquid gold.*

The whisky Dickel sold was a one-off: the cask-strength product, aged a minimum 11 years, big, without displaying any of Daniel's characteristic oiliness. It did not possess the finesse of the younger Dickels, especially the eight-year-old No. 12 brand: that would be almost impossible. For that particular whisky displays an extraordinary grace, starting as all truly great whiskies do, with the nose. To capture the intricacy of this is like trying to grasp a rainbow: the spectrum is astonishing and clearly defined, but you can never quite touch the beginning or end of it. On the palate it is no less enigmatic and is at its sportiest at 90 proof. The 11-year-old has been replaced by a 10-year-old called Special Barrel Reserve which is more oily and sweeter too. Even the youngster of the pack, the five- and six-year-old Old No. 8 brand, boasts beguiling citrus and cocoa riches despite matching neither its brothers' intensity nor complexity.

The distillery manager doesn't wave a special wand to produce whiskies as pulsating as these; instead, he relies on a 90-year-old formula of 81 per cent maize, 11 per cent rye and eight per cent malted barley, house yeast and two stills. This recipe could be a clue: the closest whiskey in style to Dickel is Ancient Age, which shares a similarly high corn mashbill, and where, perhaps crucially, Dickel was made for 21 years. The beer still is, like all others in Kentucky and Tennessee, of the unremarkable and efficient column variety. The spirit still, however, is a doubler pot still and it is in there that the magic is probably performed: although the still is stainless steel, the heating coil is copper. The filtration is slightly different for Dickel, though following the Tennessee style of filtering through charcoal. Here, pure wool blankets are used at the top and the bottom to stop the charcoal clogging and for the spirit to run more evenly throughout rather than through drip-worn holes.

Maybe it is in the maturation that Dickel's complexity lies. It is the only distillery in the states of Kentucky or Tennessee to have single-storey warehousing so the casks each have the same exposure to the elements. Also, the warehouses have been built on a ridge high up behind the distillery where Cascade Hollow can be victim to sharp winter frosts and stifling summer heat. However, the warehouses are always ventilated by winds which have a gentler impact on the valley floor. No one is exactly sure why Dickel's Tennessee is so fine – probably not even old George himself, whose life, just like that of Jack Daniel, ended painfully from complications, long after an accident – in his case on a horse. But if the distillery manages to keep the quality of its whisky up to these same high standards, eventually more and more people will be wanting to find out.

Connoisseur's Selection

No. 8 – Beguiling citrus and cocoa richness.

No. 12 exudes finesse and extraordinary grace. To capture the intricacy of this is like trying to grasp a rainbow.

Special Barrel Reserve – Alongside Wild Turkey, Dickel produces the most complicated and sophisticated whiskey in the United States.

RYE

Of the world's numerous whiskey styles, rye is the one that is least understood. Ask most people for a rye whiskey and, if they respond at all, they will probably get you a bottle of Canadian Club. Yes, that is a rye, inasmuch as Canadian is often called rye rather than whiskey. But, with the exception of one distillery, Alberta, Canadian whiskey is made from corn, rather than rye. Canadian may contain rye whiskey, but it may have been blended in to give it a desired personality.

The finest rye whiskeys the world has to offer are made in Kentucky, and also, now, California. Once it was Pennsylvania and, to a degree, Maryland which, among fellow whiskey-makers, enjoyed a reputation second to none. Among drinkers in the United States, though, they lost their appeal. This was mainly thanks to Prohibition when a generation had the opportunity to get used to drinking no alcohol at all or, if they broke the law, something that was much lighter than their indigenous bourbon and rye.

Most distilleries in North America have made rye whiskeys at one time or another, though often only for flavouring purposes. One of the best ryes was made at the Seagram plant in Indiana and was tipped into Seven Crown or the occasional bourbon whiskey blend. Today only three Kentucky distilleries bother to market a rye: Jim Beam, who have two; Heaven Hill, who have two brands but just the one style; and Wild Turkey, who have just the one brand – though at 101 proof it's one you are unlikely ever to forget once tasted.

Even in Kentucky it is rare to find a straight rye whiskey in bars and restaurants. When I do, that is my choice, no matter what bourbons are available. The reasons are twofold: first, you never know when you might see one again; second, it is probably my favourite whiskey type.

I remember first entering the Talbot Tavern in Bardstown and there was the rape-flower yellow label of the Jim Beam rye shining from the back of the bar like a beacon and calling to me like a siren: I couldn't take my eyes off it or my nose from the glass. In Britain not one single rye whiskey is marketed and that is not unusual. Outside the USA only a handful of countries import straight rye. It has no image, and because sales are so small anyway no marketing force or rep wants to put any effort behind it. It is regarded as an anachronism and a curiosity. To me it's nothing less than a wonder of the world; a rival to the very finest Islay whiskies in that the towering, powering complexity of the spirit has to be tamed to be understood. And when it is, you unearth treasures almost beyond comprehension.

Oddly, it was not the sturdy peoples of Pennsylvania and Maryland who invented rye whiskey as such. In the earliest distilling days of the New World the rye spirit would, from necessity, have been drunk when days, weeks or, at best, just months old. We are now entering a zone where spirit definitions become blurred. Five hundred years before Americans began savouring this potent brew, it had already become a staple of the peoples of central and northern central Europe. It was later to be called vodka. The difference is that in those lands, though, there was no attempt to barrel the spirit and let it mature.

By the time rye spirit was made in the United States, it was appreciated that, like corn whiskey and the whiskies of Ireland and Scotland, time in the wood allowed the spirit to mellow and take on extra, softer flavours. In Kentucky the corn-based whiskey became known as bourbon, after the county where the best distillers were said to be. Likewise in Pennsylvania, rye took the name of Monongahela, after the river which runs through Pittsburgh and down along the western parts of the state, and the little settlement of that name which sprouted beside it: the region where the best rye whiskey was made. The town and river still exist but the name for the rye has been lost; perhaps it was just too much of a mouthful.

These days there is only one commercially sold rye which is made from 100 per cent rye grain. Just as American law states that bourbon has to contain a minimum 51 per cent corn in its mashbill, so the law demands that straight rye whiskey must contain no less than 51 per cent rye. But whereas bourbon producers have few qualms about taking their corn percentage up to the 80 per cent mark, there is no matching inclination to take a rye content up to such levels. First, rye is a lot more expensive to buy than corn; second, it is more difficult to control; third, the powerful, intense nature of the grain means that distillers are frightened that too much taste might frighten off customers. Only the Anchor Distillery in San Francisco has taken the decision to produce a rye-only whiskey, as we shall see.

Already by the first few years of the nineteenth century, some American commercial distillers had discovered that they obtained what they felt were the best results by using two-thirds rye alongside a third of corn. This rye, though, would have been malted, imparting a softness of flavour which is not evident in

Under filled: *Sadly, rye whiskey is put into barrels at Wild Turkey only once or twice a year.*

today's Kentucky ryes. If rye is an expensive commodity, then malted rye is even less of an economic winner. For that reason, all Kentucky rye mashbills contain a similar percentage of malted barley, between 10 and 12 per cent, to assist fermentation; the remainder is corn. The rye remains unmalted. The result is a whiskey with the oily heaviness in body of an Islay, but with the crisp, hard fruitiness of an Irish pot-still, where another unmalted grain, this time barley, is used.

During fermentation, rye whiskey cannot be mistaken. It is darker in colour than bourbon and emits a richer, fruitier, more pungent odour. The oil from the grain gathers at the top of the fermenter, but is brown rather than blood-red, as is the case with bourbon. Fermentation time is the same with rye as it is with bourbon, and the speeds through the still are the same, but the new spirit is markedly different. At Wild Turkey, for instance, that fruitiness is evident and gives the spirit a hardness that cannot be detected in bourbon, even though the corn character is not that far behind. To taste, the contrast is even more marked: the rye is sharper, sweeter and leaves an almost sour, unripened yet delicious fruit residue; the average new-make bourbon, meanwhile, is flatter with less spice. It only stands to reason that, fully matured, this rye whiskey achieves nothing less than enormity.

In the case of Wild Turkey, Jimmy Russell feels that four years is all that is required for rye to reach its peak. And, at his cherished level of 101 proof, this is one of America's most spectacular spirits. It jumps out at you from the glass, the oiliness evident as in the fermenter, with the trademark Wild Turkey honey-wax adding great depth and a slice of ginger on the finish.

But just as bourbons show different character traits from distillery to distillery, so, too, do ryes. Some way different to Wild Turkey is Heaven Hill's offering, which goes under the names of Pikesville and Stephen Foster. This presents a different nose altogether, with the rye hiding behind butterscotch and leather. But on the palate the rye character is much more forceful, with lots of sweet oils trying unsuccessfully to contain its hardness. There is a sprig of mint to lighten things a little, but the finish is complex with first a defiant spurt of fruit juice before the drying finale. For those who find the Wild Turkey style just too full-blooded and dashing, this is a relatively supine but delicious alternative.

It is Jim Beam, though, who are really doing their bit to keep rye alive, and hats off to them. They produce two, almost chalk and cheese in character. One is the most famous straight rye of them all: Old Overholt, named after a Pennsylvanian farmer-distiller who had been producing Monongahela since 1810. Almost certainly because of yeast strain, it has a creamy nose. Almost certainly because of the type of grain, there are citrus notes. Almost certainly because of the generous quantity of the principal ingredient, there is very hard rye. To taste, it remains remarkably creamy and, paradoxically, the rye takes longer to make its mark than the other flavours. When it does, it is momentarily moist and sweet before going on to perfect the driest, crispest finish of its genre.

If that isn't wonderful enough, Beam also

makes the finest rye whiskey money can buy. It is under the Jim Beam label, which claims that the contents inside are "Mild and Mellow". If that is the case, I really don't know what mild and mellow is. This is a rye that refuses to take prisoners, a volcano of flavours erupting over the tastebuds, making for one of the world's super-great whiskeys. And mild and mellow it ain't. The supreme nose is rye-rich and oily, with perhaps a sprig of lavender for balance. As soon as it lands on the palate, the rye oil spreads itself across the mouth for bitter-sweet fruitiness. The finish is rock-hard as the rye really gathers pace and some oak gets through as well. This is at 80 proof! I'd love Beam to take a gamble and bring out a 101 version.

All these ryes are four-year-olds. In the case of Wild Turkey, the rye content will be around the 54–55 per cent mark, depending on the grain, with malted barley a constant 12 per cent; Heaven Hill's are 52 per cent rye with 12 per cent barley malt; while Jim Beam's is 51 per cent rye. The big boy is Old Overholt with an impressive 61 per cent rye. Where Wild Turkey, Heaven Hill and Old Overholt are made just once a year, Jim Beam may be made twice and, in the case of the Beam brands, either their Claremont or Boston distilleries will be called into action, depending on which is available.

It's the old traditional rye states which are the biggest markets for these magnificent whiskeys, with Pikesville hardly seen outside Maryland. Only Wild Turkey flies the flag with any confidence outside the USA, with about 40 per cent of all that is made going to Japan. That the rest of the world does not get a chance to savour these astonishing whiskeys is ridiculous. If my whiskey writing achieves nothing else, I hope it goes some way to restoring rye to where it truly belongs: on the bar of every drinking establishment you enter. Anything less is sacrilege.

Connoisseur's Selection

JIM BEAM RYE – A VOLCANO OF RYE-RICH FLAVOURS. ONE OF THE WORLD'S SUPER-GREAT WHISKEYS, IT TAKES NO PRISONERS.

WILD TURKEY RYE – THE DISTILLERY'S TRADEMARK HONEY WAX ADDS GREAT DEPTH WHILE THERE'S EVEN A SLICE OF GINGER ON THE FINISH.

OLD POTRERO

There are some grand whiskey moments in Hollywood history. There are even great ones.

Grain train: *Rye and other cereals are brought to Jim Beam's Clermont Distillery by railroad.*

For me, though, there is one scene without parallel, one of the most captivating pieces of cinema ever. A two-minute slot in *The Big Sleep* has it all: a dusty, Californian, second-hand bookshop, a book-ish, intelligent, sharp-witted and beautiful female shop assistant. And no one else around. The moment is not lost on Humphrey Bogart as he watches the rain pouring down outside: "You know, it just happened I had a bottle of pretty good rye in my pocket." It's an offer the girl in the Acme bookstore can't refuse. She locks the door, he loosens the screw-cap and they drink together ... It has to be my ultimate fantasy. He's 38, the same as me. She's younger. There are books. California. And rye.

Because product placement had not yet taken hold of the film industry it is not possible to see which brand of rye he pours, but one thing is certain. It would have been shipped from way out east: Pennsylvania or Maryland. Even in Los Angeles and even in the 1940s the one place that rye wouldn't have come from was California.

But now if film producers ever commit the mortal sin of re-making this classic, the rye they use might just be local – if you regard San Francisco as local, that is.

Yes, San Francisco has its own distillery, though very few yet know of its existence. At the moment it has just the one brand, Old Potrero. The fact that it is made in California is not the only thing that sets it apart: it is pot-distilled and, more amazingly, consists of 100 per cent malted barley. For that alone, it is one of the rarest, commercially marketed whiskeys on earth.

Strictly speaking, until the spring of 1996, San Francisco could boast only a single indigenous whiskey: Buena Vista, a blended Irish made by Irish Distillers at Midleton exclusively for that famous old café down opposite the beach on Fisherman's Wharf where the clanking trolley cars congregate. Until then no one in that beautiful city would have been able to tell you that there was a distillery in town, such was the secrecy with which the setting-up of the apparatus and experimentation with the first distilled spirits had been conducted. Even in the building where the distillery sits, in the city's Potrero district, very few people working there knew what was going on, the tiny pot still being hidden in a no-go area behind a screen.

In fact, the distillery is housed in a brewery, and not any old brewery. The beer made within its thick, proud and elegant post-Prohibition walls is held in veneration by connoisseurs the world over. It is the Anchor Brewery, purveyors of the famous Steam Beer, the luscious Liberty Ale, a chewable Porter and teasingly complex Christmas Ales. With such a heritage to follow, you might expect their whiskey to be something rather special. And you would be right.

Like those distinctive, truly classic beers, the whiskey is the creation of Fritz Maytag who, wearied a little by the micro-brewing revolution which swept the USA following the success of his Anchor Brewery, has thrown himself heartily and with a passion into distilling. The Maytag name is well-known in the USA. There is the Maytag washing machine empire, now part of the Hoover group, but begun by his great grandfather. It was his father who gave his country Maytag Blue, one of the great cheeses of North America. Now Fritz is following on the family tradition of creativity.

But his interests don't end there: I can think of no other distiller in the world who is

Anchors away! *Fritz Maytag proudly displays America's newest – and oldest – whiskey style.*

responsible for the making of whiskey, beer ... and wine. His home is in magnificent country north of San Francisco where the Napa and Sonoma counties meet. It is amid California's top wine-growing country and his farm is a vineyard, his York Creek red wines (as his beer already does, and as his whiskey certainly will) enjoying a reputation for excellence.

Fritz will talk long, hard and openly about his beers and wines. He is less expansive about his rye. The openness with which he discussed his beer may have slightly backfired and you would swear that both he and Jerry Dalton, once of Barton, were blood brothers.

When I first visited the Anchor Distillery in 1995 it was under a cloak of secrecy: I had to swear not to write, broadcast, or discuss anything whatsoever about what I knew until the rye was on its way into the market. And even now I have no idea where the rye originates (though I enjoy the fun of guessing – perhaps it is North Dakota), or where it was malted (maybe very quietly through those responsible for supplying the malted barley for his beer), the distillation times and so on. But this was a fair swap, because I had the privilege of seeing what will become a world-class whiskey in its embryonic state, and of being the first writer to sample it. I tasted some maturing spirit that was just six months old and already it had developed massive character, far above any rye I had tasted of less than three years old. I guessed it was partially because of the malting of the grain. Also because of the still (the singular is used here on purpose).

One of Fritz's dreams was to recreate a whiskey which some of America's earliest settlers might recognize. As well as being a possible commercial enterprise, it was also to be a celebration of America's great whiskey-making tradition. He discovered that rye was among the earliest grains to be successfully distilled. And many of those early settlers, especially the Scots-Irish, had learned in their native lands how to distil from the single, small copper pot.

That is also the case at the Anchor Distillery. Old Potrero, his first whiskey to hit the streets, had been double-distilled in the same pot, though earlier trials, which began in 1994, saw some strange concoctions being made. He admitted: "We single-distilled, double-distilled, triple-distilled and more. Though not on purpose. Our first efforts were not exactly covered in glory: half the time we didn't know what we were doing." In the build-up to the distilling, however, they knew exactly what they were doing. Rather than fermenting in old barrels, as was the case 200 years ago, mashing and fermenting was carried out in stainless steel vessels, thereby keeping things under strict twentieth-century control. Oddly, many Scots distillers prefer to ferment in large washbacks of Oregon pine: this distillery is the closest to those old forests.

Fritz is a man who prefers to do things his way. He will seek advice – the best he can find – and he will listen carefully to that advice. But only he will decide what is to be done. And what he has done is create a whiskey that is simply magnificent. The only whiskey it can seriously be compared with is the malted rye from Lawrenceburg, Indiana, which at eight years eclipses it on the nose yet, incredibly, is its inferior for taste. That is some achievement because Lawrenceburg malted rye is itself something very special, indeed.

It would be wrong to think Old Potrero is any slouch on the nose. It has been matured in virgin oak to give full depth and, once that glass is warm, there is honey, honeysuckle and spice; yet the youth is always evident. It is on the palate that this whiskey truly excels: massively intense, the rye offers fruit and delicious oils and the malt adds a richness of complexity which no whiskey this age should even attempt. The lengthy, oily finish adds even more honey, now with chocolate and a tell-tale rye hardness. It is nothing short of brilliant.

The whiskey is as sweet as Fritz's humour is dry. It is even called Old Potrero, a jibe against the absurdity of America's laws which prohibit the use of certain words to describe a product's age – except the world "old". Old it certainly isn't, yet there is no other 13-month-old whiskey like it anywhere else in the world.

However, there is one criticism that can be levelled at the whiskey: it is near-impossible to find. Knowing that he had only 1,448 bottles from that December 1994 distillation, Fritz resisted the temptation to place it into the world's top liquor stores where, if it really took off, he could not fulfil demand. Instead you might find it in the top restaurants of the rye heartlands of Baltimore and Washington as well as New York and, fittingly, San Francisco. But such pleasures don't come cheap, as you may have to pay anything up to $17 a shot. Another batch distilled in December 1995 is due to be sent in as reinforcements during 1997, and Fritz is looking at developing older whiskey and from different barrel types.

All this is further proof of a renaissance in the American whiskey world. Coincidentally, the last time I drove out of the gates of the Labrot and Graham Distillery in Kentucky, having witnessed the first pot-still whiskey to be made there, the radio in my Lincoln broke off from its music to give me a message or two: the first was to buy a Maytag washing machine. Maytag, pot stills, whiskey. You can't get away from them.

Now I eagerly await the follow-up rye to their extraordinary first attempt. As Humphrey Bogart might have said: "Play it again, Fritz".

Connoisseur's Selection

Old Potrero – Honey, honeysuckle and spice. Massively intense and complex.

6 

CANADIAN WHISKY

There is a barely detectable, though perhaps understandable, paranoia among Canadian distillers. They have been taxed, with a crippling 83 per cent duty on each bottle, almost out of existence by successive home governments. And, like the Kentuckians, they fall into the trap of believing that, as good as they know their whisky to be, a perceived lack of history means that it will never be taken as seriously as Scotch, or even Irish.

It would of course be ridiculous to compare Canadian whisky with, say, Scotch single malt, but only because they are made from different grain materials. There is no similarity in the distillation methods and there are other things which alter the whisky's behaviour, such as maturation. Likewise, it would be inappropriate to compare Irish with Scotch. It has nothing to do with quality; it is all about style. And style is something that Canadian whisky has in abundance.

The many long and arduous journeys which took me from the western seaboard through and over the Rockies, the Prairies and on to the uplifting greenness of Nova Scotia not only made me the first writer ever to undertake a detailed visit of every working distillery in a country whose vastness is barely imaginable, but also confirmed what I had long suspected: Canada boasts an array of whiskies of all shades of character. Generally, the quality is high; sometimes it is superb.

It is also a country of caution. From the onset of Prohibition in the United States, to the boom years after the Second World War and then into the confident 1970s, the world was awash, it seemed, with Canadian whisky. New high-tech, super-efficient distilleries were built to cope with the upsurge in demand and it was as if Canadian whisky could do no wrong. But then the demand for spirits the world over began to tumble and in Canada one distillery after another started to close until, today, just nine remain, of which only three – Walkerville, Valleyfield and Alberta – were in operation when I was born in 1957.

It has to be said that Canada has lost some rather good distilleries and, as far as quality is concerned, none better to my mind than Beaupré, Seagram's outpost in Quebec. While in Montreal during the writing of this book, I witnessed bulldozers tearing down the same La Salle Distillery that the legendary Samuel Bronfman lovingly built and developed to form his Distiller's Company, and which produced massive amounts of the booze smuggled into the United States during those dark years of the long thirst.

There is more than a touch of irony in the fact that Seagram should be flattening its former distilleries. In many ways, it has done more than any other company in the world to get the message of distilling heritage across. At Waterloo, Ontario, three warehouses made of beautiful yellow sandstone still survive. Two are close to demolition unless someone comes along with a realistic programme to put them to use. The other has been converted into a wonderful museum which any whisky-lover visiting the country should take the small detour to see. But of Waterloo Distillery itself, once one of the most impressive in the world until damaged by a blaze after already having been closed, there is nothing to be seen. When I asked why, the reply was, "What can you do with a shut distillery?"

Perhaps the answer lies in Toronto, where there remains the oldest whisky distillery still standing – not just in Canada but in the entire North American continent. Gooderham and Worts ended its 120-year-long, whisky-making career in 1957, but carried on producing rum until 1990. The distillery, today owned by Allied Domecq, is a remarkable testimony to Canadian distilling – the buildings date back to vital periods of expansion up until the turn of this century. The maltings, built in 1863 and still completely intact, is probably the most important and atmospheric relic of a bygone whisky age that I have seen at any distillery. But the caretaker escorting me around, joyfully told of his plans to knock this down, remove that, demolish here and put shops in there.

One can only pray that these crazy plans are stopped in their tracks, since some of the priceless ancient apparatus inside has already been ripped out and pointlessly sold for scrap. The Gooderham and Worts Distillery affords the last chance that the Canadian whisky industry has of proving that its whisky has as remarkable a heritage as any other. Moreover, since it is so close to the very centre of Toronto, tourists in their hundreds, or even thousands, would have the opportunity to discover this for themselves. If they do, it is to be hoped that they will be tempted to find out just what treasures are still to be found among the country's many famous but underestimated whiskies.

THE WHISKY DISTILLERIES
OF CANADA
KEY
DISTILLERIES
Cities
BRITISH COLUMBIA
ALBERTA
MANITOBA
ONTARIO
QUEBEC
NOVA SCOTIA
USA
Vancouver
Calgary
GIMLI
GLENORA
Quebec
Montreal
Toronto

BRITISH COLUMBIA
ALBERTA
ALBERTA (Calgary)
Vancouver
OKANAGAN
PALLISER

QUEBEC
ONTARIO
Quebec
Montreal
VALLEYFIELD
CANADIAN MIST
Toronto
KITTLING RIDGE
WALKERVILLE

THE HISTORY OF CANADIAN WHISKY

Finding the exact moment when a country became a whisky-distilling nation is a pretty hit-and-miss affair at the best of times. Finding when the legal stuff became available is much easier, thanks to government licensing records. For some reason, though, it is the story of pioneering distillers which attracts the most attention from whisky-writers and advertising men. Take, for instance, the rather over-romanticized early history of Scotch. This can be traced back at least 500 years, when we are presented with the vision of Friar John Cor, presumably a gentle, God-fearing man, receiving his "eight bolls of malt ... wherewith to make aqua vitae". The picture for many, rightly or wrongly, is one of a learned figure putting the spirit to good use, perhaps by administering it to the sick both internally and externally. It was thus that it became the Water of Life.

Compare that, then, with some of the earliest references to whisky in Canada through the diaries of the trappers who traded with the Indians some 200 years ago as, acre by acre, the wild lands were opened up to "civilization". These tales have never been told in the context of Canadian whisky history. Yet they do underline how the history of a great nation and its spirit travel hand in hand and are inextricably linked. One of the more prominent and literate trappers, William Henry, caught fur in southern Manitoba for the North West Company. His diary for 1802/3, for example, leaves little to the imagination about the effect whisky and other liquors had on the war-minded native population. It was, in effect, the Water of Death.

"January 1st: I treated my people with two gallons of high wine... My neighbours came visiting and before sunrise both sexes of all parties were intoxicated ... the men were fighting and quarrelling all night.

May 14th: In a drinking match ... yesterday, Gros Bras in a fit of jealousy stabbed Aupusoi to death with a hand dague... Soon after this Aupusie's brother, a boy of about ten ... took the deceased's gun ... and approached Gros Bras' tent. Putting ... the gun through the door the boy fired the two balls into his breast and killed him dead... Little Shell found the old woman, Aupusoi's mother, in her tent; he instantly stabbed her. Ondainoiache then came in, took the knife and gave her a second stab. Little Shell, in his turn taking the knife, gave her a third blow. In this manner did the two rascals continue to murder the old woman, as long as there was any life in her. The boy escaped ... and was kept hid until they were all sober.

April 20th 1803: Indians drinking. Le Boeuf quareled with his wife and knocked her senceless with a club.

May 6th: Indians arrive daily and drink continuously."

The natural look: *At times, Canada actually seems more Scottish than Scotland.*

As the first licensed distillery to be built in Canada was onstream by 1769 for the making of rum, the liquor which Henry had at his disposal was probably a mixture of rum (which might possibly have been delivered by his parent company with provisions when they came to collect the furs) and, from the reference to "high wine", a whisky spirit made from whatever grains were available. Since Henry also had access to sugar, some crude rum might have been made as well. As he often referred elsewhere to "mixed liquors", it is possible that this whisky was added to rum as a supplement, or the rum was added to the homemade whisky to add flavour. However, it appears that quality of taste had little to do with early Canadian whisky; it was the effect that made it so popular.

Yet it would be misleading to suggest that the influence of whisky on this embryonic nation was all bad. Indeed, it became a quite vital staple for a hardy people, enabling them to survive an unforgiving climate and terrain. Because of the massive influx of Scots into Canada, it is hardly surprising that whisky distilling became the norm throughout the land as the wilderness and the tribes who inhabited it were slowly tamed, cut down, or both. The Scots and Irish had discovered in their far-distant lands of origin and later in Virginia and Kentucky that, if there was any

Corby's: *The name lives on, but it is not as dominant as it used to be.*

grain going spare after it had been sold or made into bread, it made more sense to distil it into whisky. It reached a better price, was easier to carry and did not spoil with age – in fact quite the opposite. With so much whisky about, it was not long before it had overtaken rum as Canada's favourite spirit.

There was beer to be found, though by the 1830s wine was so scarce in Canada that a bottle of it cost as much as an acre of land. So the drinking of whisky, which was cheap and plentiful, became part of a Canadian's routine. And, as farmers looked for ways to supplement their unguaranteed and scarcely adequate income, thoughts of building a distillery frequently came to mind. The letters of one farmer in Upper Canada show that, while he referred to "that detestable stuff Canadian whisky" in 1834, 10 years later he had changed his tune radically. A letter he penned in 1844, as he planned a scheme to alleviate the financial strains of farming, was remarkably perceptive in showing how the industry was to change in forthcoming years:

"A distillery on my own creek in connection with the farm, and a store principally intended to buy grain for the distillery would I believe produce enough [profit], but there are objections in the way of this. My mother is most decidedly and strongly opposed to it on the score of morality, as she thinks a facility of procuring whisky would be an injury to the country. Beside this, a bill has been introduced into our House of Assembly for imposing an excise of sixpence per gallon on whisky (about 30 per cent of its value), which I think will have the effect of throwing the business into large establishments."

He was right on every count. Excise duty was to hit the smaller distiller hard and it was the larger concerns like Gooderham and Worts in nearby Toronto which, by introducing wooden continuous stills for the purpose of making the whisky in the most efficient way possible at the time, could produce sufficiently high profits to absorb the heavy taxes. The making of Canadian whisky in pot stills by commercial concerns was the exception rather than the rule, as is still the case.

The reference to his mother shows the first signs of the puritanical thinking which led eventually to Prohibition. And it was the fairer, church-going sex, through The National Women's Temperance Union, which set the ball rolling in the 1870s after half a century of rumbling protest. Contrary to popular belief, Prohibition was not confined to the United States. During the First World War, many Canadian provinces went dry but there was outright Prohibition on a national level only from March 1918 to November of the following year. It proved to be unworkable, unenforceable and unpopular, but the unfortunate consequences of Prohibition in Canada failed to teach a lesson to the Americans. The following year the manufacture, drinking and selling of alcohol became illegal throughout the United States, except for medicinal purposes. The passing of such a naive and intellectually challenged law led logically, as the darker side of human nature was bound to dictate, to a network of underworld crime which still survives. Each day, enormous quantities of Canadian whisky would be smuggled across the border. The river linking Lake Erie to Lake St Clair became a freeway for illegal hooch as organizations such as the notorious Purple Gang tried to outwit, usually with success, the American authorities; sometimes on the doorstep of the Canadian Club Distillery at Walkerville which, legally, went about its business of making its renowned whisky. Canadian whisky had never been so popular. Indeed, it was the theft by a rival gang of a shipment of Canadian whisky, originally destined for Al Capone via the Detroit River, that led to the St Valentine's Day Massacre in 1929.

There is more than a touch of irony in the fact that, for its first 100 years, the gentlest of the world's whiskies should have inadvertently been linked with so much violence. And the Canadians reckon that their whisky doesn't have a history…

BRITISH COLUMBIA

OKANANGAN DISTILLERY

If there is a more naturally beautiful spot on earth where the glorious evolution of the earth's geology combines with its flora to such awe-inspiring effect, I have yet to find it. This is British Columbia, the furthest point west Canada can go and, for those in search of a land whose rugged magnificence not so much lifts the soul but sends it merrily on to another planet, about as far as you ever need to go. It is a land of racing rivers and waterfalls, mountains, thick forests and islands which rise sheer and dramatic from the sea. Its grandeur reminds you of the west of Scotland, but in truth the Highlands are tame, tidy and tiny by comparison. Here, the elements have combined to create a natural whisky-making region. In fact, until the 1970s, British Columbia was even the home of the Britannia Copper Mine, once the largest in the British Empire, and from where, doubtless, smelted ore went on to provide the raw material for any number of Scottish and Irish pot stills.

Some still list British Columbia as a whisky region, which I suppose it is – but not in the way they mean. A century or two ago traders made their money, and ensured that they could spend it in safety, by selling whisky to the Indians. The trade still goes on. On the outskirts of Vancouver I know one man who makes his own hooch in order to sell to the city's Hindu population. But, alas, with the demise of Hiram Walker's Okanagan Distillery at Kelowna in 1995, following the closure of the Seagram plant at New Westminster, the legalized making of whisky in the province is a thing of the past although, officially, there is still a distillery in operation. This is Cascadia, also in Kelowna. Travelling by road from Vancouver, the journey, which takes you past Langley where the company began distilling as Potters in the 1960s, is nothing less than spectacular, the route watched over by an array of peaks which grow closer to the heavens the further inland you go.

Kelowna is a boom town where the standard of life is believed to be as high as anywhere in North America, a belief obviously shared by the ever-increasing number of people moving into the neighbourhood. Even the ending of local whisky production appears not to have dampened their enthusiasm for the area. As you enter the town by

British Columbia: *Although Canadian whisky is no longer produced here,it certainly doesn't lack the water it needs to do so.*

the floating bridge across the Okanagan Lake, you do not have to go very far before a left turn takes you into Richter Street, and eventually on the right you will find a brewery and winery. Once a year it is also a distillery, where the manager, Scotsman Nick Bennett, produces enough spirit during the course of a day for the distilling licence to be kept. But the spirit is not matured into anything meaningful. The brewery's beers, sold under the Granville Island Brewing label, are quite acceptable, especially a pretty tangy Amber Ale, and their respected wines can also be found in the shop. However, the whiskies marketed under their name, such as Potter's Old Special, with its prawn-cracker, melt-in-the-mouth character, have been blended from whiskies made at distilleries elsewhere.

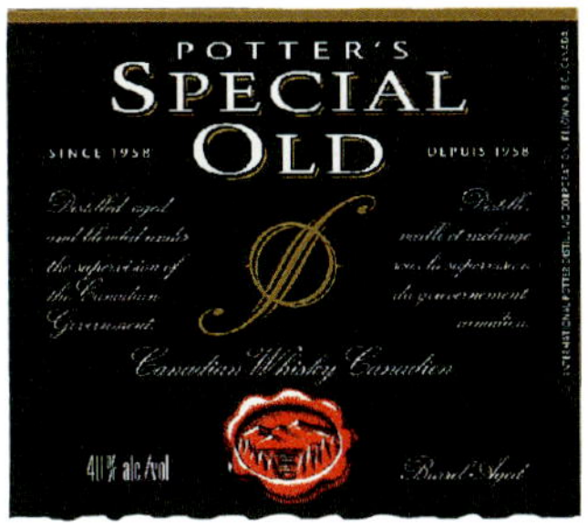

What, however, can be said about its whiskies? Well, on the whole, they are better than average. Its standard brand is Potter's Old Special which apart from displaying the qualities of a prawn cracker, having that magical ability to melt in the mouth, also leaves behind a delightful array of fluttering sensations. It is easily one of the softest, silkiest Canadian whiskies to be found, but it would be too easy to dismiss it as bland. There is a fat sweetness, doubtless thanks to a generous amount of locally made "sherry" (and here, remember, we mean fortified wine, not whisky matured in former sherry casks) and a complexity which makes for a very more-ish whisky. This is a Canadian whisky with a bit of style.

For the Taiwan market there is Royal Canadian Whisky, much more rye-heavy and oily. Again, it retains the tell-tale Potter's sweetness, but the finish is much harder and feels as if it has been chiselled as opposed to the weathered sensation of the Old Special. Once, though, pride of place in the company went to their eight-year-old, which added oak to all the other character traits. A new marketing person was brought in who decided to revamp the traditional old label and call it "Time" in designer script to appeal to younger drinkers of either sex, while upping the age to 10 at the same time for good measure. There is not too much wrong with the whisky. It is drier than one has come to expect from this company, although it never short-changes you in the complexity department. Setting it apart from the rest, it also had a lightly roasted, Costa Rican coffee feel to add to the extra spice. Unfortunately, the image was wrong and the whisky was a flop. The bottle I have in my library, though off the production line as late as 1995, is one of the last you are likely to find anywhere. A sad end to a very decent Canadian whisky.

By far Potter's finest whisky, though, is Bush Pilot, sold only in the United States. As the only single-cask, Canadian whisky to be found, it already holds a special place in the genre. But that apart, this is a magnificent whisky and it is not surprising that Cascadia is looking at the possibility of launching a similar brand on to an unsuspecting Canadian market. What they will find is a Canadian whisky that has taken on a wonderful, relaxed spiciness on the nose thanks to the oak, and equally understated bourbon characteristics on the palate. The big surprise is that it has also allowed a cream-toffee sweetness to develop which can be detected in some of the better Canadian whiskies. However, its strength lies in the soft oiliness which sticks to the palate, allowing a slightly refined sugary sweetness to deal with any grain bitterness which tries to creep in. In the space of three years, demand for this 13-year-old whisky has increased fourfold and it is not hard to see why. This must be one of the easiest whiskies to drink anywhere in the world and is one of unarguable excellence.

No one is quite sure where the casks used for Bush Pilot originated, but the chances are it was just a few miles over the other side of town, past the airport and on to Winfield. There stand the now silent stills of Okanagan Distillery, built by Hiram Walker in 1971 to take the pressure off their Walkerville Distillery as the demand for Canadian rye showed no sign of abating. That demand has now not only abated but shrunk and Okanagan is silent and up for sale. To walk around the distillery is a salutary lesson to the effect that nothing can be taken for granted. Complete with its 16 massive fermenters, it is state-of-the-art and remarkably similar to the all-purpose Midleton Distillery in Ireland. Whereas that distillery works almost flat-out, the chances of Okanagan ever making whisky again are virtually nil. When sold, it will probably be for the production of industrial alcohol.

The whisky that had been made there was claimed to be identical to Walkerville. But it wasn't. The claims were understandable: anything called Canadian Club and sold in western Canada or the United States, or in the Pacific Rim, was supposed to be the same as the whisky made and sold in the east. But I found Okanagan Canadian Club a slightly heavier, more flavoursome proposition. If you are ever in Vancouver or Seattle and someone has a 1980s bottle of Canadian Club, it is well worth persuading them to part with it.

The most remarkable thing about Okanagan are the four pot stills to be found there, built to a design similar to that of the Inverleven Distillery at Dumbarton, Scotland, which, until 1991, made rye flavouring whisky. But back in the 1980s they made pure malt whisky in them, pretty full-bodied and with a massive maltiness which does nothing but delight. It was sold for a short time to an unappreciative Japanese market as Glen Ogopogo single malt, named after the legendary beast of Okanagan Lake, the native American Indian's version of the Loch Ness Monster. Vaguely Speyside-ish in style but full of delicious chocolate-orange character, what is left of this malt is deserving of a legend of its own.

Connoisseur's Selection

POTTER BUSH PILOT – DISTILLED AT OKANAGAN, IT TAKES OFF WITH GLORIOUS CREAM-TOFFEE. SUPERB.

ALBERTA

PALLISER DISTILLERY, LETHBRIDGE

Okanagan sits as close to the 50th parallel as makes no difference. Just a few minutes further south, but a long distance six degrees to the east, is the Palliser Distillery at Lethbridge. To get there you have to cross the biggest obstacle the North American continent has to offer – the Rocky Mountains. It can be negotiated painstakingly by car. But the view from the air is exhilarating and at one point you are sure that you can spot the very point where two continents have collided – a line where the mountains on one side have an altogether different feel from those on the other. And when those mountains have been crossed there is nothing but flat lands and rolling plains as far as the eye can see. You have entered the Alberta prairies.

The distillery at Lethbridge is part of a new-age industrial site. No towering chimneys here, no deep-red, capitalist cathedrals of brick. Palliser Distillery blends perfectly with its prairie environment, low-slung save for the stillhouse and anonymous amid its anti-Gothic surroundings. It is the home of Smirnoff vodka and, truth to tell, the whisky made here really takes second place to the Great White Spirit. Even so, since it is part of the Gilbey empire, you would be right in thinking that its whisky output is large, but wrong in believing that it supports a whole host of brands. In fact, there is only one of note – Black Velvet. This is a name which reverberates around the North American continent, echoing from the nearby Rockies all the way down to the Appalachians.

One thing is certain. If a brand-new distillery is standing, the chances are that one or two have closed down elsewhere to make way for it. Gilbey's Palliser Distillery is no different. The original distillery, in New Toronto, was opened in 1933 to produce gin. It was another six years before it turned to producing whisky as well, though the outbreak of the Second World War halted production within months. In the one month of each year during hostilities when it was permitted to produce potable alcohol, the distillery only made gin. However, when the war ended and the 1939 make was considered mature enough to bottle, both of which conveniently happened in 1945, there were questions regarding the whisky's quality. Adjustments were made and in 1951 a far better whisky was available.

At first it was going to be called Black Label but, fearing legal action from Johnnie Walker, the distillery wisely decided upon the name Black Velvet. Sales of this whisky rocketed and in 1973 the Palliser Distillery was opened to serve the expanding western US markets and make use of the local corn and rye. Unfortunately, just as with Hiram Walker, contraction meant closure, only in the case of Gilbey it was the old distillery which made way for the young. Again, there was a marked difference between the two whiskies produced so far apart. Six-year-old Black Velvet from Toronto had a more clearly defined rye character, with greater pepper and spice intensity. The current six-year-old from Palliser still retains traces of what was known as the "Lethbridge Character", a rather earthy, unattractive nose which has now been eradicated from production. But there is nothing really wrong with the taste – an easy-going, gently oiled and sweetish whisky. This is to be found everywhere, except in the United States where a four-year-old has just been introduced and, I must say, it's awful. It doesn't even particularly nose like whisky; a rather heavy dose of distilled orange juice as part of the 9.09 per cent has seen to that. The taste offers more, but not much, and is rather fiery.

There is an excellent eight-year-old called Triple Crown which, by comparison, is stunning and, despite the curious saltiness one normally associates with single-malt Scotch from a coastal distillery, heads healthily toward the toffee effect that you would expect

Palliser Distiller: *The distillery reflects the flatness of the prairies.*

Alberta Distillery: *On the fringe of Calgary, it is the producer of Canada's true rye whisky.*

from a fine Canadian. No nasty surprises with this one. But the best whisky Palliser has ever produced was a 10-year-old called Red Feather Saloon, blended especially for that famous old Gold Rush landmark of the Yukon. This is magnificent Canadian whisky, bursting at the seams with oaky complexity and delicious rye fruitiness. Typically, though, the whisky did not sell and is to be discontinued. Palliser may not yet have come of age as a great whisky distillery, but if Gilbey can do more with Triple Crown and Red Feather it won't be long before that day arrives.

The slightly off-putting aroma of the mashing wheat which permeates every nook and cranny of the building has nothing of the sweetness you will find with corn, rye or barley. It is, nevertheless, a fascinating distillery, especially the tall, spinach-green washbacks which can be viewed from the bottom only, unless you want to take a vertical ladder to the top. The stills are relatively state-of-the-art, perhaps one reason why the initial spirit has such little character. Even if its whisky is not among Canada's most exciting, one can only hope that the contraction in the demand for Canadian whisky will not eventually bring about the demise of wonderful distilleries the size of these, the priceless little one-offs.

ALBERTA DISTILLERY, CALGARY

The journey from Lethbridge back up toward Calgary offers a fascinating survey of two of North America's most remarkable land features. To the left, the Rockies, to the right the start of an interminable expanse of flatlands, the prairies. They both contribute something toward the making of whisky: water from the mountains, rye, wheat and corn from the farmlands. Provided the clouds stay high, it is an impressive journey at any time of the day, but at dusk the sun burns crimson to highlight the profoundly jagged, dagger-sharp peaks.

As one passes the silos and grain stores which dominate the small towns en route, there surely has to be a distillery somewhere amid this exhibition of fertility. And there is. One of Canada's lesser-known whisky providers, Highwood, is located in the dusty town of High River which takes its name from the waters nearby. Highwood is small-scale, once drawing water from its own wells but now dependent on the mains supply to mix with its meal of wheat. It is the only distillery which makes its base whisky from wheat, and does so in order to create the cleanest of vodkas. In so doing, it produces the one neutral grain spirit which is just that: at around 95 per cent ABV, it is the only one I have tasted anywhere direct off the still which, spirit burn apart, is characterless, even tasteless.

Of all Canada's distilleries producing in their now traditional column stills, this is by far the smallest and most detached. As it is not the Canadian arm of any of the world's big drinks companies and has been operating independently since Sunnyvale Distillers set up in 1974, this is a distillery much more likely to feel the vagaries of consumer demand than most. The Highwood name was launched on its products from the beginning, and two years after the 1987 takeover by Calgary businessmen it became a limited company called Highwood Distillers.

Their own-made whisky is found only in Canada's west. They have recently doubled their rye portfolio with Centennial. Considering it has a higher proportion of rye, I find it slightly disappointing and have much more fun with their usual brand, a four-year-old called, simply, Highwood.

As delightful as it may be to find such a small-scale distillery in such a backwater, for me the most fascinating distillery in all of Canada is located not far from the perplexing, one-way-dominated city centre of Calgary, a half-hour's drive due north. Just off Ogden Road, as commerce gives way to industrialization, Alberta Distillers are celebrating their 50th anniversary by continuing to produce Canada's one and only true rye whisky. No special celebrations had been decreed by parent company American Brands of Jim Beam

fame – a pity really, because the whiskies of Alberta are worth whooping with joy over.

Their whisky is not to everyone's taste, thankfully. While Canadian distillers sheepishly ganged up together to produce a uniform softness to appeal to the widest range of unadventurous palates, Alberta has always been cavalier and nonconformist. Other distillers may dismiss this as simply a consequence of the distillery's location. There were grants to be had when setting up in the west in 1946 and the area was always too cold to produce corn, so it would buy rye from local markets – a source of even more subsidy.

Nevertheless, if Alberta had wanted to do so, they could have changed their mash bill by now and joined the corn league. Instead, they have continued to produce the most uncompromising, flavoursome whiskies Canada has had to offer, for the last couple of decades at least. These come in all shapes and ages, from three-year-old own-labels found around the world (among the best being British Halewood Vintners' seminal Canadian Gold which offers magnificent breadth to a country criminally ill-served in Canadian whisky) to their own four-, five-, six- and even 10-year-olds. However, it is the five-year-old, the Alberta Premium, which I rate among the world's very finest – even higher than their famous Alberta Springs 10-year-old.

From the outside, with its massive silos which store nearly two weeks' production in case the snow takes an unyielding grip, the distillery looks like any other in this part of the world. Inside, however, there is a feeling of underfinancing over the years which manages to convey charm and tradition in even measures. The two hammer mills are not of the dustless variety; the cooker looks tired; the 20 ageing fermenters are uncovered, allowing a grand view of the bubbling brown meal turning into a low-yield beer; the continuous stills pass muster but the pot still, looking like a kicked-over tin can, has definitely seen better days.

There are rumours that the dilapidation of the plant could bring about its eventual shutdown. However, it is this very patina of age, and of wear and tear, which puts Alberta visually on a higher plane than most, and when you taste the whisky, either as it matures, or in its final blended state, you can only pray that not too many changes are in the offing.

As with Canada's other continuous-production distilleries, two types of whisky are made, which will later be blended together. There is the base whisky, distilled to between 94.5 per cent and 96 per cent ABV, which is then flavoured with a second, heavier, more pungent spirit made from rye. With the exception of Highwood, which produces from wheat, the base whisky made by Canadian distillers is almost always from corn. In the case of Alberta, though, the base whisky is rye which is sent through two continuous stills. The whisky used for flavouring is also made from rye but it is distilled just the once to a relatively weak 65 per cent ABV. This means that the whisky has had fewer of its natural oils and flavours stripped away by a second distillation. And to add even more character to this whisky, it is then filled into either brand-new, unused oak, or wood which has held bourbon just the once and for no longer than four years.

The result is that even its youngest whisky, Carrington, is a three-year-old with an aggressive streak, not so much from its spirity youth, but from the hardness of the rye which has refused to be tamed by the oak. The four-year-old Windsor is not named in honour of Hiram Walker's flagship distillery – the frightfully British royal guard depicted underlines that. It does, however, show that an extra 12 months in a warehouse can hone some of those rougher edges. At the end of that year it has reached a form of perfection in Alberta Premium which is boosted with a dribble here and there of six-year-old. The way in which this whisky fills the mouth and its irresistible mixture of sweet, melting vanillins on a stratum of granite-like rye hardness are almost too good to be true. The finish is about as long as that of any non-peated whisky of this age that does not hail from south of Cincinnati.

There is no doubt that Alberta Springs adds a touch of extra honey to the proceedings and is light enough to allow the rye to have its bitter say. But maybe that's its problem: it is a fine whisky, but a tad too soft, a mite too bitter, too like cognac. With Premium you know where you stand and, because it is so big in the mouth, the balance is that much better. This is the only distillery anywhere in the world capable of making an outstanding 10-year-old which is nevertheless hammered by its whisky half that age. Alberta has pandered to the sweeter tastes of America with its new Tangleridge brand by putting something in the 9.09 per cent (by law Canadian distilleries can include that percentage of flavourings other than Canadian whisky) which adds effect rather than quality. Despite its age, which matches that of Springs, Tangleridge is a sop to the chattering masses – which rather goes against the grain as far as the pedigree of the magnificent Alberta Distillery is concerned.

Connoisseur's Selection

PALLISER TRIPLE CROWN – STRANGELY SALTY, YET PLENTY OF TOFFEE SWEETNESS. BRILLIANT.

ALBERTA PREMIUM – PREMIUM BY NAME AND NATURE. AN ASTOUNDINGLY COMPLEX MIXTURE OF OAT AND RYE GUARANTEES A TRUE WORLD CLASSIC.

MANITOBA

GIMLI DISTILLERY

Of all the distilling countries of the world, Canada is perhaps the only one able to boast of distilleries stretching from east to west. There is even one in just about the dead centre of the country where the prairies seem to be at their prairiest. It is called Gimli and takes its name from the small town a couple of hours' drive along the straightest road you can imagine north of Winnipeg. It sits on the shores of Lake Winnipeg and, as such, is an inland resort complete with beach. Not only does it attract tourists, but in the warmer months hordes of vicious, bloodsucking gnats. To help counter this blot on such an idyll, the town has erected condominiums of bird houses which successfully encourage the purple martin as far north as it is willing to breed. And purple martins are as partial to bloodsucking gnats as the world is to the whisky made in the north of the town. For Gimli is home to Crown Royal.

The people are, as is so often the case in Canada, a friendly bunch and the reddish-blond manes of many of the local young women reveal the strong Scandinavian connection with the area. The manager of the distillery, Chris Magnusson, can also trace his roots back to Iceland. And tracing the lineage of the Gimli Distillery is perhaps even more fascinating.

Today Gimli is Seagram's one and only distillery in Canada. This may not seem much of a surprise, since no distilling company currently has more than one operating distillery in the country. But to appreciate Seagram's heritage, it is best to read the words of Sam Bronfman, the man who raised the company from parochial respectability to world eminence, who in 1970 wrote his own version of the formation of his company and how he continued to acquire distilleries – a couple in British Columbia, the tiny Amherstburg in the south of Ontario and Beaupré in Quebec. All this was to supplement the glorious, original Seagram Waterloo, Ontario, distillery dating back to 1857, and the distillery he built himself in the 1920s, LaSalle in Montreal, complete with the Kentucky-style chimney carrying the company's name in coloured brick. By the late 1960s, with Seagram producing around a third of all the Canadian whisky drunk in the country, which represented a paltry 7 per cent of the company's global sales, it was hardly surprising that these distilleries were required to feed the apparently insatiable demands of the Seagram empire.

The lonely Gimli Distillery: *Located by Lake Winnipeg and fed by the chill waters running to Lake Manitoba.*

Although every distillery but Gimli has now been consigned to history, Seagram's blenders still have more than just their Manitoba grains to call upon when making up recipes for the many brands still marketed by the company. Of all Canada's blenders, none has the same range to work from as do the blenders based in what remains of LaSalle. The ryes, barleys, bourbons and continuous makes of Waterloo, LaSalle and Beaupré can still be added, though those whiskies become rarer as each day passes, and by the year 2000 will be exhausted altogether. One of the most complex that I found among their stocks was a mouth-watering continuous from Canada's one and only Coffey still at LaSalle. All round, Beaupré's whiskies are the most impressively balanced, just oozing finesse, while those of Waterloo, even on the continuous, possess an all too rare and welcome oiliness. In many ways, Gimli offers the cleanest of all Seagram's maturing stocks. Considering the extraordinary similarity I have discovered between Seagram's VO dating back to 1913 to the present-day six-year-old VO, it is going to take massive work from Walter Jonke and his team to keep the character profile on course. There will be subtle differences, as is always the case over time. But the high quality of Gimli's make and some very hard work which is going into the development of different yeasts to alter some flavour components toward heavier, more flavoursome bodies should see them through – just. It will not be a perfect match, but the addition of some rich bourbon and rye flavouring should also help disguise the join. However, their strict adherence to high quality does not make things easier. There is a company policy that none of the 9.09 per cent used can include non-whisky substances like sherry and other merger flavours. Instead, sometimes a dash of Kentucky bourbon from the Four Roses Distillery might be added. In the same way Canadian Mist is fortified slightly by bourbon from its sister, Early Times Distillery in Louisville.

There are also plans to re-create a Coffey-style whisky at Gimli, but at the moment the plant is run on traditional lines. It has to be said that, light as the base Gimli spirit is, it is the perfect ingredient for a skilled blender to make some truly classy whisky. For proof you only have to look at the younger Seagram brands, even Lord Calvert, a surprisingly active three-year-old make for the Scandinavian market – a whisky which, bearing in mind the origins of the local settlers, goes home. There are three four-year-olds in the shape of Seagram's Five Star, Melcher's Very Mild and Canadian Hunter. Five Star outperforms the rest, thanks to a sweeter, richer body and a long, almost fruit and chocolate pudding finale. Hunter is not without its toffee-sweet moments and the finish is quiet and dignified, with surprising oak for its

176 **Hard sell:** *Seagram's owner Sam Bronfman believed in building empires. Here he gives V.O. the full treatment.*

age. Melchers has a stunning nose for such youth and this grace is found also on the palate where perhaps it is let down by the final over-dry finish.

Seagram's "83" is the only five-year-old, perhaps lazy on the nose and less inclined toward complexity. But wait until it sits on the palate, with an almost Waterloo-esque oiliness, and here we have style again. Once we arrive at the six-year-olds, Adams' Private Stock and legendary VO, we are entering the realms of classicism. Adams' keynote is a dry, grainy simplicity. VO, on the other hand, is the kind of whisky any blender worth his salt would be quite delighted to work on. It peaks and troughs on the palate, one moment rolling over the tastebuds, the next creeping up behind them and giving them a sharp jolt. Here whisky from other distilleries is coming into play, especially Waterloo and LaSalle, and, although the minimum age is six, you can't help but notice that there is something more mature in there with it.

When we come to aged Seagram's whisky, we are talking about Crown Royal, which is (with the exception of one 10-year-old of limited demand, the Adams Antique) perhaps the sweetest of the entire Seagram range. The nose is about as sexy as they come, full of heavy oils, sweet corn, deft spices and topped off with hints of oak. It is lush and full-bodied on the palate; something akin to a Macallan in its rounded fruitiness, and again, there are touches of spice on the finish. There is amazingly little oak to ruin the proceedings – it is in the control of the wood effect on their whiskies that the Seagram blenders are ranked among the best in the world. In Scotland, blenders will hide oak in old age by possibly some liberal use of peat and sherry-cask whisky to swamp any overcooked vanillins. At LaSalle, Walter will use heavier ryes and bourbon whiskies to soften the oak blow. This is magnificently demonstrated with the Crown Royal Special Edition, which uses whisky aged a minimum 12 years and Crown Royal Limited Edition (15 years). In both whiskies, these heavier whiskies can be detected which give greater depth. Adding to the complexity in no small measure is the addition of flavouring whiskies from Seagram's four recently lost distilleries. All can be found in the Limited Edition, though Amherstburg is no more than a trace in Special. Both whiskies, though, are stunners and manage to capture the softness and complexity that is Canadian whisky. When I produced these whiskies on a BBC television programme, showing them alongside some of the finest examples of whisky made the world over, significantly it was Crown Royal that the guests appearing with me nearly all plumped for – usually with more than a hint of surprise when they realized the country of origin.

But if I had to pick a single whisky from the Seagram stable of thoroughbreds as the finest of all, perhaps surprisingly it would be the ordinary Crown Royal. This embodies Canadian whisky at its finest: there is a lightness which just flits about the tastebuds and its properties are simply pastel-shaded rather than painted in oils like the Adams' Antique and the glorious older Crown Royals. There are times, especially just before I go to bed and on average perhaps once a week, when a Crown Royal Limited or Special Edition will wind me down brilliantly. But, when just sitting with friends and enjoying, or closing my mind and concentrating on, the whisky in hand, the stylish, blossom-delicate, ordinary Crown Royal not only takes the palm, but introduces a natural gentility that is purely and uniquely Canadian.

If there is such a thing as a classically new Canadian distillery, Gimli is it. It was built so far from anywhere simply because the water supply, tapped from an underground river running between Lakes Winnipeg and Manitoba, is so clear and unlimited. Flat-roofed and built with a minimum of fuss, the distillery can still be seen for many miles before you reach it. It finds itself with the lake on one side and, during early autumn, an ocean on the other. But this is an ocean of corn, stretching as far as the eye can see, complete with waves as the wind forms ripples which roll along an expanse of flatness found nowhere else in the world.

When Sam Bronfman wrote "From Little Acorns", Gimli's whisky was too young to be used in the Seagram blends and he talks with particular affection of LaSalle, "To this day, I look forward with pleasant anticipation to my visits to the LaSalle plant. I have a strong sentimental attachment to this, our first distillery." And of Waterloo he said, "This great distillery has about it a great, indefinable aura, the like of which I have not encountered anywhere else."

He does not, however, record what – if anything – he thought about the fledgling Gimli Distillery. To me, located as it is in a world unlike any other, it is a place I yearn to return to. A few miles' drive north up the shores of Lake Winnipeg there is, appropriately enough, a place called Drunken Point. It is so named, the older locals tell me, because sailors from the Hudson's Bay Company could not, for some reason, take their liquor any further and had to drink it on the spot or dump it. The place is at its most beautiful at sunset in early May when all that can be heard is the eerie, creaky cracking of the ice which had covered the entire lake and the hauntingly sad and lonely call of the loon in the ice floes beyond. Sitting there on a rock, drinking in this most natural and timeless of atmospheres, together with some 15-year-old Crown Royal of equal delicacy, made partly from these very same waters, was one of those moments which will stay with me as long as I live. Never had I encountered such inner peace. There was, as Sam might have said, an indefinable aura.

Connoisseur's Selection

GIMLI VO – A TESTAMENT TO THE BLENDER'S ART, THIS IS AS SUBTLE AS THEY COME.

SEAGRAM'S CROWN ROYAL – LIGHT AND ALLURING IN A UNIQUELY CANADIAN WAY. A CHARMING WHISKY.

ONTARIO

WALKERVILLE DISTILLERY

On the banks of the Detroit River a building of startling, tile-smooth, red brick faces directly across to Detroit on the distant bank, seemingly cocking a Canadian snook at its American neighbour. To the right of the red brick is a château-like office and further on a number of white-painted silos on which the words "Canadian Club" can be easily made out by thirsty Americans.

This is Walkerville, in some ways now the national home of Canada's sole indigenous spirit. True, those red bricks were skilfully assembled only as recently as the 1930s, but the site on which the whisky is made dates back to 1858. With the demise of Gooderham & Worts and Corby (both while part of the same company), and Seagram's Waterloo, Beaupré and La Salle, this leaves Walkerville the only remaining home of Canada's great founding distillers. Sad, shocking even, but true.

A century ago, Walkerville was a community at the heart of which the distillery pumped away. When, in 1894, Hiram Walker opened their new suite of offices, more than 1,500 businessmen and worthies assembled from all over Ontario and Detroit to join in the celebrations. As a commentator at the time observed, "... it was a revelation of what wealth, combined with a refined taste, can accomplish". It still has the Florentine-style building, unchanged in the century that has passed. The carved oak panelling and pillars and capitals of Namibian marble are just as splendid now as they must have been all those years ago.

For the owners to have made such an investment, the business must have been good. Hiram Walker also had interests in shipping and tobacco, but it was his famous Canadian Club whisky which guaranteed his fortune. At first he called it simply Club Whisky, but Kentucky distillers protested and insisted that somewhere it should be made clear that the product was Canadian. It was not one of Kentucky's smarter moves: the success of a whisky which was clearly marked as Canadian helped the country's other distillers to win respectability in foreign markets.

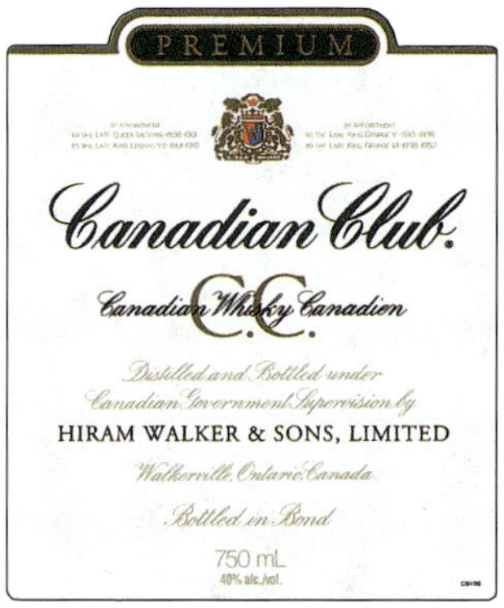

Originally, and certainly until the 1880s, Hiram Walker produced his whisky in wooden continuous stills and to a set mash bill of about 60 per cent corn, the remainder being rye, malted barley and oats. At some stage, though, the company switched to distilling corn to high strength and mixing with rye, malted rye and malted barley, distilled separately and to a lower strength. Take a trip around the distillery today and you will see that is how it is still done. And just like that first bottle of Canadian Club whisky to be filled in 1884 it was six years of age.

Much of the distillery's equipment dates back to when it was rebuilt on the same lines as the sister Dumbarton grain distillery in Scotland. The pot stills which once made a Scotch-style single malt called Highlander have gone, but there remains a pot still attached to beer still No. 1 which helps produce the heavier rye whisky.

As at Alberta, descending into the workings of Walkerville is a journey back in time. The yeast tanks are not as busy as they once

Hiram Walker: *The entrance is a lot more imposing than its gentle whiskies.*

were, but still produce a strain derived from the original 1858 yeast Hiram Walker used when he began converting his excess supplies into whisky. Nowadays that yeast is utilized only for the flavouring rye whiskies. There are high-tech pressure cookers for the corn, but traditional ones for the rye, and the bottomless fermenters installed in 1955 are there, with others added 17 years later to take on the extra pressure of producing the Gooderham brand. Again, the rye has its own section with the sticky, oily mash being pumped exclusively into numbers 33 through 38. Throughout the daily cycle, the whisky – especially the rye – is made using predominantly 1930s technology and, although new plant manager Gord Carlton has been in the post only a year or two and is a lot younger than his predecessor, he admits that he would not dream of changing a thing.

There are matching warehouses, again like the ones at Dumbarton, but these are redundant now. Instead, all barrels are matured eight miles away at Pike Creek. Before they go out there, though, they undergo an unusual process. Nearly all Canadian Club whisky is blended together as new make before it is filled into barrel. Sometimes, however, aged flavouring whiskies are added if required nearer the bottling stage. And the barrels that this blend goes into are also slightly different. With the onset of palletizing, Hiram Walker devised a method in which barrels of matured whisky are drilled through the head and the liquid inside is sucked out into holding tanks. The barrels are then conveyed on to the next stage where they are filled with new spirit. Dumping has become obsolete but, because it is almost physically impossible to empty a cask entirely, a little of the old spirit mixes in with the new, forming one of whisky's very few, though accidentally created, *solera* systems.

Despite this combination of tradition and pragmatism, Canadian Club has been universally scorned by the world's whisky connoisseurs, and I must confess that there is little in the standard six-year-old which demands my further attention. After the initial spurt of attractive, sweet butteriness it is dry with a bitter finish and, beyond a touch of oak, a little mean in its constitution. But those who have written off the whisky, and the distillery, and probably Canadian whisky as a genre with it, have short-changed themselves. In just the same way as its sister distillery, Laphroaig, has hit the duty-free market with a 100 proof version countless times better than its normal self, so Canadian Club has come up trumps. Where Laphroaig has escaped chill-filtration, the towering Canadian Club has not, which makes its extraordinary leap into the high-class bracket all the more remarkable. That toffee-butteriness now envelops the palate, with the rye coming into its own, and all this is dominant enough to see off the late, grainy bitterness which is smothered at birth.

Arguably, the classiest of whiskies under the Canadian Club banner is found in Japan. This is an eight-year-old that rightfully luxuriates in its own grandeur. It has a rich, creamy fatness giving way to a wonderful rye and oak hardness toward the finish, which the more common, yet surprisingly shy, 12-year-old sadly fails to match. The 15-year-old is a much better effort: there is less rye here but the vanillins from the oak have been drawn out to give the mouth a delicious coating of lightly peppered sweetcorn and toast. A word, though, about the 20-year-old – the word is: disastrous. This big shaker in the Japanese markets is about as poor a Canadian whisky as you are ever likely to find. Here part of the 9.09 per cent is locally-made sweet sherry. The start is not too bad, with some pleasant spices lulling you into a false sense of security. From then on it's downhill, except perhaps for a little in-built black coffee which wipes out some of the more chilling moments that the tastebuds are forced to endure.

As is always the case, some of the best whiskies are reserved for the home markets; the Wisers 10-year-old is an attractive brand for its outwardly delicate simplicity alone. Further and prolonged study, however, reveals a classy intricacy. Yet, for all that, my favourite of the entire distillery output is, would you believe it, a four-year-old. Called, oddly enough, Special Old, it is renowned for being the preferred choice of the country's rednecks and fishermen. Apart from a liberal dose of caramel which adds to not only the colour but the taste, this is a glass of young corn and rye which snaps away at the tastebuds with the aggression of a rabid husky. It is one of the most upfront whiskies in Canada and, if proof were ever needed of how cruel life can be, you have to go to Canada to get it.

From the banks of the Detroit River, you can only admire the sturdy outlines of a distillery which has survived Prohibition, recession and, latterly, contraction. It brings in millions of dollars in export earnings annually, especially by selling its older whiskies to the world's well-heeled and privileged. Meanwhile, up in the lonely hills and valleys of the Yukon an angler is in combat with a salmon almost half his size and, when his quarry is seized, he celebrates with a four-year-old whisky as fine and as much fun as anything those talented, good-natured folk inside those stark walls facing Detroit can produce. There are times when a Canadian passport can be an invaluable possession.

> *Connoisseur's Selection*
>
> **WALKERVILLE SPECIAL OLD** – GLORIOUSLY MOUTHWATERING, RUGGED NATURE.

Founding father: *Hiram Walker (above) found fame with his Canadian Club whisky.*

CANADIAN MIST

The journey between Toronto and Collingwood is one that could probably only take place in Canada, of all the world's whisky-distilling regions. For over 60 miles the road runs dead straight, correcting itself only now and again as if to make sure that the driver is still awake. Roman engineers would have considered it an absolute masterpiece. And at the very end of this straightest of all straight runs is Canada's straightest whisky, Canadian Mist.

Situated only a stroll away from Georgia Bay, which boasts the longest stretch of freshwater beach in the world, the distillery was built in the late 1960s on the fringe of a town with a population of just 9,000 (now 15,000). The speed at which it was erected – the foundation stone was laid in May 1967, the first distillation came in the following September – is perhaps the greatest testimony to the boom years of Canadian whisky, when sales figures on wall charts finished somewhere on the floor above. So there is nothing about the appearance of the distillery which much captures the imagination. However, contrary to popular mythology, there really is nothing straightforward about Canada's distilleries.

When the then owners, Barton Brands, built the distillery, they had two years earlier launched Canadian Mist on to the American market with mind-boggling results. So good were sales that, instead of allowing Melchers to continue distilling for them under contract, they wanted all the action themselves. This particular location was selected because, with high unemployment in the area, some tax benefits would be forthcoming from the government. Since they were in the centre of the Great Lakes region, communications were good both within Canada and with their biggest market, the United States. There was plenty of water and they were close to the Canadian grain belt.

Now the distillery is owned by Brown-Forman, makers of Jack Daniel's. Even after all those years, there are still only two brand names and three different whiskies. Canadian Mist remains top of the US ratings, with three million cases a year against two million each by VO and Canadian Club. It would be reasonable to assume that Canadian Mist is made the same way as those whiskies, since it has not only lasted the course for so long but has successfully stayed ahead as spirit sales receded. In fact, the Canadian Mist distillery is truly unique, not only in Canada, but among the world's leading distilleries. For a start, it is the only whisky made in Canada which uses a mash of corn and malted barley. The reason is simply that the distilling apparatus has problems dealing with enzymes and prefers to allow the malt to act as the catalyst for the yeast. It has nothing to do with adding taste: on the contrary, if they could they would remove the malt to give the spirit an even more neutral initial flavour. Second, Canadian Mist is the only Canadian distillery which does not produce its own rye for flavouring. Instead, it relies upon rye produced by its sister distillery, Early Times in Louisville, Kentucky, to do that job for it by being part of the 9.09 per cent. Straight Early Times bourbon is also added, but together they probably total less than 4 per cent of the whisky.

However, there is one other quite remarkable trick which the Canadian Mist Distillery has up its sleeve and, if you look closely at its whisky, you can spot what it is. The whisky sold in the United States, which is a three-year-old, and the four-year-old found in Canada share a hardness to the finish which might easily be associated with rye. It is not so prevalent in the four-year-old, which is richer, sweeter and fuller-bodied. But confirmation that something strange is happening comes in the Canadian Mist 1885 Special Edition, an eight-year-old launched at the back end of 1995 to mark, somewhat belatedly, the centenary of the completion of the trans-Canadian railway. This is a quite superb whisky with not a single drop of bourbon or rye added. After starting with a fine display of gentle oak complexity and spiciness, corn-sweetness and some cream toffee, it suddenly runs into that metallic wall which makes for a bumpy landing at the end. If it is not rye that is causing this, then just what is? The answer is simple: not an ounce of copper is to be found in the stills or condensers. The entire apparatus, from cooker to the small, narrow fermenters, to the six closely packed column stills, is made of sparkling, silvery non-corrosive, indefatigable stainless steel. Selling three million cases of whisky with not a piece of copper in sight confounds whisky-making law, but Canadian Mist do it, and do it well. Curiously, maturing somewhere amid the thousands of pallets to be found on the site, are around 500 casks of pure rye malt, distilled just the once through the beer still. For this experiment they introduced some copper to

Steel appeal: *Canadian Mist makes relatively decent whisky despite shunning copper.*

the beer column, though obviously not enough. Although this rye as a five-year-old is simply voluptuous on the nose, with a teasing honey sweetness to the normal rye fruitiness, and although the first four or five waves which crash against the palate are mouthwateringly delicious, that metallic hardness returns toward the end with a vengeance.

As for Canadian Mist, I cannot say that I have ever been a great fan of their US export. It is far too undisciplined and abrupt for my liking, especially on the nose and finish. The older whisky found in Canada has much more assurance and style. And, yes, 1885 is a splendid whisky though it almost pains me to say it. I'm 80 proof positive that a spirit distilled to almost 95 per cent ABV, containing just a handful of malted barley, no rye whatsoever, cooked in the town's mains water where the chlorine is blasted off at high temperature and pressure, and distilled in a soulless, copperless continuous still, has (like the Canadian Mist) a tad of some local sherry added and yet – after all this – ends up, after eight years in decent ex-bourbon casks, as a whisky with unmistakable finesse and complexity which tantalizes the palate with its charm and delicacy.

The Americans undoubtedly love it. The purists may loathe it but, in and out of the bottle, Canadian Mist is simply a phenomenon which is unmatched by any other distillery in the world. I, for one, hope that they don't one day add copper to the condensers, to the head of the still or to both. If an entire nation, and one as large as the United States, regards it as their favourite Canadian whisky, that's good enough for me, whatever I think. And without Canadian Mist's idiosyncratic stance, there would never be breadth to the world's whiskies and one would never find that eccentric exception which always proves the rule.

Connoisseur's Selection

CANADIAN MIST 1885 SPECIAL EDITION – RYELESS YET FLAVOURSOME AND STYLISH, A FAR BETTER AND MORE LINGERING FINISH THAN ORDINARY CANADIAN MIST.

KITTLING RIDGE DISTILLERY

The availability of water has always been an essential condition as far as the location of a distillery is concerned. On a freezing winter's day when snow is falling from battleship-grey skies, when the beaches of Lake Erie are being pounded by waves that any self-respecting ocean would be proud of, and the Niagara Falls are gushing into an icy river, sending spray that rises above you as liquid and rains down on you as hail, you know that no place on earth has quite so much fresh water as this area, an hour or two's drive southeast of Toronto.

And yes, there is a whisky distillery nearby, though very few people know about it – yet. Kittling Ridge takes its name from the location above Niagara where raptors take lift-offs from accommodating thermal currents to help them migrate across these massive inland waters. At one time Kittling Ridge Distillery was known as Reider's, after the man who set up the winery and small-scale distillery at Grimsby. He specialized in eau-de-vie and brandies, though he had begun experimenting with whisky. Today the distillery is in the hands of John Hall, a wine man who, while continuing the fruit spirit custom, is daily becoming more fascinated by and knowledgeable about whisky. Since he bought the plant in 1992 he has seen his whisky become top dog in Taiwan with a sweet, unwrinkled four-year-old called Canadian Company, which has even scooped two consecutive Gold Awards in Brussels. This is backed up by an even smoother, sweeter 10-year-old version and a basic (but sweet) three-year-old for the Canadians called Pure Gold. Yet, really, these are not his whiskies. For mass markets like this he buys in new make from other Canadian distillers and blends accordingly. But part of the stock which came with his investment in Reider's were two copper pot stills, one small with a rectifier, the other quite tiny. It is the larger pot still which has become the focus of his attention. He has already produced a pure rye whisky from it, buying the grain in from a nearby farmer ready crushed, sending the beer from it through the still once and then a second time to bump the ABV up to 82 per cent maximum. In the next year it will be on sale in his boutique and, he hopes, some specialist retail outlets around the world. He has also produced a pure corn whisky which he is experimenting in rounding off in casks that once held sherry that he himself had made. Some of these genuine Kittling Ridge whiskies have already found their way into his three existing outsider Canadians as flavouring agents, though you would be hard-pressed to spot them.

His rye, not yet marketed, really is a world one-off: it is easily the fruitiest, least obtrusive whisky made from this aggressive grain that I have ever experienced, although it may fill out with time. The oils you expect from the genre build up rather slowly and, although it is a touch feinty, the overall feel is of a whisky of subtlety – one which will surprise you with its refusal to strike fear into the tastebuds. Instead, that is left – amazingly – to the corn whisky. At 72 per cent ABV from the cask, it is a concentrated mouthful of delicate spice and sweet, buttery, vanilla tones. The nose could almost have been imported from an open Kentucky fermenter. This, at five years old, is the best they have in stock and it will be fascinating to see if that sherry cask can take some of the oaky dryness from the finish, although even in its present state it is well worth the experience.

As a wine man, John Hall wants to create what he neatly calls a range of "New World Whiskies" and is beginning a programme of producing Canadian from a number of grain varieties and permutations. His aim has been to produce something entirely different from other Canadian distillers. And in that he has already succeeded beyond his wildest dreams.

QUEBEC

VALLEYFIELD DISTILLERY

When the outside of a distillery tells you *Les Distilladeurs Unis*, then you have an inkling that you may be in for something completely different. And when you listen to the distillers, warehousemen and blenders discuss day-to-day matters among themselves in rapid-fire French, that inkling is confirmed. This is Quebec. Its culture and traditions are far removed from those of the rest of Canada, so much so that in a recent referendum it came within a whisker of an official severing of its allegiance to the Maple Leaf. And this is the only whisky distillery in the world where French is the first language. Indeed, the vast majority of the workers there cannot speak English at all.

Just 40 years ago there were eight distilleries in Quebec. Now there is just the one, Valleyfield, owned and operated by United Distillers but known as the old Schenley plant. Its geographical location is remarkable. Drive the 30 miles or so to Valleyfield from Montreal and you will notice that the closer you get, the greater the number of bridges. However, it is only if you look on a map, or you are told, that you discover that the distillery is located on an island in the middle of the St Lawrence River. But there again, you may not have known that Montreal was on another island, roughly the size of Islay in the Hebrides.

Of all the Canadian distilleries making their whiskies from a corn base, Valleyfield's is by far the most distinctive. Where Gimli, Palliser, Canadian Mist and Walkerville in particular possess a latent dryness to their brands, unless a special flavouring agent has been added to mask it, Valleyfield's predominant theme is a toffee sweetness. Not all their brands are faultless, but some rise as high in the quality league as it is possible to go with this particular genre.

The distillery stands on the site of an old biscuit factory which burnt down, making way for two breweries, before the 54-acre site was swallowed under a welter of neat red bricks as the tall stillhouse and broad warehouses were erected during 1945. The plant has barely changed in its 50-year existence. The same wide, open-topped fermenters are still in place, complemented now by an equal number in stainless steel erected during expansion in the boom years of the 1960s. It always lifts the heart to see a distillery operate this way. The smell of the bubbling corn and the vivid red of the corn oil lying on top, punctured by a rising bubble of carbon-dioxide which momentarily mixes the garish yellow of the near-exhausted cereal with it, shows that a distillery is a living thing, that nature is in a state of animated excitement behind the cold-steel engineering which is the external appearance presented by most Canadian distilleries.

Valleyfield differs from other Canadian distilleries by operating a Kentucky-style, copper pot still doubler for the rye flavouring which it makes four times a year. Sad to say, it is hard to get a really good view of this one-off piece of apparatus. It is swathed in massive amounts of insulation, with an outer shell of corrugated aluminium. That rye flavouring, which is sent just the once through the beer still before being finished in the doubler, contains 25 per cent corn and 10 per cent malted barley, and this mixture is used to make one of the most sensitive of ryes produced in Canada. Another flavouring preferred by the blenders is made from pure corn. But that distinctive house style is not down to the flavourings at all, but to the base spirit. Nowhere in the world have I encountered one so sweet, especially one distilled to nearly 95 per cent ABV. It should be nearly neutral in flavour. In fact, it is not only sweet but very full-bodied and is even sweeter than the rums they make at the plant from molasses. Quite simply, it is incredible. Not to be outdone, the rye, too, is sweet, showing some biscuity character which seems to have lingered from a previous life. The corn noses like sodden tortilla chips but with a dash of honey on the palate. I wondered if this sweetness was caused by the yeast, which was changed slightly six years ago. Apparently not – this sweetness shows up in the whiskies, irrespective of age.

The final result is three warehouses full of whisky unlike anything else in Canada. Among its younger whiskies that house style is most easily identified in Schenley's Golden Wedding, which contains whiskies between 36 and 42 months, but tastes a little older. In addition to doing well in Canada, it is a whisky which has built up a cult-like status in Bulgaria, perhaps because of its lightly spiced finish.

One which seems to have some bourbon character creeping in is Gibson's Sterling Edition, a six-year-old with a splash here and there of 25-year-old. Again, there is something well-refined about this one, a characteristic which seems to be lacking a little in its two whiskies intended for the US market, Schenley's OFC and the four-year-old MacNaughton's. The latter is quite rich and fat to start with but dies off, a most unusual Schenley trait, while the OFC is pleasant enough, with a deep, dark chocolate finale from the oak, but otherwise does little to excite.

However, there are four Valleyfield

whiskies which must rank among the best Canada has to offer, and one in particular is easily world-class. In some ways the most striking is Order of Merit, a 12-year-old which leaps at you from the glass on nose and palate. Fruity and juicy, it's a big, bosomy, buxom Canadian, never trying to be coy but thrusting its spicy attributes at you from the off. It's all great stuff, as is Royal Command, proudly displaying the ill-fated Vancouver distillery of Park and Telford on the label. All whiskies made at Valleyfield contain the spirits produced there. Stocks from other distillers vanished long ago. Park and Telford never made a whisky to this standard and one of the peculiarities of this mixture of eight- and 18-year-old whiskies is a slight Speyside maltiness that has crept into the nose, despite the barley being no more than a trace constituent. This is probably the most full-bodied of all Valleyfield's whiskies, and perhaps of all Canada's corn-based spirit. Legendary blenders Luc Madore and recently retired Jacques Loiselle, with over 50 years of blending experience between them, refuse point-blank to include raw sherry in their whiskies, so the heaviness cannot be due to that. In some ways it is the most dangerous whisky in Canada, since it is the easiest to drink thanks to its sweet, rich oiliness.

Jacques' favourite is his creation, the 12-year-old Gibson's Finest. The nose is one of distinction and delight. Absolutely everything about this whisky has an understated quality about it: the creamy, slightly molassed aroma; the fluttering nuances of oak upon the palate; the gentlemanly power struggle between sweet and dry. Perhaps because of the oak, some of which is 14 years old, and maybe because of a stinting on the flavourings, the dryness wins in the end, which is a pity because a bitterness then follows. That is the only flaw in a whisky in search of perfection. Which leaves what I think is the finest of all Canada's traditional whiskies: Schenley OFC. This is not the one that is sent south of the border, which is a six-year-old. This proudly

Vive la différence! *Valleyfield, the world's only distillery where the stillmen speak French.*

boasts an eight-year-old statement and is the one that Canadians drink, including Luc Madore who regards it as the best. Whatever anyone might tell you, Canadian whisky does have style. Look closely and you will see that the thread which binds the various brands together is a butter-toffee creaminess. I think if any Canadian whisky truly encapsulates that style, this is it. OFC is brilliantly complex, though only insofar as the tastebuds are at full stretch to cope with all the flavours directed at it. Yet the brain is hard-pushed to identify just what it is that causes this surge of pleasure. The balance is exemplary for whiskies the world over and the toffee-raisin fruitiness is supplemented by short-lived spice and chewable vanillins. Where the Gibson's fell short of perfection, OFC found it.

Yet, inevitably in this country, there is a question mark hanging over the future of these great whiskies. It comes not in the shape of the bulldozer, which seems to work overtime around Canada's great distilleries; this threat is political. In the provinces of Quebec separatist feelings run high. In the distillery workers voted against one another, and even in the blending room the crosses for separation were marked both for and against. At the time of the referendum the lines between Valleyfield and United Distillers headquarters became red-hot. If Quebec does finally make the split and form its own country, Valleyfield will no longer be making Canadian whisky. Should that happen, they will have the choice of braving it out and using six years of stock matured in Canada to try to create a market for Quebec whisky, or they will have to up sticks and distil elsewhere – not a straightforward matter in a country where distilleries are flattened minutes after the spirit still is shut off for the very last time.

One thing is certain. If they did move, no other distillery currently operating, or any possibly built in the future, could make a spirit with such voluptuous, magnificently classic characteristics. Once again, Canadian whisky would be the loser.

Connoisseur's Selection

VALLEYFIELD SCHENLEY OFC – THE 8-YEAR-OLD IS THE FINEST WHISKY CANADA HAS TO OFFER.

NOVA SCOTIA

GLENORA DISTILLERY

During the long, dark winter and early spring months, as often as not snow disguised as rain falls lightly upon the whitewashed buildings topped with a weathered pagoda and the nearby warehouses sheltering maturing single malt. Glazed with an icy sheen, this is a distillery of classic dimensions set back from the main road and standing in a glen of ethereal beauty. With that road heading to Inverness in one direction and Aberdeen in the other, this just has to be Speyside, the ancestral home of Scotch whisky. Well, not quite. Not even close. Listening to the local folk greeting one another in Gaelic is a giveaway clue: a Scottish west coast distillery – an island one perhaps?

Indeed, this is an island, though not on the west coast but on the east. And not of Scotland, but of Canada, a little matter of 3,000 miles distant. In a country where the column still is king, this is the one outpost, literally, where the art of the founding fathers has not so much been preserved as rediscovered. Glenora Distillery is on Cape Breton island, Nova Scotia (New Scotland). The Scots settled there in droves in the late eighteenth and early nineteenth centuries, with the Irish not far behind. Listen to the older, kindly people of this most unnervingly Hibernian of lands who were not so influenced by television in their formative years and you will hardly find a trace of North American accent: their accent is a strange mixture of Scots and Irish.

Despite the timelessness of the area, one which seems to have broken off from the Scottish mainland and drifted across the North Sea, the distillery has been operating only since 1990. In a culture where the kilt is a recognized form of evening wear, where clannishness is proudly preserved, where the haggis is revered, where young love has flourished under the accordion and fiddle of the ceilidh, where the bagpipes drone the start of the local Highland games, it was regarded an unfortunate oversight that no one had ever got round to founding a malt distillery. If there is something odd about this part of Canada, it is the fact that these people of whisky-making stock preferred to drink rum. One tradition that survived was the making of moonshine, and that of Cape Breton is the closest I have ever tasted to the poteen of Galway. An illicit distiller I met explained why: their recipe of malt and sugar is very similar. At one time nearly everyone on the island seemed to have their own still and their pungent spirit was dubbed Cape Breton Silver, a pun on the colour of the maple trees in the winter months which cover the many hills.

An ancient aura: *Yet the Cape Breton island distillery of Glenora commenced distillation as recently as 1990.*

The idea of a legalized malt distillery began to take shape in the mid-1980s and building finally began in 1989. Bruce Jardine, a local civil servant, had brought in Nova Scotia businessmen and obtained government grants to fund the project, which included nine hotel-like apartments to attract tourists, one complete with a four-poster bed. Fittingly, the technology and expertise for the building and distillation was all Scottish. Morrison Bowmore helped plan the plant, Forsyth's made the mash tun and stills, and the Scottish architect, the late David Forsyth, was responsible for creating a distillery which certain Scottish companies would give their eye-teeth for, following the oft-regretted renovations of the 1960s and 1970s.

Distillation began in September 1990. By December the distillery was silent. The company had failed. Bruce managed to mount a rescue operation, so that it was up and running again by 1991. However, two years later the money ran out again. The stills of Glenora were silent once more and the site was up for sale: a different continent, but the same old story. What had perhaps caused the greatest problem was the fact that malt whisky has to be matured a number of years before it can be sold. For a century this has been responsible for failures in Scotland. In Canada, where a home-produced single malt whisky is an unknown quantity, without sufficient capital to see it through the lean years, the financial pressures on a distilling venture can become overwhelming.

It was against this background of uncertainty that Cape Breton-born but Halifax-based businessman Lauchie MacLean made a tentative bid for the distillery, not remotely expecting to succeed. He once told me, "I made the offer, half forgot about it and then woke up one morning to find I was the owner of a distillery. I remember thinking: 'what the hell do I do now?'" His first priority was to work out a market for the whisky, as well as make sure that it was of good enough quality to sell. At the moment they are redistilling some of the maturing spirit simply because it has a feint problem. With insufficient training of staff at the distillery, mistakes were made in selecting which cuts of the run off from the spirit still to use exclusively for maturation. Ways of overcoming overactive fermentation have still to be found.

During 1995 and 1996, as well as making new malt, they also redistilled their stock which fell below standard. This triple-distilled spirit bodes well for the future. In addition to a clean maltiness, there is a delightful sweetness which should work in tandem with the oak – provided the barrels chosen are good enough. Here, too, Glenora have been working hard at dumping barrels that are too old and bringing in casks with a lifetime ahead of them.

But what is so impressive about Glenora is not just the outside and its location. Inside the distillery you could so easily be back in Scotland. The malt, when peated to phenol levels between 2 and 5 ppm, was bought from Britain, the three wooden washbacks were crafted in Scotland and the two dwarfish copper pot stills, like the mash tun, made in Rothes. For these reasons Glenora whisky is not quite as cheap as it might be. Originally the two pots were to be the spirit stills running off a much larger wash still, but during the building of the distillery when funds ran out, the wash still was scrapped, the stillhouse was reduced in size and one of the spirit stills was given the task of providing the low wines for the spirit still.

In a way it has worked to the advantage of the quality of the whisky. The stills give a healthy ratio of contact between the bubbling wash and low wines against the copper and

Spirited revival: *Glenora is back.*

this is reflected in the richness of the whisky. They have 20 barrels of 1990 maturing. It is perhaps a little feinty, but no worse than many malts I have tasted from Scotland. Its strength lies in that sweetness, which, even by that age, has taken on a honey-tinge. Oddly enough, the distillery that looks a little like Edradour and tastes a little like Edradour, with a fine, full-bodied feel which belies the angle of the lyne arm to the condenser. There are stocks of 1992 which also shows promise, and some of this is being blended into 8-, 10- and 12-year-old whisky from Palliser in a joint venture with IDV. Launched in the USA in April 1997, the whisky Breton's Hand and Seal is priced above Crown Royal.

I hope they leave the 1990 intact. Instinct tells me that it will become something of note when it reaches its fifteenth or eighteenth birthday. And as for the whisky to come? One thing is certain; it has the weight to become a malt of character. No decision has yet been made as to whether it is to be called Canadian single malt or Cape Breton single malt. Perhaps it should be called Nova Scotia single malt – the new malt from the new Scotland.

Connoisseur's Selection

GLENORA – BRETON'S HAND & SEAL HAS ENOUGH OAK TO BUILD A LOG CABIN. BUT BEAUTIFULLY BALANCED, SAP-FREE AND DELICIOUSLY AND MOREISHLY SWEET. AROMATIC AND WORTH FINDING.

7 INDIAN WHISKY

It comes as a major surprise to most people to discover which nation boasts the most malt whisky distilleries outside Scotland. It is India. There are at least 15 of them, across the length and breadth of the great subcontinent. Some of the malt whisky made by Indian distilleries is excellent and worthy of an international audience. Some is adequately pleasant. Some is near disgusting. The fact is, however, that Indian malt whisky production is growing steadily and the quality is improving year on year, thanks to some top-rate, independent Scottish expertise along the way. In the years to come it is likely Indian whisky will be available around the world, but for that to happen it would help if national and state governments would make life a little easier for both distiller and consumer alike.

For a start, it would be helpful to have an exact definition of what constitutes whisky in India. At the moment most of it is made from molasses spirit: what is called whisky is really rum with not a single grain in sight. As it costs 7.5 rupees to produce a litre of molasses spirit against 52 rupees for malt, you can see why most distillers would not welcome legislation tightening up the definition.

Some distillers at least make an effort to include malt in their whisky somewhere along the line, but if you are in India and you see a whisky claiming to be malt, read the label carefully. Actual 100 per cent pure malt whiskies are few and far between, and even then may include non-pot-still, unaged malt, though the quality is better than it sounds. Some whiskies using the description "malt" may also contain malt extract or enhancers. You will certainly know things are not as they should be when you taste these.

In most countries whisky labels are carefully and tastefully designed. In India, however skilled the artwork, the labels ends up looking something like used postage stamps. Each state is responsible for its own taxes on spirits and that information is mandatory on every label. So the labels will have stamped over them, by law, the date the spirit was bottled, its price, which states it can or cannot be sold in – and all of this on top of a pre-printed health warning! The states' Excise officials also give their distillers a bit of a rough time. Some distilleries would love to age their whiskies but are prevented from building warehouses away from the distillery grounds. Such a practice only encourages distillers to bottle their malt at a very young age, if it is aged at all.

In one or two states there is total prohibition in force and the movement across the country is getting stronger. However, one state that has enforced prohibition has already begun running into financial difficulties because of the sudden loss in revenue. Rumour has it that there is bad blood among the politicians and what was thought to be a good vote-winner may turn out to be a poisoned chalice. The battle between prohibition and practicality will be a close-fought

Hot air: *Indian whiskies like Bagpiper sound like Scotch but are made from molasses.*

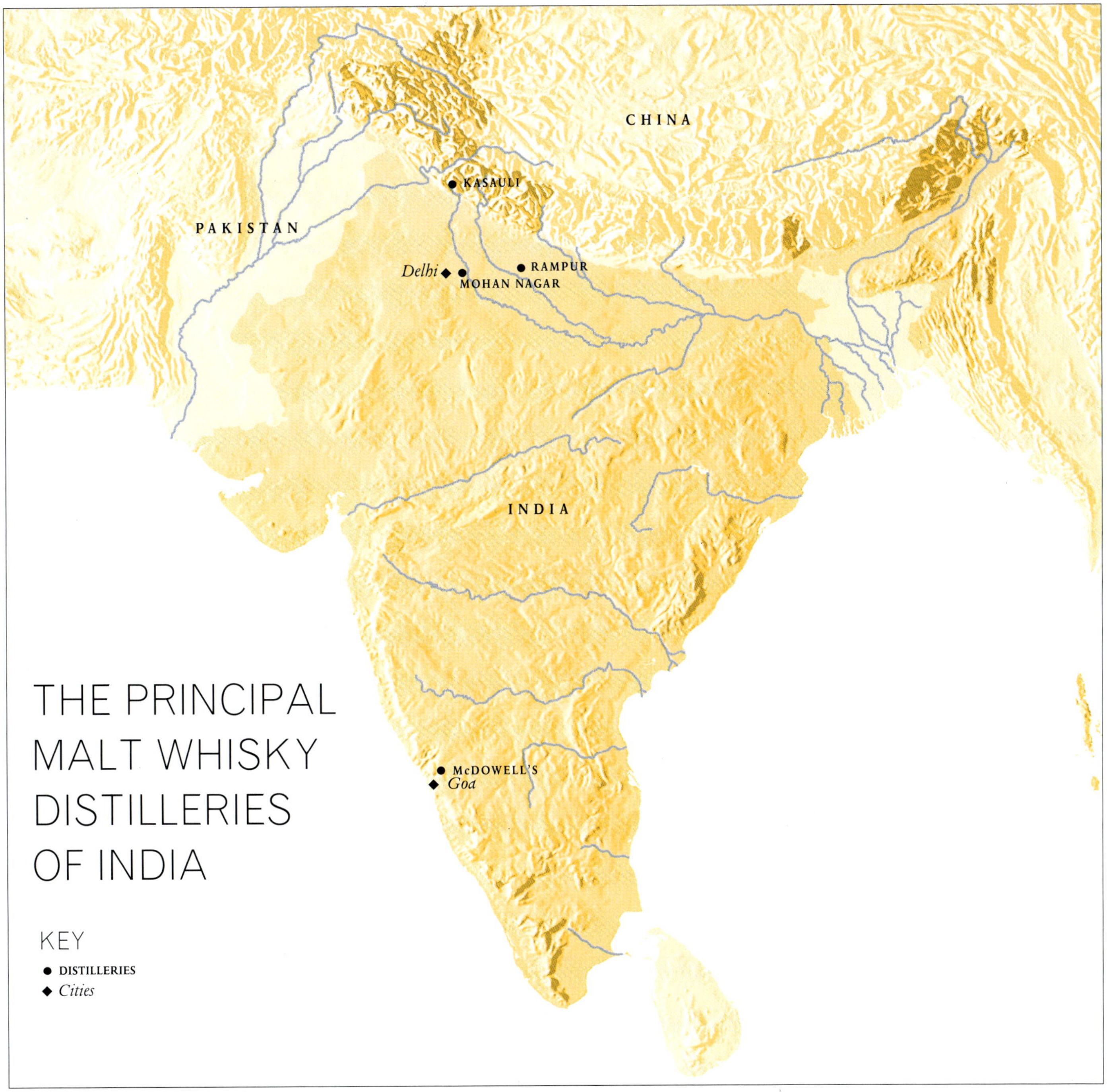

one in a number of states in the years to come.

However the whisky is made and whatever laws apply, in a country where the population is likely to reach the billion mark by the year 2000, distillers the world over are keeping close tabs on a nation which drinks 50 million cases of the stuff every year. Scottish distillers in particular have been moving into joint ventures: United Distillers flirted with United Brewers; Whyte and Mackay have gone into malt production in a big way with the Rampur Distillery; Seagram have been chasing Shaw Wallace; Glenmorangie are working alongside Mohan Meakin and numerous other Indian malt-whisky producers have been in constant dialogue with Scottish counterparts.

The biggest malt whisky distillery is found in the north of India at Jagajit Nagar's. Located at Hanira in the Punjab, some of its malt finds its way into the popular Aristocrat brand. Though it calls itself malt whisky, the malt is fleeting. They are also responsible for the dreadful Bonnie Scot whisky – "Special Malted Whisky". Maybe there is malt whisky in there somewhere, but it's hard to find. Could this be malt extract…? Also in the Punjab are Mudi Distilleries. In neighbouring Uttar Pradesh, Narang have a distillery which makes a reasonable pot-still malt, while there are two particularly fine distilleries: Whyte and Mackay's part-owned Rampur Distillery and Mohan Meakin's Mohan Nagar. The latter is particularly well-known for its Black Knight brand, which is over-sweetened by its molasses content, but at least it is possible to spot the malt.

The centre of the country is well served by malt distilleries. Below Delhi, in Madhya Pradesh, the Som Distillery at Bhopal produces 21st Century malt whisky, though here too the malt is difficult to identify. In Maharashtra state there are three distilleries, two of which are found in Aurangabad – Shaw Wallace and Sinclair. The third is the Seven Seas Distillery.

Down the west coast two sets of pot stills can be found. At Goa, there is the United Brewers' Ponda Distillery and further south they have another in Kerala. Their third is inland in the plateau city of Bangalore, which also happens to be home of Khoday's distillery, responsible for the one all-Indian blended whisky that is a must in every household: Peter Scot. For this you pay top dollar – over 300 rupees (around £6) – but it is worth it. The label says malt whisky and the malt bursts through on the nose, displaying untold riches. Some peppers and sympathetic vanillins intermingle with the glowing malt and on the palate it is as perfectly balanced as anything you will find in this part of the world: hints of spices, mouth-sucking malt, toffee (perhaps some caramel) but, best of all, the wonderfully long finish.

Despite all the molasses sloshing around the country, there is some very drinkable whisky to be found – even away from the Scotch admixes. But it would be great if all Indian malt distillers had the confidence to ignore the generally held conception that their countrymen have sweet palates and that straight malt would be too demanding.

I have long held the view that the Indian palate has to be the most sophisticated in the world. Nowhere have I experienced a cuisine so subtle, flavoursome and wide-ranging. Even when cooking traditional western food, the Indians manage to find some herb or spice that adds a hitherto unknown dimension to what had previously been a quite straightforward meal. My opinion of this advanced palate has only been strengthened by the fact that just about every Indian whisky drinker I know says that Johnnie Walker Black Label is the finest whisky he has tasted: no blend on earth shares that brand's striking complexity. And in the Indian whisky trade, it is Black Label that is held as the benchmark of the world's whiskies.

Still, some distilleries do believe in themselves – and produce an excellent product. To find out how, we must first visit a distillery in northern India. India's acceptance as a serious whisky producer may begin here …

KASAULI *(Cuss-awe-lee)*

It is not unusual to find a malt whisky distillery which began life as a brewery. You can unearth them the world over, from Glenmorangie in the Scottish Highlands to Wilson's Distillery in New Zealand, round the other side of the Pacific to the Anchor Distillery in San Francisco (which proudly remains a brewery, as well) right back to Scotland with Glen Moray in Speyside.

There is only one of which I am aware, though – located 5,500 feet up the Himalayas, which is closer to Tibet than some Scottish malt distilleries are to each other – which still uses its original apparatus dating back to 1855 and which operates its own floor maltings. Kasauli is not so much a distillery you have to visit as one you make a pilgrimage to.

The journey starts in Delhi by train. The station is located at the point where New Delhi, with its imperious governmental buildings, up-market industrial headquarters and residences and plush hotels, meets Old Delhi. The teeming people, the fume-belching autorickshaws clogging up the narrow streets and the dilapidated and overcrowded houses squeezed in on all sides emphasize that the old station is just on the wrong side of the tracks.

The first 20 miles or so north of the station is like no other journey to any other distillery. Beside the track lives a small portion of the nine million people who make up Delhi, and the number of people per square foot rises alarmingly for the first mile or two. Entire families live in tents, mud huts, shanty slums and assorted hovels, vying with oxen and pigs for land that has been illegally re-claimed from the railway company. Yet there seems to be a community spirit: people gathered around camp fires and laughing children playing on or between the tracks with makeshift toys.

However, while the first, short leg of the three-hour journey shows you the downside of the subcontinent, the remaining two and three-quarter hours leave you spellbound with the richest images of India. You are now on the plains where there is not so much as a hill to be seen for hundreds of miles, yet never is the journey dull. You pass through many villages and between them fields of bright green and the occasional irrigation canal, as broad as a river, which guarantees the vivid, early spring colour. Or there might be fields of flowers of gold, crimson and blue. Everywhere, though, there are people, usually brightly dressed women, sometimes working in bunches, or alone with their young children in a field, bent double, picking something to eat or sell. And then there are the birds, too many even for a keen ornithologist to keep track of with hoopoes, avocets and redwattled lapwings being some of the more conspicuous of the feathered guard of honour.

The train terminates at Chandigarh, the city built to become capital of the Punjab after Lahore was lost to Pakistan. The next bit of the journey is the most dangerous for a whisky writer: by car towards Solan in the foothills of the Himalayas. The road cuts across the northernmost tip of Haryana state – bad news, because in July 1996 it became the third state in the country to enforce prohibition. My car was stopped by police as they carried out what they call a "whisky search", and for one of the few times in my career I was glad I was travelling dry. Even if they had not found anything, I might have been arrested simply for

Top of the world: *Kasauli's ancient pagoda sits high in the Himalayas.*

entering the state with alcohol on my breath.

At bustling Kalka, the atmosphere begins to change. The town is set against a backdrop of the very first folds of the Himalayas and the camels carrying loads show that things are beginning to get a little tribal. From then on it is uphill, past people trudging in both directions, with more cramped little villages, and as every car is passed a horn is tooted, almost to the point where drivers seem offended if they are not given a short but resounding blast. The road zig-zags ever upwards and if it is not people you see standing and sitting beside the walled verge, with a drop of up to 1,000 feet below, then it may be a platoon of monkeys. Beyond them, the view is exhilarating with snow-capped peaks in the distance, while below are carefully manicured terraces leading down to the valley bottom.

Dotted here and there are "English Wine Shops", a term which has to be displayed for liquor stores. In reality, there is no wine at all. Just whisky – around 35 varieties of it – rum, and beer. Finally, before Solan is reached, the road takes a sharp left fork near Dagshai and it's uphill again until the road ends at Kasauli. The distillery is found on a narrow turn just before you reach the old British army outpost, and the sight which greets you is astonishing. Over the years I have seen dozens, if not hundreds, of old Victorian line drawings of British breweries and distilleries. What stands before you at Solan, set into a hill, is just such a sight. Even the malting chimneys are of the ancient, oblong type which everywhere else gave way to the late-Victorian and Edwardian preference for pagoda-style elegance. Word has not yet reached the Himalayas, apparently.

What is made at this time-warp distillery is one of the country's most famous brands, Solan No 1. In fact, its entire output, bar just a few drops, goes into this pure malt whisky, but even that is not enough to meet demand and its annual, 300,000-case sales cannot be increased by the distillery as it stands. Why it is called Solan No 1 is as confusing as most things arein India. The label clearly states it is made at the Kasauli Distillery, yet the carton shows a photograph of the Solan Distillery. Such a malt distillery does exist, a functional-looking thing built in the early 1970s, but it has never made a single drop in 25 years of existence because the state government of Himichal Pradesh refuses to give it a licence.

This distillery is a lot easier to reach than Kasauli. The narrow-gauge railway from Chandigarh to the old British colonial resort town of Shimla, 7,500 feet above sea level and complete with mock-Tudor buildings and English country church, passes through no less than 103 tunnels, some a mile long, and stops at umpteen points, one of which is the Solan Brewery, where the distillery is located. This is one of the great railway journeys of the world and it is a pity you can't hop off the train for a little local juice.

Where the virgin Solan Distillery is state-of-the-art for the '70s, the infinitely prettier Kasauli Distillery is still geared towards the '50s – the 1850s, that is. If the belted apparatus used in the milling is primitive, the mash tun is positively prehistoric; rarely have I seen anything quite so beautiful. It is an 1855 original made of cast iron, though it is surrounded by green wooden lagging and for good measure – and an extra dollop of charm – has hinged wooden doors to keep it all neatly self-contained.

Next we come to the heat exchanger, of the type cooled by running water on the outside, which I had seen only in nineteenth-century brewing and distilling textbooks, and then it's into the fermentation room. Here is a clue to the distillery's previous life: as well as five very old wooden fermenters, there are two iron ones, of the square shape preferred by brewers. These fermenters are also part of the distillery's production problem: their output is so small that they cannot supply the needs of the pot and column stills they have on site. If one set of stills are working, then the other cannot. Fermentation time is alarmingly quick: 35–40 hours in high summer, around 45 hours at all other times.

It is invariably the pot stills at a distillery which quicken the heart most when you see them for the first time. And here I was particularly fascinated to see their style. Although Kasauli had not been converted into a distillery until just after the First World War, there were hints of an Irish influence at work.

Silent: *The never-used Solan Distillery has waited for a government licence for 25 years.*

The thick but slightly bowing walls give a broad clue to the building's 1855 heritage. After its construction by Scotsman Edward Dyer, it became the first brewery in the whole of India, supporting a very large and thirsty British army. He also constructed what is now the Solan Brewery soon after, though it is believed it started life as a distillery ... as I said, things in India are seldom straightforward.

An Irishman called Meakin also entered the brewing business in India and bought the Solan Brewery from Dyer. Exactly what happened during this period is a bit hazy, but certainly the two joined forces to form Dyer Meakin and Company. The present company is called Mohan Meakin, after the powerful N.N. Mohan who took over the firm in 1949. Intriguingly, their brochure produced in the 1980s shows a drawing of Irish pot stills, almost identical to those found in the old Jameson Distillery in Dublin. Furthermore, I knew that until just a few months earlier they had been using triple distillation. Not only that, Solan No 1 is the only whiskey in all India spelt with an "e". So, would the Kasauli stills be Irish in style, I wondered?

The answer was no. There are four stills in all, none particularly large, two pretty small. They are neither bulbous in the traditional Irish style nor onion-shaped in the Scottish. Rather, they are straightish in a coned kind of way, with thick necks and a lyne arm angled sharply downwards towards the condensers in order to produce the heaviest spirit possible. Proof of a little modernization is the use of steam heating within the stills: below them are disused coal furnaces. The capacity of the wash still being used is 14,000 litres and the spirit still holds 500 litres less. Both were once wash stills. The old intermediate still of 10,000 litres is redundant, as is the 8,500-litre former spirit still. It is obvious the character of the whisky is likely to change.

Connoisseur's Selection

KASAULI SOLAN NO I – DISAPPOINTING AT THE MOMENT WITH TOO MANY OFF NOTES, BUT MIGHT IMPROVE WITH TIME.

It appears that the distillery is operating on the ancient gravity system, as at Glenturret in Perthshire, where the next stage of the whisky-making process is held below the previous one. Certainly you have to walk downhill to find the pot stills, though they are on the same level as two very small and entirely copper patent stills which were installed in 1955. Until then, it is believed, the distillery had made nothing other than pot-still, Indian malt whisky. Remarkably these column stills continue to make from malt only. In fact, they contribute 93.5 per cent of what goes into Solan No 1.

This patent spirit is nothing short of glorious. Its trademark is its cleanliness yet it still contains enormous character with surprisingly rich malt and a lingering sweetness. It is more than evident that this plays a key role in Solan No 1 and what is more remarkable is that the only maturation it undergoes is the couple of weeks spent in a marrying tank. Never does it see a barrel.

Yet it is not this new make, or fresh spirit as the Indians refer to it, that weakens the brand's character. Solan No 1 is an attractive whisk(e)y, but flawed. Its nose is its Achilles' heel: somewhere some heavy, oily foreshots have crept in. Because of the cleanness of the fresh patent spirit, and the crispness of the malt which accompanies it, the finger of suspicion points accusingly at the pot stills.

Certainly, as the continuous spirit proved, there is nothing wrong with the malt itself. That is made just a few minutes' walk downhill and round another Himalayan hairpin bend at the distillery's own maltings where there are no less than eight floors, of which six are working. During the hottest part of the year, however, malting is suspended as the heat plays hell with germination. So about 60 per cent of the distillery's malt is bought in from Haryana – to the consternation of puritanical state officials. Coal is used in the kilning – never peat – and there is no mechanization. As was the case in Scotland, wooden shovels are used ("shiels" in Scotland, "showels" in Kasauli) and, to guarantee the malting barley is treated with the utmost respect, the maltmen wield their showels barefoot. Like the main distillery building, the maltings is truly unique.

If there had not been surprises enough during my visit, the one to cap them all came at the warehouse, called the "Mature Room" under Excise orders. The casks sitting two or three high were predominantly 1995 and 1996 makes, but astonishingly there were at least two dated 1969. Considering they had undergone 27 summers where for three months the temperature hovers somewhere around the 100 mark, I was expecting little more than sap. Instead, I was greeted with faint sherry tones and enormously sweet malt, with oaky notes delicately seeping through here and there. The colour was a healthy tan and the taste was every bit as well balanced as the nose. For one horrible moment I thought the power of the oak would overwhelm all else, but then it just faded away leaving a magnificently long finish of ripe fruit, chewable malt, nut-toffee and toffee-apple. It was nothing short of sensational. Taking into account its location, it was miraculous.

Following on from that, a four-year-old malt I tasted from a neighbouring cask was a bit of a disappointment. Certainly the middle and finish enjoyed a malty exuberance, but the nose and greeting to the palate were hard to take. Without doubt, in an effort to meet demand, either by accident or design, the middle cut has been made too long and some unwanted alcohols that should have been destined for re-distillation have crept in. What was heartening, though, was the evidence of the 1969 and the finale to the four-year-old: Kasauli is more than capable of making above-average malt whisk(e)y.

I discussed the whiskey with two rather impressive people. One was distiller Omparkesh Dayagi, the other was deputy distiller and blender Ish Kapoor. Ish had been at the distillery 35 years, Omparkash a mere 32 years, yet they were delighted to analyze their whiskey with me because in all that time not a single writer, drink or otherwise, had made the expedition or pilgrimage to their fairytale distillery.

As a man who obviously has high standards, Ish agreed with my diagnosis: the malt was being stretched too thin and he wished he could find a way round it. With experimentation I found at least one way to get the best out of the whiskey: put a glass of it in front of a roaring fire and leave for half an hour. By the time you return, the worst of the volatile and heady alcohols have evaporated, leaving a seductive, sweetly malted dram. To give the whiskey the short middle cut it deserves and maintain the same output is a problem not quite so easily solved.

As it is, the distillery is operating at a loss. And with 170 people working there, it is hardly surprising. Yet Mohan Meakin's managing director Rakesh "Rocky" Mohan is not losing any sleep. "There is more to life than making money," he told me. "What we have at Kasauli is unlike anything else in this country and we feel we have a responsibility to keep a tradition alive and create something of unmistakable quality. And we have a responsibility to our workforce and the community in which they live." It's a pity he's not on the board of a few other distillers elsewhere in the world.

Barefoot in the dark: *The ancient practice of floor maltings is still carried out at Kasauli.*

It is hard to tear myself away from a distillery at the best of times. When it is in a place where no distillery should ever contemplate being, among the steepest of mountains where the air is sweet and the birdsong sweeter; where the people are gentle and the stillmen and mashmen spend their lunchtimes sleeping on cliff ledges bathed in the warm spring sun; where pride is taken in the ancient artistry of making malt whisky, then leaving is much more than a wrench. It had taken me near on 40 years to find this most sacred of shrines. It will be nothing like so long before I return there.

MOHAN NAGAR

Solan No 1 may be Mohan Meakin's most famous pure malt whisky, and one of three in the country, but the company have other brands containing pot-still malt whisky and for that they invariably use the spirit of their second malt distillery, Mohan Nagar.

It is found a short distance outside Delhi, due east. The half hour's journey by car takes you over the Hindon river towards Ghaziabad in the state of Uttar Pradesh. Within this city there is another city, quite self-contained. It is called Mohan Nagar – Mohan City – and is named after the Mohan family who in 1962 began constructing a self-sufficient industrial site in which their cornflakes are made, their apple juice crushed, their beer brewed, their whisky distilled and in which their workers live. It has a population of between five and ten thousand people, some of whom are responsible for making quite a decent malt whisky.

That wasn't always the case, as distillery manager Jitendar Mohan (yes, he is related to the company chairman Brigadier Mohan) will honestly admit. For a time there were fermentation problems and the maturing three-year-old spirit verges on the unpleasant. The present spirit, thankfully, shows no sign of contamination whatsoever.

The distillery dates back to when the city was built in 1962 and is every bit as ugly as Kasauli is beautiful. It is a concrete construction not even pretending to be anything other than a protective shell for the distillation process. But even so, Mohan Nagar is a fascinating and highly individual distillery, going about things in a way no other malt distillery can ape.

For a start, the first three processes – the malting, milling and mashing – are not carried out at the distillery at all, but across the quadrangle at the brewery famous for its Lion and Golden Eagle brands. No floor maltings here, just three enormous Saladin boxes and, sad to relate, it is the inferior barley which is used for the whisky, the beer getting the cream of the crop. Even these mechanical maltings cannot provide for both a brewery and a distillery and, as at Kasauli, some malt is bought in. But, as I discovered when I visited the kiln, the coal used in drying gives off enormous amounts of smoke and guarantees the smokiest non-peated malt I had encountered.

Nor had I ever found a large commercial whisky's mashing process being carried out in traditional brewing coppers – but it is here. There are 22 fermenters, painted green on the baffling insistence of the unpredictable Excise, which hold between 60,000 and 80,000 litres, though some have rotted into disuse, perhaps exhausted by the terrifying 24-hour fermentation time. Next door is the stillhouse for the continuous stills.

Jitendar Mohan has been at the distillery for all but one year of its existence and he is as solid a whisky man as you are likely to find. It was great to see that a man with all his experience holds stainless steel stills in nothing short of contempt. He had put in a pair during the 1970s when news was filtering through that these were the new way forward and would never wear out. They have worn out and are about to be replaced while the original copper columns keep going strong. Not only that, he felt that the spirit produced off the stainless steel columns was vastly inferior to that produced from the copper columns and banished them to making spirit from molasses only: "We tried malt; we were wasting malt." So, irrespective of the extra cost the replacements will be copper: hearing such words, I could have kissed him.

Connoisseur's Selection

MOHAN NAGAR SUMMER MALT– BRIGHT YET WEIGHTY ON THE PALATE WITH LOTS OF OAK.

The four pot stills are also all copper. They are not exactly stylish, being straight where they should be curved and displaying necks like Arnold Schwarzenegger. They were also once used in triple distillation; now it's just a double distillation with three of the pots acting as washbacks.

It is in the maturation room that you are once more reminded that this can only be India. The malt whisky is matured in oak, but not barrels – the Excise, for some reason known only to themselves, won't allow it. Actually, it is probably because they don't like the sun claiming so much alcohol. Instead, the whisky has to be poured into large oak vats where it matures at a much slower rate. A 29-year-old I tasted was a very classy act, full of spices, herbs, malt, fruit and soft vanillas. A seven-year-old was a little weird and showed signs that not all was right at Mohan Nagar at the time; enough has been said about the three-year-old already. The fresh spirit, though, was impressive stuff. So too was the malt made from the patent stills, though perhaps, with just 100 plates to Kasauli's 55, it is hardly surprising more character had been stripped away and was not a patch on its Himalayan partner.

Burning ambition: *A kiln blasts dry the malt to be used in Mohan Nagar's improving whisky.*

The malt from Mohan Nagar already makes an appearance in two well-known Indian brands, Black Knight and Colonel's Special, though molasses provide the bulk for both these whiskies. However, it will be better demonstrated in a new brand to be launched during 1997, Summer Hall – named after the spectacular old colonial residence of the Brigadier in the hills of Solan. As recently as late 1996 the Brigadier got out of his car there to be confronted by a leopard. A couple of days later it was captured.

There is nothing untamed about Summer Hall whisky, though. As well as containing pot and continuous malt spirit from Mohan Nagar, there is also malt from Kasauli and some pot- and Coffey-still malt from the Lucknow distillery which has not made whisky for some years now. This 100 per cent pure malt is quite weighty on the nose and shows bright malt on the palate. It hangs together deliciously despite rumblings of heavy woodiness from some of the very old malts used. Great stuff, though.

Incidentally, if you are looking for the animal within you, the maturation room at Mohan Nagar might have just the thing: a single vat of 20-year-old Aphrodisiac spirit made from Jagri (lump brown sugar) and 128 types of herb. Never have my tastebuds been so ruthlessly assaulted and then tenderly caressed by wave upon wave of multi-textured flavours. It was certainly a turn-on for me. Now they are thinking of marketing it. By Indian standards, it probably qualifies as a whisky, so you had better watch out!

At the double: *Mohan Nagar has switched from triple to double distillation.*

RAMPUR *(Ram-pour)*

Having already taken the road east out of Delhi, it is well worth staying on it for another four hours to find one of India's newest malt distilleries. This is at Rampur in deepest Uttar Pradesh.

It is not quite as pretty a journey as the one by train to Chandigarh, though the landscape – especially when the sun is rising – is no less beguiling, and there are numerous colourful villages and towns to pass through. At times the countryside is so flat you could be in the heart of the East Anglian region of Britain. But that is only a fleeting sensation because the road is perpetually clogged with lorries, ponies and carts, oxen and people. It is also littered with vehicles which didn't quite make it through the weaving traffic where the only rule seems to be: give way to the person who got to the space first. When I went there, just yards from one disintegrating bus, a squadron of 20 or so longbilled vultures sat patiently as if waiting for the next, horribly inevitable calamity. It was all rather unnerving.

Roughly halfway between Delhi and Rampur you ford the major natural obstacle of the plains, the mighty Ganges, its fortified crossing patrolled by soldiers. There are guards, also, at the gates of the Rampur Distillery, though these are armed only with a smile and a salute. The last town you have to fight your way through is Moradabad, famous for its brass. Rampur is likely to become famous for its copper – or at least the gleaming, new copper pot stills that have been working since 1993.

The distillery was built by the Rampur Distillery Company which, until then, had been making a self-styled "whisky" from molasses. They then made the bold move to go into malt production and began an operation which greatly impressed Scotch distillers Whyte and Mackay, who set up a joint venture buying 51 per cent of the shares of the malt distillery – but wisely had nothing to do with molasses-spirit production.

Just a single taste of the maturing whisky there shows why renowned blender Richard Paterson has been spotted in Delhi of late. He has been working hand-in-hand with legendary Indian distiller and blender Jolly Bhargava, now managing director of Whyte and Mackay (India).

Paterson is not the first Scottish blender to have worked among the Rampur stills, though. Jimmy Lang, once of Seagram, was instrumental in the distillery's earliest days and helped get the plant running. And, rightly, he is pleased with the outcome.

To look at the distillery, it's hard to believe that it is of 1993 vintage. Seen from beside the enormous fermenters in which the treacly molasses are frothing away at its sister distillery next door, the shape of the building and the type and coloration of bricks used for the construction make the distillery look a century older.

Once inside, however, such thoughts vanish. The mash tun in stainless steel, as are the six small fermenters, each holding a miserly 16,031 litres. But they don't have to be big, not with the two tiny pot stills close to the mash tun. These are a couple of little beauties and in February 1997 they came back on stream after a three-month break to make Whyte and Mackay Indian whisky for the very first time.

The distillery manager, R.B. Singh, is as fond of them as a father is of his children. He has been in charge since the distillery began production in September 1993. To learn his trade, he undertook a course at Edinburgh's Heriot Watt University and trained at Whyte and Mackay's glorious Dalmore Distillery, long before they even knew where Rampur was, and at Invergordon's Tullibardine malt and Invergordon grain distilleries – before Whyte and Mackay's takeover of that company. No other Indian distillery manager has undertaken so much formal training.

It appears that his study and travel have paid dividends: the spirit he produces is of a very high standard. He is probably helped by having such tiny stills to work from. The wash still holds just 7,000 litres, the spirit still 4,000. And although both stills were born together, twins they most certainly are not. While the wash still is a pretty unremarkable affair, the spirit still is a bit of a show-off, catching the eye and demanding constant attention. It has the most busty of "Balvenie Balls" – the second bulge above the bottom one. Here it is slightly alembic in style and is as pronounced as any in the world.

The only reason I can think of for it to be shaped this way is to counteract the heaviness normally associated with small pots: the smaller the still, the more contact the spirit has with copper, the more character the whisky has and the oilier it seems to be. In this second bulge, it is possible that some of the condensation forms on the upper side and runs back into the heart of the still. Likewise, the lyne arm is at an exaggerated angle upwards – in fact, it is the exact opposite of the one at Kasauli. This again looks as though the designers were trying to lighten the spirit by allowing as much condensation as possible to run back for re-distillation. Also, because of the size of the still, having the arm at such an upward angle prevents the boiling fluids from spilling over through the lyne arm into the condenser. It is, at least by sight, a canny little still.

R.B. Singh reckoned the spirit it produced was medium in build, with the two character-forming actions cancelling each other out, but when I tasted the spirit at 18 months I had to disagree: this is a weighty little chap with bags of muscle and personality. It may only have been 18 months old, but the Indian subcontinental sun had done its work: this had all the complexity of a six- to eight-year-old Perthshire malt and was lacking none of its grace and charm. While the nose wasn't exactly faultless, with perhaps the tiniest trace of something that has crept in that shouldn't, the most dominant characteristic on the nose was a big, confident maltiness holding hands with soft vanilla and the most delicate hint of liquorice. To taste, though, it is flawless. This is a malt for those who like their whisky deep, fully textured and rich in oil. In fact the malt it most reminds me of is that from little Edradour in Scotland – just an extra taste of honey and I might have mistaken it. As it is, Rampur is chewy stuff, a whisky that moulds itself to your mouth, and its finish is long with a hint of burnt honeycomb at the finale. No matter which part of the world it comes from, this is brilliant stuff.

Jolly Bhargava won't say one way or another whether there are plans afoot to release it as a single malt. They are waiting to see what further maturation brings. Even in its present form, though, it is certainly worth bottling – and I think the great man of Indian whisky would like to see that. His pride in what has been achieved in his country is evident, but, like the true whisky man he is, he shudders at most "whiskies" found on the Indian market and has little time for the cheap-and-nasties full of molasses and flavouring which take the name of malt in vain.

Connoisseur's Selection

RAMPUR– NOT YET AVAILABLE, BUT KEEP AN EYE OUT FOR IT.

And he has put his money where his mouth is by joining Whyte and Mackay, despite having officially retired after years with Shaw Wallace. Jolly has seen more active service in the industry than anyone else alive and it thrills him that he is now working only with grain whiskies – made from wheat – and pure malt.

So far he has put Rampur malt into White Hall, mixing three per cent with Indian grain and Scotch malt, and the same amount into a strikingly attractive blend, Genesis, which enjoys a much bigger Scotch content. It is also found unaged in the uninspiring Moghul Monarch brand produced by Shaw Wallace and bought by thrusting young executives holidaying in Goa on the strength of its claim to be "Finest Malt Whisky". Yes, there is malt whisky in there somewhere, but the body of the whisky is moulded around molasses spirit. At least with White Hall and Genesis, the Rampur malt used is 18 months old, which will add – even at three per cent – a sturdy, honeyed richness.

It will be interesting to see how Rampur malt whisky pans out over the forthcoming months and years. It may be yet to peak; it may already have done so. One of the most exciting things about a brand-new distillery is that you never know what is going to happen. Rampur is on a learning curve and, taking into account that they have the Indian climate to deal with as well, it makes for a very interesting learning curve, indeed.

Instant ageing: *The Rampur Distillery may look a century old, but it was built in 1993.*

McDOWELL'S DISTILLERY

It would be wrong to assume that good-quality or historically interesting Indian malt whisky is found only in the north of the country. Theoretically that should be the case: there are mountains, plentiful water supplies and cooler air to slow down the maturation process.

However, to find the maker of India's one and only pure, pot-still malt whisky (currently, anyway) you must travel a long way south, down to the resort state of Goa. It is a long haul from Delhi – days by train, a few hours by plane – but, once you arrive, you are taken aback by what you find: same subcontinent, different world. Whereas in the Himalayas you found pines, here you find palms. Whereas up north the roads take you either on long, flat journeys or up steeply climbing mountains, the road from Goa's airport to the town of Ponda snakes along single-track lanes, up and down shaded glens, past little inlets where the Arabian Sea bleeds into the countryside and where multi-coloured birds, short-bodied and long-winged, swoop low with the sun glinting on their feathers of metallic blue and red. The Himalayas may be dramatic, the Scottish Highlands may be romantic, the undulating expanse of Kentucky may be majestic, but the balmy, southeastern seaboard of India is exotic.

Eventually you reach Ponda. Like most towns in India, it is crammed full of people, all shoe-horned into a relatively small area. The architecture in the centre is typically functional and painful on the eye. A few miles further in either direction, though, and for miles around it becomes much more attractive, elegant even, with straw huts sitting alongside old, usually crumbling, and newer, brightly painted, Romano-Iberian-style homes.

Everywhere are dotted little icons of Catholicism: whereas India was ruled by Protestant Britain, until 1961 Goa was a tiny dependency of Catholic Portugal. Yet today the locals speak Hindi and English (albeit falteringly): Portuguese has all but vanished from the land. The people look different, too. Their faces are rounder and a little softer; the men's hair is a little wavier; the smiles of the girls and young women are readier and the glint in their eyes shinier – mischievous, even. It is here, in the south, that the peculiarly Indian swivel of the head when considering or taking home a point has been truly perfected.

Liquid gold: *The sun sinks into the Arabian Sea, a few miles from Goa's McDowell's Distillery.*

The distillery can be found just a few miles past Ponda on the Panaji-Belgauam road at a tiny village called Bethora. At first you wonder if you have found the right place. The initial impression is that you have discovered India's version of Kew Gardens. Surrounding the two rows of neat little office buildings are tropical rose bushes and other butterfly-attracting flowers in full bloom. By contrast, the distillery building is something of an ugly duckling. Actually, it houses the column stills which make the molasses spirit used in the blending of their whisky brands. The one brand it doesn't enter, thankfully, is McDowell's Single Malt Whisky.

Why this beautiful little Eden was chosen for United Brewers' venture into single malts is quite curious. They have other plants around the country, but it was felt that the climate of Goa was as good as they were going to get. Since 1971 they had been making their famous Kingfisher beer here and had also built the molasses distillery. The malt plant was added in 1988 as it was reasoned that maturation would not be a great problem. Elsewhere in India temperatures can fluctuate between 5° and 47° C. In Goa it is warm all year round with temperatures ranging from 29° to 38° C, but at least that means controlling the stocks is a lot easier.

At Rampur, as we have already seen, the malt is ready to drink at 18 months. Here it can take three to four years, though no longer, and some two-year-old I have sampled is already more than drinkable. Another thing the distillery enjoys is humidity. Even in the cooler months it is about 65 per cent. When the temperatures rise, humidity reaches 95 per cent, a phenomenon that reduces the bones and muscles in your legs to mush. But, again, it probably helps even out the maturation within the warehouses which endure the same kind of pounding from the sun as those in Kentucky and Tennessee. For that reason, as in those two states, the whisky at the top of

McDowell's: *Attractive malt is made here.*

the Goan warehouses matures much faster than that at the bottom.

The inside of the distillery is more interesting than the outside which, being of corrugated steel, looks remarkably similar to the ironclad warehouses to be found in Lawrenceburg or Louisville, Kentucky. One or two distilleries in India found next door to breweries allow them to carry out their mashing and fermentation. Not at Goa. The mash tun is of stainless steel, as are the six fermenters, but there are one or two curiosities about them. The malt production is very high up in the distillery building and the mash tun finds itself sharing space with the very top of the column stills. Meanwhile, on a floor below, the fermenters are squeezed next to the two pot stills.

Fermentation time lasts 48 hours here. Very unusually these days, the distillery manager, K. R. Shankaranarayan, allows a secondary fermentation of a further 24 hours to impart what he is certain are extra flavours and character to the eventual spirit. The stills themselves also do their bit. Made completely of copper, they are conical in shape with the neck of the wash still dumpier than that of the spirit still, which is also quite long. The resulting spirit is clean, malty, mildly spiced and not too heavy in body.

The warehousing at Bethora is probably the most attractive feature of the distillery. Sometimes, when tasting the spirit of Scottish malt distilleries at source you wonder if you can detect coconut. At Goa it would be surprising if you didn't: the warehouses are set among a small grove of coconut trees, which abound in the region as a whole and provide offerings to Buddha, which the workers give in a special shrine situated at the base of the column stills.

Inside the warehouses can be found row upon row of ex-bourbon casks. Sometimes a sherry effect is required (as can be found in the McDowell's Single Malt): these barrels will be filled with sherry for a day or two to impart some, though limited, character. Taking into account Goa's history, you might have expected port casks to be used.

From one or two barrels, though, you can also smell the unmistakable richness of something else: peat. The distillers have begun importing Scottish peat which their maltsters use to add extra weight. This is a very brave thing to do considering sales of malt whisky have so far failed to take off as hoped, partly on account, it is believed, of the Indian preference for lighter whisky. This, though, doesn't tie in with the Indian passion for the mighty Johnnie Walker Black Label.

McDowell's is a distinctive malt of the Highland style. It reminds me a little of pre-sherry Bunnahabhain only without the salt. Certainly, it fills the mouth comfortably with rich toffee-malt but there is the slightest spirit kick that lightens it a little. After some food, it doesn't sit too well, but when the palate is clear the malt is received welcomingly and its outstanding characteristic is its excellent ability to offer sweet and dry tones in quick bursts. This is a form of complexity, yet beyond the subtle shades of vanilla there is little else. Even so, it is delicious stuff.

How the blender arrives at whisky of this style is fascinating. At McDowell's I was able to do something that is virtually impossible at any other Indian malt-whisky distillery: taste the spirit as it matures over four years. The journey the malt takes through its maturation is really a revelation. The fresh spirit has a tiny hint of mint (which can also be found in the bottled single malt) and clean malt. In Scotland it would be regarded as sound blending whisky. By five months it has already taken a big oak character from the cask with a solid sweetness forming. At a year old the whisky has travelled a long way in a short space of time. The sweetness has intensified, but so have the malt and oak. Six months later, the whisky is very Scottish in character, having made another enormous jump, and is almost ripe to be bottled as a single malt on its own as there is now genuine balance between the sweet malt and drier oaks.

At 24 months the very first sign of a bourbon character has arrived with some fruitiness, oranges perhaps, also giving some needed lightness. At 30 months the colour has taken on an intense golden hue and the bourbon character has been confirmed but has become oilier and fatter. A complexity develops and the whisky hangs on gamely to some semblance of a Scotch dram. At 36 months the battle is lost. It is now entirely bourbon in style, and what style! This is mind-blowing, massively intense stuff like a 10-year-old Ancient Age, and shares with it great balance and style.

Rare sight: *Women employed at the Goan lab.*

Connoisseur's Selection

McDowell's Malt – A touch fiery but very malty and deliciously well-balanced.

A taste of the exotic: *The warehouses of Goa's McDowell's Distillery are set among beautiful hills and shaded by heavily laden coconut trees.*

Curiously, the 42-month-old malt is a lot lighter than the three-year-old and has returned to the simplistic, Scotch-style maltiness. The four-year-old was back to bourbon with intense oak.

I have heard other distillers in India complain that McDowell's uses enhancers for its taste. Having travelled on the roller-coaster ride of its malts at various ages, I can vouch for its authenticity. The man in charge of production, Devendar Sapra, points out that they don't even bother to add caramel for colouring – the bottle is green. Mr Sapra is pretty pleased with his product. His father was distiller at Kasauli during the 1950s so as a child he grew up in the grounds of the great old malt distillery and brewery at Solan. He feels he has a point to make.

He is particularly excited about the peat whisky coming along, and I don't blame him. Some I have tasted from the cask is lacking, but one, at 22 months, was about as close to perfection as you are likely to find in this part of the world. The peat may be powerful, but like the finest malt of that genre it allows the barley to surge through and additional sweetness to balance things out. It's so good they don't yet know what to do with it.

McDowell's has been given a name that imparts Scottishness. The label and carton are unashamedly Glenfiddich in style, and the malt, despite the bourbon traits found in certain casks, is also rather Scottish, thanks to some assiduous use of lower-floor casks. With glass in hand, you only have to look around at the Western Ghats, the beautiful hills which encircle the distillery, and the coconut-bearing palms, and you realize that, for a whisky lover, you really are truly experiencing a taste of Paradise.

Nearly there: *The maturing Goan malt.*

8  WHISKY FROM THE REST OF THE WORLD

The majority of whisky-drinkers in the Western world would probably expect this book to end where the Canadian chapter finishes. Scotch (grain, malt, blend); Irish (pot-still, pure malt, blend); bourbon; Tennessee; rye; Canadian … yep, that about covers it. Or so they might have thought. A few will know about Japanese whisky. Some about Indian, perhaps. But Pakistani? Czech? New Zealand? Turkish? Tasmanian? Spanish? Hardly anyone will have heard of them; some may refuse point-blank to believe in them. But tasting is believing.

Just about every whisky-distilling nation has set about trying to copy the Scots in producing malts of outstanding complexity. Some have succeeded – more than the Scots will happily admit – but others have failed, even to the point, as with the South Koreans and Finnish, where the industry has vanished altogether.

If proof of distillers' quest for this Celtic holy grail were needed, the evidence is in the number of phone and fax lines ringing all over Scotland. Richard Forsyth, managing director of the famous old coppersmiths at Rothes in the heart of Speyside, seems to spend as much time working out quotes on pot stills for foreign customers as he does for those at home. And his expertise is urgently sought. Likewise, the leading scientists from the independent whisky research company Tatlock and Thomson of Glasgow always seem to be winging their way around the world helping sort out a fermentation problem here, a distillation problem there. Retired distillery managers and blenders also have their passports regularly stamped by the distilling nations.

Bourbon and Canadian distillers, too, have on occasion been asked for advice here and there (though nothing like as often as their Scottish counterparts); even this author has been known to help out when needed. The world, it seems, wants to make whisky and distillers who have gone it alone without bringing in experienced hands have met with mixed fortunes, as we shall see.

The average drinker will probably stick to his Scotch or bourbon. But, for me, the fact that whisky is made in so many corners of the globe has long been a reason for celebration and exploration. Now perhaps it's time for people to wake up to just what whiskies there are to be found around the world.

After all, whisky is made in some of the world's most extraordinary geographical locations, from the Japanese island of Hokkaido to the Himalayas, even to a spot on earth where a mile or two down the road penguins emerge from the sea after a hard day's fishing. In this chapter, we discover just what surprises the world's distilleries have in store.

Dram of Pakistan: *Barrels at Murree.*

What's your poison? *The whisky connoisseur has plenty of choice in this Tokyo bar.*

WHISKY DIASPORA

Wherever you look around the globe, there appears to be a nation that once made whisky, or has just begun to do so. When I say whisky, I mean something other than grain spirit distilled to a high strength in continuous stills and then barrelled, or added to Scotch. Countless nations do that, and some might argue that, for this reason, the Canadians should be excluded. Maybe, but I still haven't tasted a grain spirit which matches that found in Canada: perhaps it is all in the climate. Or the heritage.

What we are looking at here are distilleries which work with a small grain to create a spirit of quite intense flavour. It has recently been argued by archaeologists that the first distilling nation was Wales, which was distilling from malt even before the Scottish and Irish got in on the act. I need to look into that more closely but, certainly, the Welsh were distilling in 1888 when the massive Frongooch Distillery was created by businessmen in nearby Liverpool, England. Wales has all the main ingredients required for making whisky: mountain waters, barley, peat. Yet the distillery close to Lake Bala died the same year as Queen Victoria and no longer stands.

There is a Welsh whisky distillery now, though. It is found on a small industrial estate on the outskirts of the town of Brecon, overlooked by the forbidding Brecon Beacons. They began distilling during 1996 from stills designed by students at Surrey University, though the first year's output was tiny and further work was required in fine-tuning the coppers. Some people are convinced that they have drunk Welsh whisky before: well, they have and they haven't. The same company have produced a couple of brands called Welsh Whisky but the spirit is distilled in Scotland and blended in Brecon with some herbs being infused to give a unique tang.

Similarly, there is a white whiskey called Glen Kella produced in the village of Sulby on the Isle of Man, a spirit created by re-distilling malt whisky made and matured in the Highlands of Scotland. It is a practice the rather twitchy Scotch Whisky Association have taken a dim view of, even to the point of winning court action – banning it from being called whisky in the UK – despite the practice falling within the statutes of the Manx Whiskey Regulations 1995. There is a six-year-old single malt and, indeed, the malt does come through, though so does a touch of feintiness; sometimes a lot of feintiness. It is still odd, though. You could swear that a splinter of oakiness has withstood the re-distilling process, yet this is whisky to be enjoyed by vodka drinkers. For me it's just a bit too dry; it badly needs some sweetness to balance. The 12-year-old, by contrast, does start sweetly and enjoys a definite, if limited, character build-up – and there is little sign of the offending feintiness. But at least it is distilled in the Isle of Man.

I have met buyers convinced, for whatever reason, that Red Rose whisky was distilled in Lancashire, England, the red rose being the symbol of the county. It is Scotch. The only thing that comes from Lancashire is the water they reduce it down with for bottling. There is no such thing as Lancashire whisky, or any other English whisky at present, unless you consider adding water to whisky makes the town where it is added the heart of a whisky region. If so, Wellingborough is now the centre of Northamptonshire whisky.

A true European producer of malt whisky is Turkey with its Tekel Distillery in Ankara, though its product is rarely, if ever, seen outside its own country. This, with India, is the hottest malt-whisky distilling region in the world, though in South America the Brazilians, Uruguayans and Argentines have all tried their hand with varying success.

Scandinavia has so far been a graveyard for all distilleries which have tried to make a malt, despite its much colder climes. Finland recently gave up the ghost and Sweden was subjected to a malt whisky between the mid-1950s and 1970s which few lovers of whisky latched on to. Despite this, whisky enthusiast and occasional writer Hans Wicchel is working hard to create a new pot-still, malt distillery somewhere in or near the town of Umea, which looks out on to the Gulf of Bothnia dividing Sweden and Finland. Being close to the 64th parallel and a skidoo ride from the Arctic Circle (albeit a long one), if the Umea distillery does get off the ground Highland Park in Orkney will be robbed of the position it wrestled off the Alcoa Distillery in Finland a few years back as the world's northernmost malt-whisky distillery.

A nation that has gone the same way as the Finns is South Korea. Back in the early 1980s, three distilleries were built there, the first in partnership with Seagram, the second with the Baikwha company, the final one in 1983 by Jinro. In the process, the town of Ichon became one of the main distilling centres of Asia, with two distilleries being built there because of its water supply. Because of the cost of production, those plants are now silent, the Forsyth stills still in place, and in the case of Jinro, the last to close, there are little more than 300 barrels left. It has been some 10 years since any malt was made there, giving the country one of the shortest production periods in distilling history.

Despite these heroic failures, another country has entered the malt-whisky fray over the last couple of years: Australia, or to be exact, we should say Tasmania, now the home of two malt distilleries. Australia did have its own whisky heritage, brought over by colonists, but that vanished some time ago and it has been two vastly different concerns which have revived the art.

The bigger is in Hobart, the island's capital. It is officially registered as the Gasworks Distillery but trades as the Tasmanian Distillery and can be found near the waterfront in Davy Street by Constitution Dock. Like the Welsh Whisky Co, with their small distillery in Brecon, the set-up is designed to attract visitors: in the case of the Tasmanian company with a whisky museum. But what is most remarkable is the still, a French-style alembic built to an 1861 design. It began distilling Tasmanian whisky in 1995, preparing for the launch in 1997 of a two-year-old called Sullivan's Cove Single Malt Australian whisky. This is not to be confused with a blended Scotch they also marketed to bring in the cash while the spirit was maturing for the minimum two years demanded by Australian law. Owner Robert Hoskin currently runs the stills fortnightly. No other whisky in the world is legally made in an alembic still.

The first Tasmanian Distillery to be up and running, though, was a much smaller concern at Ulverstone, on the north of the island, which is probably why they call themselves the Small Concern Whisky Company. They are preparing to bottle their very first cask, distilled in November 1993. The sample I have tasted from it is rather feinty, though the malt character buzzes through after a while. The distillery itself is a galvanized iron shed and the tiny still's capacity is a mere two to three barrels a month, making this the smallest legal whisky distillery in the world. They use unpeated barley and the still's body is stainless steel, which shows a little in the character of the whisky. The head is of copper, however. The water comes from nearby Cradle Mountain, which is the proposed name for the whisky when it is finally bottled.

Already seven barrels of their whisky have gone around the world, or at least as far as the Springbank Distillery in Campbeltown, whose warehouses are used to mature stocks of whisky for the independent bottlers Cadenhead. Three of the barrels originated from a Jim Beam distillery in Kentucky, while the others had contained local Cabernet Sauvignon wine. Having tasted samples of all seven as two-year-olds, I am sad to say that only one is up to scratch. They make for a strange set of whiskies; some have too much feintiness, some are overly estery, while some have a cabbage-water aroma associated with too little copper contact. Yet, having said that, one or two are quite attractive on the nose at least, with a Tia Maria-style coffee or cocoa sweetness wafting through and usually evident on the finish. Those maturing in the wine casks are closer in style to rum at that age than whisky. Still there is a long way to go in the maturation of these whiskies and doubtless some of the bumps will be ironed out over the next eight years while some of the oilier notes may be absorbed into the wood. The one thing that has to be said is that not a single barrel is short of character and that has its advantages.

However, the one which is showing the greatest promise – a bourbon cask – is gloriously perfumed, scented like an evening country garden in full bloom while being rich and oily on the palate with an effervescent spiciness holding closely to the malt. The finish is also a treat with unmistakable cocoa and toffee. And this at two years. Amazing! With a malt like that, there is clearly hope for this tiny distillery down under – and hope for every potential whisky distiller in the world.

Turkish delight: *Tekel's impressive malt distillery at Ankara.*

PAKISTAN

MURREE

Empires can be useful things, even when they are gone. The Romans gave us straight roads and aqueducts, theatres and baths. Two thousand years on they can still be either used or marvelled at. The British Empire was nothing like so spectacular, but thanks to it there are railways and cricket, breweries and distilleries. And in this case, all are still with us today.

The unenlightened might say that none of the aforementioned triumphs of the British Empire bear comparison with the extraordinary achievements of the Romans, and they might be right. Except for possibly one example, the Murree Distillery in Rawalpindi. You will already have gathered that just about every single distillery has a little foible that makes it different from any other. If you were to measure the utter uniqueness of this particular distillery on the Richter Scale of Unusual Distilleries, this one would wobble itself right off the graph. You see, Murree is the world's only distillery operating in a Muslim country.

For those outside the Islamic world, that may not sound like much, but in the history of whisky-making it has to be one of the greatest feats of survival against the odds of all time. In India, the government forces distillers to carry warnings on whisky labels which typically read: 'Consumption of liquor is injurious to health'. The Pakistani authorities don't make such a demand, but perhaps they should, because if one of their citizens is spotted drinking the stuff he or she will probably end up with a two-year jail sentence, a heavy fine and several lashes. In other Muslim countries the penalty can be more severe.

How, then, can this distillery be allowed to produce whisky and, what's more, be part of a brewery complex? The answer lies in the Pakistani constitution, created when the country was formed some 50 years ago. It came about as part of the protection of the non-Muslim population's rights, which included being allowed to drink alcohol, though these days they need a licence and are subject to quota. Thus non-Muslims are allowed to own the Murree Brewery Company, and Muslims can be shareholders but are barred from being paid any dividends on their investment. There have been several near squeaks, especially in the 11 years after hard-line Muslim President General Zia ul Haq came to power in 1977. It was he who signed the death warrant of Prime Minister Zulfikar Bhutto, who was living at a residence that was once owned by the distillery. His execution was carried out just 100 yards or so from the distillery, on land that has now been turned into a park to his memory.

During much of that time a sword hung above the distillery's head. It is a well-known fact that Zia disliked the distillery's existence, especially when Bhutto publicly announced that he once drank alcohol. The fact that Zia's Minister for Religious Affairs for the Minority was one Minoo Bhandara might just have helped a little. Bhandara also happened to be – and still is – managing director of the Murree Brewery Company, his father having been chairman between 1950 and 1961.

Leaving aside Murree's peculiar religious and political situation, it remains a highly unusual distillery. The Murree Brewery Company began life in 1860 some 50 miles north of Pindi in the Himalayan foothills. Just like the Kasauli Distillery, which pre-dates it by five years, it was built to serve a British army in need of something a bit stronger than mountain water and a bit fresher than some of the supplies which made it from Old Blighty. Being located on either natural or man-made terraces on the side of a steep hill at Ghora Gali, 5,000 feet above sea level and a few miles from the hill fort of Murree, it commanded a view far more rugged and barren than does Kasauli.

The buildings were attacked and torched during the battle for independence in 1947. Even now there is soot remaining on some of the higher bricks in one of the buildings. Or perhaps that was the result of 70 years of malting. Just above it the gauze used for the kiln can still be seen. In fact, just about everything can be seen. When they built things in the 1860s and 1870s, which is when the maltings was added, they were certainly built to stand the test of time.

Had the distillery been located at Ghora Gali, then there would probably be no Murree whisky today. But, in fact, it was erected in 1899 beside the Rawalpindi Brewery which the Murree Company had founded 10 years earlier. It was called the Rawalpindi Distillery, but the name was probably changed to its present one when brewing ceased (though malting continued) at Ghora Gali in 1927.

The Murree Distillery is an absorbing place to visit. Just as at Mohan Nagar in India, the distillery carries out part of its operation in its brewery. Also, just like Mohan Nagar, it has a Saladin mechanical malting system. And, just like Kasauli, it also has a floor maltings which means that, to my knowledge, it is the only distillery on earth which carries out both traditional floor and new-fangled mechanical malting. And just like those two distilleries, it also has to buy in malt from outside – in this case Baird's in Britain – to meet demand: Pakistan is not well blessed with barley.

Mashing is carried out in a semi-lauter tun hidden away in a wall. Fermentation is in the brewery. It may take place in any of the brewery's 26 fermenters, though six are specially given over to it, painted black and overlooked by an extraordinary stained-glass window: usually it is the stillhouse that exudes the atmosphere of a cathedral, here it is the fermentation room.

In fact, the stillhouse is a pretty poky affair with two large copper pots, allegedly of Scottish style, but actually something a little removed, with little of the swanned curvaciousness (or goose necks, as the Indians call it). They are not made any prettier by the lagging that surrounds them so not a single bit of copper can be seen. These are both the spirit stills. So where are the wash stills? A touch of the Irish, here. Now and again they were known to have their pots working out in the open, and that is just where you will find them at Murree. These are big, ugly brutes, four of them, with any charm they might possess wrapped like a bar of chocolate under a layer of silver, mild steel lagging. If you peeled that lagging away you would first reveal glass fibre and then beneath that ... stainless steel. These stills are not made from copper, or at least their straight body isn't, nor is the thick neck, but the head is and so is the condenser.

The warehousing is a bit of a shock, too. There are no warehouses. Instead, cellars are preferred and these go deep underground away from the summer's broiling sun. Rawalpindi may be high up at 1,900 feet on a plateau before the first shrubbed and ravined Himalayan foothills are reached, but that is hardly any protection against frying temperatures. So, for good measure, for the last five years there has been a cooling system added to keep the temperatures at an all-year constant. This is possible because there are only two cellars holding just 700 or so barrels, but, as at Mohan Nagar, there are vats as well, holding much, much more. The majority are around 50 years old – as apparently are some of the barrels in use. Four or five new vats have been installed, made from Australian oak, and it will be interesting to see how those whiskies pan out.

Absolutely everything I saw at the distillery pointed to the whisky being unbelievably light in character. First, the malting kiln is heated by gas and barely a particle of smoke is produced. Second, the wash stills are made from stainless steel, which means negligible contact with copper – at least in the first phase of the distilling process. Third, the stills themselves are very large. Added to this, the wood in which the whisky is being matured is, on average, pretty ancient. Finally, vats are being used (by choice), which means the maturing spirit has minimum contact with wood. And all this in temperatures that were never higher than cool.

So how was the whisky when I finally tasted it? Light. The one good point is that, unlike in India, the whisky has been matured for a number of years. Until recently they actually produced a 12-year-old. Now it's an eight-year-old. This is called Murree's Malt Whisky Classic and the blurb on the carton reads: 'Every drop contained in this bottle is distilled from barley malt in traditional Scotch-type pot stills and matured for a minimum period of eight years in oak cask or vat. We claim this single malt whisky classic compares favourably with Scotch malts of equal age.' Usually on reading such a claim you would sneer at its presumptuousness: remember, never believe anything you read on labels or cartons. But this time the claim is spot on. Not only does it compare favourably, it is much better than a number of lesser Scotch malts, which come nowhere near matching this whisky's crisp and delicate maltiness.

This has not always been the case. Until a year back the eight-year-old was a lot flatter in style and darker in colour. The two went hand-in-hand because the caramel used masked the beauty of the malt. Now caramel is kept to just a pinch and the whisky benefits in both looks and taste. So good is this whisky that it passed the 'morning after' test with flying colours: leave a drained glass of it overnight, smell it in the morning and you are swamped by its fabulously honeyed riches.

They also make a whisky called Gymkhana that is not worth exploring: it is a mixture of malt and rice whisky spirit with neutral molasses spirit. They also have another malt called Vintage, a three-year-old, though this is not being pushed in order to preserve stocks for the eight-year-old. Worryingly, it has a distinct off-note on the nose, a result of allowing in too much foreshot, and I hope just a one-off. Strangely, though, before the caramel takes charge it does reveal a rustic spicy-maltiness. It is not a patch on the complex yet brittle Classic, a malt that would not be out of place in Speyside, but is unlikely to be seen there because of the Pakistani government's ruling that the whisky cannot be exported.

What a pity, as well, that the distillery is not be found where the proud and sturdy remains of the old Murree Distillery still stand. Then, not only would it make a fine, Scottish-style malt whisky, but it would be located in a spot more spectacular and truly wondrous than any other distillery. And be the very faintest and sweetest echo of a now-lost empire.

Elementary: *Murree's open-air wash stills.*

Connoisseur's Selection

MURREE– MALT WHISKY CLASSIC. A STRANGE GREEN TINT DOES NOT MASK ITS CRISP MALTINESS.

JAPAN

SENDAI *(Sendie)*

The mysteries of the East don't come much more mysterious than Japanese whisky. It is not that this whisky leaves you hypnotized and spellbound (though in fairness, it occasionally does); it is more to do with trying to work out exactly where the spirit of the rising sun begins and where the spirit of perpetual rainbow ends. It seems as though Scotch and Japanese whisky are inextricably linked.

There is only one set of blenders in the world more paranoid than the Scots about letting on what goes into their blends and malts, and that is the Japanese. For the best part of ten years I've been trying to find out what is going on, and my failure rate has been spectacular: worse than the rest of the world put together.

It all stems from the fact that the Japanese have been continuously told that their whisky is a Asian form of failed Scotch. This myth has been embroidered, spun and told by a large section of the public who have never tasted the stuff and fanned by sections within the Scotch whisky industry understandably keen to protect the great name and exclusivity of their product. The big mistake that the Japanese have made is believing it.

The fact is, some single malt whisky made in Japan is head and shoulders above certain single malt whiskies made in Scotland, though exactly how much is I'm still not sure. The Japanese spent the last couple of decades first buying Scotch into their country to mix with their indigenous malt spirit, and then went the whole hog of buying Scottish distilleries themselves. The result is 'Shot Bars' wall to wall with Japanese whiskies, and no-one being exactly sure which is pure Japanese and which is a mixture of Japanese and Scotch.

A few years back, I asked someone I knew working in the drinks industry in Japan to bring me back samples of single malt whisky from each working Japanese distillery. This, after a few months, he dutifully did. When I rang him a few weeks later to say that I was getting some weird results against other samples I had, he confirmed that he was beginning to have doubts about what he had been told he had been given. As a result I scrapped my notes.

For that reason, I'm not sure what to say about probably the two most famous Japanese malts of all, the 12-year-olds of Suntory Yamazaki (Yama-sarki) and Suntory Hakushu (Hack-Shoo). Both are lovely distilleries, each set in spectacular forest and mountain. And both have vaguely similar styles, though for me the Hakushu, situated in the very heart of main Honshu island, lords it over its sister from the south on account of the peat, giving extra depth and balance. Both are very enjoyable whiskies, but neither on the label claim to be single malts: they are Pure Malt whiskies and astonishingly Scottish in style. The label also tells us that the whisky is made and bottled by Suntory, but what cannot be overlooked is that they own the Scottish

Twin peaks: *A dramatic backdrop to a mountain of barrels at Sendai.*

Out in the cold: *Sendai's charming distillery has also seen demand for its whisky slacken.*

distilleries of Bowmore, Glengarioch and Auchentoshan – the first two being pretty peaty beasts. It is very likely they are single Japanese malts with not an atom of Scotch, but the noises I get from Suntory are as conflicting as the signals I get from the whiskies. So your guess is as good as mine. The Yamazaki Distillery is Japan's oldest, dating back to 1923 and her stills are a mixture of straight, conical and double bulbed. It appears to produce a lighter style. Hakushu's, on the other hand, are more uniform, perhaps slightly more elegant, which seem to yield something weightier even without the peat. Hakushu may sound like a sneeze but its whisky certainly isn't to be sneezed at. It is well worth sampling.

There is another wonderfully situated distillery on Honshu and that is Kirin Seagrams' close to the old, snow-capped, dome-cratered volcano Mount Fuji and with access to superb water supplies. When I managed to get an alleged sample of that, it was extremely light, chalky and flowery. The San Raku Distillery near Hakushu has been re-named Mercian which (I believe) is slightly fuller bodied and with a sweeter, maltier edge. For an age the Noheji Distillery overlooking Mutsu Bay on the northern tip of Honshu, has been in the process of being built, but it has still not yet been completed.

For that reason, it is always a delight to visit the Sendai Distillery, further south. At least this is one distillery of Honshu which is unambiguous about its whisky. It produces a single malt whisky and, what is more, is proud of it.

Although it is called Sendai, it is quite a distance from that large city close to the Pacific Ocean. Instead, you have to drive half an hour inland to reach the mountains which stretch a long way southwards towards Tokyo, offering glorious scenery and good skiing.

Even at this distance out of the city centre, the distillery is found in the environs of Sendai but in the Prefecture of Mayagikyo (Mee-ya-Gee-Kyoe) and the whisky can be known under both names. The distillery itself dates back to just 1969, but the river running past, the forests of bamboo and the steep climb of the mountains to all sides, gives the impression that nature has been awaiting its arrival since time immemorial. So sharp is one hill behind Mayagikyo, one is immediately put in mind of that most charming of little Highland distilleries, Glengoyne, set in the shadow of Dumgoyne.

But there the similarity ends. The Japanese are nothing if not efficient and the distillery is an exercise in spick and spanness as well as a showplace of highly efficient – and new – distilling apparatus. The 23 fermenters, like the two large mash tuns, are stainless steel but the stills, naturally enough, are made of nothing other than copper. These are stills designed on classic Scottish lines, the gleaming contours accentuated on a plinth of rose-coloured marble. The sight is fabulous.

The size of the stills heads the spirit towards a certain lightness which can be detected in the new make. The waters from which the distillery draws has some limestone dissolved into it, though the type of barley used can vary in its peat content, sometimes heading up towards a hefty 17 ppm phenols. When tasting the new spirit from moderately peated barley it begins well, with a fresh aroma and delicate malts. It tastes sweet to start but as it pans out on the palate a very hard, almost metallic, wall is reached. It is not unpleasant, but certainly a surprise. Five years into maturation it is still an awkward whisky refusing to stand on its own feet and falling about the palate with little grace. By the time it reaches 12, one of two things will have happened. It will either be quite ordinary, or very attractive indeed.

Each time I taste Sendai it seems a little different. One or two I have had have been downright disappointing; others have been quite delicious. It has picked up some extra body in the intervening years and become big and fat with a really chewy maltiness.

The next trick is to try to introduce a regular standard within the vatting of the 12-year old. At its best it is a whisky that can make the mouth water. It still has a long way to go, though, to match its sister distillery – the finest in all Asia.

Connoisseur's Selection

SENDAI – 12-YEAR-OLD: A FIRM-BODIED WHISKY WITH A CHEWABLE MALTINESS.

YOICHI *(Yoych)*

Whenever anyone knocks Japanese whisky, writing off an entire generic style in one sweeping statement, I tend to ask them if they have ever tasted Yoichi whisky. Not a single detractor has so far said yes.

If all Japanese whisky were just 75 per cent as good as this malt, the Scots really would have something to worry about. As it is, though, the Japanese economy has undergone several lean years and the country's malt distilleries have not been producing as much as was the case during the boom years of wealth and expectation.

This decline – which saw Japanese whisky sales halve between 1989 and 1996 – has left some observers wondering just what the future holds for Japanese malt distilleries. There is even the possibility that within 10 years it could go the same way as South Korea: that is, fail to exist at all. Japanese malt whisky is about the most expensive to produce in the world as labour and natural resource costs are so high. So, the logic goes, it is cheaper to import from Scotland and, after all, Scotch is perceived as the superior and more fashionable whisky.

Doubtless, there is probably some truth in the rumours being bandied around the industry but if, heaven forbid, these fears were realized, the world would have lost at Yoichi not just a good distillery, but a great one. Already the recession has seen the distillery take longer breaks from distilling so stocks can be whittled down a little.

Great Expectations: *Yoichi's maturing malt.*

Benign spirits: *The door of a Yoichi warehouse is decorated to ward off evil influences.*

Oddly enough, despite making the country's finest malt, it is situated in the least dramatic of locations, being something of an urban distillery. Even so, Yoichi is surrounded on three sides by mountains and on the other by the Sea of Japan. It is the only distillery on the northern-most island of Hokkaido, which itself is within touching distance of Russia. This is volatile country: every other day, it seems, Japan feels the rumble of the earth's restless crust and near to the distillery are hot springs where you can bathe naked to relieve aches and pains and, it is said, restore a life-weathered skin to a more youthful condition – preferably with a glass of Yoichi. Just 70 kilometres away is an active, venting volcano.

To reach the distillery you must first travel to the city of Sapporo which, for all its neon, exudes a charm thanks mainly to its people. The train journey onwards is a slow one, at times running right next to the seashore. But the distillery is the closest to any main railway station in the world – less than a minute's walk in the summer or 10 minutes during one of the all-too-frequent blizzards.

Japan is, of course, a land of pagodas, so how right it is that the moment you step through the archway at Yoichi it is the malt-house pagoda chimney which greets you. Yet why the distillery exists, exudes so Scottish a feel and is located in what was once such a backwater part of Japan is a very romantic tale.

The Nikka company, which owns both Yoichi and Sendai, was founded by the legendary distiller Masataka Taketsuru. He had come from a long line of *sake* makers and was sent to Scotland in 1918 to study the art of brewing and distilling at university. While there, he married a Scots lass, and brought her back to Japan where he began work for Suntory. He was part of the team which first introduced malt whisky to his country but, so the story goes, left because they refused to build a new distillery in a location where he felt the very best whisky could be made.

Taketsuru was convinced that the bitterly cold winters and the plentiful water at Yoichi would be perfect for making malt whisky, so he quit Suntory and went it alone, building the Yoichi Distillery in 1934. One of the stranger reasons he chose to establish another distillery at Sendai was because each year the sea would turn white with herring. This also reminded him of Scotland, and in particular of Campbeltown where he had worked at the Hazelburn Distillery. This was part of the

White Horse group which also taught him his trade on Speyside, at Craigellachie, and on Islay at no less a distillery than Lagavulin. No wonder he preferred his whisky to be peaty in character. Amazingly, even after all this time, the whisky remains true to his preferred style.

He would be delighted to see that malting is still carried out at the distillery today, but it only occupies the maltings for a single week in the year to satisfy government rules, though local peat is still used. Otherwise the malt is brought in. Yet while the buildings remain the same, he might not recognize the inner workings of the plant, stillhouse apart. The mash tuns are identical to those at Sendai, though the 10 fermenters are styled more like pepper pots than the original vat shape which he would have encountered when he worked in Scotland.

However, the stillhouse is as impressive as you might wish to see, with six mighty copper pots, adorned with traditional decorations to ward off evil spirits (alcoholic and non-alcoholic, one presumes) and the lyne arms protruding at varying angles, perhaps to counteract each other in the first stages of condensation. The curves on the stills are gentle. One still does stand out – a tiny still which dates right back to 1934, visible proof of how the distillery has grown in that time.

The distillery's very first malt whisky was bottled in 1940, but soon afterward Japan became embroiled in warfare. The distillery was forced to make alcohol for the war effort, making life unbearably difficult for Taketsuru's wife, Rita. She may have adopted a Japanese way of life, even worn traditional Japanese clothes, but she remained a Scottish lady at heart.

These were hard times at the distillery, which had no sooner begun than it was forced to abandon whisky-making. To survive in its earliest years it distilled from fruits, and still does so today. After the war, however, the sturdy, low-slung, stone warehouses, complete with the gravel floors which help keep the inside moist and cool, began filling up with malt spirit. Today inside those warehouses the secrets of Yoichi's magnificent whisky can be properly inspected.

One of the things I have long admired about this distillery's whisky is its complexity of style, yet its ability to keep woodiness in check. This is achieved because of the extraordinary array of whiskies that the distillery produces. Nikka have obviously taken wood management very seriously because in one warehouse alone I was able to sample the malt at varying degrees of maturity after it had been in fresh sherry cask, re-used bourbon cask and even virgin bourbon cask. The whisky in the fresh wood was only nine years of age yet had taken on a distinctly bourbon character. This attack of complex vanillins was something I had not bargained for.

Nor had I bargained for the 10-year-old matured in sherry wood. For me, this is a type of whisky that distillers get wrong more often than not: keep the whisky in sherry barrel too long and the wine takes complete hold, and

Freeze frames: *Entering Yoichi.*

then not only are a whisky's more subtle nuances lost, but the character of the whisky is obliterated altogether. Here, however, the soft peats and the rich, malt tones pierce through the sherry with ease and peppery spices make for a deliciously complex dram. Then there is the heavily peated Yoichi, like Sendai roasted up to 17ppm phenols, and so chewable and deep that you wonder if the finish is ever going to recede.

What makes this whisky so different to Sendai is that there is no hard shield to break through. The whisky yields on the nose and palate with ease and at five years old has none of the ungainliness of that from its sister distillery. There is, however, a rawness which indicates it has a long way to go yet.

At the distillery only you can buy it as an eight-year-old. This is relatively peat-free and depends on its clean, sweet maltiness to win over the palate, something it accomplishes with almost frightening ease. This is like a Northern Highlander with a touch of fruit here, a touch of spice there. It can be bought, nationally, at 10 years old. Here the peat is upped a little and the balance is as near perfection as you might wish: there are hints of apples, raisins and grassiness on the nose, while the sweetness on the palate intensifies, leaving the malt and peat to fight it out on the finish. This is a better-balanced whisky than the massive 12-year-old, a whisky where the peat can be cut while still in the glass and the malt and toffee add even further weight. All three whiskies are classics of the highest degree; malts with the confidence to show their character to the full.

There is another, rather unusual, pure malt whisky blend in which the Yoichi character can be found. It is called All Malt and mixes Yoichi pot-still with 100 per cent malted barley that has been distilled in Coffey stills at their distillery in the south of Honchu at Nichinomiya. There is an almost rye-style sharpness to this whisky, and the peaty notes of the pot and the ethereal barley from the Coffey combine in a beguiling mixture of light and heavy, hard and soft characteristics. They thought it was the only whisky like it in the world, until I broke the news about Kasauli's Solan No 1 brand.

Yet as good as the hybrid pure malt is, it's only a sideshow to the great whisky of Yoichi, which deserves a world, rather than a national, showcase. Yoichi is not so much the jewel in the Japanese whisky crown, as the crown itself.

Connoisseur's Select

YOICHI – 10-YEAR-OLD: HINT OF APPLE AND RAISIN SIT ALONGSIDE THE MALT AND PEAT. EXCELLENT.

THE CZECH REPUBLIC

You may be surprised to learn that there is a malt whisky distillery in this most central of European countries. To discover that there are three almost borders on the absurd. But when you think about it, and add a spoonful of logic, perhaps you should not be quite so amazed. The Czech nation is famous for the high quality and range of its beers. Malted barley holds no fears for a people who have learned how to make such good use of it. Even less of a surprise, then, to discover that Czech whisky can be nothing short of lip-smacking.

Yet it would be wrong to think that because of this beery background, the Czech Republic has a long history of whisky-making. It hasn't, but it certainly has one of the most remarkable. Perhaps one of the oldest 'whisky' distilleries in the country is Dynybyl. It is believed that it was responsible for a malt whisky up until the outbreak of the Second World War. Even during the Nazi occupation, Emil Dynybyl, the company's founder, distilled 'whisky' specifically for the invading army. What they may not have been aware of was that he was making it from weeds and flavouring. Whatever, they were appreciative enough to turn a blind eye as he hid a number of Jewish families.

Dynybyl was one of a number of distilling companies which, in the 1970s, was ordered by the ruling Communist government to produce whisky in order to earn some hard currency. Ironically, their Private Club label was scrapped following the fall of Communism, when the Dynybyl family regained ownership. They recognized that its quality was simply too poor.

The same cannot be said though of the whiskies produced by the large food and drink concern, Seleko. They have two distilleries satelliting the glorious city of Olomouc to the north-west of the country, close by the Slovakian and Polish borders, themselves patrolled by gentle mountains. It is a peculiar thing, but whisky distilleries always seem to find themselves situated in charming countryside and near attractive towns of architectural or historical importance. The Tesetice and Dolany Distilleries are both so located. These, in reality, are the Czech Republic's two most important distilleries, although there is a third just where you might expect to find it. It can be located just 30km from the world-renowned brewing town of Plzen (Pilsen) in the village of Pradlo west of Nepomuk, a short drive from the German border. The distillation of malt here is sporadic and the owners, Stock, use all its produce for their blended Czech whiskies. The malt is slightly peated, and comes from the same Czech maltings which supply Suntory's Japanese distilleries. Another Pilsen distillery, Halberg, also made malt whisky for a brief time during the 1970s, but that seems to have vanished altogether.

It is at the other end of the country at Tesetice (pronounced Ti-esh-e-tee-ce) that the country's one and only single malt is produced – King Barley. Of all the former Communist countries, it was the Czech Republic which embraced Western and capitalist culture with the greatest ease. For this reason younger drinkers have found themselves seduced by the slick advertising of the Scottish distillers. The Czech distilleries have felt the effect. Because of the lack of demand within the country for their own whiskies, Tesetice and Dolany spend most of the year silent.

Still aired: *Tesetice's copper pot.*

TESETICE *(Ti-esh-e-tee-ce)*

Tesetice is quite a remarkable distillery in many respects. Once it was a brewery – nothing unusual in that – but it is now split into two distinct halves. At one end there are stills which have nothing to do with whisky and concentrate on supplying the locals with their national drink *slivovitz* or *slivovice*. Here, people from the neat little village and neighbouring districts bring the excess fruit that they have grown to be distilled into a potent, tasty spirit. These stills tend to be busier than the two at the other end of the distillery. Those appear to be related to the Lomond type of still seen in Scotland rather than conventional pot stills. Manager Jan Bartos seems to operate them with ease and invariably makes good spirit. However, he is helped by being able to draw upon high-quality basic ingredients; the water, drawn from 30 metres below ground, once supplied the brewery and the malt benefits from peat brought in from southern Bohemia.

The fermenters are stainless steel, covered on the outside by a strange bean-green paint which might well be appreciated at Scotland's Port Dundas grain distillery. After a 72-hour fermentation period, at a relatively weak six per cent ABV, the wash is pumped through to the stillroom, brightened by a blue and white checked tiled wall. Not only are the stills a little odd on the outside, but inside they possess rummagers despite being heated internally by steam. Obviously, nothing is left to chance.

However they wish to go about creating the end product it should not be knocked, because Tesetice makes very good whisky indeed. Its flavour is given a startling lift by the type of casks it is matured in. Made from Czech oak (as are the casks at Stock), from day one they impart a richness which distillers in Kentucky and Tennessee would much admire. The warehousemen are not quite so impressed, though, as the barrels do not have bungs, being stoppered instead by large pegs which make them impossible to roll. Curious, but all rather charming.

DOLANY

The Dolany Distillery, which you have to reach from Tesetice by travelling along Olomouc's spine-jerkingly cobbled roads, is found in a much prettier village six kilometres north-east of the town. Yet Dolany is the uglier of the distilleries by far, though the stillhouse with its four stills, against Tesetice's two, makes for an impressive, if rather cramped, sight. At Dolany the stills are similar in shape and design to its sister distillery, but as you will have learned by now, that really counts for nothing. The whiskies they produce are markedly different, even despite the energetic intervention of the local oak.

For a start, Dolany's whisky seems to be feintier, as if slightly less care has been taken over which part of the run from the spirit still is regarded as good enough for maturation. But at least those oils impart an oily character which gives weight, and although those feints are also to be found on the palate, once you are past them the whisky sweetens remarkably and is buried under an avalanche of powering malt. Not too bad, considering.

But Tesetice is better. It is rare to find any feintiness here at all and, although it is a lighter whisky in character, the balance between sweet and dry is a much more subtle affair. At two years old, Tesetice shows promise; by the time it has reached 12 it is a highly polished act. Even at 20 years old Tesetice whisky remains first-class, but has now taken on the style of a top-notch bourbon. The oak has taken command, yet this deeply golden liquid is not even slightly sappy. The malt, however, has taken on the role of the rye in giving the bourbon taste a mouth-watering sharpness and complexity. Certain Kentucky distillers would kill for such stuff.

Great oaks: *Czech whisky maturing.*

At 12, that bourbon character has taken shape but it is the malt which still dominates, starting sweetly but drying for a beautifully lingering finish. The whisky found on sale, though, is half that age. King Barley enjoys a striking red and black label and benefits from being at 43 per cent ABV rather than the usual 40 per cent. This really is a one-off whisky because it enjoys the best attributes of single malt and bourbon: it is a halfway house between the two. The result is not just good whisky, it is monumental. The tastebuds are tweaked in every conceivable way as the complex malt and oak tones intermingle and traces of smoke and spice drift in and out. The creaminess of the rich cocoa finish on top of that oak is something that you can savour for three or four minutes. Of all the world's whiskies, I place Tesetice's – and especially the 20-year-old – easily in the top dozen. Even the blend they make from these malts, Gold Cock, is unusually flavoursome with a silky grain smoothness. Outside the established distilling nations, the Czechs, with the brilliant whiskies of Tesetice, seem way ahead of the rest. The added bonus of visiting these distilleries is that you can take in the delights of Olomouc, dating back to the ninth century and the one-time capital of Moravia. You can explore by tram and discover a spectacular array of squares, fountains and cathedrals; the richness of its architecture always being given space to express itself by the generous width of the roads. It is not long before you realise that the startling treasures of this old city do not come exclusively in liquid form.

The Czech people are also a delight to know and it is difficult to be in their company long without tuning into their sharp sense of humour. The man in overall charge of distilling operations at Tesetice, Frank Dvorak, employs a humour as dry as the finish of his whisky. He is rightfully proud of King Barley and his country. It is a pity the Czech nation don't seem to value their home product in the same way. King Barley sells for only two-thirds the price of most Scottish single malts, but has every right to stand proudly beside them, while Gold Cock sells for less than half the price. Even so, sales could be better.

It wasn't always that way. Once it was not so easy to obtain the standard international whiskies and the nation was more dependent on the output of its own distilleries. As a Seleko director told me with the wryest of smiles: 'It was whisky that the government ordered us to make. Therefore it was ideological whisky. Fortunately, once you drank it, it was an ideology destroyer.'

Connoisseur's Selection

TESETICE – KING BARLEY: EXTRAORDINARY MIXTURE OF BOURBON AND SINGLE MALT STYLES. EXCELLENT.

DOLANY– PLEASANT, THOUGH TOO OILY AND HARSH EVER TO BE REGARDED TOP RANK. BEST AT 10.

SPAIN

From Olomouc in the Czech Republic you have to travel a long way to find another mainland European malt-whisky distillery. A crow making the trip would have to cross Austria, Germany, Switzerland and France, traversing the Alps and Pyrenées, before homing in on a stillhouse full of bubbling copper pots.

This one is found in Spain and is yet another of the industry's little gems, largely unnoticed in the shadow of the Scotches and bourbons of this world. Yet the Distilerio Molino Del Arco (The Distillery of the Mill of the Arch) is responsible for the malt and grain which makes up the DYC blends, two million cases of which are sold in Spain every year. It appears that Spaniards love their national whisky, as much as bullfighting and soccer.

DISTILERIO MOLINO DEL ARCO

This is not just some functional distillery found on a nameless industrial site. It is set in open countryside just six kilometres or so from the breathtakingly beautiful town of Segovia. Whereas Olomouc is large and expansive, Segovia is a relatively small town that still thrives within its ancient walls and has barely changed for a century. And not even Olomouc can match Segovia's *pièce de résistance*, a 2,000-year-old aqueduct, built with astonishing skill by the Romans to pipe water into the city. Nearly 200 feet high, with one tier of arches built upon another, the entire structure is hewn from granite without any form of cement whatsoever: few sights in Europe quite match the entrance of Segovia for sheer drama. Once you pass under one of those arches, the town is cramped with narrow streets, though the principal square is worth finding as you can drink DYC at a bar there until the very early hours of the morning. Or, if you prefer, you can walk around the cathedral, remarkable for its numerous pinnacles and enormity of presence: it was the last Gothic building of its style to be completed in the country.

With Segovia being just an hour or so by car from Madrid, a charming journey of peaks and plateaux, the town is a popular haunt for Spaniards looking for an aesthetically pleasing day out. A number of them head past the old bullring towards the village of Palazuclos de Eresma. There, on a plain, the whisky warehouses, green with rust-red roofs, can be spotted. There are 18 of them holding the majority of the 200,000 barrels in stock. They are similar to Canadian warehouses in that you notice a lack of the black fungus that grows wherever alcohol is to be found. Instead, the warehouse is thick with whisky fumes, just like in Canada, though some is allowed to escape through vents in the roof. When last there, a red kite soared overhead. The bird was probably a look higher than it seemed.

The distillery is a few hundred metres further on down the road. And it is now things start getting very interesting. There is a touch of *déjà vu* as you take the hairpin, down-hill, left-hand bend: it is almost identical to the one in Speyside that takes you from Cardhu to Tamdhu. By then you have already seen the distillery and the pulses are racing: it has a pagoda. Not any old pagoda, but one absolutely identical to the very finest found in Scotland. At the bottom of the road in Scotland is the Spey: here is the Rio Eresma, which in mid-winter sweeps down furiously from the Sierra de Guadarrama, the mountains (nearly 7,000 feet high) which act as a natural barrier between Segovia and Madrid. It is from these mountains that the distillery's water needs are served.

As for its malt, the pagoda chimney is not there as an ornament. The distillery actually makes all the malt it needs, some of it even being peated in the kiln below. At first a

Classic malt: *Spain's malt whisky is made near Segovia's stunning Roman aqueduct.*

Plane spirit: *DYC distilleries are dwarfed by the Sierra de Guadarrama.*

breakdown in communication meant that I thought that they had their own floor maltings; that would have been something. In fact they work a Saladin method, where the malt is germinated in large metal vessels and turned mechanically. Only one distillery in Scotland actually produces all its malt this way and it's ... Tamdhu. Spooky!

Actually, the maltings is hard pressed to keep its place at centre stage because the still-house is something else again. However, the process takes you first into the maltings, where 80 per cent of the malt is air-dried before being mixed with the kiln-dried malt. This is roller-milled before being mashed in the normal way. The wort is sent into 1,635,000-litre-capacity stainless steel fermenters which are split into two rooms. Then it's down to the business of distilling. And here you are rocked back on your heels once again.

There are no less than seven pot stills in all, though it has been some time since they have all worked in unison. Some have bulbous Balvenie balls, some are straight. No two, though, are the same. Looking at them, you would be convinced that the name Forsyth, Rothes, would be found all over them. Instead they have been made by Martinez of Madrid. It is hard not to believe that someone travelled to Scotland before they were made. After the heads run for 45 minutes, the spirit runs for four hours before the tails are reached. This is thanks to the large capacity of the spirit stills – 25,000 litres and 15,000 litres running off two 35,000 wash stills. Theoretically the spirit should be quite light. The distillery's charming manager is tempted to try running off the spare 10,000-litre stills to see what difference there is. But he is more than happy with the spirit he produces. This is not the only still-house found at the distillery. There is a grain plant here as well. They make from corn but sometimes, when it has been cheap, from rye – though only in small amounts. The first still is entirely copper-free, but the spirit is saved by the second still employing a few strategically placed copper plates as well as copper in the head. The result is a grain spirit which when matured actually outperforms the malt.

With grain of this remarkably high standard, it's little surprise that the DYC brands are so popular. There are two, the straightforward DYC and a rarer eight-year-old. Both are blends and as yet there is no Spanish single malt available on the market. DYC stands for Distilerias Y Crianza del Whisky, a company which owns – and has shut down – the Lochside Distillery in Montrose; malt from there traditionally went into its blends. Today the company is part of the Allied Domecq group and Scottish malt still finds its way in, but from a number of different distilleries. It is far more noticeable on the eight-year-old which contains the same 75 per cent grain content as standard DYC, but of the malt 15 per cent is Scotch against 10 per cent Spanish; while the standard is 20 per cent Spanish and five per cent Scotch. In particular, the eight-year-old shows a lot of Islay and this really is a delicious little blend with excellent sweet and bitter balance and good oak from the ex-bourbon casks.

Standard DYC can be a little more raw, though the five- to seven-year-old Spanish malt has character enough to come through early on before being rather swamped by the grain in the finishing straight. By the time the grain has matured to eight years it has taken on enormous character, not unlike the excellent cream-toffee whisky from Quebec's Valleyfield Distillery. Certainly one Canadian distillery manager I know, Gord Carlton at Canadian Club, rates it as highly as I do. Oddly enough, it is much better than the straight malt at that age, though having said that when it is reduced down to 46 per cent ABV it has an impressive barley character that links well with the oak. The malt spirit is naturally fiery at all ages though the faintest whiff of smoke adds extra depth. It is certainly worth an outing in its own right.

Spain did have another distillery at Cuenca, south-east of Madrid as you head towards Valencia, which, ironically, belonged to the Hiram Walker group. It has been closed since 1991 and all its malt, apparently, consumed. So the distillery of the mill of the arches is all Spain has got, and it should be proud of it. Even its offices are quite stunning, a courtyarded former villa of some 300 years' standing. In fact, it was also the very first distillery. In 1957 the owner installed stills into a part of the building, and the pits where they stood can be seen today, as can the site of the original concrete fermenters. Two years later the new distillery was built a few yards away. If you were in Scotland, you would take a look at the pagodas and reckon you were looking at the work of late-Victorian craftsmen, not those of the 1950s.

Connoisseur's Selection

DISTILERIO MOLINO DEL ARCO – THE DYC 5-YEAR-OLD IS A SOUND, CONFIDENT, SMOKY BLEND.

NEW ZEALAND

It is here in this most scenically astonishing of countries that our journey around the world's whisky distilleries ends. We began 12,000 miles away on Scotland's windswept Orkney Isle, where the (currently) northernmost distillery, Highland Park, can be found. Heads are often scratched, however, when the question of the world's southernmost whisky outpost is considered.

For the uninitiated it is in Dunedin, New Zealand. And here's the rub: there is something about the city which is as Scottish as Aberdeen's Union Street or Edinburgh's castle. Look in the telephone directory and there are pages of 'Macs' and 'Mcs'. And you only have to wander few minutes from the distillery, located opposite the city's beautiful Botanic Gardens, to see that the entire area seems to have been named after Scotland's distilleries and their blends: Dundas Street, Dalmore Street, Mackenzie Street. As you head in towards the city centre, you might spot the streets of Oban, Leven and Moray.

Even the name Dunedin was taken from the ancient name for Edinburgh – some will tell you it is a combination of Dundee and Edinburgh – and the city was swelled by expatriate Scots seeking a new life away from the toil of the Highlands. Indeed, the community in the whole southern half of the South Island grows from Scottish roots; during the winter you might spot curling contests, that most Highland of pursuits. A function involving some of Dunedin's senior citizens at the hotel nearby offers a quite remarkable sight: the tweeds, the sturdy, weatherbeaten faces, the kindness of the eyes below the white or greying hair could make you believe you're in Elgin, Fraserburgh or Inverness. With so much apparent Scottishness, the city could never have been complete without its own real-life malt distillery. It has been in operation a full quarter of a century now, something of an achievement for a distillery which got off to such an ignominious start.

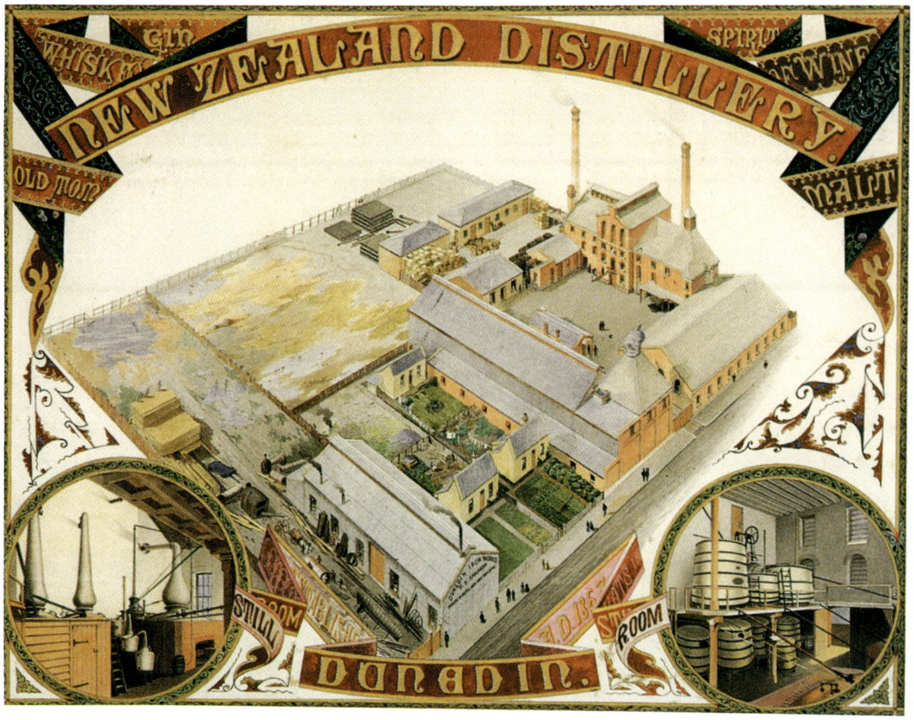

New World malt: *Notice that, in 1867, New Zealand made "whiskey".*

WILSON DISTILLERY

The Wilson Malt Extract Company had been operating in the city since at least 1926 but, although they were linked to a brewing company, it was a further 40 years before the idea of beginning their own distillery was taken with some seriousness. There had been precedents. An illegal trade in poteen-style whisky had been operating all over the island since the South Island was colonized, though one particular region, Hokonui, was famed for the quality of its whisky. This is an area of unparallelled beauty, through which the Hokonui river runs, where the silver fern grows unmolested and fantails follow your every move, dancing their little expansive jig just yards from where you are walking.

But legal concerns were developed on the island as well, most notably the New Zealand Distillery, an impressive contemporary painting of which can be seen at Wilson. It was by all accounts a large concern, boasting pot stills recognizable from earlier drawings made at Ardbeg on Islay and was located in Cumberland Street, close to the city centre. Now it has been swallowed whole by the Cadbury's chocolate factory complex and not a brick of it can be seen. Its life was a short one, being up and operating from some time after 1867, but silent by 1873. Another distillery, the Crown Distillery in Auckland, was closed at the same time after just three years of trading.

A problem was that New Zealand was then still part of the British Empire and publicans were loath to sell anything other than Scotch, or so they said. It was commonly thought that the well-known Scotch brand names being sold over the counter may well have contained New Zealand whisky. One thing was for sure, the Scotch distillers resented two businesses doing all they could to make inroads into their trade and pressure was put on the country's ruling body at the very highest levels. Legend has it that the hard-up New Zealand government closed down the distilleries in return for money to finance the building of the nation's railways. Extra tax was imposed on these two distilleries so that they were forced to abandon their ventures, though some financial compensation was made. So much for capitalist enterprise.

These rather sad stories confirm Wilson's as the most successful whisky distiller in New Zealand history. Yet when the first spirit was produced in 1969, few thought it would survive. Their biggest problem had been in acquiring the know-how to make good malt spirit. When a representative from Wilson's flew to Scotland on a fact-finding mission, the distillers were a more closed shop than today and he found himself cold-shouldered wherever he went. By the time he arrived back at Dunedin, he knew little more than when he had set out.

It was for that reason that an awful mistake was made when building the stills. These days a quick call to a number of coppersmiths in Scotland or Kentucky might give a clue to what was needed. Then, they went it alone and decided to make their stills from stainless steel. There was no copper in the system at all and the spirit was predictably, even after maturation, pretty awful stuff. Their first blend, a whisky called 45 South, referring to Dunedin's geographical location, earned a name so poor in the country that it was many years before the nation's whisky-drinkers trusted the distillery again. However, the international giant Seagram spotted the distillery's potential and acquired it. The first thing they did was to replace the condenser – the new one was of copper. The spirit changed dramatically overnight.

So good is the malt made there that for the last few years they have even marketed it as a 10-year-old. It is called Lammerlaw, named after the mountains through which their water supply runs. This water originates in Deep Creek and runs down the Taireri River before being piped into the distillery. Curiously, the distillery's warehousing complex is in the village of the same name.

When I told a coppersmith at Forsyth's that the stills were made of stainless steel, his first comment was that they would be a strange shape. He was right. In fact, the closest resemblance is to the cockpits of the *Apollo* spacecraft. The room they are in is quite cramped, but some of the distillery is attractive and old, having first been a brewery. Some of the old buildings reveal charred timbers, evidence of a serious fire nearly a century before.

The malt hails from Australia. What is more, it is peated. This will be noticed by anyone who has tasted the malt as it has been bottled over the last couple of years. In fact, the malt has changed styles several times. First it was a touch too chalky as some rather old whisky made its way into the bottles. As the age approached 10 years it became slightly fizzier on the palate – doubtless something to do with those stills – and more mouth-watering, with the malt taking on a rather fruity character.

But as distillery manager and blender Peter Martin, an Englishman originating from the Roman town of Colchester, showed me samples of his maturing stock, it was obvious that the character of Lammerlaw was likely to change radically. Certain years' distillations, especially the 1986 and the 1990, were excellent: indeed the 1990 was sublime. The peatiness was heavy and had done a fine job of toning down any off-key notes from the stainless steel stills.

Further good news is that the grain whisky made there for the Wilson's blend is pretty sound as well. But grain stocks are low and over the last year the malt content has been upped, which has done the blend no harm whatsoever.

It is the Lammerlaw, though, which grabs my attention. There is something almost infuriatingly attractive about this whisky: it has certain fleeting aspects as it curls around the tongue which make you believe that it will be sub-standard malt. In fact, your tastebuds keep discovering more and more unique qualities about it that keep you coming back for more. It has charm and lightness tinged with darker, peatier edges; it has delicate sweetness; it has excellent oak weightiness on the palate and a tell-tale Wilson's fizziness. Most of these are qualities that are common to certain Scotch whiskies, and Lammerlaw is like a Scotch … except there is a deliciously indefinable something about this whisky which sets it apart.

Even so, the Wilson Distillery has been going through an uncomfortable period. For a couple of years up until 1995 the stills had been kept running hard to meet a large order from the South Koreans. But the deal fell through, leaving warehouses full of surplus stock. Those stocks are falling monthly as case sales of Lammerlaw have risen around the Pacific Rim.

So the Wilson Distillery is sleeping right now. Some, incorrectly as it happens, have told me it has closed for good. They are wrong. Like the volcanoes which are found studded around the North Island and islands off it, it is merely dormant. And with a river running past the distillery called, of all things, the Water of Leith, how can it fail?

Connoisseur's Selection

Lammerlaw – 10-year-old Single Malt.

Incredibly peaty, with soft, sweet edges.

APPENDIX: HOW TO ENJOY YOUR WHISKY

Slàinte: *Whisky is enjoyed around the world.*

People come in all shapes and sizes. And so, too, do their whiskies. How people drink their whisky is a very personal thing. There is nothing wrong in taking it long on the rocks for a cool, refreshing, entirely delicious drink, if that is your preference. Nor putting a splash of ginger, lemonade, cola, orange, branch water; whatever you fancy. Whisky is not something to get snobby about and has been put on this earth for mankind to enjoy.

But there are one or two tips you might like to try. My own preference is for whisky to be taken straight, without ice and at body temperature. Then I feel I am extracting all the natural character of the spirit and discovering its true depth and intensity. Lifelong bourbon drinkers I know who have had never before drank their native spirit without pouring it over the rocks were pleasantly shocked when they tried it for the first time neat. It was something they previously thought you would only do with a malt. I also prefer to use a glass which is tulip shaped to hold in the aroma and stemmed so I can get my hands underneath to warm the golden spirit. Tumblers I find too thick and with minimum possibilities of discovering the nose; likewise expensive whisky glasses which have recently been "specially" designed but with only the faintest of stems to be equally useless . . . and a little pretentious. If all else fails, settle for a brandy or red wine glass.

Also, if you are using whisky as a mixer, there is no problem in using an expensive well-aged straight whisky if you wish. But you might find it more economical to use younger whiskies or blends for the purpose and spend a bit of extra time exploring the bigger whiskies as nature intended them to be. Naked.

Nose it: *Blender and whisky drinker alike can learn much about a whisky from its aroma.*

GLOSSARY: AN A-Z OF WHISKY TERMS

Age: The age of any bottled whisky refers to the very youngest whisky used in the vatting.

Ageing: The process by which whisky gathers its individual character by maturing within the confines of an oak cask and, in some countries, a vat. The ageing process ends once the whisky has been bottled, irrespective of the time it may spend in that bottle.

Alcohol by Volume: Also known as ABV. The alcohol strength of the whisky measured as a percentage part in relation to the liquid as a whole, e.g. 40% ABV equals 40% alcohol, 60% water, congeners, etc.

Angel's Share: The name given to the whisky which each year evaporates from barrels stored in warehouses. On average this works out at around 2% of the barrel's contents per annum, most of which is alcohol.

Backset: Peculiar to North American whiskeys, this is the "Thin Stillage" added to both the "Mash Tub" and fermenter to an amount totalling no less than 25% of the overall mash. This is carried out to help prevent bacterial contamination.

Ball of Malt: A peculiarly Irish expression for a glass of whiskey.

Beading: A rough method used to tell the alcoholic strength of a whisky. When a bottle is shaken bubbles, or beads, will form. The bigger they are and longer they last, the greater the alcoholic strength of the spirit.

Beer: "Wort" or "Mash" that has had yeast added which is either partly or completely fermented. Known also as "Wash".

Beer Still: Mainly North American term for the first still to be used in the distillation process, whether pot or continuous.

Blending: In general terms the mixing together of a straight whiskey (be it pure malt, bourbon or rye) and grain whisky. In Canada, the blending process allows for 9.09 per cent to include non-Canadian whiskies (i.e. distilled fruit juices, fortified wine or whiskies from other countries, e.g. bourbon). The result is a blended whisky.

Bond: The warehouse(s) in which whisky stocks are held until excise duty is levied against them.

Bothie: A small, usually one-roomed building, sometimes even a hidden underground den, in which illicit distillers in the Scottish Highlands made their whisky.

Bottled in Bond: North American (nearly exclusively bourbon) whiskey which is bottled at four years old and at a minimum of 50% alcohol by volume.

Bourbon: A whiskey produced anywhere in the United States made from a mash of a minimum 51% corn, distilled to a strength of no more than 80% alcohol by volume (160 proof) and entered into new charred oak barrels at a strength not exceeding 62.5% alcohol by volume.

Bourbon Whiskey – A Blend: A whiskey containing a minimum 51% straight bourbon whiskey with the remainder being made of whiskey matured in used casks or neutral spirit.

Brewing: The process of infusing cereal grains in hot water (mashing) which, with the aid of yeast (fermentation), produces alcoholic liquids (wash/beer) from the dissolved sugars present.

Canadian Whisky: A grain spirit made within the boundaries of Canada and matured for a minimum three years. Uniquely, by law, Canadian whiskey is allowed to contain non-Canadian whiskey, which could be whiskies from other countries, pure sherry, distilled fruit juices, etc. (see "Blending").

Cask Strength: A term used for whisky which has not been reduced by water to a standard strength of, say, 40% ABV before bottling. Often, however, the strength may have been reduced down fractionally to perhaps 57% ABV in order that labels do not have to be constantly changed.

Charcoal Mellowing: The process which sets Tennessee whiskey apart. The spirit runs off the stills into tanks holding around 10 feet of charcoal. Only after it has been filtered through this is it entered into barrel. Some whiskey is also filtered a second time after maturation but before bottling.

Charring: The dramatic firing of the inside of a new barrel. The contact of the naked flame on the oak opens fissures into which the spirit can run and form types of sugars which will assist the flavouring and colouring of the maturing spirit. The term sometimes applied to the process being carried out on old barrels is re-charring.

Chill Filtration: The removal by the chilling of whisky of congeners. It is a purely cosmetic precaution used to prevent hazing when the bottled whisky is stored at cold temperatures. The more the spirit is chilled during filtration, the greater the number of congeners will be removed.

Congeners: Chemical compounds found within whisky and formulated during fermentation, distillation and maturation carrying properties that have direct relevance to the taste and smell of the sprit. Some of the more delicate congeners can be lost during chill filtration.

Column Stills: Also "Continuous Stills" or "Coffey Stills". These are used in the process of continuous distillation, a cheaper and faster method than batch-distillation pot stills. These stills work by the use of plates, made from either copper of stainless steel, through which an upward thrust of steam meets alcoholic liquid, thus stripping the alcohol as it passes.

Couch: A second tank in which barley is placed after it has been taken from the steep and dries sufficiently before being spread on the floor.

Distillation: The process of extracting alcohol from a fluid substance by the application of heat. Because alcohol vaporizes quicker than water, it can be collected during condensation.

Doubler: A pot still used for the second distillation off a beer still in order to increase alcoholic strength.

Draff: The Scottish term for spent grains after it has been exhausted of all sugar-like properties during fermentation. Used as nutritious food for livestock.

Dram: (Scottish) A small glass of whisky.

Enzymes: Carried within grain, especially after malting, acting as an organic catalyst which converts large non-fermentable molecules of starch into smaller, fermentable ones. During mashing, brewers must beware that the grain does not enter the waters at too hot a temperature as these enzymes can be destroyed or damaged.

Feints: Also known as "Tails", this is the flawed end portion of the run from the final distillation. Being unpotable, re-distillation is required.

Fermenters: These are vessels, made from either metal or wood, used for the mash to be turned into beer. This is achieved by the addition of yeast which feeds off the soluble sugars held within the wash. Because of the energy created by the activity of the yeast, fermenters are never filled to the brim. Distilleries using all malt in their fermentation use either switchers to help keep down the foam, or use temperature control.

Fillings: Barrels containing spirit freshly run off the still and which is to be allowed to mature into whisky.

Foreshots: The very first runnings off the still during the second distillation (see "Heads").

Floor Maltings: The building within a distillery in which the practice of malting is carried out by hand. Very few distilleries now continue this ancient practice.

Fusel Oil: One of the principal and heavier congeners produced during fermentation.

Gauger: The old name given to the exciseman, whose job it was to put down illicit distillation and smuggling.

Grain Whisky: A whisky distilled by a continuous method to a high alcoholic strength from either wheat or maize and used to blend with a straight whisky.

Green Malt: Barley that has begun germination but has not yet been hot-air dried either by kiln or in a drum. This is sometimes used in the making of grain whisky.

Grist: Ground grains that will be used in mashing.

Heads: The very first runnings off the still, an undesirable distillate containing compounds even more volatile than alcohol. These are unsuitable for whisky and must be re-distilled.

High Wine: The alcoholic product from the first distillation which is ready to be pumped into a second still for re-distillation.

Indian Whisky: As the Indian government does not give a specific definition of whisky, a bottle of Indian whisky may be found to contain pure single malt, a blend of Indian malt and grain whiskies; a mixture of Indian and scotch whiskies; a spirit distilled from molasses or a mixture of all of these.

Irish Pot Still Whiskey: A spirit produced in a copper pot and made from a mixture of malted and unmalted barley.

Jigger: A now disused name for an illicit distillery which has lived on to mean an American measure of spirit, usually one and half fluid U.S. ounces.

Kieve: The Irish term for mash tun, these days rarely heard.

Leaching: One of the most common terms applied to the to the filtration process carried out in Tennessee Whiskey, the others being Charcoal Mellowing, Mellowing and sometimes, though accurately, The Lincoln County Process (see "Tennessee Whiskey").

Liquor: Hot water that is specially prepared for the mashing process.

Lomond Still: A type of pot still, squat in shape, designed to produce a heavier, oilier spirit. Named after the Lomond Distillery where first used.

Low Wines: The third and final portion of the distillate from the first distillation following High Wines and the middle cut. This is relatively weak in alcohol and joins the High Wines for re-distillation.

Lyne Arm: Pertaining to pot stills, this is the pipe which slants from the head of the still to condenser or worm along which the alcoholic vapours travel.

Malt: (1) A name given to a grain – usually barley, sometimes rye – which has undergone a process of artificial growth. This is a achieved by steeping in cold water and then allowing to germinate. The growth is arrested by rapid drying. The grain will then be rich is sugar-type chemical compounds on which yeast can feed to produce alcohol. (2) The simple name given to malt whisky; a whisky made entirely from malted barley, be it single malt or vatted malt.

Maltings: The building in which malt is made.

Marrying: A process, a lot less common than of old, when blended whisky is given time to mingle in large containers of either wood or stainless steel before being bottled.

Mash: A sweet, yellow-brown liquid containing the sugars extracted from the crushed grains that is cooled before passing into the fermenter.

Mash Bill: North American term for the percentage make up of the ingredients (corn, barley, wheat, rye, etc.) that is being used for mashing.

Mashing: The process by which the grist is added to hot water in order to dissolve the fermentable starches.

Mash Tub: The large metal vessel in which milled grains (grist) are added to hot water in order to soluabelize all grain starch in preparation for fermentation.

Mash Tun: (Scottish) see "Mash Tub".

Middle Cut: The fraction of the spirit which runs from the stills through the spirit safe which is regarded as potable. Also known as the "Heart of the Run".

Mouth Feel: The term applied to the effect a whisky has on the palate. It could be smooth, fiery, soft, light, cloying, etc.

Nose: The aroma of the whisky.

Noser: One who smells whisky usually within the distillery or for the distilling company to ensure that its quality meets the required standard.

Organic Whisky: Made exclusively from barley gown in ground free of inorganic fertilizer and a treated with natural, non-chemical pesticides.

Peat: Known as "turf" or "moss" in Ireland, this is a combustable fuel made from compressed vegetable matter. Unlike coal it is soft enough to be cut from bogs and is dark brown, sometimes black in colour. It produces a very pungent smoke, known as peat-reek and it is this that is sometimes used in the malting of barley, especially on the Scottish island of Islay. Waters that have run over peat used in distillation will also pick up certain peaty character traits.

Peated Malt: Malt whisky showing strong, smoky flavour characteristics peculiar to a spirit made from barley kiln-dried with peat.

Piece: The term given in Scottish distilleries still practising floor malting to the barley that has been spread on the floor to germinate at one particular time. Therefore a floor maltings may have a number of pieces at any one time.

Premalt: Used in North America. Here malt is added to the grist before cooking in order to help agitation. The enzymes within this malt will be damaged and unusable so far as fermentation is concerned.

Pot Stills: Containers, usually made of copper, occasionally stainless steel, used for the purpose of distillation.

Quaich: An ancient two-handled Celtic drinking vessel; its use these days synonymous with whisky.

Reflux: Alcohol-rich vapours that have already undergone the distillation process and which for reasons of control in column stills or, in pot stills, the individual shape of the lyne arm, return into the still for additional distillation, usually to produce a lighter spirit.

Rummager: Found only in coal-fired pot stills, a mechanical device consisting of arms and chains which rotate within the bottom of the still to prevent solids sticking to the bottom and burning in the direct heat.

Run (or Runnings): The colourless spirit at various strength and purity which passes from the still through the spirit safe via the condensing apparatus.

Rye Whiskey: A spirit produced in the same manner as bourbon but with the mash bill containing no less than 51% rye.

Saladin Box: Found with a mechanical maltings; the trough-like container named after its French inventor in which barley germinates while being turned by mechanical rather than manual means.

Scotch Whisky: A spirit made exclusively in Scotland either from barley, wheat, maize or a mixture of all three which has been matured for a minimum three years in oak casks.

Single Barrel Whisky: A whisky from an individual cask and which had been made at a single distillery.

Single Malt Whisky: A whisky produced exclusively from malted barley and neither blended nor vatted with any other whisky.

Small Grains: The term applied to all cereal grains used in the making of Bourbon, Tennessee and Rye whiskey which are smaller than corn.

Sour Mash Whiskey: Bourbon or Tennessee whiskey which during its making met prescribed government requirements. These include the mash containing a minimum 25% backset stillage; the use of a lactic bacteria soured yeast mash and a minimum fermentation period of 72 hours. In fact, all Bourbon and Tennessee is Sour Mash, irrespective of whether the label tells you so or not (see Backset).

Spent Beer: See "Stillage".

Spirit Still: The second still (or third when triple distillation is practised) which takes the high wines from the previous still and re-distils them. It is from this final distillation that the potable spirit is entered into cask.

Steep: The tank found at a maltings in which barley is soaked – steeped – in cold water to begin the process of germination and then malting.

Stillage: Pertaining particularly to North American distillation, the residue at the bottom of a still; beer that has been stripped of alcohol and containing solids (see "Thin Stillage").

Sweet Mash: A mash where yeast only has been used in fermentation without the addition of backset.

Tails: The last runnings off the spirit still, weak in alcohol (see "Feints").

Tennessee Whiskey: A type of whiskey made and matured to the same specifications of bourbon but with the exception of undergoing a filtering process before barrelling. This consists of the spirit passing through at least 10 feet of charcoal made from burned sugar-maple wood.

Thin Stillage: The alcohol-free liquid that remains when solids have been removed from the stillage.

Thumper: A type of doubler, this contains water which vapours from the beer still passes through causing a noisy, thumping effect.

Uisce Beatha: The Gaelic name meaning "water of life" and the derivative term for whisky: "*uisce*" was corrupted to "*uisgey*" and then whisky.

Vatting: A term used for the mixing together of malt whisky from one distillery or more. Likewise with grain whisky.

Vatted Malt: A bottled whisky made entirely from malt whisky but from more than one distillery.

Wash: See "Beer".

Wash Back: Scottish term for "Fermenter". Made either from wood or stainless steel.

Wash Still: Performing the same job as the continuous beer still, this is the first pot still used in the distillation process, producing high wines to be re-distilled in the spirit still.

Wort: The liquid high in dissolved sugars which is the product of the mash-tun; a liquid sweetened usually by malt by mashing and cooled before entering the "Wash Back" for fermentation (see "Mash").

Worm: The coiled copper tube along which alcoholic vapours travel and assist in condensation by being submerged in cold water. Most distilleries these days prefer to use condensers, also made of copper tubes, but smaller in area used through not being coiled.

X-Waters: An ancient term for distilled spirits in Ireland.

Yeast: A living micro-organism of the fungi family vital for the purpose of fermentation. By feeding on sugar it produces alcohol and carbon-dioxide as a by-product.

Zzzzzz: The happy and peaceful result of drinking too much whisky ...!

INDEX

H

I

J

PICTURE ACKNOWLEDGEMENTS

The publishers would like to thank the following sources for their kind permission to reproduce the pictures in this book:

Alberta Distillers Ltd; Allied Distillers Ltd; Anchor Distillery; Austin, Nichols Distillery/Wild Turkey; Barton Brands Ltd; Jim Beam Brands Co; Ben Nevis Distillery (Fort William) Ltd; The Bowman Companies; Brown Forman Ltd; Burn Stewart Distillers Plc; Campbell Distillers Ltd; Canadian Mist Distillers Ltd; The Chivas & Glenlivet Group; Cooley Distillery Plc; Corbis-Bettmann/UPI, Douglas Peebles; Corby Distilleries Ltd; Martin Corteel/Sarah Schuman; Doe-Anderson PR/Makers Mark; Mary Evans Picture Library; Four Roses Distillery; Glen Catrine Bonded Warehouse Ltd; Glenora Distillery; Glenturret Distillery Ltd; William Grant & Sons Int. Ltd; Gordon & MacPhail; Robert Harding Picture Library/Adam Woolfitt; Heaven Hill Distilleries Inc; Highland Distillers; Hiram Walker & Sons Ltd; Samantha Lyn Hodges; Hulton Getty; Images Colour Library; International Distillers & Vintners UK Ltd/Jack Daniels Distillery/ Justerini & Brooks; International Potter Distilling Corporation; Inverhouse Distillers; Irish Distillers Ltd; Michael E Jones; Kentucky Distillers Association; Kittling Ridge Ltd; Leestown Company Inc; John Lock & Co Ltd; Macallan-Glenlivet Plc; MacDonald & Muir Ltd; J & A Mitchell & Co Ltd/Vincent Leloup; Morrison Bowmore; Jim Murray; Palliser Distillers; Phipps Public Relations/Highland Park Distillery; Pictor International; Science Photo Library/Manfred Kage; Scotland In Focus/G Dey, A G Firth, A G Johnston, B Lawson, V Lowe, D McKinnell, J McPake, M Moar, W Ross Napier, W S Paton, J Stephen, J Weir, R Weir, Willbir, G Williams; The Seagram Co Ltd; Speyside Distillery Company Ltd; Springbank Distillery; Ralph Steadman; United Distillers; The Welsh Whisky Co; Whyte & Mackay Group; Wilson Distillers.

Special thanks are due to Bob Lawson and his intrepid team of photographers at Scotland In Focus.

Every effort has been made to acknowledge correctly and contact the source and/copyright holder of each picture, and Carlton Books Limited apologizes for any unintentional errors or omissions which will be corrected in future editions of this book.